ESSAYS ON AMHERST'S HISTORY

Happy Birthday to Nelson.

1979

Mother and Dady

ESSAYS ON

Amherst's History

1978

Published by

The Vista Trust

Amherst, Massachusetts

ESSAYS ON AMHERST'S HISTORY

FIRST EDITION

Copyright © 1978, The Vista Trust

Library of Congress Catalog Card No.: 78-8117

ISBN: 0-9601712-1-5

Printed in the United States of America

Contents

Preface

Everything happens faster nowadays. People had lived in Amherst for more than a century and a half before Edward Carpenter and Charles Morehouse compiled the first *History of Amherst* in 1896. Sixty-two years later Frank Prentice Rand published his own personal version of the town's history in *Amherst: A Village of Light,* timed to appear just before the town's official bicentennial in 1959. Now, less than two decades later, a group of about two dozen Amherst residents brings forth this present review of Amherst's past. Obviously the pace of history is quickening in this New England town and more people are becoming involved in Amherst's past as well as in its present.

This book began at the initiative of Mike de Sherbinin, publisher and editor of *The Amherst Record,* and of Polly Longsworth, biographer of Emily and now of Austin Dickinson. They called together about a dozen interested persons (town and gown, men and women, young and old) and proposed that the Carpenter and Morehouse history should be brought up to date. Everyone approved the idea, but no individual was willing to undertake the task. Whatever could be done would have to be a collaborative project with many different authors writing separate pieces.

Our first concern was to agree upon some common theme, some continuing questions which might run through many of the separate essays and provide a coherent "plot" for a reader of the whole volume. In 1974 when our deliberations developed Amherst was still suffering from the effects of tremendous expansion and cultural revolution during the previous decade. For three years Kim Townsend, a regular member of our group, had been teaching a course on Community at Amherst College. His students had interviewed scores of residents about their sense of change in the town's life and had discovered a pervasive feeling that Amherst had somehow lost in recent years *that sense* of community which it *presumably had known* in the past. We decided to ask as our central question in this book: "What kind of a community has Amherst actually been at different stages in its life?" What had been the lines of division and of relatedness? How successful had the people of this town been at acting together for common purposes? What had been their attitudes toward difference, differences of politics or religion or race or sex or age or class? Had they been conscious of some special identity for their town? What had they felt as the relation of their town to the larger world? In short, had there been some simple, idyllic sense of community throughout Amherst's past which has been suddenly lost in its hectic present?

Our next task was to define as well as we could the natural stages in the town's development so that assignments for writing essays could be made more intelligently. For almost a year a group of us met monthly to share our limited, partial understandings of Amherst's past and to argue good-naturedly about where the significant lines of change should be located. A glimpse at the divisions in our Table of Contents will reveal that we arrived at no very original stages of history, but this process of friendly debate did help individual authors to sense more clearly how Amherst during the period of their particular essays compared with the town at other times. Finally Ted Greene drew up an outline of five stages (now reduced to four by treating the nineteenth century as a whole) and suggested the plot line for the nature of community at each stage along with suggestions for the individual essays to be assigned within each period of history. In return for these pains—and in the absence of any other willing soul—he also found himself left as general editor of this volume, a function which he has fulfilled only in a loose and general way.

Most of the authors of these chapters early became members of our group and participated in the process just described. A few others we sought out because of their special knowledge and interests, as in the cases of George Taylor's essay on Amherst's economy up to 1860, David Booth's chapter on town government from 1900 to 1950, and Rhoda Honigberg's review of the Amherst schools. One essay had actually been written strictly for the author's own personal interest several years before anyone thought of this present volume. Two of us who had read Theodore Baird's reflections on the contentiousness of New England communities and of Amherst in particular knew that his essay should be preserved for other readers for it raises in its own way some of the questions that run through these chapters.

Within each of the three early parts of this history we planned to follow the interpretive essays with some piece which gave a direct, firsthand impression of Amherst life in that period. Because we could find no adequate original writing for the earliest period, Hugh Bell has employed his disciplined historical imagination to recreate "A Day in 1800." The most fortunate discovery of this whole enterprise came when Jean Mudge and Polly Longsworth, two scholars of the Dickinson family, unearthed Sue Dickinson's immensely engaging, heretofore unpublished account of the foibles and features of Amherst society during almost sixty years in the nineteenth century. We are particularly grateful to Houghton Library of Harvard University, where the original manuscript now resides, for permission to let it appear in this local community history. Finally we heard, almost too late, that Edward Landis, now a lawyer in Springfield, had come to Amherst as a very young Jewish immigrant boy in 1904, had grown up here until leaving in 1928, and that he could recall much about Amherst life during those years from his rather special perspective. We thank him for making public the moving, appreciative memories which are transcribed in Chapter 10.

The result of this collaborative process has been a rather unusual kind of local history. In this volume a variety of individual voices speaks out about what life has been like in this town. They are the voices of men and of women, of natives and of newcomers, of longtime residents and of ex-residents, of the living and of the dead. Some are professional historians or speak from other academic perspectives. Some have never before seen their words between the covers of a book. The town of Amherst has historically offered the space and the opportunity for individual identities and perspectives to become known to fellow citizens. This volume attempts to do likewise.

At the same time these separate essays on Amherst's history generally pursue aspects of a common theme. The changing forms of community, of relatedness, the changing conceptions of a communal identity, of the town's links with the larger world—all these matters become clearer than we were able to perceive them in our prelimi-nary discussions. While the book does serve to shatter any nostalgic images of some idyllic community in the past, it has clarified, en-riched, and complicated our sense of how people have managed to live together in this place at different times. In short, this book reflects—just as it reflects upon—the continuing human urges for individuality and for community as these had developed in Amherst by 1977.

Those whose words appear in this volume are identified in the proper places. Anyone with any experience in publishing collabora-tive volumes knows, however, that many other persons have had equal or greater shares in the responsibilities of this enterprise. Eugene Worman has sought out and selected appropriate illustra-tions. Ann Gross has applied her professional ability to produce as much consistency of format and punctuation as individual authors allowed her to impose. Carlton Brose has assumed major respon-sibilities for publication of the book and in a gentle, persistent way has maintained momentum for the enterprise.

Robert Grose has continually provided stimulus, interest, and energy to sustain the project, particularly in assisting Sheila Rainford to list available unpublished writings in the bibliography. Tom Looker participated in many of the planning sessions, edited or tran-scribed several chapters, and assisted in research upon the changing character of Amherst life in our most recent period. Winthrop Dakin not only wrote the chapter on town government since 1945 but also established the Vista Trust, the non profit organization which pro-duced this historical volume.

Philip Ives, a native and long-term Amherst resident, in addition to writing the concluding essay on Amherst's climate, wrote exten-sive comments on many initial drafts of the last six chapters which were often gratefully incorporated into later versions.

Thanks to the cooperation of the Jones Library, and specifically Winifred Sayer and her successor as Curator for Special Collections, Philip Cronenwett, information and pictures critical to the comple-tion of this volume have been readily available. Donald Frizzle, Superintendent of Schools, and members of his staff along with Katherine Emerson and John Kendall at the University of Mas-sachusetts Libary and others at Amherst College and Hampshire

College provided valuable help and information from their respective institutions. Virginia Dewey Lapworth perfomed the difficult and indispensable task of indexing this volume. Typing or proofreading by Friederike DeWitz, Mary J. Greene, Lois A. Hill, Rosa Roco, and Marcia Kendall were performed at crucial stages.

Since this is a collaborative history of a community there is a sense in which all residents of Amherst, past and present, have contributed to this volume. We hope many of them will enjoy reading in it for many years to come.

THEODORE P. GREENE
Amherst
July 1978

PART ONE

The Factionalism of the Founding Fathers 1730–1800

CHAPTER ONE

EARLY AMHERST

HUGH F. BELL
ANDREW RAYMOND

Hugh Bell teaches and writes about early American history on the faculty at the University of Massachusetts. Andy Raymond, as a graduate student at the University of Massachusetts, wrote a long research paper on the divisions within early Amherst and, in the process of this research, discovered long-neglected town records on this period in the basement of town hall. Under a special grant Andy Raymond was employed by the town to put its historical records in order and under proper preservative safeguards.

The story of early Amherst has been told many times. It has been told by the indefatigable Sylvester Judd, by *Amherst Record* editor Charles F. Morehouse and his publisher Edward F. Carpenter, by Frank Prentice Rand, and by Alice Morehouse Walker among others. Each author chose a different approach in picturing the town and its history, as is an author's privilege, but in this age of discontent new questions are being asked about the past of our institutions. Community pride is a cohesive force, and Amherst has much to be proud of, but in the earlier histories of the town there has been the implicit assumption that Amherst was a community, a group of individuals who thought, felt, and acted as an entity. Is this assumption warranted? What happens to "my little village," as Ray Stannard Baker described it, when viewed from atop a university skyscraper? If Amherst is, or was, a community, how did it evolve? Let us take a new look at early Amherst in a search for this nebulous thing, a sense of community.

No one knows the identity of Amherst's first white settler. It may have been the legendary Mr. Foot whose Folly, a swamp, was a local landmark as early as 1703. It is reasonably certain, however, that settlement began in earnest in the late 1720s, for by 1731 some eighteen families were listed as living in what is now Amherst. These settlers became the third *precinct* of Hadley, the mother town, in 1734, a *district* in 1759, and finally a *town* in 1775 almost as an afterthought under a general statute passed by the rebel Provincial Congress.

To a student of colonial New England these formal terms are standard and recognizable milestones in the development of a town. A precinct was analogous to a parish, a separate church congregation within an established town. A district took on all the governmental functions of a town except that of electing representatives to the General Court of the province. Town status, the final step, brought a settlement into the family of towns that was, and still is, the basis for local and representative government. That this process stretched out over nearly half a century in Amherst may have been significant in determining the true nature of the community that evolved within the legal framework of a town.

The Puritan New England town in the seventeenth century was a *covenanted community* in which the building of homes, the formation of a congregation around a "learned and orthodox minister," and the grant of town status by the General Court were nearly simultaneous. In the early days the recommended minimum of seven "visible saints," or communicant members of an existing church, and their families would negotiate with the General Court for a grant of land, select and "call" a minister, and enter into a covenant with each other "to walke in all our wayes according to the Rule of the Gospell, & in all sincere Conformity to His holy Ordinaunces, & in mutuall love, & respect to each other, so neere as God shall give us Grace" (to borrow the phraseology of the Charlestown church). Though there were bewildering variations on this theme, the theory was clear enough. As a result such towns would be made up of remarkably homogeneous and like-minded people, "knit together," said John Winthrop, by religious belief and often by similar English geographic origins and occupations. They had been through a double winnowing process, first, the decision to take part in the great exodus from England, and second, the formation of a separate settlement away from crowded Boston. This process, seemingly so simple and so logical, was bound to generate its own complications, but both the model and the ideal of homogeneity remained in the New England mind.

When the model is projected into the eighteenth century, the sharp lines become blurred, and Amherst is a good example of this loss of clarity. From one point of view Amherst should have been the epitome of homogeneity and cohesiveness. Instead of two siftings Amherst's original inhabitants and their forebears had been through multiple refinements. There had been the break from England, the dispersion from Boston to Watertown, New Town, and Roxbury, the 1636 trek to the Connecticut River under Thomas Hooker, and the founding of Wethersfield, Hartford, and Windsor in Connecticut. After Hooker's death in 1647 there was a decade of contention, and then a group of dissatisfied *strict Congregationalists* left the three towns for Hadley, Massachusetts led by the dominating minister, John Russell.

Amherst grew out of Hadley. The families that formed the early population of what is now Amherst did not move to the new ground under the impetus of any recognizable religious or political schism, but rather oozed to the east as part of the natural expansion of Hadley's population and the need, or desire, for more land. It could be argued, therefore, that the eighteen heads of families who were listed as "east inhabitants" in 1731 represented as pure a strain of Connecticut Valley orthodoxy as could be imagined, a unit of cohesiveness tempered by tradition, belief, and common agricultural occupation. But there were significant factors militating against this ideal.

Each of the winnowings may have been a purifying event in one sense, but each involved a departure which left in the minds of both groups an awareness of dissension and separation as an alternative to conformity to the community will. This paradox was of long standing; as early as 1632 it had been a source of anguish to Governor Bradford of Plymouth Colony as he watched his "Christian and comfortable fellowship . . . suffer many divisions." Hooker's departure for the Connecticut Valley, leading parts of at least three congregations from the heart of the colony, was similarly a cause of grave concern to John Winthrop and his fellow magistrates of the Bay Colony. The removal of John Russell and his flock from the Connecticut towns was even more traumatic, as evidenced in the many attempts by church councils to arrange a reconciliation, or *pacification* as they termed it. Thus purification and divisiveness seemed to go hand in hand.

Another factor that tarnished the seventeenth century image of a tightly knit community was the profound change in methods of land distribution and settlement. Land had always been dear to the hearts of English colonists, and the prospect of more land was indeed a factor in Hooker's move to Connecticut; but the real change became apparent nearly a century later. An expansionist tendency was fueled by such developments as the population increase, the evaporation of the Indian menace, and the decline of the church as a focalizing influence. Land speculation emerged as a popular occupation at about the time of Amherst's founding. One by-product was an important change in the classic conception of the New England village with its central common surrounded by houselots under the benign presence of the meetinghouse spire.

If this conception of the New England town was an anachronism by 1730, Amherst presents a puzzle for it had a common and the "learned and orthodox minister" required by the General Court, and soon a meetinghouse overlooked the common from Moot Hill (a singularly appropriate nickname). In 1759 the "eastern inhabitants" of Hadley acquired the name Amherst (in honor of the hero of the second taking of Louisbourg) and the authority as a district to create a local government complete with selectmen, assessors, tithingmen, constables, surveyors, fence viewers, and hogreeves. These would seem to be the trappings of a New England town of the classic mold. But a closer look reveals important differences. The *common* was quite literally a wide place in the road, the so-called west street. The Amherst common was following precedent in this regard, for Hadley, and before it Wethersfield, had used a small section of road forty rods wide as a common, but the west street of Amherst stretched all the way from the foot of the Holyoke Range to Mill River, a distance of some six miles. And instead of the normal eight or ten acre houselots circling a common with outlying fields and common grounds, most Amherst lands were divided into sizable, separate, scattered farms from the beginning.

This variation from the seventeenth century norm was neither irrational nor unique. Initially the land in question was merely surplus land which lay on the east side of the New Swamp and was thus separated from Hadley proper. In 1703 this surplus was parcelled out to Hadley residents as farmland, with little expectation that the tract would become in time a separate town. As a result, when serious settlement began in the 1720s, the homes were scattered over some fifteen square miles without the traditional focal point or

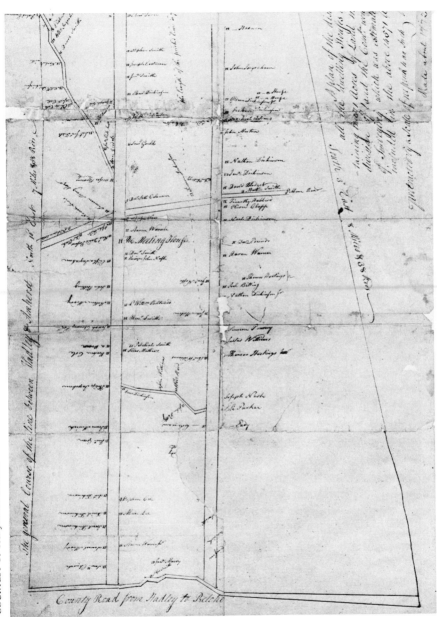

THIS 1772 MAP IS THE EARLIEST KNOWN MAP
OF THE TOWN OF AMHERST.

center. Thus Amherst because of its slow progress from outlying Hadley farms to full town status was deprived of that important cement of community—an initial focal point.

The lack of focus can be seen in the nature of the inevitable controversies that became a matter of record. No sooner had the east inhabitants moved beyond the sound of the Hadley meetinghouse bell than they started agitation for a minister and a place of worship of their own. At first Hadley offered no objections so long as its distant brethren continued to pay four-fifths of their regular tax for the support of Hadley's Reverend Isaac Chauncey. The tax exemption was soon raised to one-half, but by 1734 even this concession was not enough, and the east inhabitants petitioned the General Court for the creation of a separate precinct, a request that was granted despite the efforts of an agent sent to Boston on behalf of the mother town.

After settlement of this issue the new precinct had to provide the *quid pro quo,* a "Convenient House for the Publick Worship of God" and a "Learned orthodox Minister." At the first regular precinct meeting held on October 8, 1735, one committee was chosen to "hire a Minester," and it was agreed that the "Meating House" should be forty-five by thirty-five feet in size and "Set upon the Hill East of Jno Nashs House," or Moot Hill. That agreement lasted only six weeks; it was then voted that the earlier decision "be Revoaked" and that the building be erected "neare the Hartling Stake so Called" (the northeast corner of North Pleasant and Main Streets). This was rejected a month later in favor of a site at the east end of Noah Smith's lot, which was well south of the present common.

Despite numerous votes at precinct meetings, it was not until November 1738 that the meeting finally decided to abandon the Noah Smith site and return to the original choice, "the Hill East of John Nashs House." There was more at issue than just a suitable tract of land for the meetinghouse. There was also the silent, or at least unrecorded, contest as to where the focal point of the settlement would be. In comparison with South Hadley, however, the lengthy argument in Amherst was insignificant. South Hadley, another precinct offshoot of Hadley, went through an eleven-year battle over the meetinghouse site, a battle that was ended only by a council that recommended the formation of two churches.

The laying out of Amherst lands in 1703 had complicated a seemingly simple problem. The Hadley fathers had laid out the tract in three parallel strips, or divisions, with two north-and-south streets, each forty rods wide, as dividers. The west street (now West Street, South Pleasant, North Pleasant, and East Pleasant Streets) could lay some claim to superior status from its closeness to Hadley. Running east and west was "the Roade Leading to Brookfield" (now Bay Road) at the southern extremity of the precinct. The only other entry was present-day Amity Street. Being close to the middle of the north-south dimension of the precinct, the intersection of this highway with the west street was a natural focal point, but only a shade more so than the intersection of the same highway with the east street at the foot of the hill. But by 1744, when Nehemiah Strong built his imposing house near the west street intersection, this neighborhood had accumulated great weight in terms of large property owners and influence. So in one sense the meetinghouse and the houses of the well-to-do determined the center despite the rather uniform scattering of homes throughout the precinct.

Notwithstanding this centralizing influence, there was still an air of uncertainty as to whether the configuration was to be centrifugal or centripetal, and this was manifest in the question of schools. The precinct managed to restrict its educational program to *dame schools* until 1761 when a district meeting voted to build two schoolhouses. The meeting had not been completed before another vote cancelled the first and called for the selection of a committee to determine whether two or three schoolhouses would be appropriate. The committee dutifully reported three months later recommending three schoolhouses, but educational ardor had cooled to the point where the meeting voted "to Stop all Proceedings Respecting the schoolhouses for another Year." Two years later, four schools were authorized, one at each corner of the district. But neighborhoods were still unhappy and squabbled over allocation of school monies and scheduling for a decade. It is reasonably clear that the schoolhouse arguments were rooted in neighborhood jealousies and the fear of being left on the fringe of village life.

If these geographical concerns indicate a diffuseness in the village's conception of itself, its selection of a minister did not. It was during the arguments over the site for the meetinghouse that the Reverend David Parsons came on the tiny stage. He and his son, the younger David Parsons, as successive ministers of the First Church were to occupy for a total of eighty-two years a position of central importance in the creation of Amherst's character.

From the earliest days the ministers of Massachusetts were men of unique importance, especially considering their lack of any formal political power. They led emigrating groups from England; they were usually the best educated men in their respective towns; and

COURTESY OF THE JONES LIBRARY

DAVID PARSONS THE ELDER, MINISTER OF
THE FIRST CHURCH OF AMHERST.

despite a myriad of theological disputes they on the whole had done much to set the tone of the Bible Commonwealth. John Russell ministered to Hadley for more than thirty years, and his successor, Isaac Chauncey, held the office longer than that, without serious dissent. By the time of Amherst's founding, however, the position of the minister was in decline. The *declension* of religious zeal, the growing importance of mundane economic concerns, the loss of the political monopoly that full members of the church held until forced into a liberalization of the franchise by a more tolerant England, all combined with the unnerving effect of paper money inflation on ministerial salaries to make the traditional seat of local influence an uneasy one.

David Parsons was a mere twenty-three years of age when he first preached in Amherst in 1735, but the infant settlement apparently liked what it heard for he was brought back repeatedly on short-term arrangements. In April 1737 the precinct issued him a formal call to become the settled minister, a call that he accepted, but only after two years of complex negotiations. The precinct finally committed itself not only to a salary tied by formula to sterling currency, but also to a house of certain specifications and an incredible supply of firewood (about ninety cords or 120 wagon loads every year). The records are silent, but there must have been those who muttered that the money changers and woodchoppers were infesting the temple. On November 7, 1739 the young negotiator was ordained as the spiritual leader of the Third Precinct of Hadley with its sixteen communicant members. One interesting deviation from the traditional procedure was the absence of any church covenant entered into by the members.

To this day David Parsons remains an enigma. He was reserved and austere in bearing, the soul of orthodoxy in the doctrinal sphere, conservative in politics, and unquestionably the voice of Amherst. Yet in some ways there is something of the unexpected about him. He was, of course, a Harvard graduate, nearly a prerequisite for the office at the time, and the only college educated man in the precinct. While at Cambridge Parsons had known as college mates such men as Thomas Hutchinson, Israel Williams of Hatfield, Peter Oliver, and Jonathan Belcher, Jr., men who were to operate on an imperial scale in later years and who would in the crises of the 1770s become leading Tories. After settling in the third precinct Parsons married a girl ten years his junior, Eunice Welles of Wethersfield, the heiress of a prominent Connecticut family, who brought to the marriage considerable economic benefits to augment the groom's ample salary and gigantic woodpile. It was agreed that Parsons was "strictly Calvinistic" and an adherent of the doctrine of salvation through faith rather than works, but by nature he could not share in the evangelical fervor and "enthusiastic" religion of Jonathan Edwards's Northampton and other valley towns. His ownership of a slave, the giant Pomp, was not unique for some of his parishioners—Zechariah Field, Richard Chauncey, and the Kelloggs—were also slaveholders, but one wonders how the members of the church, not to mention other inhabitants viewed this man who was so atypical. There is the old and probably unanswerable question as to whether the New England ministers of the period were molders of society or merely reflections of it. It is impossible really to understand the relationship that developed between this man and his flock of hardworking yeoman farmers over the forty-two years of his ministry. Perhaps the contrast echoes in a sense the split image of the village seen by its inhabitants.

There was occasional bickering between the minister and his parish over salary and wood supply, and there were signs of unhappiness over the pew assignments, the *seating* of the meetinghouse, some always taking umbrage at their ranking, but it was a rare New England town that did not indulge in some of this unchristian contention. Despite such ripples the Amherst of 1770 was calm, but the decade that followed revealed for all to see the divisiveness beneath the surface, and David Parsons, the unofficial arbiter of village attitudes, found himself in the middle of a situation that he could neither ken nor control.

The American Revolution is viewed by nearly all modern students as involving two main issues, the "question of home rule" and the "question of who should rule at home," to borrow historian Carl Becker's often quoted phrases. Amherst provides an admirable case study of both problems.

In terms of chronology the question of who should rule at home arose first, and it became visible as a result of tension-producing changes within the village, changes that with hindsight seem less surprising than they were to the participants.

Like nearly all of the "outgrowth" towns of western Massachusetts the tiny nucleus that became Amherst district in 1759 had been growing in population. The land was good, and Amherst participated in the great population explosion that pushed Hampshire County from a 7 percent share of the Massachusetts population in 1765 to 16 percent in 1790. By 1790, in fact, Hampshire County, which then included today's Hampden and Franklin Counties, was the most populous in the Commonwealth. When David Parsons first settled in Amherst, there were perhaps 130 people living within the bounds of the precinct. By 1776 this figure had increased to over 900.

There was an accompanying trend that did not affect all towns in the same way—a significant change in the distribution of wealth which saw, for example, the wealthiest 10 percent of the population controlling an increasing proportion of the property in the town. When compared to other Hampshire County towns with similar population growth, Amherst showed a higher rate of wealth concentration, particularly toward the end of the revolutionary era.

With this factual picture before him a social historian would expect to find increased signs of internal tension, and the decade of the 1770s in Amherst did produce signs of malaise, the first being the "division" movement, which not only reveals some of the currents at work beneath the hitherto calm surface of village life, but also points up the tenuous position of David Parsons, who could only stand by helplessly.

The division movement appeared in January 1772 in the form of a cryptic vote in a district meeting to "Take sum Measures to divide the District into two Pearishes." In terms of population the Amherst of 1772 was large enough to support two churches though there were parishes in the province with a larger population base. The usual grievance leading to the splitting of a parish was the excessive distance between the meetinghouse and outlying residential clusters, and this point was raised by the people of Amherst who favored the division. But as the contest developed it became more complex.

In a meeting held in March, the January vote was reconsidered and laid aside by a tie vote, but in April the proponents of division packed a district meeting and not only voted to build two meetinghouses but also turned down a petition by "Sundry of the Inhabitants" to be relieved of this expense. These Sundry Inhabitants were not to be silenced so easily, however, and they filed a lengthy petition with the General Court in Boston, protesting the proposed division and making explicit the nature of the real trouble in Amherst.

To begin with, these petitioners, seventy in number, were the social and political elite of the center and their supporters, including such village leaders as Josiah Chauncey, Simeon Strong, Jonathan Cowles, John Field, John Nash, the Boltwoods, Kelloggs, Colemans, and some Dickinsons. The petitioners took pains to point out that of the total taxable valuation of the district of £7,800 they owned £4,220, or 54 percent. The petition also complained that the proponents of division had transferred enough property to otherwise ineligible sons to enable them to vote and thus become a "majority party" bent on pleasing "their own humor at the expense of your Petitioners ruin."Woven through the petition was the vaguely articulated theme that seniority and estate deserved the protection of the General Court.

The tactics of the opposite party marked them as experts in the craft of politics. Tactical maneuvering could hardly have been absent before this date, and the multitude of earlier decisions of land and school questions must have called for politics of a fairly sophisticated variety, but their complexity and the lack of detailed documentary evidence makes analysis impossible. In 1773, however, the progress of the dispute can be traced because the names of the contestants are in the town records and on the petitions for all to read and count. The fact that people were willing to stand up and be counted may in itself reveal the growing intensity of feeling.

No legal division of the district could be accomplished without the approval of the General Court, but the dissident majority temporarily avoided this hurdle simply by voting to build two meetinghouses with no mention of two parishes, though that would have been the practical result. The old guard recovered some of its lost ground in January 1774 when the General Court, in answer to the antidivision petition, issued a *citation* halting all proceedings pending further consideration. Not to be denied, the "outlyers" took control of a district meeting, appointed a committee to draft an answer to the petition, and gave the committee plenary power to act "as they Shall think best for the Town"—a delegation of power unusual for Amherst. At the same meeting a "Large Majority" voted to divide the district into northern and southern halves with "the Centre of the

Meeting House" to be the demarcation line, certainly a symbolic gesture of defiance. Eventually the General Court appointed a committee to investigate the charges and countercharges on the spot.

The significant feature of this confrontation is the way in which the village divided over the issue, and it represents the first instance in which there is enough surviving factual information to permit present-day historians to examine the cracks that were appearing in the societal structure of Amherst in some detail.

The antidivision petitioners were correct in stating that they represented property. Of the eight wealthiest men on the tax list seven signed the petition. Yet this was more than a rich man's problem, for some of the low men on the economic totem pole also signed. The petitioners were also correct in complaining that the proposed division would leave them on the outskirts of either of the new parishes. A mapping of their homes shows a distinct clustering around the center they had in a sense created. This particular argument was an old one in New England and recurs in the records of town after town. It was, of course, an inevitable result of settlement patterns whether the center developed first, as was the case in older towns, or as a postsettlement development as was the case in Amherst. The complaint that the opposition party was accumulating votes by transferring enough property to sons to enfranchise them may have been true, but the number of father-son combinations on the antidivision petition generates the suspicion that it was a case of the pot calling the kettle black.

But there was a larger issue that pushed the division problem into the background; it first appeared in the minutes of the same meeting of January 26, 1774 that chose Moses and Reuben Dickinson as the town agents to fight the antidivision forces before the General Court. At the end of this session there were three actions that catch the eye. First, it was decided to "Chews a Com^tee of Corrispondance to Refer with the Com^tee of Corrispondence in the Town of Boston." Second, the meeting once again chose Moses and Reuben Dickinson, together with Joseph Williams, Jacob McDaniel, and Nathaniel Dickinson as members of this committee. Then the committee was directed to "Draw up a Letter" for the Boston committee.

The simultaneous appearance of the division question and the Committee of Correspondence on the meeting agenda must have been more than mere coincidence, but the connecting links are difficult to discern. Whether or not the two issues were connected, Amherst was officially acknowledging for the first time the existence of trouble between the colonies and the mother country and, for that matter, the existence of the outside world. There had been Amherst men in the French and Indian War; but it was a Hadley rather than a district matter, and the hardships and heartaches of these men and their families are not visible in the official records. The inhabitants of Amherst cannot have been ignorant of the crisis generated by the Stamp Act of 1765 or the Townshend Acts of 1767 or the landing of British troops in Boston in 1768 or the Boston Massacre of 1770. Amherst men had served in the General Court as Hadley representatives, and Boston newspapers must have been passed around at the tavern. Yet these events which seemed earthshaking in Boston, New York, Philadelphia, and Williamsburg, Virginia, did not distract the Amherst district meetings from their methodical consideration of the best location for a school, the precise boundaries of Deacon Simeon Clark's lot, or the pressing question of whether hogs could run at large if properly ringed and yoked. The impression of calm is, of course, deceptive. Traditionally the district meeting dealt only with district business, not the expressions of opinion on other topics of the day, and the old hands were not easily persuaded to change their ways. But the total absence of reference to the storm clouds on the horizon reveals a side of the American Revolution that is often ignored. The population of Boston and its satellite towns only represented some 10 percent of the province, and the tens of thousands of farmers scattered through the villages and towns and districts like Amherst were parochial, conservative, and inert.

Samuel Adams, the chief incendiary, well aware of this fact, never ceased in his efforts to arouse the country and to bring to these people some of his sense of urgency. He might control Boston, but without the support of the country towns he was bound to fail; to gain this support he faced a monumental and frustrating task. The Boston Committee of Correspondence was his propaganda machine and in December 1772 had distributed its first clarion call to every selectman in the province in the form of a pamphlet reciting the usual catalog of grievances against the English government and its minions in America, Lieutenant Governor Thomas Hutchinson in particular. Though Amherst farmers may have been oblivious to the Vice-

Admiralty Courts and the impact of the Iron Act, they might react to more general appeals couched in terms of "taxation without representation" and to warnings of threatened encroachments on the "Civil and Religious Liberty, which in the face of every danger, and even death itself, induced our fathers to forsake the bosom of their Native Country, and begin settlement on bare Creation."

The Boston committee asked for responses and did receive acclaim from 119 towns and districts by April 1773, but not from Amherst. In fact, fewer than a quarter of the towns and districts in Hampshire County bothered to reply. It is little wonder that Samuel Adams's less dedicated followers despaired of generating patriotic fervor in the western towns. Paradoxically it was the Tea Party of December 1773 that supplied the catalyst for the new men of Amherst. During the spring of 1774 some twenty hitherto silent towns, Amherst among them, wrote letters to the Boston committee.

The actual author of the letter which the meeting of March 14, 1774 accepted and forwarded to Boston is unknown, but, whoever he was, he had drunk deep at the well of revolutionary rhetoric. Samuel Adams himself could have done no better. It was full of "Diabolical Designs of our Mercenary and Manevolent Enemies Foreign and Domestic" and "abhorence of that tame submition which tends to Entail on our Posterrity that worst of Curses Slavery." The people of Boston were thanked "in a Perticular manner for the seasonable Indeavours & mandley opposition to prevent the Landing of the East India Companys teas."

The letter is as curious as it is amusing. The Tea Act itself could hardly have aroused much concern in Amherst, certainly not the fiery language of the letter. Neighboring Montague, for example, sharply criticized the Boston mob for its unseemly behavior. On the other hand, it would be rash to ascribe this outburst to the animosities created by the division question. Here we find the mystery of the Revolution. There was obviously a group of men who had become sensitized to the increasing encroachments of an unfeeling and faraway government. "Every Avenue to the Royal Ear seems to be blocked up," wrote the committee. Many of this same group, fresh from their battle with the old guard at the center, were also asserting their right to a place at the core of the local power structure. Thus both questions, "home rule" and "who should rule at home," came into the open at the same time. That the sentiments expressed by the Amherst meeting fell short of unanimity goes without saying, but the fact that it went on the record gives some indication of the effectiveness of the new men in assuming local command.

Revolutionary sentiment became institutionalized later that year when the meeting voted to make the Committee of Correspondence a standing committee and chose Moses Dickinson, Joseph Eastman, Jacob McDaniel, John Dickinson, and Nathaniel Dickinson, Jr., as members. It was significant that the seventy signers of the antidivision petition gained not a single seat on this committee. Two months later Amherst sent young Nathaniel Dickinson, Jr., as a delegate to the rump Provincial Congress meeting at Concord, thus committing the village to the common cause. This commitment was rapidly implemented with the purchase of gunpowder, lead, and flints, then relief collections for beleaguered Boston. These moves were followed by refusal to pay town taxes to the official treasurer of the province and the creation of a Committee of Inspection to enforce the boycott of English goods urged by the Continental Congress.

Despite this splurge of patriotism the American Revolution in Amherst had an ambivalent quality. On the one hand the town officially committed itself to independence and the war being fought to confirm it. A large number of Amherst men answered the call for troops that followed the skirmishes at Lexington and Concord, and the recurring calls for soldiers always produced Amherst men, some bound for glory at Saratoga and some for defeat and disease in Canada or galling garrison duty at Providence. Very few local men served for the duration, but this was the New England pattern. And if Amherst had no roll of honor of men who gave their lives for their country, the town did make its share of sacrifices in terms of heavy taxes, losses through inflation, and family separations.

Yet the divisions in the town persisted. John Dickinson, a leading patriot, estimated that half the town was either loyalist or neutral. He may have ascribed neutralism to anyone who failed to match his own zeal, but even after making allowances for such overstatements it is obvious that the town was deeply divided over the issues of the revolutionary era. That these cleavages cut through earlier groupings, neighborhoods, and even families, seems certain, though a really detailed study remains to be done. The 1772 petition against division of the parish, with its significant property and neighborhood orientation, might serve as a starting point. Of the town's twenty suspected loyalists, for example, fifteen had signed the petition; and the Reverend David Parsons, another loyalist, would doubtless have signed the petition had his signature been appropriate. But as a warning against facile stereotyping it should be noted that thirteen of the signers answered the call for minutemen and marched off to join the siege of Boston, a group that also included two suspected loyalists. And a check of men serving at one time or another on the Committee of Correspondence during the war turns up seven of the antidivision petitioners.

If this complexity is bewildering today, it may give some comfort to know that it was no less so in 1776. The patriot leadership of the town fumed and sputtered. They first determined that thirteen of the suspected group were "unfriendly to their country" and placed them under house arrest until the General Court suggested that this zeal infringed upon the realm of the courts. Another attempt in 1777 to blacklist persons "supposed to be Inimical to the Interest of the United States" ran aground in a town meeting, with the admonition to the accuser, Elijah Baker, to produce the evidence first.

David Parsons presented a more difficult problem. The minister made no secret of his loyalist sympathies, but the office of the minister seemed to be sacrosanct. A complaint was lodged against Parsons, criticizing his failure to pray for the patriot cause, and in 1777 the town voted "That the conduct of the Rev'd David Parsons is not friendly to the Common Cause." Yet the minister continued to preach, and the town continued to pay his salary, an intriguing situation that has no ready explanation. David Parsons rode out the storm, and one can only speculate that the townspeople chose to remain with this frail vessel as the only known quantity and symbol of identity in a world turned upside down.

The capture of Burgoyne's army at Saratoga in the fall of 1777 marked the end of active warfare in New England, and as the war moved south beyond Amherst's field of vision, the heated concerns with loyalists cooled. There were continued calls for money, supplies, and men till Yorktown, calls answered by the town in depreciated currency and an apparently increasing percentage of bounty soldiers from outside the town. In Amherst the Revolution seemed just to fade away, and parochial concerns resumed their place in the town consciousness. The embroglio created by Berkshire

County men to the west over their demands for a new state constitution elicited no response from Amherst until after the 1778 Massachusetts constitution had been rejected by the towns, and then the town meeting merely voted that the town "was Desirous" of having a new constitution.

If the division controversy of 1772 is accepted as a kind of benchmark indicating the way in which Amherst was dividing, the Revolution added puzzling features. In one sense it was an outside force, an intruder, that created new fracture lines that cut across old ones. But at the same time the Revolution reflected local concerns, reinforcing and widening the cracks already there.

The end of the war brought a resurgence of internal conflict in Amherst. On January 1, 1781 David Parsons died after preaching to, and leading, his congregation for forty-five years. One of his longtime parishioners, Doctor Seth Coleman, referred to the "melancholy days" that followed and wrote of the meetinghouse as "an empty place." It is little wonder that the town had approached his loyalism so gingerly. But his death suddenly removed his potent stabilizing influence from the scene, and the ties with the past snapped, or almost snapped.

The vacuum in the pulpit of the Amherst church sucked in the flotsam remaining from the division struggle of 1772 and also elements of the newer alignments brought about by the Revolution. In tracing the paths of the new division as they developed in 1781 and 1782 it must be remembered that more than religion was involved. Despite the decline of religious influence as a predominating force, a decline that accelerated in most of America during the Revolution, there was still an essential unity between church and town in New England. The town as a political entity still supported the church with general taxation and held on to the right to select the minister. Thus the choice of David Parsons's successor was a town meeting matter, and some understanding of town political currents is vital to an understanding of the final split of the church.

In analyzing town politics we must examine the economic status, rate of turnover, location of residence, and the known proclivities of the selectmen over a period of time. Viewed in this way, Amherst's selectmen of the 1780s do give us some hints as to the trends in local sentiment. Traditionally Amherst selectmen, like those of most Massachusetts towns, came from the wealthiest 25 percent of the inhabitants, but they exhibited a more rapid turnover rate than the norm. In Amherst they served an average of only three and one-half years as opposed to four and one-half years in a random selection of towns. In the seven-year period from 1779 through 1785 only two Amherst men were elected to two consecutive terms. In 1779 three of the five selectmen were divisionists, or outlyers, of the 1772 contest and can be classed as avid patriots. In 1780 this coalition broke up, for in that year the all-new board included three representatives of the old center and no outright divisionists. In 1781 the board was again all new; and three of the five had been signers of the center petition of 1772, although two of them, John Billing and Elijah Baker, were among the most rabid patriots during the war. Did the vacant pulpit in the meetinghouse affect this election? There is no certain answer, but it must be considered as a strong possibility.

Lightning finally struck during the summer of 1781 when none other than David Parsons's son, also David, began to preach at the request of the town "for the present," an invitation that was renewed periodically until the following year when young Parsons was invited to become the settled minister of the Amherst church. The invitation was voted by a clear, but hardly overwhelming, majority, and on October 2, 1782 the second David Parsons was ordained at a service in which seven neighboring ministers assisted, four of whom happened to be loyalists. The committee charged by the town with arranging the ordination service was probably dominated, in terms of weight if not in numbers, by such old center loyalists as John Field, Josiah Chauncey, and Ebenezer Boltwood. But this is too simple a picture, since Nathaniel Dickinson, Jr., a sterling patriot, was also a committee member.

Regardless of the town vote and the bipartisan arrangements committee, the ordination of young Parsons was too much for a substantial segment of the town to swallow, and a month later a Second Church was organized at a meeting of dissidents in the home of Ebenezer Mattoon on the east street. Thus appeared a schism that according to some contemporaries was to have ripple effects for three generations.

It is tempting to look upon this otherwise sudden breach as a mere continuation of the division fight of the previous decade with a hiatus for the Revolution, but the surviving records of 1782 and the geography of the break pose a further problem. The outlyers who favored division in 1772 did indeed have a geographic argument in terms of the distances from their homes to the meetinghouse, but when the Second Church was framed up in November 1783 with the aid of "one barrell of rum" the structure was in the east common and at about the same distance from the north and south ends of the town as was the First Church. It is not that distance had ceased to be important, for the decision as to location was based upon measurement "from every man's door, to find the center of travel," as well as the recommendation of arbitrators from surrounding towns. But the ninety-degree shift from the east and west demarcation line proposed in 1772 to the north-south orientation of 1783 indicates the complexity of the fracture lines generated by the formation of the Second Church.

If one attempts to ascribe the break of 1782 to a confrontation between conservative old money and a rising group of new people who were being excluded from places in the local power structure (a plausible explanation of the earlier division attempt), there is more confusion, for the "aggrieved brethren" of the Second Church could hold their own in terms of wealth and old names in the town. Each church had its rich men and its poor men, its 1772 divisionists and antidivisionists, and its center residents and outlyers. The only label that gives a solid clue is that of Tory. The First Church congregation included both patriots and loyalists, but not so the new congregation. There was the blunt accusation from that quarter that the elder Parsons felt "that the Whigs were as unfit to come to the Communion table as the Pagans or infidels" and that the patriot Whigs could expect little "under the Second Reign; but to be censured." To the Second Church leaders it was a question of "like father, like son," for young David Parsons shared his father's political ideology. The schism does lend credence to the idea that the Revolution, the outside force, had indeed penetrated the shell of localism that marked Amherst's early years.

There may have been a less tangible but equally important force at work—plain mistrust or dislike of the young minister. Like many a son who tried to fill his father's place, Parsons could not come to his ministry as a finished product and create his own particular image and office from the day of his ordination. When he stepped into the pulpit, his congregation would not see him as a handsome and learned man clothed in his black gown and white bands, but rather as one of the village boys of twenty years earlier, always underfoot and probably no more sedate than his playmates. The transition would have been difficult at best and certainly was not aided by Parsons's political stance. It is suggestive that one of the most outspoken opponents of Parsons and one of the aggrieved founders of the Second Church was Nathaniel Dickinson, Jr. Dickinson was a classmate of Parsons at Harvard, from which they graduated in the tempestuous Boston year of 1771, and probably knew him better during those formative years than anyone in Amherst. What there may have been in their shared college experience that soured a normally supportive relationship can only be guessed. Perhaps it was nothing more than the Harvard ranking system, a somewhat mysterious formula for divining social rank which placed young Parsons eleventh in the class with young Dickinson far below, forty-eighth in a class of sixty. Some of the missing pieces in the puzzle of the Second Church may in the long run be found only in terms of a clash of personalities or a series of back fence arguments that defy the sophisticated methods used by historians and sociologists of this sophisticated age.

One interesting and perhaps instructive aspect of the confrontation of the 1780s which bears upon the underlying question about the Amherst sense of community can be found in the documentary arguments of the contending groups. In May 1784 the First Church adopted a letter addressed to the "withdrawing brethren." It was patronizing in tone and full of explicit assumptions as to the culpability of the Second Church. But in addition it raised procedural points which revealed a significant change in the traditional patterns of settling disputes. The Second Church was accused of separating "suddenly and percipitately . . . without requesting our assent, or . . . giving us regular Notice." Second, the withdrawing members "neither endeavored to heal the breach . . . nor allowed any time for Reconciliation." Third, the separators "repeatedly rejected . . . offers of healing the supposed offences in ye ancient and Christian method of a mutual Council of Sister Chh^s." It would seem that the Second Church had violated an ancient rule for the resolution of disputes within a town and had broken the bond that would otherwise have signified community. It was perhaps symptomatic of revolution and the increased secularization which Amherst, and most of America, was undergoing.

But the separators stayed separated, and finally the General Court put what amounted to the seal of state approval on the breach, a poor substitute for local consensus. That no man of the second parish served as selectman until Ebenezer Mattoon, Jr., Amherst's own war hero, broke the spell in 1789 may be a reflection of the bitterness arising from the precipitate schism.

It was an age of discontent in western Massachusetts. Hardly had the Second Church raised its meetinghouse and called its minister, Harvard-educated Ichabod Draper, when a new and shattering blow was leveled at the strained ties that held Amherst together. This was Shays's Rebellion, named after its almost unwilling leader, Daniel Shays of Pelham.

Western Massachusetts had been simmering since 1780 under what its inhabitants, with some justice, termed a tyrannical government. No longer the British ministry, but now an unfeeling and unresponsive seaboard oligarchy that controlled the government of the Commonwealth. The unrest could be traced to no single cause; it was more a general malaise. There were specific grievances, of course, such as the tremendous burden of debt brought on by the war and now laid on the taxpayers. Massachusetts, along with the other states and the Continental Congress, had adopted printing press money as the only way to finance the struggle for independence, and this policy, despite price controls and tender laws, had generated a galloping inflation. This inflation was reflected in Amherst's valuation lists of the period. In 1776 Amherst's taxable property was valued at £7,662, but in 1781 this total had jumped to £56,678. By 1786, due to a devaluation of Continental bills, Amherst's valuation plummeted to £3,159. The property had not changed, but its value in terms of a nearly nonexistent currency had fluctuated wildly. The effect of these gyrations, together with an on-again, off-again status of paper currency as legal tender raised havoc with normal debtor-creditor relationships. The General Court did adopt a law permitting the payment of judgments with commodities, but its cumbersome operation and continually threatened repeal exacerbated an already bad situation.

There were also persistent complaints against the high costs of justice, but beneath the multiplicity of specific grievances lay a basic distrust of the commercial-cosmopolitan interests of Boston which were, in the eyes of Amherst men, being enriched at the farmers' expense. There was more than a modicum of truth in this argument; the archaic tax system with its heavy reliance on the poll tax was regressive, and the state impost duties went for the payment of interest and principal at face value on the state obligations held largely by the suspect group.

There were signals of discontent in the town meetings of Amherst. In January 1782 Elijah Baker and Joseph Eastman were chosen to represent the town at a rump convention in Shutesbury, one of the gatherings of dissidents that passed resolves as a prelude to the later outbreak of violence. Later that year Amherst sent John Billing, Elijah Baker, and Martin Kellogg to a county convention at Hatfield. In 1783 the pattern was continued, and in that year Amherst did not even send a representative to the General Court despite the urgings of the county conventions. It was becoming clear which way the wind was blowing in Amherst.

While these protest conventions were attempting futilely to catch the ear of government in Boston, the old answer to such woes began to emerge—mobbing. In 1782 a mob led by Samuel Ely of Conway disrupted the courts in Northampton. When Ely was jailed, another mob freed him; when hostages were jailed pending Ely's surrender, yet another mob appeared to free them, led by none other than Reuben Dickinson of Amherst. The courts at Northampton were closed again in 1786 by a mob, one of whose leaders was Joel Billing, a former Amherst selectman. According to reports Billing led his group "with sword drawn."

This was just the beginning. The tragicomic story of Shays's Rebellion need not be retold here. It is enough to say that a goodly proportion, if not the majority, of Amherst's population sided with the Shaysites. When General Benjamin Lincoln at the head of the state militia marched through Amherst on the snowy night of February 3, 1787 in pursuit of Shays, he found few Amherst men at home. Lincoln's troops captured the main body of the rebel force the next morning at Petersham, and the rebellion died with a whimper.

Fortunately, the message that the unhappy and alienated western Massachusetts farmers had been trying to get through to Boston finally reached receptive ears. A wave of voter sympathy substituted the politic John Hancock for the law-and-order governor, James Bowdoin, and brought a majority of new faces into both the Senate and the House. In Amherst the election results were difficult to

DANIEL SHAYS, LEADER OF THE REBELLION OF 1786.

fathom. Only twenty-one votes were cast instead of the usual thirty-five to forty, and this skimpy turnout favored Bowdoin thirteen to eight. The choice of General Lincoln for Lieutenant Governor was unanimous. This apparent contradiction can be explained by the disfranchisement of known rebels, and there may well have been an informal boycott of the election.

The rebellion raises other questions about Amherst. All the supporters of Shays were required to take an oath of allegiance, and 113 Amherst men did so. The sheer number gives some idea as to the pervasiveness of the movement. Supposedly not all of the oath takers were actually under arms, and the taking of the oath may have been motivated by invisible reasons, but it is a curious list nonetheless. The movement attracted not only soldiers of the Revolution such as Joel and John Billing and Reuben Dickinson, but also prominent Tories such as John Field and John Nash. The cause also found adherents in all social classes. One computation indicates that 38 percent were from the upper economic stratum, 32 percent from the middle, and 30 percent from the poorest sector, proportionate to the population as a whole. Debtors seemed little more prevalent than creditors. When the same curious list is compared to the earlier line of division, the formation of the Second Church, no more light is shed upon the problem. First Church families provided about one-third of the Amherst rebels while the Second Church proportion stood at about 40 percent. One cannot be certain as to the meaning of this event. For a moment, at least, it would seem that the earlier internal problems were entirely subordinated to a broader issue.

The sense of isolation and resistance to faraway authority evinced by such a large number of Amherst people during Shays's Rebellion was reinforced a year later. During the long hot summer of 1787 the delegates to the Philadelphia convention had hammered out a new frame of national government, and with the other states Massachusetts faced the task of ratifying or rejecting their handiwork. Along with New York and Virginia, Massachusetts was considered to be an important pillar in the structure of the proposed republic. The General Court, after some preliminary maneuvering, requested the towns to choose delegates to meet in Boston to debate and act upon the matter. Amherst town records are silent as to the choosing of its delegate, but the choosing was done, and Daniel Cooley was the man. Cooley was born in Sunderland, graduated from Yale, and after serving as an Amherst tavern keeper began to work his way up through the local hierarchy of power. He served on the David Parsons ordination committee and on the town committee charged with convening a church council in the futile attempt to bring the separating brethren back into the fold of the First Church. He also did his civic duty as hogreeve and committeeman for the survey and sale of unneeded town road lands. But in 1787 Cooley suddenly stepped to the front as moderator of the town meeting, representative in the General Court, and delegate to the ratification convention. Not enough is known of Daniel Cooley. He did not appear on the valuation list of 1776 nor in any list of Amherst soldiers of the War for Independence. He was a member of the First Church but played no visible role on either side during Shays's Rebellion. He was apparrently a man of the middle and thus ripe for positions of public trust in a town that was exhausted by the turmoil of the preceding years.

At the convention, Daniel Cooley was articulate in asking such key anti-Federalist questions as how the proposed national government would apportion direct taxes. He voted, as he said, in accordance with the instructions of his town and the "dictates of his conscience" in opposing the constitution. Amherst was in an anomalous position. Hadley, the mother town, as well as Northampton and South Hadley favored the new frame of government, but not Amherst. Historians have been intrigued by the belt of proconstitution sentiment in the river towns and have tended to ascribe it to the commercial orientation that paralleled this water highway. Amherst, however, joined the hill towns of Belchertown, Pelham, Shutesbury, and Leverett in voting nay. These towns had apparently had more than enough of big and distant governments, and their votes on this question would seem to confirm the sentiments of the Shaysites.

In his farewell speech to the convention Cooley stated that, "as it had been agreed to by a majority, he should endeavor to convince his constituents of the propriety" of the new constitution. His advice was adopted, but it would be twelve years before Amherst would put forward her own candidate for a seat in the national legislature, General Mattoon.

As Amherst entered the nineteenth century calm once again prevailed. The strains created by the Revolution, the separation of the Second Church, and Shays's Rebellion slipped into the past. The wounds were outwardly healed though the scars were still there. As the generation that had precipitated these struggles retired from active town life, died, or moved away, the village settled down as a tiny speck on the map of the new republic. Mr. Parsons preached to one congregation and Mr. Draper to the other. The town meeting reverted to debating questions of schooling, boundary lines, the building of bridges and, more significantly, attempts to build a road to Shutesbury or turnpikes to the east or west. It would be tempting to state that Amherst had retreated within its shell after two disrupting excursions into the world outside. This could not have been wholly true, for once that door had been opened it was very difficult to close. But Amherst was clinging to the old ways. The Federalist Party, though declining nationally, still held the allegiance of this conservative town. Jeffersonian Republicans were no more welcome than turnpikes or new religious sects, Boston Unitarians included.

The last clear index of town attitude during this period was again the result of an outside force, this time the backwash of the Napoleonic wars of Europe which eventually sucked the nation into its second war with Great Britain, Mr. Madison's War as it was termed in New England.

In terms of European depredations against New England shipping and the attendant publicity, it should have been New England's War, but this was not the way that New England, and western Massachusetts in particular, viewed it. Following Jefferson's embargo of 1808, the Amherst town meeting dropped its parochial mask and adopted a ringing resolve against the Republican administration, employing the best Federalist rhetoric and viewing with "deepest concern . . . that cool and deliberate tyranny, which at present pervades our public councils, and which, unless arrested by the genius of New England, will inevitably lead to a more confirmed despotism, or to a division of these United States." Despite Amherst's veiled threat of secession the war eventually came in 1812, and all of Hampshire County united against it. At a Northampton meeting chaired by Ebenezer Mattoon, Samuel F. Dickinson presented and secured the adoption of a resolution deploring a war "neither just, necessary, nor expedient" and asking that peace commissioners be appointed. The Peace of Amiens in 1815 did not stop Amherst's suspicion of the outside world, but in 1815 there was peace in Amherst too.

We are left with our original questions as to the existence and the nature of the Amherst community. It would be a mistake merely to equate contentiousness and controversy with lack of community. What one must examine are the methods by which controversy was resolved. Amherst controversies there were aplenty, ranging all the way from the shadowy probing for the proper location of the meetinghouse and its subconscious by-product, the center, through the traumas of the Revolution, the breaking away of the Second Church, Shays's Rebellion, and the rejection of national concerns attendant upon the adoption of the federal Constitution and the War of 1812. In some cases there was eventual consensus and in others a tacit agreement to disagree. But in no case was there a complete breakdown of societal structure or a mass exodus. What had happened, we must suppose, was a subconscious internalization of the Revolution, a process that "unhinged the principles, the morality, and the religion of the country more than could have been done by a place of forty years," as President Dwight of Yale put it.

Erik Erikson, in dealing with national character, has made some observations that might well be applied to early Amherst:

One may begin rather than end with the proposition that a[town's] identity is derived from the ways in which history has, as it were, counterpointed certain opposite potentialities; the ways in which it lifts this counterpoint to a unique style of civilization, or lets it disintegrate into a mere contradiction.

Early Amherst's salvation and its ability to survive in spite of its unhinging may have rested in its geographical diffuseness, for from its beginnings the town slipped with relative ease into a form which modern urban experts term *multinucleated*. At the time this diffuseness was an accidental rejection of the older norm of *knit-togetherness,* though with hindsight it appears to have been a herald of the future. As a mechanism for the damping of the centrifugal forces generated in any growing society, it succeeded. Instead of a forced melting pot it became a salad bowl, a mosaic of life-styles and interests bound together in a flexible confederation.

But what of community? Such an entity does not exist in a vacuum; it must have an awareness of boundaries and of something different beyond these boundaries. The harsh outside world that Amherst had discovered was really too foreign to provide such a comparison. It motivated a certain withdrawal, to be sure, but did little to make Amherst aware of itself. In 1815 there was a lack of conscious community in this sense, for the feeling of the town was defensive and negative. What was still lacking was a positive image of self, but there did seem to be what the Romans called *genius loci*—the spirit of the place.

NOTE: The writers have drawn freely from a variety of sources too numerous to list. Aside from such standard sources as Carpenter and Morehouse, *History of Amherst,* Sylvester Judd, *History of Hadley,* and Robert J. Taylor, *Western Massachusetts in the Revolution,* the editors have borrowed from, and wish to acknowledge, the work of numerous students at Amherst College and the University of Massachusetts, particularly William Doubleday, David N. Smith, Andrew Rapp, Mary Wardwell, and Sheila Rainford. The documentary and manuscript materials to be found in the Amherst town hall and The Jones Library, are, of course, invaluable.

CHAPTER TWO

A DAY IN 1800

HUGH F. BELL

It was a cold January morning, bitterly cold. The soapstones at the foot of the bed which had been so warming the previous evening were now nothing more than cold soapstone. As Joshua Warren swung out from under the quilts, the cornhusks of the mattress rustled, and the hempen webbing of the bedstead creaked. He donned his thick stockings, deerskin breeches, and homespun shirt and stumbled into the kitchen. His wife Silence was bending over the fire with little Abigail in the crook of her left arm, stirring the contents of a steaming kettle. Joshua moved to the fire, chucked Abigail under the chin, and looked for a moment in wonder into her eyes, so wide open as only a year-old child's can be. Then after dashing some water from the bucket onto his face he moved to the settle to pull on his big cowhide boots that had been warming by the fire.★

"You had best waken Josh if he isn't already frozen to death. I can hear the creatures moving about." Silence did not even turn her head from the fire. Joshua rose, walked to the ladder leading to the half loft, and rattled it. "Come on boy, do y' want the stock to kick the barn down?" He was answered by the appearance over the edge of the loft of the tousled head of his ten-year-old son, Josh. Soon the boy descended the ladder, clumped across to the root cellar trapdoor, disappeared, and came up with a bucket of potatoes. As Josh was putting on his heavy jacket, his father briefly examined the potatoes. "Well, if these are the worst you can find they are keeping better than I thought." Joshua, with a growing number of his skepti-

---

★The characters, places, and events described here are real, except for the Warren family, the schoolmaster, and the peddler—and maybe they were real at that.

cal neighbors, had been trying the potato, for his own table and as a winter feed supplement for his stock.

Now attired in his jacket, mitts, and wool cap, young Josh retrieved the bucket from his father's critical inspection and opened the door to face the morning gloom. The snow squeaked under foot with the cold but the air was still. The eastern sky over the Pelham Hills was just beginning to turn pink, and the winter stars still glittered overhead. The smell of wood smoke in the air was replaced by the sweet-sour odor of a barn as Josh swung open the door. He was expected and greeted with snuffling and the thudding of hoofs on the dirt floor. First in line for attention was the cow, Jerusha, named for a fractious maiden aunt, though Josh's parents would quickly deny the connection if queried. Jerusha was due to freshen shortly and thus demanded and received special attention. Josh forked down some fresh hay into her stall and then doled out a generous portion of potatoes. Next came the old ox, always just called that, Old Ox. This trusted servant of the family got only hay. Finally there was Brigadier, the horse recently acquired. Brigadier was of indeterminate age and bloodline and for that reason perhaps was used indiscriminately under a saddle or in front of a harrow or cart. He had a mean cast in one eye which was the source of some concern to Josh, who did his best to hide it.

After taking care of the creatures, Josh threw a few handfuls of corn to the hens in their winter coop in the corner of the barn and then visited the big sow. She was hungry as always, but would have to await kitchen scraps. Next came the unpleasant chore of getting water. During the summer Joshua had spent several days constructing a canopy roof over the well and replacing the cumbersome sweep and bucket with a proper windlass that Josh could handle. Though he deeply admired his father, Josh could not help wondering if the construction of the windlass was really a scheme to shift the burden of the water chore to his young shoulders. No matter—the task was now to break the skim ice with the bucket, carry water for the stock, and bring two buckets into the house for his mother. That chore completed, the family was ready to partake of the contents of the steaming kettle which Silence ladled out into wooden bowls for her menfolk. It was hasty pudding, the Yankee version of cornmeal mush, just as it was every morning, but still delicious with a dab of butter from the crock and molasses. Abigail, now seated on her mother's lap, was being weaned and fussed a bit at this new food, but after spitting some out she became aware that this brought frowns of disapproval and settled down to eat. The minds of Silence, Joshua, and Josh were all turning over the same thoughts, thoughts of the two little girls that Silence had borne between Josh and Abigail and who had succumbed to the throat distemper one after the other. Would little Abigail of the big eyes escape that fate?

Joshua finally broke the reverie to announce the plan for the day. "Josh, wash your face and get your copy book while I saddle Brigadier. I have to go to the mill and then to the center. You can ride behind me to school. Silence, I figure to get two bushels of corn ground at the mill if the wheel isn't frozen."

"And why, then, are you going all the way to the center—to drink rum with the high and mighty?" Joshua merely growled that he had business to attend to, knowing that it was an answer that would turn Silence's mouth into a tight, straight line—well named, that woman. After struggling into his coat, mitts, and hat Joshua headed for the barn and saddled Brigadier. He then shovelled Indian corn from the crib into two big tow sacks, tied them together, and heaved them across Brigadier's back behind the crude saddle. By this time Josh had appeared, bundled and ready with his well-worn copy book in his belt. Riding behind his father, even on the corn sack knots, was a rare treat.

As he gave his son a hand to hoist him up to his precarious perch behind the saddle, Joshua asked about schooling. "What is Mr. Nott teaching you now?" The boy mumbled that all week would be spent on "cyphering." As Brigadier plodded across the rickety bridge which carried the Sunderland road across Mill Creek, Joshua quizzed the boy on simple multiplication which was all the cyphering Joshua knew anyway. When they crested the rise from Mill Creek hollow they could see Mr. Nott, the schoolmaster, carrying a load of wood into the little school house. Smoke was already drifting up from the chimney into the still air, so there was some hope of enough warmth inside to permit writing without mitts. As the father of a scholar, Joshua had grudgingly provided his share of school firewood, "so long as it wasn't wasted." This year the three-month session of school for North Amherst children fell in the dead of winter, but at least they didn't have to trudge all the way to the north east school out near Kimball's place.

In front of the school Josh slid expertly from Brigadier's back, and Joshua turned east on the road to Shutesbury. It was full light now, but there was no sign of life except for the hanging plumes of smoke from the two houses he passed before coming to the west street. Once again he turned left, along the wagon track to the mill. Banging on the door brought Ebenezer Dickinson out of the gloom. Dickinson, though a part owner, did not do much actual milling, but his lack of expertise mattered little since the mill wheel proved to be frozen solid, just as Joshua had feared. After some brief negotiations, it was agreed that Joshua would leave his shelled corn and on his way home pick up its equivalent in meal drawn from a bin Dickinson had accumulated from earlier tolls. Joshua, in turn, would contribute a tenth of his corn in payment for the milling. Ebenezer's son Rufus, one of Josh's good friends though three years older, had been standing quietly behind his father. To Joshua's question as to why he wasn't in school, the lad came up with the ready answer that his mother thought he might be coming down with the ague, but Joshua, remembering some of his son's comments, suspected that Rufus just did not take to cyphering.

Joshua, mounting the less heavily laden and much happier Brigadier, rode south on the west street. He passed Ebenezer Dickinson's house and then still another Dickinson farmstead, muttering to himself that the Dickinson clan grew like weeds, then John Eastman's and the old Mattoon place, and so on. As he rounded the shoulder of Mount Pleasant and neared the center, the sense of winter loneliness dissipated. The scattered houses were now closer together, and the packed snow showed signs of increased traffic. As he passed the fork where the road to Sunderland branched away from the west street he could see the gambrel roof of Judge Simeon Strong's house at the top of the rise to the south, and past the Clark place the Reverend David Parsons's house across the Hadley road came into view.

On reaching the center, Joshua dismounted and hitched Brigadier to the post in front of Hezekiah Strong's store and paused a moment to take in the scene. Caterwise stood Joel Dickinson's little tavern, and behind the tavern the Parsons's house. To the south across the wide part of the west road, the meetinghouse overlooked what people were beginning to call the common. Down the hill to the east was Zebina Montague's house. All in all Joshua could count about twenty plumes of smoke, and he thought to himself that Amherst was becoming quite a village. But it was Hezekiah Strong's store that was the center of his attention. Hezekiah was adding more wood to his fire as Joshua entered, and the blaze was cheering after the cold ride from North Amherst. But before Joshua could remove his coat and hat, Hezekiah gave him something more important to think about. "General Mattoon was in yesterday looking for you, Joshua. He has some work he needs done."

Now Joshua Warren bowed to no man, but when General Mattoon, Amherst's war hero, sheriff of Hampshire County, and prospective candidate for representative to the federal legislature wanted to see one, one did not delay. Furthermore Joshua had an idea as to the reason for the summons, for the General had been talking during the fall about the necessity of enlarging the barn given by his father-in-law along with his daughter. Like most Amherst farmers Joshua was a jack-of-all-trades, but in addition he was a master of the mysteries of barn building and was often called upon for advice and skilled labor in that art.

After telling Hezekiah he would be back for an important purchase, Joshua mounted Brigadier once again and turned east down the road to Pelham. At the foot of the hill in the east village, which was called Sodom by folks at the center, he turned south down the east street and soon arrived before the Mattoon house. Mary Mattoon (yet another Dickinson) answered his knock and, after inquiring as to Silence's health, directed him to the barn where he found the General. It was as Joshua had expected. General Mattoon's expansion of his farming activities had made the old barn too small, and he wanted Joshua to take charge of adding two bays to the rear of the existing structure. "I know it's too cold to be raising a barn, Joshua, but I have had my men squaring up some timbers and sledding them in. What I need to know now is whether you can do this work early in the spring and whether these timbers are proper for the job." Using the time-honored methods, Joshua found a long pine pole and was soon up under the rafters measuring the existing beams and queen posts, cutting notches in his pole at appropriate points. He followed the General into the yard where the timbers had been laid out and broad-axed roughly to proper dimensions. After scrambling over the pile with his measuring pole, Joshua announced that everything necessary was on hand and that he would be ready to "frame the bents," or construct the sections of frame on the ground with mortise, tenon, and pegs during the first thaw. Doing work for the General was a mixed blessing, for he was an exacting task master, but he usually paid in real money, a rare commodity in the valley. There was one other possible problem. "General, the man I like to work with on framing is old George Aries over Mount Warner way, if that is agreeable with you." Now George Aries was an old Hessian soldier who had drifted away from Burgoyne's convention army after Saratoga, settled in Hadley, and brought his wife over from Germany. The General's eyes glinted for a moment. He would never forget Saratoga, and for that matter he would never let anyone else forget it. Many a tavern gathering had been lulled to sleep as Mattoon related once again his story of the great battle, a story which grew longer and more detailed as the years went by. Joshua had been a mere lad during the Revolution, and it was little more than legend to him, but he was well aware of the general's sensitivity on the subject. But Mattoon had no objection to hiring George Aries. From all reports he was a quiet, God-fearing citizen of Hadley, and that was what counted.

The bargain concluded, Joshua returned to the center and reappeared in Hezekiah Strong's humble emporium, a not very general general store, but all that the center could boast. Today was Silence Warren's birthday, and Joshua had a gift in mind. He had Hezekiah dig out his box of notions, as they called them, and after some thought selected three yards of blue silk ribbon that matched the color of Silence's eyes. She would never believe that he had chosen it for that reason, but beneath his rather taciturn exterior there beat a heart with some romance in it. With his gift carefully wrapped and the transaction recorded on the debit side of his running account with the storekeeper, Joshua tucked the package inside his jacket and was free to cross the street to the humble but convivial tavern presided over by Joel Dickinson and his good wife Eunice. The windows were fogged over from the heat and condensation of much conversation within; as he approached the door, Joshua could see the glow of the fire, and his mouth started to water at the thought of a mug of hot rum punch. The tiny room contained about seven or eight customers, some of the regulars and a stranger or two. David Parsons, the still controversial minister of the First Church was there, together with Zebina Montague, the perennial town representative in the General Court who lived across the common from the tavern, and Judge Simeon Strong. These worthies were deep in conversation around one table. At the other table a stranger, or to put it less charitably, a peddler, was regaling his auditors with stories of his travels. Joshua, after making small talk with Eunice Dickinson and filling a mug with her justly famous punch, joined the latter group. The hawker, Silas Poor by name, was heading west despite the season. He came from Taunton, had filled his pack in Boston with pins, "best London pins with heads that won't fall off," needles, scissors, pewter spoons, spools of thread, packets of "Genuine Billious Pills," and what not. Poor was bound, according to his story, for the Mohawk valley, where eager buyers were waiting in line to buy his merchandise. He was asking about stories he had heard of Levi Dickinson of Hadley and his broom corn. According to rumor, Dickinson had been growing broom corn and was making the best brooms available anywhere. Poor was anxious to acquire some of these miraculous brooms for sale on his way west, and, if they were as good as reported, he might employ himself as Dickinson's agent. Simeon Strong had caught the drift of this conversation and told Poor that indeed Dickinson was making those brooms, that Mrs. Strong would have none other, but that there would be no more brooms available till fall.

Soon tiring of the peddler's chatter, Joshua retrieved a copy of the *Hampshire Gazette* from the seat under the window and idly turned the pages. Several items caught his eye. The Amherst-Shrewsbury Turnpike Company was advertising its stock at $25.00 a share. Was this another will-o'-the-wisp, or would there finally be a good road to the east? What changes would it bring? Would it affect his land or its value? There seemed to be some men of estate behind the scheme, Ebenezer Hunt of Northampton and Major Conkey of Pelham. Building on these speculative thoughts, Joshua turned to an advertisement by the Great Western Turnpike Company for bids on a section of its toll road at Schoharie on the Mohawk. What a heathenish name! Remembering the peddler's talk of the Mohawk country, Joshua paused a moment. What would Silence think of moving west? Joshua could well imagine the answer to this and dropped that thought for the time being at least.

Joshua then skimmed through a whole black-bordered page of

eulogies delivered from Boston to Savannah on the death of George Washington. His feelings were mixed. Washington was a name to conjure with, yet Joshua had a Yankee farmer's inherent distrust of the great Virginia plantation owners with their slaves and coaches, and now they were saying that President Adams might not be able to beat that Jacobin Jefferson in the upcoming election. Maybe New England should just up and leave the union of states if those southern potentates were going to occupy all the seats of power forever and a day.

Ah, here was something of real interest, an advertisement for an apprentice to learn the trade of printer and bookbinder. Josh would be too young he guessed, but in a year or two this might be something to think about. On the other hand, he was going to need all the help he could get on his farm, particularly if he could buy or rent some more land from his neighbor John Dickinson. Enough of this daydreaming—the afternoon was wearing on, and Silence would be unhappy enough as it was.

Thoroughly warmed, within and without, Joshua put on his jacket and hat and prepared to leave the society of the tavern but was detained by the Reverend Dr. Parson's hand on his arm and a quip or a question, one could never tell which with this minister. "I hope to see you at meeting Sunday, Joshua." Joshua was not a member in full communion of the First Church, and was, in fact, a bit of a backslider despite the efforts of both Silence and David Parsons. The only retort he could articulate was a question as to whether it was worse to freeze in meeting or roast in the eternal fires. Parsons laughed, but continued the inquisition. "I understand you may be helping our high sheriff add to his barn. Is the addition to the east or the west?" Without thinking Joshua told him it would be the east end that would be extended. Later, as Brigadier was plodding northward around Mount Pleasant, it dawned on Joshua that Parsons had perhaps been voicing his suspicions that General Mattoon was luring his parishoners to the Second, or East, Church. No matter, thought Joshua, let the clever Dr. Parsons go on wondering. He was too sly for his own good.

Joshua stopped at the mill, roused Ebenezer Dickinson from his warm spot by the fire, loaded his bags of ground meal behind his saddle, and headed for home. Brigadier, sensing the end of his work day, broke into his lackluster version of a trot and needed neither guidance nor urging. As the pair turned north on the road to Sunderland, the gray of the eastern sky was beginning to darken, and a dusting of snow all but obscured the spark of light from Silence's kitchen window. Joshua remembered her face when he had completed that window with real glass, wavy as it was, her window to the tiny world in which they lived.

Brigadier went right into his stall and was soon munching on some of the all too rapidly diminishing supply of hay that Joshua forked down for him. Old Ox and Jerusha had been fed, so that boy was worth something after all. Even the sow and the chickens were quiet, or at least the soft sounds they were making were contented. The contentment of the evening was pervasive, for when Joshua entered the house Silence showed a trace of a smile as she turned from the kitchen fire, Abigail's wide eyes reflected the flames as she lay in her trundle, and Josh was enthusiastically telling his father that Mr. Nott was going to teach him some Latin as a reward for good work.

The Warrens' dinner of a salt pork stew, boiled potatoes, and cider was occasionally interrupted by Joshua's account of his day at the center. Silence shot a disapproving glance at her husband on hearing about the conversation with the minister, but she could readily understand how vexatious Dr. Parsons could be with his jokes and double meanings.

Josh needed some prodding, but he bundled up to go out for firewood and another bucket of water. As his last chore of the day, he lined up the soapstones near the fire in anticipation of a cold night and settled down with a rush light sputtering at his shoulder to work on his copy book. Joshua, a bit taken aback by the boy's enthusiasm over Latin and his obvious concentration now, wondered if perhaps apprenticing him to a printer might not be best after all. That old fox, Franklin, had done pretty well in that calling.

While Silence fed Abigail some of the potato mashed up in the stew gravy, Joshua fished some sticks out of the corner and sat on the settle whittling and scraping with his prized knife on the mysterious pieces of birch. Silence glanced at her husband from time to time, her natural curiosity as to his work nearly overcoming her natural reticence, but in the end her name won out, and she said nothing. Joshua was well aware of the struggle going on and chuckled to himself. Finally the pieces satisfied him and, using a ladle, he extracted a rib bone from the bottom of the iron stew pot and proceeded to rub his sticks assiduously with it. Soon the smooth birch began to glisten. When he had achieved the finish he desired, Joshua fitted the three sticks together, a middle piece with crossed pieces at each end. At last it was recognizable. "A niddy-noddy for me," blurted Silence, all smiles. Joshua replied that it was nothing fancy but that it would give her something to measure her yarn on till he could make her a proper winder like that one of Mrs. Nash's she was always prating about. Josh was distracted from his copy book by the exchange, took his mother's new acquisition over to the fire to examine with admiration the finish of the device and the tight fit of the tiny mortices and tenons on the crosspieces. Was there anything his father couldn't make? Silence was suddenly embarrassed by her own enthusiasm and covered it by ordering Josh up to the loft to bed. Grumbling Josh gingerly wrapped a soapstone in a piece of blanket and ascended to his nest in the loft.

Soon the crackling of the last wood in the fire was the only audible sound. Silence couldn't wait to try what she thought was her present and was skillfully transferring a ball of yarn to the new measurer. "Niddy noddy, niddy noddy, niddy noddy," she whispered to herself as she swiftly ran the yarn up and back and up and back from crosspiece to crosspiece.

At this point Joshua brought out his little package and handed it to Silence without a word. Her fingers shook a bit as she unwrapped it and shook even more as she unrolled the blue silk before the fading firelight. She was already picturing how it would look threaded around the sleeves and neckline of the white linen dress she had brought with her when she married Joshua. Vanity was a sin, she knew, but it would be so pretty.

Abigail's wide eyes were now closed in sound sleep, and Silence smiled.

PART TWO

The Enterprises, Contentions, Civic Consciousness, and Customs of Nineteenth Century Amherst

CHAPTER THREE

THE RISE AND DECLINE OF MANUFACTURES AND OTHER MATTERS

GEORGE R. TAYLOR

George Taylor is Professor of Economic History, *emeritus,* at Amherst College. One of the founders of the American Studies program at Amherst, he also served as Editor of *The Journal of Economic History.* His book *The Transportation Revolution* is considered the best analysis of American economic history during the period covered by this essay.

BEGINNINGS, 1750–1810

Economic aspects of Amherst's development are best approached in relation to its geography and history of settlement. Hampshire is the middle of three Massachusetts counties which constitute a broad ribbon extending from north to south and spanning the Connecticut River. Its central section includes the alluvial meadows on each side of the river, and to the west and east it extends into the rugged Berkshires on one extremity and to the Pelham Hills and their southern continuation on the other side. Three river towns, Northampton, Hadley, and Hatfield were settled in the last half of the seventeenth century and continued to grow into the first third of the following century. Then in the 1730s, as fear of Indian raids disappeared, Hampshire County attracted a growing influx of pioneering farmers; waves of migrating families found their way over the broken hills of western Massachusetts on rough roads often little more than trails through the forest or alternately poled clumsy flatboats or rafts along the banks of the winding Connecticut River.

Amherst, originally the East, or Third, Precinct of the town of Hadley, had been parcelled out to Hadley yeomen who for the most part disposed of their holdings to new settlers. By whatever route they came they sought tillable land beyond the settled valley where the best locations had already been taken up. Even the hilly areas well beyond the alluvial plain, towns like Worthington on the west and Belchertown on the east, had attracted more than 1,000 inhabitants at the time of the first federal census in 1790. By then the great migration to Hampshire County had about run its course. That so many migrating farmers should have attempted to make a living on the stony and forbidding upland slopes comes as a surprise. But they sought unoccupied lands and well-drained fields which were preferred over wet areas commonly believed to be unproductive and unwholesome. Some came as religious groups like the Pelham Presbyterians. Others came to such towns as Belchertown, tempted by Northampton promoters who sought to dispose of their extensive land grants at a profit.

The quality of Amherst's soil varied, rich and fertile in some areas near the Hadley line but less so in the upland fields rising in the south to the Holyoke Range and to the east toward the Pelham Hills. Even in the latter new arrivals cleared and cultivated stony fields which often defied their best efforts to produce paying crops on land soon exhausted after a few years of cultivation. Also, in most communities there were patches of swampy land, *wet meadows,* which until drainage projects were carried out later could not be cultivated and yielded only coarse hay with little nutritional value. Lawrence Swamp in the southeastern part of the town remains to this day unavailable for agricultural purposes.

Town valuation lists of the Revolutionary period permit a partial view of Amherst's colonial economy. One hundred twenty dwelling houses and eighty-nine barns were scattered over the town in 1771. These numbers had risen to 136 and 112 by 1784. Everywhere general farming prevailed. The number of bushels of grain raised in 1771 was 6,596. Five hundred twenty-four barrels of cider made in that year rose to 862 by 1784. The fact that land devoted to mowing and pasturage considerably exceeded that in tillage indicates the importance of farm animals and dairying. It could not have been a very affluent society, for both horses and oxen were less numerous than able male voters. In 1771 the number of swine slightly exceeded the number of such voters. Meat cattle numbered 2½ times that number and sheep 3½ times. The records reflect the undeveloped state of the economy, for in 1781 only 7.5 percent of the land was in tillage and slightly over half in woodlots and unimproved. Gristmills and saw-mills on the Mill River in the north and the Fort River in the south of town catered to local needs. Between three and six were in operation between 1771 and 1784. One or two potash works provided material for soapmaking and for pot and pearl ashes to meet an export de-mand. A varying number of shops, fourteen in 1771, served the town. Sylvester Judd says these were "those of tradesmen and mechanics" (385). Finally, a distillery in East Amherst produced both gin and brandy chiefly to meet a local demand.

Although farmers and their families provided for most of their own needs, the economy of the town of Amherst was not a self-sufficient one. Its prosperity depended in no small part upon distant, foreign markets. Only by producing an export surplus could the inhabitants obtain in exchange such needed imports as salt, molasses, and hardware or such luxuries as tea, coffee, rum, dyes, pewter, and stoneware. The Amherst farmer could offer only the items of his ordinary production, the excess over his consumption needs for which a market demand existed and transportation costs were not prohibitive. So he brought to the local merchant small quantities of marketable produce, a few bushels of corn, wheat, or oats, salt pork or beef, cheese, butter, flax seed, wool, and sometimes even small accumulations of beeswax, tallow, or ashes. Or a local farmer-trader might buy up cattle which he would drive to market at Boston or Hartford, bringing back needed supplies or even currency, always a scarce item prized for paying taxes or interest on debt. Having col-lected enough country produce to make a wagon load, the Amherst merchant drove to Northampton where he traded for goods brought up the river. In turn the Northampton buyer sent his purchases by barge down the Connecticut to Springfield or more likely Hartford or Middletown, Connecticut. In one of these cities he usually dis-posed of his goods to an exporting merchant who shipped food products like corn and barreled beef to the West Indies. Flax seed and potashes more often found a market in the British Isles. As yet the small coastal cities along the Atlantic obtained ample supplies of country products from nearby sources.

Amherst farmers like their fellows in other western Massachusetts towns lived in a marginal producing area. Shipment by the Connecticut River, though ordinarily cheaper than transportation by land, involved many difficulties. When ice or flood did not close the river to traffic, the necessity of portaging around the South Hadley Falls or passing through the canal after 1795 and, except in times of high water, of by-passing the Enfield Rapids, made the first leg of the export shipment more costly than the subsequent one to the Caribbean or Europe. Even so, obstacles remained. Only small sloops could navigate the 5½ foot river canal (deepened after 1800 to 7½ feet). Some small vessels sailed all the way to St. Kitts or Jamaica but most gave up river cargo to somewhat larger ships sailing from a convenient port, often New London. Finally, foreign markets proved an uncertain outlet in an era when wars added to the usual risks of ocean navigation, and in the West Indies changing regulations, frequent delays, and arbitrary seizures laid toll on commerce. Nevertheless, these difficulties though troublesome were in ordinary times offset by the advantageous prices available for country produce in the West Indian trade.

Settlers streamed into the Connecticut River towns in such large numbers between 1765 and 1790 that they nearly doubled the population of Hampshire County. The record of Amherst's surprising growth in these years stands out in Table 1. As early as the 1750s it overtook the town of Hadley. Amherst's 645 inhabitants in 1765 rose to 915 in 1776 and to 1,235 in 1790, an increase of more than 90 percent in twenty-five years. This growth rate was exceeded in Hampshire County by only two towns, Belchertown and Pelham. Belchertown, whose acreage was the most extensive in the county, and Northampton were the two towns in the county with a larger population in 1790. Only Northampton surpassed Amherst in persons per square mile and that by less than one (see Table 1). Amherst's relatively rapid increase pre-1790 is puzzling. Of course it can be pointed out that the river towns of Northampton, Hatfield, and Hadley had been long settled so that migrants arriving in the second half of the eighteenth century looked to open lands beyond. In soil and location Amherst appears to have been superior to the hill towns. Yet considerations beyond fertility of soil must have sometimes prevailed. Why, for example, did such hill towns as Pelham and Belchertown grow much more rapidly in the twenty-five years before 1790? Or, glancing beyond towns in Hampshire County, why, despise their rugged terrain, had Conway, Colrain, and New Salem attracted more inhabitants by 1790 than Amherst? These are among the questions which invite further study of eighteenth century migration into the Connecticut River Valley.

In the two decades following 1790 the eastern cities of the United States and the western frontiers attracted increasing numbers, but the flow of migrants into the Connecticut Valley slowed. The number of persons living in Hampshire County grew by only 22 percent in the ten years ending in 1800 and 7 percent in the decade ending in 1810. For the same two decades Amherst's growth scored 10 percent and 8 percent respectively. Northampton, making up for sluggish growth in the years preceding 1790, somewhat increased its expansion tempo in this period. But for most Hampshire towns the rate of decline exceeded that for Amherst. Some, Goshen and Williamsburg, suffered an absolute loss of population while in others like Pelham and Cummington the rate of increase fell off rapidly, especially during the second decade. This retardation in the rate of population increase in the first twenty years covered by the federal census cannot be ascribed to failing markets for the valley's foreign exports. At least until 1808, the Embargo year, exports from the Connecticut River Valley as reflected in the customs house records at Middletown, Connecticut continued with but little change. Elsewhere the rates of population increase soared upward in this twenty-year period. In Suffolk County (Boston) the rates of increase became 37 percent and 33 percent respectively, and westward beyond the Massachusetts state line the population of New York State grew by 73 percent in the first decade of the national period and 63 percent in the second. And middle western states greatly exceeded these rates. The declining tempo of expansion for Amherst and Hampshire County generally reflects not only the pull of the rising seaboard cities and the new lands available for settlement to the north and west but also the maturing of the rural economy of the valley. Given the available markets and the farming methods of the time, the limits of profitable agriculture were being approached in most Hampshire towns.

By 1810 the twenty-three towns of Hampshire County had reached a remarkable uniformity of economic development as well as population density. The economy of each town duplicated that of its neighbor in the type of grain harvested, the kinds of farm animals raised, and the methods of cultivation and organization of produc-

TABLE 1. POPULATION OF HAMPSHIRE COUNTY AND SELECTED
HAMPSHIRE TOWNS, 1765–1860

	Hampshire County			Amherst*		
Year	Popu- lation	% Change Decades	Popu- lation per sq. mile	Popu- lation	% Change Decades	Popu- lation per sq. mile
1765	—	—	—	645	—	24.4
1790	18,823	—	32.6	1233	+91%	46.7
1800	22,885	+21.6%	39.6	1358	+10	51.4
1810	24,553	+ 7.3	42.5	1469	+ 8	55.6
1820	26,487	+ 7.9	45.9	1917*	+31	69.2
1830	30,254	+14.3	52.4	2631	+37	95.0
1840	30,897	+ 2.1	53.5	2550	− 3	92.1
1850	35,732	+15.7	61.9	3057	+20	110.4
1860	37,823	+ 5.9	65.5	3206	+ 5	115.7
1810 to 1830		+23.2%			+79%	
1830 to 1860		+25.2%			+22%	

*1.3 sq. mi. transferred from Hadley to Amherst in 1815.

	Hadley			Hatfield		
Year	Popu- lation	% Change Decades	Popu- lation per sq. mile	Popu- lation	% Change Decades	Popu- lation per sq. mile
1765	573	—	23.5	803	—	49.6
1790	832	+59%	36.1	703	−13%	43.4
1800	1073	+22	44.0	809	+15	49.9
1810	1247	+16	51.1	805	− .5	49.7
1820	1461	+17	63.2	823	+ 2	50.8
1830	1585	+15	73.0	893	+ 9	55.1
1840	1814	+ 8	78.5	933	+ 5	57.6
1850	1986	+10	86.0	1073	+15	66.2
1860	2105	+ 6	91.1	1337	+25	82.5
1810 to 1830		+35%			+11%	
1830 to 1860		+25%			+50%	

SOURCES: Federal and Massachusetts Census Reports. See especially *Abstract of the Census of Massachusetts* 1860 (Boston, 1863), 204, Jesse Chickering, *Statistical View of Massachusetts from 1765 to 1840* (Boston, 1846), esp. 23–24; Decennial Census, 1915 of Massachusetts, (Boston, 1918), 84 and U.S. Census of 1820, Table 6. NOTES: Changes

Easthampton			Northampton			South Hadley†		
Popu-lation	% Change Decades	Popu-lation sq. mi.	Popu-lation	% Change Decades	Popu-lation sq. mi	Popu-lation	% Change Decades	Popu-lation sq. mi.
—	—	—	1285	—	37.1	817	—	45.9
457	—	34.4	1628	+27%	47.1	759	+ 7%	42.6
586	+28%	44.1	2190	+35	63.3	801†	+ 6	45.0
660	+13	49.6	2631	+20	76.0	902	+13	50.7
712	+ 9	53.5	2854	+ 8	82.5	1047	+16	58.8
745	+ 5	56.0	3613	+27	104.4	1185	+13	66.6
717	− 4	53.9	3750	+ 4	108.4	1458	+23	81.9
1342	+87	100.9	5278	+41	152.5	2495	+71	140.2
1916	+43	144.1	6788	+29	196.2	2277	− 9	127.9
	+13%			+37%			+31%	
	+157%			+88%			+92%	

†Part annexed to Granby in 1792.

Belchertown			Goshen		
Popu-lation	% Change Decades	Popu-lation per sq. mile	Popu-lation	% Change Decades	Popu-lation per sq. mile
414	—	7.9	—	—	—
1485	+259%	28.3	681	—	39.4
1878	+ 27	36.0	724	+ 6%	41.8
2270	+ 21	43.3	652	−10	37.7
2426	+ 7	46.2	632	− 3	36.4
2491	+ 3	47.5	617	− 2	35.7
2554	+ 3	48.7	556	−10	32.1
2680	+ 5	51.1	512	− 8	29.6
2709	+ 1	51.7	439	−14	25.4
	+ 10%			− 5%	
	+ 9%			−29%	

were made in town boundaries which were sometimes of importance. Between 1810 and 1820 Amherst annexed close to 1.3 sq. mi. of Hadley land. This change has been taken into account in the computations. For boundary changes for Hampshire County towns consult *Abstract of the Census of Mass.* (Boston, 1863), 225 26.

tion, all this despite wide variations in date of settlement, soil, and location. Amherst's population per square mile in 1810 was fifty-six, Hadley's with its rich river bottom land fifty-four, and for hill-town Pelham forty-nine. Even Northampton with its double advantage of deep soil and location as the natural trading center had a square mile population of only seventy-six, the highest in the county and the only one exceeding Amherst's. Not even the most disadvantaged hill towns fell far below forty people per square mile. The average for the whole county measured forty-two. This striking similarity and evenness of development among the towns in 1810 becomes especially interesting because of its rapid disappearance in the following decades, years to which attention is now directed.

ACCELERATED GROWTH, 1810–1830

For the five decades ending in 1860 the twenty-three towns of Hampshire County may conveniently be placed in three divisions: manufacturing towns such as Amherst, Easthampton, Northampton, and South Hadley; two valley agricultural towns Hadley and Hatfield; and hill towns such as Belchertown and Goshen (see Table 1). The categorization rests on dominant characteristics. Most towns, of course, had at least a few fertile acres and some primitive manufacturing. By 1860 more than half of the hill towns had a smaller population than in 1810, and the others registered only small increases. The two valley agricultural towns, Hadley and Hatfield, increased substantially in the fifty years, 69 and 66 percent respectively. But the four manufacturing towns enjoyed higher rates of increase than all others. Each of them more than doubled the number of its inhabitants by 1860.

Amherst's unique position among the manufacturing cities is evident in Table 1. In the twenty years ending in 1830 the town's population growth rate was more than double that of any other Hampshire County town.* Then in the three following decades its expansion slowed, became erratic, and fell behind that of all the other manufacturing towns. In fact, in the whole fifty-year period following 1810, Amherst experienced the slowest growth rate of all the manufacturing towns with the exception of Williamsburg. These

*In this comparison the town of Ware has been excluded because its spurt 1820–30 appears to have resulted in large but undetermined part from the annexation of territory from two contiguous towns in 1823.

data raise interesting questions. What form did Amherst's development take in the early period of exuberant expansion, and why was the growth so rapid? Second, how did Amherst develop in the following thirty years, and why did its rate of growth lag far behind the other manufacturing towns? Some tentative answers are attempted in the following pages.

Because population data are available only at ten-year intervals, the measurements recorded in the tables are necessarily shown by decades. Yet much can happen within a ten-year span, for as new conditions arise, established trends may slow down or even be reversed. A drastic change of this nature appears to have taken place in Amherst during the 1830s; the figures for 1840 show an absolute loss of 3 percent in population for the full period. In this decade, which included the twin national crises of 1837 and 1839, the trend of population growth altered. The rate of population increase appears to have moderated before 1837 and then to have taken a nose dive. A commonly overlooked Massachusetts enumeration of 1837 shows Amherst's population as 1 percent less than in 1830. This compares with a 3 percent drop for the full decade ending in 1840. Consequently, the analysis attempted here will divide the period 1810–1860 not by full decades but as far as is possible by two roughly even time periods, 1810 to 1837 and 1837 to 1860.

Exploration of the bases for Amherst's phenomenal growth from 1810 to 1837 involves an examination of developments in manufacturing, agriculture, and the service industries. The interaction of these factors is so fundamental that it must be kept in mind throughout the discussion. Yet for expository purposes each factor will be dealt with separately.

Accounts of individual commodities or industries tell much as to Amherst's manufacturing development. But first attention is directed to the available statistical series which contribute toward an overall view of manufacturing growth during Amherst's remarkable period of expansion. Four sets of statistical materials provide helpful soundings: changes in population density, employment in manufacturing as reported in the federal census of 1820, the *McLane Report of 1832,* and the Massachusetts state industrial census which provides a statistical summary of manufacturing by town for the year ending April 1, 1837.

The relatively small differences in population per square mile among Hampshire towns in 1810, commented on above, disappeared dramatically in the following twenty years. While the average density for the whole county rose from forty-three to fifty-two, the differences among the towns became increasingly pronounced. In some, like Hatfield and Easthampton, population density gained slowly. In others, density actually declined. At the same time two manufacturing towns pulled rapidly ahead of the others. For Northampton and Amherst the figures for density reached respectively 104 and ninety-five. In the twenty-year period following 1810 Amherst's population per square mile rose by 71 percent. This advance was nearly twice that for Northampton and far greater than for other towns in the county.

As density of population and manufacturing often go hand in hand, it comes as no surprise that according to the federal census of 1820 only two towns in the county had a higher percentage employed in manufacturing than Amherst (see Table 2). In view of

TABLE 2. AGRICULTURAL, COMMERCIAL, AND MANUFACTURING
EMPLOYMENT IN SELECTED HAMPSHIRE COUNTY TOWNS IN 1820

Town	Popu-lation	Agriculture		Commerce		Manu-facturing		Total	
		No.	%	No.	%	No.	%	No.	%
Manufacturing Towns									
Amherst	1,917	362	18.9	7	0.4	128	6.7	497	25.9
Easthampton	712	151	21.2	1	0.1	26	3.7	178	25.0
Northampton	2,854	449	15.7	48	1.7	218	7.6	715	25.1
South Hadley	1,047	241	23.0	14	1.3	57	5.4	312	29.8
Ware	1,154	251	21.7	5	0.4	35	3.0	291	25.2
Williamsburg	1,087	247	22.7	8	0.7	46	4.2	301	27.7
Valley Towns									
Hadley	1,461	309	21.1	9	0.6	67	4.6	385	26.4
Hatfield	823	179	21.7	6	0.7	17	2.1	202	24.5
Hill Towns									
Belchertown	2,426	593	24.4	7	0.3	137	5.6	737	30.4
Cummington	1,060	226	21.3	4	0.4	62	5.8	292	27.5
Goshen	630	160	25.3	2	0.3	9	1.4	171	27.1
Granby	1,066	287	26.9	3	0.3	18	1.7	308	28.9
Pelham	1,278	299	23.4	4	0.3	43	3.4	346	27.1
Worthington	1,276	302	23.7	5	0.4	30	2.4	337	26.4

SOURCE: U.S. Census of 1820

the many difficulties of definition, especially in an era when the domestic system of manufacture was widespread and reporting done without trained enumerators, the returns for Hampshire towns appear surprisingly consistent with what one would expect. Even the seemingly aberrant figure for Belchertown appears reasonable, for its area was about double that of Amherst, its population appreciably larger, and its manufacture of wagons, by far its most important industry, dependent on a putting-out system which made employment reporting unreliable. In view of these imperfections only limited reliance can be placed on the information provided in Table 3. Nevertheless, lacking other statistical summations, it seems worthwhile to explore what meaning can be wrung from these fragmentary materials. Attention to data for 1845 and 1855 is postponed to the final section of this study.

Table 3 summarizes information for six manufacturing towns which can be obtained from the federal census of 1820, the *McLane Report of 1832,* and the Massachusetts state returns of 1837, 1845, and 1855. Only data which can be aggregated appear in the table. Information on the number of units produced in each industry, probably the most reliable manufacturing statistic available, is postponed for the later examination of individual industries operating in the Amherst area. The reliability of the information appearing in the table is far from satisfactory for a number of reasons: untrained reporters assembled the data; no uniformity can be assumed in the definition of terms; accounting methods were rudimentary at best; and putting-out industries presented unusual reporting difficulties. But most important, all manufacturing data are much affected by variations in coverage from year to year.

The number of factory employees in Amherst, though registering a decline from 1820 to 1832, rose in 1837 to exceed the 1820 figure by nearly 80 percent. Total manufacturing employment in Amherst exceeded that in the other towns, except for Ware and Northampton, and in number of males employed it was greater than the latter. All the manufacturing towns except Easthampton show an increase in the value of manufactures from 1832 to 1837. Amherst's value of manufactures more than doubled between 1832 and 1837; this may suggest that considerable manufacturing progress continued there. However, the 1832 figures for Amherst may be unduly low if coverage was incomplete, and data for the other manufacturing cities

TABLE 3. EMPLOYMENT IN HAMPSHIRE COUNTY MANUFACTURING TOWNS, 1820–1855

Employment (Persons)

Year	Amherst				Easthampton				Northampton				South Hadley				Ware				Williamsburg			
	M	C	F	T*	M	C	F	T	M	C	F	T	M	C	F	T	M	C	F	T	M	C	F	T
1820	—	—	—	128	—	—	—	26	—	—	—	218	—	—	—	57	—	—	—	35	—	—	—	46
1832	70	3	37	110	—	—	550	550	181	25	87	293	29	48	—	77	71	11	704	786	99	32	61	192
1837	186	—	42	228	12	—	129	141	126	—	106	232	91	74	—	165	250	—	312	562	72	—	140	212
1845	127	—	111	238	14	—	12	26	—	362	481	843	215	12	—	227	120	—	219	339	119	—	254	373
1855	172	—	194	366	119	—	171	290	—	525	161	686	354	278	—	632	532	—	718	1,250	359	—	122	481

Value of Manufactured Products (Dollars)

Year	Amherst	Easthampton	Northampton	South Hadley	Ware	Williamsburg
1832	$59,000	$65,000	$286,656	$81,000	$384,000	$178,700
1837	$200,026	$55,300	$296,350	$237,650	$644,621	$196,867
1845	$211,793	$7,060	$248,546	$207,120	$289,571	$297,307
1855	$223,234	$359,652	$619,108	$414,890	$780,482	$416,272

Capital Investment (Dollars)

Year	Amherst	Easthampton	Northampton	South Hadley	Ware	Williamsburg
1832	$66,800	$136,000	$181,850	$57,000	$519,500	$83,660
1837	$74,300	$22,400	$248,000	$148,700	$417,300	$90,550
1845	$39,700	$2,800	$117,500	$80,500	$57,325	$146,100
1855	$37,350	$275,800	$417,000	$335,700	$657,750	$195,900

*KEY: M = Male; C = Children; F = Female; T = Total

SOURCE: U. S. Census 1820, 120; McLane Report on Manufactures, Documents Relative to Manufactures in the United States, House Document No. 308, 22d Congress, 1 Sess. (Washington, 1833). I, 294–311; Massachusetts State Reports on Industry 1837, 1845, and 1855.

indicate value product growth generally greater than for Amherst. Capital investment, probably the least reliable of all the figures, shows that, except for Easthampton, Amherst had the lowest total in 1837. About all that can be concluded, and that with no great certainty, is that Amherst continued its manufacturing development into the 1830s although at a slowing rate. Apparently as late as 1837 Amherst could claim close to a middle rank among the Hampshire manufacturing towns.

The data in Table 4 supplement those in the previous table and point up the importance of carriage manufacture as well as cloth production in 1832 and 1837. The data are no more or less reliable than those in Table 3 but the general tendency of values and number of employees to rank about the same lends some credibility to the data. The last two columns will be commented on later.

Amherst's grist- and sawmills continued essential to the town's economy well into the nineteenth century, though potash works tended to disappear as the forest land was cleared. Other small operations catering to local needs continued; cider mills and a brandy distillery were recognized as common necessities as were carding mills to prepare wool for household processing. One of the latter was reported at North Amherst in 1802. At about the same time a tannery began operating to provide leather not only for shoes but for various farm and home needs. This like other small neighborhood industries then to be found in most Hampshire County towns disposed of its output locally. Valuable as were these operations, they did not propel Amherst into its era of rapid population growth and manufacturing leadership.

With its population of only about 1,900 in 1820 and a little over 2,600 in 1830 Amherst could not by itself absorb the output of even a small, specialized manufacturing plant. Indeed, for a factory of any size its products had to be marketed not only outside the Connecticut River Valley but beyond the borders of the state. An examination of the chief manufacturing enterprises which grew up in Amherst between 1810 and 1837 now claims attention.

Papermaking was one of Amherst's first industries. Beginning at least as early as 1795, it flourished moderately for nearly a century. Familiarity with the techniques of papermaking appears to have been widely diffused in the valley. The supply of water both for power and for the manufacturing processes proved ample for the modest Amherst operation. But as Carpenter and Morehouse comment, the

TABLE 4. LEADING AMHERST MANUFACTURES, 1832, 1837, 1845, AND 1855

Rank in Value of Product	1832		1837		1845		1855	
	Product	Number of Employees	Product	Number of Employees	Product	Number of Employees	Product	Number of Employees
1	Carriages	30	Carriages	100	Bonnets and palm leaf hats	70	Bonnets and palm leaf hats	173
2	Cotton cloth	45	Woolen cloth	52	Kentucky jeans	55	Kentucky jeans	20
3	Paper	14	Palm leaf hats	N.G.	Mechanics' tools	22	Paper	25
4	Wagons	9	Boots and shoes	14	Childrens' wagons and velocipedes	N.G.	Mechanics' tools	20
5	Shoes	8	Paper	18	Miscellaneous vehicles	16	Childrens' wagons and sleds	18

supply of rags had to be gathered "through all the counties of the state." For efficient operation this industry was located rather far from the center of population of the state. Moreover small amounts of rags procured from Leghorn, Italy had to be transported across the ocean and then nearly 100 miles inland from the coast. Nor was Amherst's marketing situation advantageous, for outlets for the paper had to be sought in the south and west. Carpenter and Morehouse report that in about 1809 writing paper manufactured at Amherst reached Albany "by team." Boston, which a little later became an important outlet for Amherst paper, also was reached by wagon transportation. Paper produced annually at Amherst in the early 1830s was apparently valued at around $7,000, but Northampton and South Hadley were already more important producers. By 1837 the latter town with its abundant power and water supplies produced paper valued many times more than that of Amherst. Yet despite obvious disadvantages papermaking persisted at Amherst for some time; in 1855 it ranked third most valuable manufacture of the town (see Table 4).

Though records are fragmentary, they leave little doubt that cotton yarn manufacture took first place among Amherst industries in the years 1810 to 1830. Distant events had their impact on the town; when the Embargo and Non-intercourse Acts stopped the importation of English textiles, Ebenezer Dickinson, a well-to-do Amherst farmer, was caught up in the popular enthusiasm which swept New England to establish spinning mills. With financial help from his neighbors he built in 1809 a three-story wooden building at Factory Hollow to spin cotton yarn by machinery. Having no experience in the business he soon encountered difficulties, and the property passed from his hands into those of a group of Amherst citizens who became incorporated in 1814 as the Amherst Cotton Factory. The new owners had no more knowledge of cotton spinning than the originator, but they wisely secured the services of an Englishman named Odber, under whose management factory-spun yarn was provided to families for weaving on hand looms. The business was somewhat extended for by January 7, 1818 it advertised in the *Hampshire Gazette* that it could "supply machines of all kinds for cotton and wool manufacture." Apparently the mill was operated on what has become known as the Waltham System; the *McLane Reports* describe how extensive supplies were secured for operating a boardinghouse for the workers.

THE NORTH AMHERST PAPER MILL, ON MILL RIVER
BETWEEN FACTORY HOLLOW AND CUSHMAN.

The Amherst Cotton Factory did not prosper, but neither did it fail and go out of business like most American small textile mills faced with a flood of British exports after the War of 1812. A foot-note in McLane's 1832 *Report* states that the concern suffered serious losses and misfortunes and paid no dividends until 1831, adding: "Its only good fruits have been in rearing and sustaining an intelligent and moral population of sixty-six souls. . . ." (I, 298). No cotton mill at Amherst appears in the state census for 1837, but two woolen mills are reported. One of these may be the original cotton mill converted to the manufacture of woolen yarn or cloth. The sub-sequent history of textile manufacture records a discouraging series of fires and bankruptcies.

The surprising fact about the Amherst cotton manufacture is not its later disappearance. In explaining the decline of early cotton man-

ufacturing in Hampshire County, a writer in *McLane's Report* correctly ascribes it to "want of proper machinery, want of skill, and expense of transportation." (I, 102). In addition to these disadvantages Amherst's water power was pitifully small, and, unlike the mills in Ware and Chicopee, the Amherst factory did not attract the financial and marketing expertise of the Boston magnates. Giant textile mills such as those at Lowell and Chicopee which came into production in the 1820s sealed Amherst's doom as a textile center. But this should not overshadow the town's pioneering effort in this field nor obscure the fact that for a couple of decades Amherst's textile mill contributed to industrial leadership in Hampshire County.

The manufacture of carriages joined cotton yarn as a leading Amherst industry in the late 1820s. In December 1826 Lyman Knowles advertised in the *New England Inquirer,* Amherst's earliest newspaper, that, at his place of business near the South Amherst meetinghouse, he made "coaches and waggons," had patterns to show interested customers, carried on blacksmithing in all its branches, and would take lumber and produce in exchange. Four years later he moved his business to a location on the Pelham Road not far from the East Street common. A multifamily house still in use at this location probably formed a part of the carriage factory. There he continued his operation in association with Asahel Thayer, a deacon in the Second Congregational Church whom Carpenter and Morehouse describe as a sagacious businessman. They also state that the products of this industry were "of superior workmanship" and that the establishment included "shops for woodworking, iron making, upholstery, and painting." (295–99). Although this indicates a rather centralized production complex, it seems likely that at least to some extent parts of the carriages were made by local farmers at their own homes, much as Belchertown's important wagon making industry was carried on. In Belchertown, according to the *McLane Report:* "The various parts of the wagon are made in all parts of the town, some employed on the wheels, some on the bodies, seats, etc." (I, 294). The carriages turned out appear to have been mostly light, drawn by one horse, with seats for one person (sulkies) or two (chaises), although some enclosed carriages (coaches) may have been manufactured.

This Amherst enterprise grew remarkably in the ten years following 1826. The value of coaches, chaises, and sulkies amounted to $30,000 in 1832 and $100,000 in 1837. Thirty men were employed in the earlier year, 100 to 150 in the later one. The business proved not only the most important in the town; in all western Massachusetts no carriage works approached it in value of product or number of employees. Unlike cotton manufacture, its chief raw material, wood, flourished close at hand, and New England farmers had developed skill in using wood by long practice. Carriages, of course, enjoyed only a very limited use in western Massachusetts where most travel was still by horseback or wagon. But the vehicles manufactured in Amherst could easily be driven to Boston or Providence, the two most important markets. After this promising beginning, carriage making as a major industry disappeared from the town after 1837, victim of the financial crisis of that year and the rise of large-scale manufacture at New Haven and elsewhere.

Like carriage making, the manufacture of palm leaf hats did not depend upon water power, but it was carried on in houses under the putting-out system. Traders or merchants secured the palm leaves from Boston where they had been imported from Cuba. Transported by wagon to centers of operation, the leaves were distributed to farm families over a considerable area. Women and children as young as ten split leaves, braided, sewed, and fashioned them into hats. Then they were returned to the merchant who paid in goods reckoned at retail prices. Completed hats brought the farm women 12 to 24 cents a hat, depending on the quality of the work. The appearance of this industry is well described by Joseph Lyman of Northampton, reporting on the town of Enfield for the *McLane Report:*

[The manufacture of palm leaf hats] has sprung up within about six years, in which time it has driven the foreign article from our market, and supplied us with a substitute of greater beauty and value for less than one-third of the price formerly paid. The hats are made in private families, the coarser kind by quite small children. . . . The manufactures here furnish, for four dollars per dozen, an article superior to the foreign one, which commanded fifteen dollars per dozen in 1826. The number of females employed in this and adjacent towns, amount to about two hundred. (I, 303).

The manufacture of palm leaf hats first appeared in western Massachusetts about 1826. The most rapid growth came originally in Barre which continued to be the outstanding leader through the early decades. But other centers also appeared: in Ware and Enfield enterprising merchants served not only local farms but those in Pelham and Prescott. Hat making appeared before 1829 in Amherst, but not until that year did Leonard M. Hills arrive from Ellington, Connecticut to begin his successful operations as an organizer in the industry. Progress was not rapid at first. By 1832 it accounted for 15,000 hats while Enfield produced 50,000 and Ware 21,000. Six years later found Amherst about equal with Enfield and Ware, though still far behind Barre which was not to be overtaken for decades, when Amherst became the hat-making center for the country.

Two crucial factors, cheap home labor and an aggressive capitalist organizer, seem to have determined the location of this industry. Amherst was well enough supplied with the first, and Hills's arrival in 1829 made a strong beginning on the second. The product was so light that the cost of transportation to New York, the chief market, was not decisive.

THE STRAW WORKS,
ON THE CORNER OF NORTH PLEASANT AND MAIN STREETS.

Five shoemakers and three wagon makers conclude the McLane
tabulation of Amherst's industries in 1832, each group being ascribed
a product value of $3,000. As in other Connecticut Valley towns
shoemakers who provided for local needs were active well before the
nineteenth century. The account books of Elisha Smith, 1784–1822,
indicate that along with operating a tavern in South Amherst, providing transportation for persons and property, and maintaining a
retail store, he made and repaired shoes. As might be expected, the
making of boots and shoes often grew out of the tanning operations
early established in this area. Thus Oliver Watson who had inherited
a tanning yard in Amherst sold it in 1832 and engaged with considerable success in making shoes largely for the local market. By 1837 the
value of boots and shoes fashioned in Amherst had increased by three
times in five years. However, shoemaking never became a factory
industry in Amherst as it did in parts of eastern Massachusetts.
    Amherst's wagon makers also produced for nearby markets

within the state and probably used a putting-out system as in Belchertown. The value product remained the same between 1832 and 1837, but by the latter date the making of children's wagons had assumed more importance, the output being valued at $4,500, and the number of employees reported as ten. The manufacture of wagons of whatever size benefited from the ample supply of suitable wood and the woodworking skills of local residents. Other workbench production using wood, often with iron or steel parts, developed in Amherst during the thirties or even earlier. Of the variety of wooden items produced, joiner's planes were most important. Here as often elsewhere Amherst craftsmen succeeded in making a high quality product and introducing ingenious innovations. Trueman Nutting built up a profitable business during the 1830s and probably earlier in a shop located in Nuttingville not far from where East Street and Mechanic Street intersect with Bay Road. Like other woodworking mechanics, Nutting secured metal attachments for planes and other tools from outside the town, perhaps from Hartford. His finished product he shipped to such places as Brookline, Massachusetts and Middletown, Connecticut or had them carried to Northampton to be sent to more distant markets by the recently opened New Haven and Northampton Canal. In the state report of 1837 planes are credited with a value of $8,000 and the employment of ten men.

Other products coming from Amherst's workbenches included faucets, pumps, axes, hammers, broom handles, chairs, cabinet ware, and even plows. Eli Dickinson began the manufacture of faucets early in the century, used horse power to turn his lathe, and made a two or three weeks' trip each year to Baltimore to dispose of his product, reported Rand (303). Amhert's mechanics must have developed some skill in utilizing metals. Not only was this necessary in constructing wooden products made partly of metals but in such small items appearing in the 1837 tabulation as tinware, stoves, bowie knives, and pistols.

Such then is a brief account of Amherst's manufacturing progress during the period 1810–1837. Ignoring for the present the local stimulus coming from agriculture and service industries, what conditions, it may be inquired, favored this early industrial development? As long as factories remained relatively small, two narrow streams contributed adequate power; wood provided abundant raw materials; a modest accumulation of wealth was available; skilled work-men were not lacking; and adventurous entrepreneurs came forward. On this scale, Amherst enjoyed a healthy economic growth. This favorable situation was also dependent upon the age of wagon trans-portation. Of course location near the Connecticut River and the New Haven and Northampton Canal gave some advantage, but floods and ice often made them unreliable and expensive avenues of trade. Wagon roads improved rapidly in the early decades of the nineteenth century. The Sixth Massachusetts Turnpike, completed in 1800, originated in Shrewsbury on the "great road . . . which leads from New York to Boston." From there it led through Greenwich, Pelham, Amherst, and Hadley and crossed the bridge to North-ampton which was completed in 1805 and replaced in 1826. Shipping goods by wagon or sleigh was after all quite inexpensive. Food for driver and horses could be carried along, inns if necessary for stop-overs charged very little, and if not employed in carrying loads, driver, horses, and wagon might well be idle.

This favorable era came to an end as the railroad connected Boston and Albany in the 1830s and was extended in the next decade up the river from Hartford to Northampton and beyond. Products of Amherst's factories could no longer compete in distant markets well-supplied by large-scale, mechanized complexes. In fact, textiles and carriages could now often be delivered to Amherst more cheaply than they could be produced locally. National markets were developing for which Amherst finally discovered one product, palm leaf hats, which could survive in the new competitive situation.

Although less obviously so than manufacturing, agriculture also played a role in Amherst's rapid growth. Unfortunately records of agricultural development in these early decades are much less full than those for manufacture. Even Carpenter and Morehouse in their stan-dard history have almost nothing to offer beyond noting the activities of the agricultural societies which gained attention especially in the 1840s and 1850s. The state report of 1837 credits Amherst farmers with raising sheep yielding wool worth $1,600, hardly an impressive figure compared with $5,400 for Belchertown, $7,075 for North-ampton, and $2,170 for South Hadley.

Yet something further can be discovered. Besides demonstrating Amherst's importance in manufacturing, a study shows that the number engaged in agriculture in Amherst trailed only Northampton and Belchertown, and that, in percentage terms, Amherst was second only to Northampton. The *McLane Report* provides the most interesting clue to the encouragement which manufacturing gave to Amherst's agriculture. Hitherto generally overlooked data appearing in this document indicate that the Amherst Cotton Manufacturing Company, like several other mills reporting in the valley, lists the products used at the factory, their place of origin, the quantities of each consumed, and their respective values. The implication is that the Amherst textile mill operated on a boardinghouse system much like that developed at Waltham, Massachusetts, where the mill owners housed and boarded the workers.

Table 5 shows the supplies for the factory operations as well as for the mill workers for the year ending April, 1832. The number of persons who consumed the food listed appears to have been between forty-five and sixty-six. The *McLane Report* indicates that the mill employed twelve males over sixteen years of age at 45 cents a day, three boys under sixteen at 25 cents, and thirty women and girls at 30

TABLE 5. AMHERST COTTON MANUFACTURING COMPANY,
COMMODITIES CONSUMED IN 1832

Commodity	Quantity	Value	Where From
Cotton	48,000 lbs.	$4,800	South Carolina
Tea and Coffee		250	Foreign Countries
Sugar and Rice		50	Louisiana
Molasses	6 hhds.	240	Louisiana
Flour	40 bbls.	300	New York
Rye Flour	120 bu.	100	Massachusetts
Wood	150 cords	300	Massachusetts
Coal	300 bu.	18	Massachusetts
Lamp Oil	130 gal.	130	(Nantucket)
Fish Oil and Tallow	200 lbs.	130	Massachusetts
An. Rep. Leather and Lumber	—	250	Massachusetts
Codfish	2 tons	160	Massachusetts
Potatoes	200 bu.	60	Massachusetts
Rye for Families	180 bu.	150	Massachusetts
Corn	100 bu.	65	Massachusetts
Pork	2 tons	220	Massachusetts
Shad and Mackerel	10 bbls.	100	Massachusetts
Beef	7,000 lbs.	280	Massachusetts
Salt	60 bu.	54	Massachusetts
Peas and Beans	15 bu.	19	Massachusetts

SOURCE: *McLane Report of 1832.* I, 298–99.

cents, all of these "boarding themselves."★ Some interesting observations can be drawn from this report. Rates of pay for Amherst
cotton mill workers appear to have been even lower than those prevailing in nearby towns. The flour listed, obviously wheat, undoubtedly arrived from New York via Long Island Sound and the Connecticut River. This entry, along with similar ones from other mills
in neighboring towns, confirms the belief that wheat was no longer
commonly grown in the Connecticut Valley as it had been in earlier
days. Advertisements in the local newspaper, *The New England Inquirer,* in 1827–28 indicate that the flour consumed in Amherst came
from Baltimore and Rochester via Boston or New York. In fact, as
early as the twenties western flour brought lower prices in Boston
than in Northampton or Amherst.

Some items of general consumption do not appear in the table for
Amherst. Similar lists for nearby towns include such commonly used
foods as butter and cheese. Doubtless many families kept a cow,
probably chickens, possibly a pig. The value of the food products
listed for the Amherst cotton mill as coming from the vicinity totals
something over $1,600 a year, a rather small sum perhaps but possi-
bly not inconsequential in a community of about 2,600 people where
local markets for farm products were always severely limited. In a
population this small a work force of sixty-six cotton mill workers
might well have been of some importance when added to thirty
carriage workers and at least thirty-five persons in other industries.
The records show the presence of 228 factory wage earners by 1837.
All this must have augmented the demand for locally grown food
products.

Comment on Amherst's agriculture would be incomplete without some notice of the craze for raising mulberry trees which swept
many towns of western Massachusetts during this time. A farmer of
South Amherst, one Timothy Smith, began raising mulberry trees in
the early thirties. By the middle of the decade many more farmers
believed that silk worms feeding on the leaves of these trees would
produce the raw materials for a great silk industry. For a time small
fortunes resulted from farmers selling young trees to others who in

---

★This seems to suggest that workers instead of living in boardinghouses received scrip payable at the country store. The effect on consumption would be
substantially unchanged. See Caroline E. Ware, *The Early New England Cotton Manufacture* (Boston, 1931), 51–52.

turn sold them again. But the bubble burst in the late thirties; the whole venture collapsed when the processes of caring for the worms and unwinding the silk fiber proved unprofitable. Why were Amherst farmers as well as other New England agriculturalists, ordinarily so conservative in their methods, swept away by this foolish venture and others at about the same time? In an era when new crops, improved methods, and western competition presented unprecedented problems, Amherst farmers turned in desperation to a chimera which seemed to promise a quick solution to their problems.*

Finally, activities connected with commerce, the professions, and the educational institutions can be examined. Even though the record is surely incomplete, the seven Amherst residents listed in Table 2 as being employed in commerce can hardly be regarded as impressive. No doubt the number grew from 1820 to 1837, and to it must be added the professional men, doctors, preachers, lawyers, and of course more humble workers such as carpenters, wagoners, stage drivers, and the like. Also Amherst has always attracted a small number of intellectuals. Noah Webster, who came in 1812 to work on his dictionary, was one of the first; the Pulitzer Prize winners Robert Frost and Ray Stannard Baker of more recent date are in all probability not the last.

Especially in the early days the presence must not be overlooked of those connected with Amherst's educational institutions. We do not know the number of administrators, teachers, students, mechanics, and construction workers these institutions brought in, the amount of outside capital made available, or their effect on stimulating trade, local agriculture, and services, but a summary of the information available suggests an appreciable impact.

Amherst Academy, which opened in 1814, averaged around 200 students, often more. About half came from outside the town. This includes the Amherst Female Academy which functioned between 1824 and 1838 when women were excluded from the earlier school. The administration and teaching staff numbered six or eight, possibly more. At the Classical Institute in the years 1827 to 1833 seven or eight teachers instructed sixty to sixty-eight boys, possibly as many as 100 according to Tyler (33). The number of students at Amherst

*Arthur H. Cole, "Agricultural Crazes," *American Historical Review* XVI (1926), 622–39.

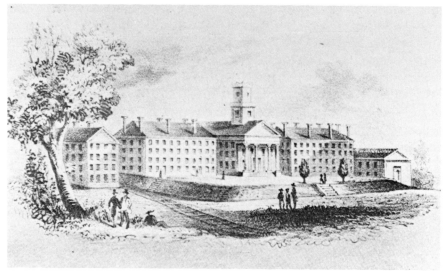

AMHERST COLLEGE IN 1855.

College rose rapidly from fifty-nine in 1821 to peak at 259 in 1837, a figure not repeated until after the Civil War. The staff at the college averaged ten to twelve. Most of the students came from outside Amherst. As early as 1827 the local newspaper reported that nearly 100 members of the college occupied rooms in private homes in the town.

Writing in 1839, John Warner Barber estimated the annual expense for an Amherst College student at $90 to $180.* If the number of students at Amherst Academy is estimated at 200, at the Institute as sixty, and at Amherst College as 250 and if we assume that 300 of these 510 came from outside the town and that each spent only $120 each year, their total annual expenses would be $36,000. As much as $40,000 may have been spent in the town if the outlays by administration, faculty, and necessary caretakers and workmen are included. A yearly expenditure of this sum added a dynamic element in a town which had numbered about 1,900 in 1820 and about 2,500 twenty years later.

*John Warner Barber, *Historical Collections* (Worcester, Mass., 1839), 511–12.

A Nineteenth Century Building Boom

Building construction also played a part in Amherst's rapid growth, and a part of this was contributed by the educational institutions (see Table 6). Much, perhaps most, of the capital for these building projects originated in Amherst or nearby towns, though outside gifts did supplement local funds. Thus the Commonwealth of Massachusetts contributed land in Maine which brought $2,500 to the Amherst Academy, and the elaborate Mount Pleasant Classical Institute was built from the private fortune of one Martin Thayer who hailed from Philadelphia.

Unusual activity in the construction of churches came at about the same time as the early surge of educational buildings (see Table 6). The capital for these buildings appears to have been contributed very largely by the members of the respective parishes. In one case, the North Church, the story has come down to us that it was built and owned by Oliver Dickinson who had for many years conducted a tavern in North Amherst.

The construction of factories and workshops was also carried forward in these years. The three-story cotton factory discussed above had been built about 1809 by Ebenezer Dickinson, partly with his own funds, the rest borrowed from neighbors. The capital involved in buildings, equipment, and materials in process is shown as $23,600 in the *McLane Report,* but the business had gone through at least one bankruptcy by 1832. The amount of the original investment is not known. Lyman Knowles's carriage factory may well have required a considerable investment, but the *McLane Report* tells us only that the machinery and apparatus was valued at $18,000 in 1832 and the average stock on hand at $15,000, but the state report of 1837 lists capital invested as $30,000. In 1832 Oliver Watson erected a building in South Amherst for the manufacture of boots and shoes, and a few years later Porter Dickinson built a shop at East Amherst to manufacture hammers, forks, and edged tools. The state report of 1837 lists two woolen mills with a total investment of $30,000. As no such mills are listed in the *McLane Report,* it may be assumed that the mills were built between those two dates. However, as no cotton factory is listed in 1837, it may be that one of the woolen mills had been converted from the cotton mill. And as appears from Table 3 investments had increased moderately since 1832. But for most of the small bench and workshop industries of the time the use of parts of houses and sheds made little new construction necessary.

One of the most enduring evidences of Amherst's Golden Age from about 1810 to 1837 appears in the fine houses then erected, many of them the showplaces of today. Two houses completed early in this period were the White Homestead (1810), now on the

TABLE 6. OUTLAYS FOR THE CONSTRUCTION OF BUILDINGS IN AMHERST, 1813–1860

Date	Educational Building		Cost
	Building		
1813–14	Amherst Academy		$ 5,000 +
1825–27	Mt. Pleasant Classical Institute		5,000 + (est.)
1820–21	South College		8,000
1821–22	President's House (first)		4,000
1822–23	North College		10,000
1826–27	Johnson Chapel		15,000
1827–28	"Old" North College	Amherst	10,000
1834–35	President's House (present)	College	9,000
1847–48	Octagon		9,000
1852–53	Morgan Library		11,000
1855	Octagon Lecture Room		1,000
1855	Appleton Cabinet		10,000
1857	Octagon Gallery		567
1857–58	East College		15,000
1857–58	Williston Hall		16,000
1859–60	Barrett Hall		15,000
			$143,567 +
	Religious Building		
1815	First Church, new cupola		?
1820	Second Church, repairs		$ 1,200
1825	South Amherst Church		3,300 (est.)
1826	North Amherst Church		2,900
1837	Baptist Church		3,500 (est.)
1839	Second Church, new building		?
1839	North Amherst Church Parsonage		1,409
1839	Second Church, new building		3,000
			$15,309 +

SOURCES: Stanley King, *The Consecrated Eminence* (Amherst, 1951) 310–15; Frederick Tuckerman, *Amherst Academy* (Amherst, 1929) 18; and Frank Prentice Rand, *The Village of Amherst* (Amherst, 1958) 46–47.

COURTESY OF THE JONES LIBRARY

THE MILL, ON THE CORNER OF SOUTH PLEASANT AND MILL
LANE.

Amherst College campus where it provides offices for the Five College Organization, and the fine edifice on Main Street, now known
as the Emily Dickinson House (1813).

Construction activity expanded rapidly in the twenties and thirties. Some notable examples in the earlier decade are the Waitstill
Dickinson House (1820) on the South Amherst Common, the
Bridgman Tavern (1822) on the Bay Road, the Horace Kellogg
House (1828) at 459 South Pleasant Street, the Snell House (1820) at
317 South Pleasant Street, and the Joseph Cowles House (1821) at
1184 North Pleasant Street. Equally distinguished houses were added
in the 1830s: the Helen Hunt Jackson House (1830) at 249 South
Pleasant Street, the Luke Sweetser House (1835) at 81 Lessey Street,
and the Justus Williams House (1835) at 706 East Street. Built mostly
by well-to-do farmers and tradesmen, their residences were evidence
of their prosperity. How much their building contributed to the
continuous stir of industry in the town cannot be measured. Though
labor and materials were relatively inexpensive in those days, we
cannot now observe the size and excellence of these houses without
marveling at the wealth and taste in this country town.

DECELERATION, 1830–1860

The years from about 1830 to 1860 provide a sharp contrast to the period 1810–1830 (1837?), when Amherst's population had increased more rapidly than any other Hampshire County town. In the later period the town's growth lagged well behind the other manufacturing towns of the county (see Table 7). In fact, Amherst's increase was only one-fourth of the average achieved by the five manufacturing towns and actually failed to equal the average population growth for the county as a whole despite the inclusion of the somnolent hill towns. Amherst's population change by decades, −3.0 percent for 1830–40, 20.0 percent for 1840–50, and 4.9 percent for 1850–60, presents an irregular record deserving a more thorough exploration than can be attempted here. The conclusion reached earlier that Amherst's decline in the 1830s occurred largely between 1837 and 1840 should be kept in mind. The rebound from the absolute reduction of the 1830s measures the change between the depression year of 1840 and the considerable recovery of 1850, while the slow gain of the 1850s began in a fairly prosperous year and ended with one of limited prosperity. So the bias resulting from decennial census data should be kept in mind. The striking contrast lies between Amherst's deceleration 1830–1860, a 21.9 percent growth and the 82.7 percent increase for the other Hampshire manufacturing towns. Or the contrast may be expressed in another way. By 1860 Amherst had the lowest population density of any Hampshire County manufacturing town except Williamsburg.

Neither Amherst nor Hampshire County as a whole could with-

TABLE 7. POPULATION CHANGE FOR SELECTED AREAS

Area	1830–40	1840–50	1850–60	1830–60
Amherst	−3.0 %	20.0 %	4.9 %	21.9%
5 Hampshire County manufacturing towns*	3.4	91.1	4.4	82.7
Hampshire County	2.12	15.65	5.85	25.0
Springfield-Chicopee	61.9	82.4	12.0	231.1
Suffolk and Middlesex Counties	44.4	51.1	33.7	191.9
United States Urban Population	63.7	92.1	75.4	451.6

*Ware is not included because of the erratic behavior of its statistics, due at least in part to important changes in the town's boundaries.

stand the population pull of the frontier or that of the great urban
centers of industry and trade in the decades under examination. So
far as Amherst is concerned, we do not know which of these magnets
was the stronger. But study of the last three categories in Table 7
suggests that many ambitious Amherst citizens may well have mi-
grated to the nearby booming textile mills of Chicopee and the expanding railroad and industrial center of Springfield. Others no
doubt contributed to the flow of workers to the urban centers of
eastern Massachusetts as well as those of Connecticut and New
York.

The manufacturing statistics for Amherst and the other industrial
towns of Hampshire County have been shown in Table 3, and their
limitations have been emphasized. The table demonstrates that while
other manufacturing towns enjoyed a vigorous if somewhat uneven
growth after 1820, Amherst lagged on each of the three measures the
table provides. In total number of employees and in the number of
males employed, Amherst usually trailed the other towns in this
group save only Easthampton and South Hadley. And in the other
two categories, Amherst's record proved even less impressive. In
value of manufactures its total for 1855 was only slightly above 1837,
and in both 1845 and 1855 its capital investment in manufacturing
was about half that of 1837. At the same time, Amherst trailed far
behind other manufacturing towns of Hampshire County both in
value of product and capital investment.

The difficulty of explaining Amherst's early flowering as a manufacturing town has been noted above. Accounting for its decline
beginning in the 1830s presents fewer uncertainties. In an age of
increasingly large scale, mechanized, production, Amherst did not
possess the minimum essentials for success. Its small streams could
not provide the necessary power for great textile enterprises like
those in nearby Chicopee, Ware, and Holyoke or those more distant
at Lowell and Lawrence. Nor as steam became important was cheap
water transportation available to bring in coal or iron. Remote from
national markets and without an abundance of local capital or the
means of attracting eastern financiers, only a miracle could have
prevented Amherst's decline as a leading manufacturing center. Even
the Amherst & Belchertown Railroad, a short span which reached
the town in 1853, brought doubtful blessings. The local hat factory
may have found its freight services useful, though this is difficult to

document, and it must have been an appreciable convenience to travelers. Yet it served also as an avenue to bring in outside competition for small concerns making such products as paper, boots and shoes, mechanics' tools, and tin ware. Lumber was the most valuable manufactured product in 1855, and other wooden products like childrens' wagons and sleds, axe handles, and the like held on for a time, but the depletion of the varieties of wood needed was already threatened. Only straw bonnets and palm leaf hats proved a growth industry. Cheap and dependable labor and aggressive entrepreneurship permitted the leaders of this business to overcome the disadvantages from both lack of local raw material and distant markets. But its mature flowering came in later decades. For the time being even such specialty products as rubber goods at Easthampton and buttons both there and at Williamsburg overshadowed the hopeful beginnings at Amherst of the factory production of hats.

While Amherst's industrial development trailed that of more fortunate Hampshire County towns, Amherst also failed to enjoy the stimulus of expansion in other sectors of the economy. As Springfield, along with its satellites, and Northampton developed into important industrial centers, Hadley and Hatfield, the two river valley towns of Hampshire County, benefited from nearby expanding markets for country produce. In the thirty years ending in 1860 both valley agricultural towns increased their population more rapidly than Amherst, Hatfield more than doubling Amherst's growth rate. Uneconomically large farms in the fertile river valley were now divided into smaller ones. Thus R. T. Wheelock, Chairman of the Hampshire Agricultural Society, stated in 1852:

Some farmers in the river towns have divided their farms with their sons . . . and have yet again subdivided with their sons. . . . This is what is meant by making two or three acres out of one.*

Intensive cultivation brought greater production of milk, cheese, butter, garden vegetables, fruit, and fresh meat to supply growing outlets in nearby markets. At the same time the two valley towns utilized their fertile acres to grow great quantities of broom corn for a flourishing new business devoted to the manufacture of brooms and brushes. Also, the beginnings of tobacco culture in the valley

*Transactions of the Agricultural Societies of the State of Massachusetts for 1852 (Boston, 1852), 308–9.

foreshadowed the coming specialization in that crop for whose production the alluvial soil of the valley proved so well suited.

Amherst farmers also sought to take advantage of changing conditions by sending products such as butter, cheese, and potatoes to
nearby markets and even began to raise limited amounts of broom
corn and tobacco. But they were at a double disadvantage compared
with the valley towns. Springfield and Northampton markets, as
well as the other manufacturing centers of the area, were relatively
more distant, and most Amherst soil was less suited for intensive
cultivation than that of the valley towns.

The few statistical compilations available on farm production
provide even less information than those for manufacturing. But
they do invite some possible comparisons. Returns of the assessors to
the General Court available for the years 1771, 1779, 1781, and 1784
provide limited though helpful information, and detailed tables
showing agricultural production for 1845 and 1855 appear in the state
industrial census for each year. Such difficulties as vague definitions
of terms used and variations in coverage present the usual problems.
But interesting comparisons are possible between the earlier and later
years and between the two reports of 1845 and 1855 (see Table 8).
Over the eighty-four years from 1771 to 1855 the population of
Amherst increased about three times. During this same interval the
number of farm animals, except for sheep, grew in about the same

TABLE 8. AGRICULTURAL RETURNS FOR THE TOWN OF AMHERST

Product	1771	1845	1855
Sheep	695	2,054	741
Horses	153	336	429
Neat Cattle[a]	506	1,668	1,668
Swine	214	625	525
Hay (tons)	1,057	3,900	3,993
Grain (bushels)	6,596	35,250	42,814
Improved land (acres, including mowing and tillage)	1,266[b]		13,529[c]
Woodland (acres)	3,693[b]		332[c]

[a] Domestic bovine animals
[b] Data for 1779
[c] Data for 1865, Massachusetts Census of 1865, 282–3
SOURCES: Sylvester Judd, *History of Hadley,* 385–87; Edward Carpenter and Charles Morehouse, *History of the Town of Amherst, Massachusetts,* 137–38; and Massachusetts Industrial Censuses for 1845 and 1855.

ratio. The hay harvest increased about four times, and grain more than six times. The acres of improved land grew by more than four times; woodland declined by about 90 percent. These last two comparisons are made possible by using data for 1865, similar figures for 1855 being unavailable. The total value of Amherst's agricultural products as reported in 1845 and 1855 amounted to $76,041 and $114,945 respectively. This jump in value of over 50 percent within ten years probably has little significance, as 1855 was a peak year for farm prices, and anomalies in the tables and variations in coverage reduce their credibility.

More meaningful probably than the foregoing is a ranking of the leading Amherst agricultural products as shown in the two census reports. In order of value, the five leading products in 1855 were hay, corn, butter, rye, and potatoes. The ranking for 1845 was similar except that rye and potatoes reversed positions. Hay's number one position reflects the increased demand to provide food for larger numbers of cattle and other farm animals. Corn provided important food for animal and human consumption both in Amherst and the growing industrial towns, and the same was true for butter and other dairy products as well. Rye furnished the straw essential to the manufacture of bonnets and some hats. The ranking of potatoes reflects the growing use of this vegetable in Amherst and nearby cities. A more complete examination of Amherst's agricultural history would take notice of the disastrous mulberry-silk worm craze which swept Amherst and other nearby towns in the thirties and also the growing attention given to the raising of fruits and vegetables. But here we must be satisfied to note that, although considerable growth had taken place in this sector since colonial days, little evidence has been found to indicate that substantial enlargement took place in the two or three decades before the Civil War.

Amherst Academy, which had done so well earlier, ceased to attract many students from outside the town after the 1830s. By 1852 Academy students numbered only twenty, and Tuckerman reports that: ". . . [a]ttempts were made in the early 'fifties to revive the now languishing, moribund Academy. . . . But it had become very largely a purely local high school, with few non-resident scholars in attendance." (123). And Amherst College also fell upon difficult times. Attendance dropped from 259 in 1836 to 118 in 1845, and although a slow recovery developed in the 1850s, the pre-1840 record was not equalled. Reduction in administrative and teaching staff as well as caretakers removed much of the former stimulus from this source.

The construction of buildings for educational purposes so important in the 1820s declined thereafter. Only one such facility was erected in the 1830s and one in the 1840s. Sums devoted to construction at Amherst College rose to a little over $77,000 in the 1850s but four-fifths of this was spent in the closing years of the period, 1857–1860 (see Table 6).

Other construction appears to have lagged behind the record activity of the 1820s and 1830s. This was especially true of new factories and churches. Though the number of fine new houses declined, some imposing residences date from this period. Among these were three on North East Street not far from the East Amherst common, the old Rectory of the Grace Episcopal Church at 14 Boltwood Avenue, William Austin Dickinson's House at 214 Main Street, and a few others. Also account must be taken of the building of the Amherst & Belchertown Railroad in 1852. Insofar as money was paid out for Amherst land and supplies and to employ local labor some temporary stimulus may have been given to the town's economy. The railroad cost about $290,000, practically all coming from local sources. A losing venture from the beginning, a reorganization of the road became necessary in 1857. Those who invested $195,000 in the stock of the company lost all, and the fate of the bond holders was little better. The building of the railroad was made possible by a tremendous civic effort, but its chief results were to redistribute the wealth of the community and to siphon into an unproductive venture local capital which might otherwise have been available for sounder investments.

CHAPTER FOUR

A DRY AND THIRSTY LAND

THEODORE BAIRD

Theodore Baird is Samuel Williston Professor of English, *emeritus,* in Amherst College.

★ ★ ★ ★ ★

This is Amherst's 154th Commencement and, although circumstances and surroundings have changed, the College motto *Terras Irradient* applies as well to the Class of 1975 as to that graduated on August 28, 1822.
Program of the CLIV Commencement

I desire to remember the saints of New England. We Americans are digging for art and intellect in Troy, in Sardis, and in Egypt. Let us sometimes dig in the old records of our own towns; and while doing so, let us pray that mind be given us to understand what we bring to light.
John Jay Chapman, *William Lloyd Garrison*

 The imagination preys upon life, as Samuel Johnson said, and in so doing moves from the mystery of human behavior to a reality it creates by way of meaning, a feeling for what being alive was like, a sense of the past. This is a complex process, and there are various ways of expressing how it works. One can say it fills in statements about past events by making new relationships possible in new directions. It alters the declarative sentence and introduces the subjunctive, the possibility of contingencies: one thing touches another and yet another, so that the imagination is able to construct in what has actually happened an area of uncertainty and perplexity, a field of choice. Alternatives still lie open, or so by a considerable effort it can be imagined, just as they do in the present when looking ahead into the uncertain future. The course of history, it then seems, has not yet been determined, even though what is being looked at is the past as it has been recorded in history. Life did not have to go the way it has inevitably gone, however that may have been.

In this experience of understanding just what it was like to have lived in the past, the imagination has to be exerted to its utmost to take in what can only be called our predecessors' ignorance. They did not know, as we do, what happened next, how the current of thought moved, where belief found its way, how human will controlled direction. It is incredible, the extent of this ignorance, to be explained only by supposing that for them it was not ignorance at all but something they, mistakenly, called knowledge. Whatever the blood did before it circulated, they knew. Their minds were richly and lovingly stored with the misinformation of centuries, and they viewed the future with resolve, as all men do, because its inevitable direction they had willed with all their might and main, misjudging it at every turn. They could in perfect confidence demand that the future must conform to their determined purpose. They could draw up a legal document stating exactly what a human institution should be doing "for all time." They could define belief as it must exist in the future. Yet in looking back it is plain how dreadfully wrong nearly everyone was about nearly everything, including the face of the earth, the shape of the universe, and most of all the way time appeared as the future became the past.

Whether ignorant or knowing, depending upon the position taken in looking back at them, our fathers and forefathers must have equalled us in love of truth and, generally, in good intentions. This is a fair and reasonable assumption to make unless we are to dismiss our ancestors with simple contempt. And no matter how kindly and forgiving our attitude may be toward them, it is the ordinary man of good will, not the great man, someone distinguished for extreme brutality or heroic self-sacrifice, who is hard to understand. This ordinary man of good will seems too near to be clearly seen, and even so not worth bothering about. His setting is local, wherever we happen to be right now, our parish, where the forefathers of the village lie in the nearest cemetery, and our great-great-grandfathers, hidden though they may be by political and economic and sociological and anthropological generalizations, ought to be within shouting distance. In fact only a few years separate us, only a few lives will take anybody back to the Revolution. But we turn away from our predecessors. We have triumphed over them as an enemy. They are the dead.

Nevertheless there are moments, perhaps of self-deception, when the immediate past seems very close, the years fall away, and all this in the course of an ordinary day. A place can be made to work magic, hence all those signs that begin, "On this spot. . . ." What happened there need not be momentous or earthshaking, when just being alive at another time and under the same conditions seems miraculous enough. A classroom will do. At Amherst College you can look out the window of Chapel 20 (which for a short period recently was the president's outer office and before that, going back to the first use of the building in 1827, had served both as the Rhetoric Room and as a place for prayer meetings) and see the brick wall and a window frame of North College and leafy branches of trees and the sky beyond. For a moment nostalgia does its work, and you know that this is exactly the sight and sense of a teacher of what is now called English a hundred, a hundred and more, years ago. Time, history, individual differences are, if not obliterated, somehow generalized in the continuous existence of an institution, as if this really did exist along with animal and vegetable as a form of life. Thus the imagination beguiled by the senses enchants the heart.

It must be enchantment. A glance at the students in the Rhetoric Room, the sound of the voices, the meaning of what is being said, the tone, all this is enough to make absolutely certain the proposition that between the past and the present no possible connection of any interest or value can be made ever again. The present is incomparable. It is unique. Even that glimpse of North College can be made by a slight shift in point of view to show a lot of genuine ivy growing on a genuine old brick wall as pretty as a picture, and there on the opposite window sill is a solid row of liquor bottles. The time is now. As for the conversation in the Rhetoric Room on, say, an April morning in 1969, as for the ideas and attitudes, the books and events alluded to, how can anyone seriously suppose that Samuel Melancthon Worcester (Professor of Rhetoric and Oratory, 1825–1834) or Heman Humphrey Neill (Professor of Rhetoric and Oratory, and English Literature, 1874–1903), each of whom may well have stood in that very place, would even begin to understand the dialogue in progress? Exactly how far back, exactly how close to that

April morning, does the date fall when everything that has gone before must be crossed off as stupid, boring, wrong, ignorant, and utterly dead? Who knows enough about a particular past in a particular place to answer that question?

Once it was supposed that the past could be looked at as a preparation for, a step in the direction of, the present, that is, the culmination of time, its very peak, but no one believes in any of that any more. Furthermore, about this particular past in a particular classroom nothing seems to be known. Curious minds simply do not turn to Samuel Melancthon Worcester, a graduate of Harvard and the Andover Theological Seminary, or Humphrey Neill, a graduate of Amherst and the Princeton Theological Seminary, and ask what they had to say for themselves as readers of literature and as critics. Plainly they have nothing to tell us. Indeed where would one look for the record of their methods and judgments? What books did they read, and how did they read them? It is possible and also it is sensible to look out that window and believe that nothing of any interest to anybody of ordinary intelligence has ever happened in that place till this very instant. The present, of course, is of overwhelming importance, for the direction the future takes depends upon us second by second. As for the past, it is not only dead, it is stupid.

So even though you may feel the past is just within your reach while standing where others have stood, while teaching where others have taught, there is also the strong awareness that any sense of a tradition in teaching is simple egotism. Teaching—and learning?— has no history, at least when places like the Rhetoric Room are considered. In the discouraging setting of a classroom where students say things about books they may or may not have read and where they more or less pay attention to whatever a teacher has to say for himself, the historical method is a feeble instrument to put into chronological order trains of thought, vocabularies used, and expectations about life and literature. After all to move to a larger and more respectable area, even the history of literary criticism, where talk about books goes on, proceeds by leaps from name to name, from Dryden to Addison to Johnson to Coleridge to Arnold to Richards to Eliot to Leavis to Winters and so on. And if this succession moves every which way what can possibly be said of a succession of ordinary teachers and ordinary students whose conversation has rarely if ever been considered interesting even within the four walls of a classroom? Compared with the not very impressive history as so far written of what is called Literary Criticism, not much in the way of a pattern can be made from the day by day teaching over a period of about a century and a half of the subject called Rhetoric and Oratory and English Literature. Can any coherent view of literature and its uses in life be discovered from the scanty evidence still available? Apparently this question is not often asked.

Behind the indifference or even contempt toward whatever has gone before in the classrooms of an educational institution there is still some obscure contradiction. While no one supposes that Professor Samuel Melancthon Worcester or Professor Humphrey Neill and their students had anything to say of the slightest interest nowadays, there is still a way of talking that makes these primitive students of literature—and the entire venture of education—vaguely dignified. So it is we love to tell the story of the early days when hardworking farmers in the hill towns, the village squire, the learned minister, joined together in clearing a bit of wilderness to create out of almost nothing a college, where, among other subjects, the study of literature might be pursued. There has never been any problem about the motivation of all those engaged in this enterprise: they were men of deep religious conviction who loved learning and truth. Such is the cant that easily disposes of the past.

The story of the early days of Amherst College is heroic in its simplicity. It is a model for what was to happen in Ohio, in Illinois, in Minnesota, when some farseeing founder struck his staff upon some rise in the ground and said, Here, on this hilltop, shall be built a college. We have it on the best authority that when the Amherst trustees voted to construct the first building on the ten acres of farm and woodland, "the timber was in the forest, the stone in the quarry, the brick in the clay," yet in ninety days South College stood ready for shingling. It was a modern miracle. Donations of lime, sand, lumber, materials of all kinds, flowed in from every quarter, that is to say, from Pelham and Leverett, from Belchertown and Hadley. (But not, apparently, from Northampton, which had just failed in its effort to establish its own college.) The people, it is said, turned out and labored day and night, "for they had a mind to work, like the Jews in building their temple, and they felt they were building the Lord's house." This is Tyler, whose devotion to the college—he knew every graduate from the founding till his death in 1897 and became its historian—was an expression of his own religious nature: he loved the college as he loved his church, for both existed to serve God. His view of what happened is utterly noble, and it has been widely shared and often piously repeated.

Almost as if recognizing the smallness, the plainness, even the crudeness of the dedication ceremonies, the sermon preached on that occasion bore the title, "A Plea for a Miserable World," in which, nevertheless, large promises were made. This college was to be unlike any other: here an education could be had free of expense to those who would enter the gospel ministry. And this ministry was to bring joy to the destitute and hope and salvation to perishing millions. Such was the language used. It was to have a surprising effect.

The idea behind the historical record is one we cherish about the past. Then, we love to say, looking back, life had meaning. Ordinary actions, like loading a wagon, driving a team, were transformed, and Yankee farmers in their physical exertions magnified the name of the Lord. A hilltop pasture and woodlot became a consecrated eminence. A plain brick building, 100 feet by 40 feet, utterly without style or ornament or comfort, was a college. A bookcase not six feet wide in the North Entry became the library. A small number of ministers became professors, exercising intellectual, spiritual, and parental authority over a few green and ignorant country boys, who in their turn became college students and finally candidates for the Christian Ministry. One of these was soon to die in a far off land and to be known as the Martyr of Sumatra.

All this is miraculous, when the demands of the present, just carrying wood and water, must have absorbed so much attention, leaving little energy for works of high aspiration. These details of ordinary existence, all those things taken for granted as necessary in order to get through a single day, these are hardest of all to piece together. It was, first of all, a world where numbers were not large, where names could be put to persons and things, and they could be counted easily for taxing, for voting in town meeting. When South College was built there were, it is estimated, about forty houses within a mile of the center of the town, and woods stretched in every direction, to the Range, to Hadley. There was one coach or wagon a week to and from Boston. Winter made extraordinary demands on everyone, and during a cold spell with the outside thermometer below zero the sacramental bread might be frozen solid, and a student could use ink only by huddling over a fire while the thermometer on the wall behind him might register as low as 16°F. The darkness of night and the inadequate means of lighting meant that the greatest demonstration possible of common joy, as over the granting of the charter for the new college or, much later, over the Emancipation Proclamation, was an Illumination, a candle or lamp in every window. It is no wonder—when we think of them at all—that we express admiration for these heroic souls, Squire Dickinson, the indefatigable Colonel Graves, President Zephaniah Swift Moore, the forty-seven students with which the college opened, and those devoted farmers. These and many more like them must have known something that we can no longer recollect by the utmost exertion of our memories, to have lived under such bleak circumstances such purposeful lives. Would that we could know this sacramental power of transforming action, of really renaming events and places and persons, of merging solitary, isolated, lonely individuals into a community.

There is only one trouble with this wistful view of the past. Wherever you touch the record of a New England town, just before or just after this extraordinary community effort of making a college, the most obvious fact is the high degree of sustained and bitter antagonisms with which extremely irritable individualists maintained lifelong, acrimonious disputes over every possible subject. They all shared, it may be admitted, the highest principles, yet they disagreed in every possible way about how they should be applied. They all agreed in defining certain ordinary evils, yet took forever in organizing themselves so they could do anything about them. A diary of the period will show how frequently houses and barns and sometimes half a town were burnt to the ground, yet efficiency in fire-fighting was to remain for many years beyond human capacity. Even the United States as a nation held together only by a miracle, its preservation due, as George Washington and others believed, to the favor of Divine Providence. In fact any organization looked at with care seems at that very moment to be about to be reorganized or in the process of coming apart and splitting in two. After all Amherst College began by taking from Williams College its president and fifteen students. Williams barely survived.

As for the town of Amherst there is plenty of evidence of local

discord. Almost at the same time the community was coming together to haul lime and brick for the college on the hill it engaged in
what was called the Triangle Street Fight. The town of Amherst had
already—having successfully separated from Hadley—split into two
parishes: the West or First Parish or Mt. Zion and the East or Second
Parish or Sodom. (It is easy to see who gave the Biblical names.) A
new road was proposed by which one could go from the north of
town to the church on East Street without having to come in sight of
the First Church. A town meeting voted to approve this road, and
then two weeks later the town meeting rescinded that vote. There-
upon the inhabitants of East Amherst with those in the north of town
came together as a community to construct the road themselves.
That night the inhabitants of West Amherst, the center of town,
gathered as another community to undo what had been done, to fill
ditches, to make the smooth rough again, the straight crooked.
There was a confrontation by day, though it was not what we would
call violent. "[T]wo men would have hold of a plank pulling in one
direction, while at the opposite end two other men would be hauling
another way." What is hard to keep in mind is the number of people
involved. Perhaps thirty or forty at most?

But if the numbers were small, why have these two churches
anyway? If any institution in the Commonwealth was in a strong
position to resist forces of disintegration and to maintain itself this
surely was the Congregational Church. It had long been established
by law. A new town or parish, when set off by the General Court,
was obliged to erect a meetinghouse and settle "a Learned and Orthodox Minister" and provide for "his handsome and honourable
support." All this was made possible by local taxation and by voluntary contribution. By law people were required to attend worship on
the Sabbath, and a tything man was regularly elected as a peace
officer to enforce the laws for the observance of the Lord's Day and
to maintain order in church. It is hard to imagine an institution—it
was not disestablished till 1833—more likely to bring people together
in a community by expressing their commonly shared hopes and
aspirations than the Congregational Church. By definition it was a
company, a gathering. Or in the language of the Cambridge Platform of 1648: "A Congregational Church is, by the institution of
Christ, a part of the militant visible church, consisting of a company
of saints by calling, united into one body, by a holy covenant, for the

public worship of God and the mutual edification one of another, in the fellowship of the Lord Jesus." The visible church was not a body of doctrine or belief or dogma or usage. It did not exist as a hierarchy or in large organization, but only as a coming together of particular individuals in a particular place, and it was said that the only principle of agreement in the Congregational Church was the granting of self-government to the single congregation. As a church it was a system of polity, of units of government, like the town or the precinct. Yet it was not simply a collection of citizens who could be taxed and who could vote but a company of saints, who, furthermore, were surrounded by other citizens more or less antagonistic to their claims of exclusive religious privilege.

From its beginning protestantism carried within itself the seeds of its own destruction, as everyone knows. The general course of movement, of division and redivision, seemed always toward greater exactitude and clearer truth. Then there were the necessities of simple convenience. The very idea of a town as a parish meant that, with growth in numbers and the consequent physical expansion, separations had to take place, and new precincts or territorial divisions had to be set off, and it was not long before churches were to be established in both North and South Amherst. So it had been from the very beginning when the New Swamp as it was appropriately called, or East Hadley or the Third Precinct was set off from Hadley by the legislature and, as usual, under protest from the parent town. This is Amherst. It is said that the original name as proposed by the petitioners had been Norwottuck but the Colonial Governor, exercising his privilege, had scratched it out, writing in the name of the friend who, as it happened, had just won his first great victory at Louisbourg. In complying with the requirements of the law to erect a meetinghouse, the town of Amherst was immediately engaged in the usual dispute as to just where exactly it should be placed, and the records of the early town meetings show vote after vote, one correcting another. The classic story about this problem tells how a town voted to employ a surveyor to determine (1) the center of the territory, (2) the center of population, (3) the center of wealth, and (4) the center of these centers, and when this place had been determined the town then voted to build the meetinghouse somewhere else. Once the building was erected, there would be the usual difficulty of just where everyone or every family should be seated in relation to the pulpit, and though the principles, by "Age, Estate, and Qualifications," were established, every few years for decades a new committee would have to be appointed to settle once more these delicate matters. As for the choice of minister here was a real problem. Who was he to be? How was he to be paid? In what money, silver valued at just what, and how much in kind? Educated ministers were in short supply and were in a position to bargain. Every year, with notable exceptions which plainly meant no good, a vote in town meeting would have to be carried for the payment of this salary. For some reason, stinginess on the part of the hunkered element, as it was called, unwillingness to pay, inability to collect taxes, a town would fall behind in the payments due the minister, and on his dismissal or death more bargaining had to be gone through by the minister or his executor to reach some kind of settlement, and then it might take a court order to exact payment. This was to happen in Amherst.

The company of saints united in one body were also citizens, yet all citizens were not church members, and this situation led to more divisions. In the constitution of a society where a state church had to be maintained by taxation, provision had to be made for variances. After all the congregation did not take in everybody, and not everybody wanted to belong to the congregation. If you were a Baptist or a Methodist or an Episcopalian or a Quaker or a Universalist, to begin to account for exceptions, it was possible to deal with the town clerk so that you set yourself off from the congregation or rather claimed for yourself membership in another church. Some mute inglorious Thoreau could always refuse to pay his tax for the support of the minister, and then the town would have to institute legal proceedings. In a Salem church the oldest communion vessel had been obtained by an act of distraint upon some unwilling taxpayer.

The very fact that the Congregational Church was established by the state proved its undoing. A church, a company of saints, having drawn up a covenant, having selected a minister whose religious expressions they approved by a majority vote might find themselves a minority in conflict with the parish, their chosen minister might be dismissed by a vote of the parish, and then, as at Dedham in 1808, the Supreme Court of the Commonwealth might decide that the very church property, the utensils of communion, its lands and holdings, the building where they and their fathers had been accustomed to worship, belonged not to them but to others, others who did not so much as believe in the Trinity, others who were somehow—it has always been hard to express how—representatives of the parish. In one way what a parish was seemed clear enough, the voters in a town or part of a town, taxpayers, citizens, male and over twenty-one, and property owners, and of course the majority of the parish might not be Congregationalists at all or even church-goers. The difficulties here are immense, and after all the whole idea of a church must be beyond an operational definition, since it is of two worlds.

A number of terms are being used here to express the ways in which society was organized, and since they are not mutually exclusive nor are they defined in the same way by different people, it was bound to be a contentious world. The idea of the parish seems clear as a political unit. The church is much harder to locate because more than one realm of experience is being talked about, and metaphor has to be drawn upon. It could be defined as a communion of saints, a society of visible saints who had publicly acknowledged the covenant, who had perhaps testified publicly to a personal knowledge of God and had known what was called experimental religion. By 1800 such persons would mostly be women, the sex, in Gibbon's phrase, most prone to devotion. Then there were members of the church who contributed voluntarily or by taxation to its support but who did not take or were not admitted to communion. There were probably some members who did not regularly attend the service of worship, and they were commonly known as stay-at-home Protestants. Then there was the minister himself. He was in the Congregational Church a "learned man," a graduate of Harvard or Yale or Dartmouth or Brown and later of Amherst, trained in the ministry by the apprentice system, studying under an experienced minister, that is, or after 1808 and the establishment of the Andover Theological Seminary, going on with his studies as a graduate student. He was licensed to preach when approved by a local association of ministers. When called or chosen by a particular church he was ordained or set apart for his office by the acts of a church council composed of ministers usually from the neighborhood. "The ministerial office is instituted by Jesus Christ for the gathering, guiding, edifying, and governing his church. . . ." In this gathering, while set off from other men, the minister was also a peer, a man of equal standing, with his congregation, and he was a minister, in theory at least, only so long as he was associated with a particular congregation. In practice a minister could be arrogant, factious, and troublemaking. He possessed by custom life tenure, though there were ways by which he could be got rid of, just as it was possible for him to move on to what he took to be greener pastures. To complicate matters of government and control still further there were or there might be proprietors who owned the land and had built the building. In North Amherst Oliver Dickinson was the sole proprietor. In the deed that accompanied the sale of a pew he stipulated that on no account could that pew be sold to a Negro or mulatto, and in formally deeding the pulpit to the first minister he stated that the minister "shall believe and inculcate the principles of the gospel as contained in the Westminster Assembly's Shorter Cathechism forever. . . ." The meetinghouse was usually paid for by the sale of pews in a *vendu* conducted by the town treasurer. (In Fitchburg in 1802 Pew Number 1 sold for $105.17, while a less conspicuous one went for only $10.00. Pews were real property by a decision of the courts and passed from owner to owner, and occasionally they were advertised for sale.) The proprietors or the owners of the pews who were represented by a committee maintained the house, replacing the weather vane when it blew down in a storm. All these terms, town, parish or precinct, church, church members, congregation, meetinghouse, and so on are ways of talking about what we would call a community, its activities, its professed beliefs, its property, and since these terms refer to an everchanging number of human beings and their activities they were not and they cannot be mutually exclusive, and in what they refer to their meanings are various. It is little wonder, therefore, that the local history of New England is made up of disputes, quarrels, feuds, separations, litigation, pamphlet warfare, eloquent and bitter sermons, all signs of dissension in a world where only uniformity, community, congregation, or gathering, ought to exist. Occasionally there were even acts of violence. More than once the doors of a meetinghouse were nailed up to prevent the entrance of the minister, and there is one instance when some parishioner took a shot through an open window at the minister. There is the pettiness of a minister's washing hung out to dry being torn up by someone's malice, and the ludicrous episode when the fire company at practice played the hose on the passing minister, who, soon after, let it be known that he had purchased a pair of pistols. More sadly, there is the minister who after forty years' faithful service announced to his parish that he was withdrawing since he was not paid enough to keep his family and himself alive. Even when a minister was dismissed by the usual forms, his parish might not then be rid of him, since he might set himself off with a few loyal souls—there were always some of these—as a new congregation, a new church, and demand for himself the use of the meetinghouse and even lay claim to the very title ("The First Church") of the church he had left. "Preachers multiply and we are overwhelmed," wrote the Reverend William Bentley, D.D., of Salem in 1807. "Sects are in all their glory in New England and through the United States. They are as thick as gulls upon our sandbar, as hungry and as useless."

Assuming for convenience that Amherst is the center of the universe, we can then see how much excitement had been going on in the neighborhood, when congregations, parishes, and towns were torn apart by the bitterest of quarrels with their ministers. Perry Miller says of the story of Jonathan Edwards' dismission at Northampton that everyone must read it "by his own lights—which is one reason why it belongs along with Harper's Ferry or Homestead to the symbolism of America," but in its essentials—it began with the usual dispute over the amount of salary—it follows the usual pattern: just how much authority did the minister have over his parish and over the precinct and over the town? This was in 1750. Nearer in time to the founding of Amherst College arose a quarrel in Fitchburg where the same issues were joined, almost as if this particular dispute had to be an essential element of the polity of the Congregational Church. If the minister's duties involved gathering and guiding and edifying, trouble was bound to occur when he was plainly leading and guiding in a direction where a number of his flock did not want to go.

The details of such a quarrel can only be brought intensely to life by the addition of virulent passion aided by the ingenuity of extreme malignity to the plain narrative. The community of Fitchburg in 1800 was small, news of the outside world was limited, the winters were long and hard, spring nonexistent, the summers almost tropical. As for manners and education—who could afford such luxuries when hell yawned and money was scarce? In such a situation the minister served a worldly purpose by supplying subjects of conversation for a whole community: giving it food for thought, by telling it what life and death looked like, by using words which somehow connected the desolate individuals in lonely farms with other places and other events, with Cambridge and the makers of the Platform, with Plymouth and London and Amsterdam and Scrooby and Geneva, and then most wonderfully by a vast leap to those wonderful events in the Holy Land. The minister brought history and theology and his own interpretation and the Bible and his observation of his parishioners' behavior all together, and this he impregnated with his own intensely felt religious and emotional life, to be expressed with whatever gifts of rhetoric and powers of voice he could summon. The minister was a source of energy in such a New England town, making it possible for people to take sides, to doubt and believe, hate and love. What he said, how he said it, what he really meant, how this applied to the peculiar situation of a particular listener, how it altered his view of his neighbor down the road, here were new ways of seeing and thinking and feeling, adding new meanings to daily existence.

Samuel Worcester was brought up on a New Hampshire farm, the youngest of five boys. The usual pattern of Yankee self-improvement was complicated for him because in all his attempts at study or reading he met the active hostility of his father, who said of him that this son was worth any two hired men. Nevertheless he was to break free, buying his time, as they used to say, by giving his father a note for the several months of labor still owed him before his twenty-first birthday. He entered Dartmouth, crudely dressed and poor even for that time in that place, and by great frugality and industry graduated valedictorian in the class of 1795. In those days a liberal education, as it came to be called, was not something many young men wanted. It led nowhere in particular, except toward the professions of teaching, preaching, and the law, and the last two could only be entered with some further preparation. Since there were then no theological seminaries Samuel Worcester managed to spend four months studying under the Reverend Samuel Austin, who had in his turn studied under Jonathan Edwards, the son, and was later to be the first editor of the *Works* of the celebrated father. What this training meant in practice seems to have been the writing out of answers to certain theological questions, the composing of sermons. Then rather surprisingly Worcester taught school for a couple of years, indecisively. As for his own religious experience, it is reported that he had "met with a saving change," though there is no record that he had known and publicly acknowledged the kind of conversion he was to demand of others when he came to occupy a pulpit. Theologically, as a pupil of Austin, he was a militant Hopkinsian, in the direct line from Edwards. There is a two volume *Life,* written by his son, the Reverend Samuel Melancthon Worcester, the first teacher of English at Amherst College.

In 1798 Samuel Worcester was ordained minister of the First Congregational Church in Fitchburg, a town which, since its founding about thirty years before, had enjoyed very little harmony, to put it mildly. The preceding minister had been "laid aside" because of "mental alienation," and behind this fact there must have been an unhappy story. Both Baptists and Universalists were active and controlled the majority of votes in town meeting. As usual a remote part of the town wanted to secede, to be set off as a precinct, and as usual this movement was bitterly resisted. There had also been some strange goings on, which were later to be described by Samuel Worcester as Bacchanalian orgies around the intoxicating bowl, a form of language which must have raised whatever these residents of Fitchburg had been doing to a new level of dignity.

Dignity the new minister certainly had. He was twenty-eight years old, which was not young in those days. He wore a tricornered hat, long hair in a queue behind, small clothes, and silver buckles at knee band and on shoe straps, quite in the style of the provincial clergy. And as if he were himself an experienced preacher he took pupils, some of whom were preparing for college, others for the ministry. His self-confidence is breath-taking. He began immediately to live over in Fitchburg the sequence of events that had occurred half a century before in Northampton: a restricting of the terms of church membership, a revival of religion, the antagonizing of a number of prominent citizens, and finally dismissal. His son was to say that Samuel Worcester should be recognized as "The Liberator of the Congregational Churches of New England." Certainly he carried a sword. But just what that liberty was he stood for is not so clear, unless it was the recognition of the right of the church council to decide finally the issues that came before it and the right of the minister and his church to act without any control from town or parish.

Immediately on his ordination Samuel Worcester upset the balance of hostilities as they already existed, and at the end of four years of incessant wrangling, on his retirement in defeat in 1802, he published a pamphlet of more than 100 pages with one of those long titles, which begins thus, *Facts and Documents Exhibiting a Summary View of the Ecclesiastical Affairs Lately Transacted in Fitchburg. . . .* There is nothing dull about this performance: it is written with a lawyer's clarity, it is documented, it records dramatic confrontations, some of which came close to physical violence, and the tone of the narrative ranges from patient forebearance to outraged indignation. The first act of his short career as minister to the First Church of Fitchburg was to abolish the Half-Way Covenant, following in this his teacher Austin, who, in his turn, had followed his teacher Edwards. He then composed a new covenant and new articles of faith, and he insisted that, while some members of his church did at this point withdraw, the church was itself unaltered from what it had been when he became minister. Those members of the church who had protested at what was going on, objecting especially to the Hopkinsian creed, those members, two of whom were selectmen and a third the town moderator, were reasoned with, prayed over, and then declared formally to be "heathen men and publicans" and so excommunicated. Worcester's position was, of course, hopeless. He had been called by a vote of the First Church, the town concurring, quite in the regular fashion, but since it was the town that provided his support he could also be dismissed by a vote of the town, even though the Church still supported him. At first Worcester resisted this proposition, that the town although it concurred in the choice of a minister could by formal vote dismiss him. But such a balance of powers was entirely traditional. Worcester finally surrendered. He acknowledged receipt of what was owed him, namely, $196.48. "And I do hereby declare my consent to relinquish, and to wholly and forever relinquish the contract made by me and by the said Town for my support." He then moved to Salem, as minister of the Tabernacle (so-called in memory of George Whitefield), where he played a minor part in the founding of the Theological Seminary at Andover and was most active in the expanding missionary movement. At Fitchburg the town records show that now two Congregational Societies struggled for existence with the town and with one another. As for the numbers involved in all this there were 181 male voters in Fitchburg, and seventy members of the First Church, most of whom were women.

Like Edwards before him Samuel Worcester preached—and then published—a farewell sermon. At one level this quarrel, where neighbors and families were divided, can be seen in its expressions of the passions of hatred and malignity, as only one more bit of evidence pointing to the monotonous horrors of human nature. By his powers of eloquence, his rhetorical gifts, his beliefs in the meaning of what had happened, Samuel Worcester raised this confused, really contemptible village fracas to a new level where principles were involved, rights existed, and the most sublime of all dramas was once more reenacted. Whatever anyone felt about these events he could now believe in his own feelings in a new way, know that they had been called good or bad, and be assured that this acrimonious experience in this backwoods community was part of the workings of divine providence. The text Worcester chose was Acts 20:27: *For I have not shunned to declare unto you all the counsel of God.* What had happened in Fitchburg was one more enactment of the Christian story. Their minister was a public teacher of the First Church of Fitchburg, yes. But what was a church? Was it an unheated, unpainted building so many feet wide, so many long, with benches on two sides, one for men, one for women? Was it the creature, a thing created, of the legislature and so controlled by a majority of the voters in town meeting, voters who as everyone knew were mostly Baptists and Universalists? Is it not "a company of saints by calling, united into one body, by a holy covenant, for the public worship of God?" Cannot this church cast out by excommunication anyone who notoriously and obstinately offends and permits the covenant to be profaned? To whom can the excommunicated appeal, and how can the town meeting have anything to say to such a matter? As for himself he was not as might be supposed by unbelievers the embodiment of a merely human will determined to have its own way but an ordained minister, a father, a watchman on the battlements, a light to the Gentiles, able to wrestle, as all men could then see, with principalities and powers, with Antipaedobaptists, Ario-Arminians, Universalists. It was said: "If thou warn the wicked of his way to turn from it; if he do not turn from his way, he shall die in his iniquity, but thou hast delivered thy soul." As for his being dismissed by the town he would remind his listeners that they would all very soon meet at the bar of God, and then it would be very terrible for them to meet their faithful minister: "Terrible, indeed, must be

their doom." Both friends and enemies, it was said, were now reduced to tears. Worcester's son comments: "They had little realized,
that they were *his* enemies because 'the enemies of the cross of
Christ.'" And at his installation at Salem, Worcester was thus addressed by his teacher for four months, The Reverend Samuel Austin: "You have, like your dear master, borne the cross. . . ."

This notorious quarrel in Fitchburg left nothing behind it except
more bad feeling. A few years later an event occurred in Deerfield
which could be seen as a portent, a threat of a monstrous future, or as
something quite different, still another triumph for the principle of
the independence of the church. For this we have in addition to a
couple of hundred pages of controversial pamphlets an admirable
document, written without a trace of bitterness or resentment, and
its author was plainly a modest and a lovely man. In 1857, fifty years
after his ordination, the Reverend Samuel Willard delivered an address in The First Church of Deerfield, entitled, *The History of the
Rise, Progress and Consummation of the Rupture Which Now Divides the
Congregational Clergy and Churches in Massachusetts.* The ordination of
Samuel Willard reversed the situation at Fitchburg by demonstrating
that a church with the town concurring could successfully choose its
own minister against the disapprobation of the assembled council
and the threat of any outside authority.

Samuel Willard's ordination was felt at the time to be a significant
act of freedom. It proved that while the ministers on the council were
allowed to pass a final judgment on the candidate's orthodoxy and
while they exerted all the pressure they could summon toward conformity, the candidate could maintain the right to his own belief. Of
course this balance between freedom and control was at the heart of
Congregationalism, and now it tipped one way, now another. The
individual church recognized Christ as its only head, the individual's
most precious experience was his own knowledge of God. Nothing
could be freer than this. But what of other men and their beliefs, and
other churches, and the past, and what of John Calvin? Somehow the
First Churches of Deerfield and Amherst and Conway and Shelburne
could be associated together, yet the question could properly be
asked whether the Congregational Church as a single institution even
existed. So far as one can make out at any given moment the emphasis moved back and forth and back again from the inner experience of the individual to the relation of one person to another, one

church to another. This process is still at work, of course, although in other terms.

There were arrangements of words, catechisms, articles of faith, platforms, confessions, but what authority an arrangement carried at a particular moment had to be proved at that moment. A minister like Samuel Worcester and many another after him felt free to compose his own version of a covenant and articles of faith, and there is no indication that his parishioners felt this a presumptuous act or that they supposed every word bore an indisputable meaning satisfying the scrutiny of every member of the church. What everyone did recognize was that the meaning of the words was to be found in the individual's wordless religious experience. Various forms of words, the Westminster Catechism, the Cambridge Platform, the articles of faith of a particular church, referred somehow as symbols to an inner experience a person did or did not know, an experience in the ways of grace. This is difficult to express but more difficult to live with. Many a minister whose life is recorded in Sprague's *Annals of the American Pulpit; or Commemorative Notices of Distinguished American Clergymen of Various Denominations From the Early Settlement of the Country to the Close of the Year Eighteen Hundred and Fifty-five* suffered fits of terrible depression because he knew himself to fall short of some article of faith easily and painlessly expressed in some verbal formula. The words were not what really mattered.

In any question about the nature of inner religious experience, appeal could be had to the past, and of all formulas of appeal the most successful in bringing different parties like the Old Calvinists and the Hopkinsians together was to speak of those doctrines "which from the beginning had been generally embraced by the Churches of New England as the doctrines of the gospel," though it is hard to see how anyone who knew about early New England could be so easily satisfied. Classic expressions did exist, most notably the Cambridge Platform of 1648 adopted by the Cambridge Synod: *A Platform of Church Discipline Gathered Out of the Word of God: and Agreed Upon by the Elders: and Messengers of the Churches Assembled in Synod at Cambridge in New England.* Therein is described "the Form of A Visible Church" as well as "the Communion of Churches One with Another," so relevant to what was to happen at Deerfield. Provision is made for consultation (as "the Church of Antioch consulted with the Apostles & Elders of the Church at Jerusalem") and for the following purposes: admonition, participation, recommendation, relief and succour, and the propagation of one church out of another. In practice consultation meant the calling of a council, when ministers and members of the congregation, known as messengers, of neighboring churches were summoned for certain purposes by *letters missive* (a very old and dignified phrase, even royal, used in Shakespeare) to settle a quarrel between a minister and his parish over a woodlot, to decide whether or not a minister should accept a call to a professorship at Dartmouth College, or whether a minister should be dismissed because of age or infirmities, extreme dullness or constant drunkenness, or to go through the forms of licensing a preacher or extending the right hand of fellowship. This last was the ritual that held individual churches together.

Suppose, however, that this right hand of fellowship was withheld, as it was in Deerfield in 1807 from Samuel Willard. Was this decision of a church council final? Could it be appealed or rescinded, and if so by whom? If it was to be enforced what police power was there available? These were questions long in dispute. The desire for some system of federalism is understandable, simply from the love of order in what always seems a world of increasing disorder. It is easy to see why Samuel Worcester in his quarrel with the town wanted the support of other churches, for there was nowhere else to appeal. As long ago as 1705 an attempt had been made to establish a stricter form of ecclesiastical government when a Convention of Ministers recommended the establishment of "standing councils." Their decisions were to be final and decisive, and if their finality was questioned the churches in the council should withdraw from communion with the church "that would not be healed." Of course these proposals met with opposition from the occupants of the pews and little support from the legislature. They also provoked two pamphlets, reprinted with much political effect in 1772, in which the Reverend John Wise of Ipswich defended, in the name of democracy, the liberty of New England churches against the domination of their own ministers. Smaller local Associations did indeed already exist, what we would call professional societies, where like-minded ministers organized themselves by town or region or county. Such was the Hampshire Association and its offshoot the Franklin Association. The latter met on the first Tuesday of February, May, August, and November, from two in the afternoon until noon the next day.

There would be a public meeting with prayer and a sermon, a discussion of theological issues which once formulated might well have practical results in the neighborhood, and an exchange of information about the running of a church, what to do about adjusting the minister's salary to the continuing inflation, and, most perplexing of all, finding a way to collect that salary in full when they professed, as did these ministers, to be unmercenary. It is reasonable to suppose that there was also much professional gossip and much political talk, for whatever this clergy was it was certainly political. One question discussed and then decided at such a gathering was the following: "Is it our duty to admit into our pulpits a man who denies the divinity of Christ?" The answer was "No." The man aimed at, to be excluded from fellowship, was Samuel Willard.

Many forces had recently been at work in places beside Fitchburg or Deerfield to deepen the rupture that was to divide the Congregational clergy and churches in Massachusetts. There had always been pressures for and against moving the Independents in England and the Congregationalists in America toward Presbyterianism, and in Connecticut and later in the Middle West the movement seems to have been away from the pure congregationalism of the fathers, for whom a minister was only a member of the congregation though set apart, and then only so long as he was set apart by a particular church, toward the idea of a minister as a member of a profession with special rights and even unquestionable authority. In 1802 and 1803 delegates from district Associations met in Northampton, and in 1804 at a Convention of Ministers in Boston it was proposed by Dr. Lyman of Hatfield that a General Association be formed. Such meetings did indeed take place in Westfield, Dorchester, and even in far off Conway. Another related event in what was the gathering of organizing forces in the Congregational Churches in Massachusetts was the union of two magazines, the *Massachusetts Missionary Magazine* (one of whose editors was Samuel Worcester) and *The Panoplist,* in which, as was currently recognized, two parties joined hands. The naming of these two parties is not easy, for they were, of course, both Calvinist and both claimed to be orthodox. There were those, the Old Calvinists, who carried their belief back to the purity of the Founding Fathers, but everyone seemed to claim to do that. Then there were those who called themselves Hopkinsians and were derisively called Hopkintonians or New Lights who professed disinterested benevolence to the point where a willingness to be damned for the glory of God was evidence of perfect submission and who insisted on what was called experimental religion, just as Edwards had done. Then a providential event was to occur that seemed to ensure the direction to be taken by Congregationalism for all time, when these two parties joined together in the establishment of the first professional graduate school for the training of ministers in America, the Theological Seminary at Andover. Up till then candidates for the ministry had studied as apprentices under some minister who might be running what amounted to his own private theological school. In as unlikely a place as Shelburne the Reverend Theophilus Packard trained more than thirty such students. Obviously this loose system had drawbacks, for it must have encouraged individual variations in belief, even though there were traditions in handing down doctrine.

After the most elaborate and subtle negotiations between the two parties and the two sets of donors an agreement had been reached, and in 1808 there was opened the Andover Seminary. It was, as such things went, a rich institution, where a poor boy of proved piety could receive free of expense a strict, controlled education, and so, leaving the farm as Worcester had done, make his way into a new world as a learned minister. According to the Statutes of the Founders, the nature, the content, the meaning of a minister's education was to be established, fixed, forever and ever, by an exactly defined curriculum and explicitly stated articles of faith that were to remain unchanged in the future. According to these Statutes every professor every five years had to make a public profession of faith in accordance with what had been written out in the Seminary's constitution. He had to proclaim his willing determination to maintain the Christian faith "in opposition to not only Atheists and Infidels, but to Jews, Mahometans, Arians, Pelagians, Antinomians, Arminians, Socinians, Unitarians, and Universalists, and to all other heresies and errors, antient and modern." It can scarcely be surprising that not everyone welcomed this new institution, and one critic immediately described it as an institution "which would have disgraced the bigotry of the dark ages." The Reverend William Bentley, a neighbor but no friend of Samuel Worcester of the Tabernacle, regularly spoke of it in the currently hostile phrase, "that Jesuit college at Andover" or "the Andover furnace." But then Bentley, if not an infidel or a Jew, was, so far as these terms can be understood, an Arian, probably a Pelagian and an Arminian, certainly a Socinian, certainly a Unitarian. He called himself "a rational Christian." He was also one of the most learned men of his day in America.

So far only half the story has been sketched in, the inclination toward regularization, organization, association, authority, the fixing of belief for all time. The other side is so complex that it is hard to sort out all the forces at work. Congregationalism, though still the established church, was especially in the eastern part of the state losing ground to the various sects, the Baptists (in several forms) and the Universalists especially, neither insisting on an educated clergy, both encouraging what was called enthusiasm. Worse than these separations was the appearance in the pulpit of ministers ordained in the usual fashion, supported by their congregations, who in their statements of belief revealed to others of different temperatures of Calvinism their heresy. The classic case, recognized as such at the time, was the appointment in 1805 of Henry Ware as Hollis Professor of Divinity by the Corporation and Overseers at Harvard, an event according to Samuel Eliot Morison as momentous in the history of the university as the appointment in 1869 of Charles William Eliot. Orthodox Calvinists saw this as an act of the enemy: "Pious families in the rural districts of New England horror stricken at Harvard's defection from their ancient faith, impelled their sons elsewhere." That meant toward Brown or Yale or Dartmouth or Williams and, in a few years, Amherst. Such was the triumph of Unitarianism at Harvard and its effect. Yet the surprising thing is how little Henry Ware was moved to controversy. He and others like him had continued to think of themselves as Congregational ministers, and it was not till 1815 that the term Unitarian was used as the name of a separate denomination, and it was Samuel Worcester in his pamphlet warfare with William Ellery Channing who insisted that there must be no compromise. From then on Unitarian churches began to form their own associations and to extend for themselves the right of fellowship. When in 1807, therefore, Samuel Willard faced the hostile council assembled for his ordination it seems reasonable to suppose that it never crossed his mind to claim that he belonged to a new and different church. The First Church of Deerfield was a Congregational Church, and he expected to be its pastor. It must have seemed otherwise to the ministers who composed that council. They were already prepared for the worst.

There had been nothing irregular in Willard's education or training. Graduating from Harvard in the class of 1803 he had taught at Exeter and at Bowdoin while preparing himself for the ministry, and one day, without any special preparation, he presented himself before the Cambridge Association and was duly licensed to preach. He had supplied pulpits in several places, even at Andover, and he had never heard a word of dissatisfaction or any criticism of his orthodoxy. When Dr. Webber, then President of Harvard, told him that Deerfield was looking for "a man of moderate orthodoxy," he went there and after preaching for a while received a call from the First Church by a vote of 40 to 1, the town concurring.

In the local situation there were the usual occasions for disunity, and there were those who did find the candidate most objectionable. Certainly the disgruntled inhabitants who lived in the southern part of the town had something to complain about, for it was easier to drive to church in Sunderland or Whately than to what is now called Old Deerfield. There were said to be unspecified theological differences of long standing to complicate matters. As for Samuel Willard, the ministers gathered for the council from Hatfield and Conway and Shelburne and Whately and Amherst had every reason to treat him with suspicion. He was a graduate of Harvard, a nephew of the late President Willard with whom he had lived, during his college course, and President Willard, everyone knew, was an Arminian. At the gathering of the council the candidate's offer of his written confession of faith was rejected by a majority vote in favor of a catechetical examination. This was not unreasonable: men seeking membership in a church were customarily expected to make a public profession of their religious experience, and it was only women who were allowed to substitute a written account of how they had felt the powers of grace. Furthermore an oral examination made it possible for church members—or in this instance the council—to ask questions and so assure themselves of the speaker's soundness of belief. In earlier days when church membership was desirable for worldly men because with it and only with it did they have the right to vote, some written testimonies concocted for the occasion had been rightly rejected, and now when party lines were being more firmly drawn how much more earnestly should a candidate's beliefs be inquired into.

Dr. Joseph Lyman, the minister of Hatfield, was a powerful figure, born, it was said, to command. It was he who turned round the people of Hatfield for the cause of the Revolution, it was he who had

Colonel Israel Williams, an old Indian fighter and a Tory magnate, smoked out (this was not a mere figure of speech) and later had him jailed. (They now lie side by side in the Hatfield Cemetery.) According to Willard it was Dr. Lyman who took the lead in questioning him, "determined to let others know the precise state of my immature mind on some of the deep mysteries of Theology, and particularly the absolute Deity of Christ, or his equality with the Father." Everyone present must have known what was going on. A shrewd and experienced questioner ought to be able to obtain from the candidate a denial of the doctrine of the Trinity, and then there would be no need to proceed further. But Samuel Willard refused to be led into a denial, insisting instead on his own uncertainty of mind about this momentous Mystery. Toward the end of the first session, "a large number of citizens," so it is said, formally appeared before the council, when an address was read in which it was insisted that the candidate was indeed their choice, ending with the threatening words, "Pause—Reverend Fathers for Heavens sake—Pause." Later, so goes the story, when the council moved across the common to the meetinghouse, they were pelted with stones. After a second day's meeting and further catechizing the candidate, the council determined by a vote of 11 to 5 that since they "did not discover in . . . [the pastor-elect] that belief of true and essential Divinity of our Lord Jesus Christ, nor those sentiments respecting the entire moral depravity of fallen man," in short, since he was neither a Trinitarian nor a Calvinist, they could not "separate him for the gospel ministry." For all their efforts they could not make Samuel Willard profess what they knew he really must believe. This decision on the part of the council should as far as they were concerned have ended the whole matter.

Within a few days the First Church of Deerfield voted 28 to 8 that the profession of faith made by Mr. Willard was satisfactory to them, and by a vote of 27 to 12 they renewed their invitation, the town concurring, 114 to 34. Another council was called, from Lincoln, Concord, Wendell, Warwick, and so on, and by unanimous vote proceeded to ordination. The right hand of fellowship was extended. "I must expect some inconvenience," Willard said. He also said he would not "withdraw communion" from those who had disagreed with him on what he called points of "speculative theology." (This particular phrase was to the orthodox an outrageous thing to say.) Willard went out of his way to maintain civil relations with his neighbors, the ministers of Hatfield and Shelburne, his very worst enemies, and he took some satisfaction that in later years the Reverend Joseph Lyman sought him out as an attentive listener to the usual complaints of an old man.

The immediate effect of this ordination was to antagonize the members of the first council. For them it was perfectly clear that "when one thinks his neighbor radically defective in Christian doctrine he ought to say so and act accordingly." Here again was the issue that had troubled men's minds for over a century: what was the relation of one Congregational Church to another? If a council was called was not that council's decision final? Immediately the members of the Franklin Association and of the Hampshire Association voted, mentioning no names, that it was not their duty to admit to their pulpits anyone who denied the divinity of Christ. When an occasional person moved from Deerfield to a neighboring town and brought as was customary a letter of recommendation which ought to have admitted him to membership in another church, that person was rejected. At church councils in Montague and then in Greenfield when Willard appeared as invited all other business was suspended while the other members expressed at length their reasons why he should not be allowed to sit with them, yet in both places Willard refused to countenance their objections by withdrawing from the meeting even when the only business transacted was a vote to the effect that fellowship with the pastor and church at Deerfield was refused.

Lines were heavily drawn. Neighborhoods, churches, families were soon torn apart. South Deerfield was immediately set off as a new town. And by 1819 there had been established a new association, this one Unitarian, which could also extend the right hand of fellowship, composed of ministers from Deerfield, Pelham, Charlemont, Brattleboro, Springfield, Orange, even Northampton, all towns from that part of the state where orthodoxy was strongest. There were also some distinguished names to be mentioned: Dan Huntington of Hadley, Preserved Smith of Rowe. And during the next few years Unitarian churches were established in Bernardston, Conway, Greenfield, Heath, Montague, New Salem, Northfield, and Leverett. The Connecticut Valley was no longer the unbroached stronghold of Calvinism. Amherst was pretty well surrounded.

In 1829 Samuel Willard, having lived in harmony with his congregation, asked for his dismissal, giving his reason in three short words, "I am blind." The First Church in its final address to him after paying proper respect to their pastor's qualities stated that what had lately happened there had been a historic event. They said that they—and especially their pastor—had been subjected to "obloquy and persecution." But this is only one side of the story. "This Society was the first in this region," they said, "practically to assert the rights of conscience, and your settlement with them was the first step toward the establishment of the principle of religious freedom." Not only did the church members have that freedom but so did the minister himself, and no outside authority or power could control them. It is remarkable that although the events at Fitchburg were very different from what happened in Deerfield the same appeal was made in both places to the name of freedom.

In the small world of ecclesiastical quarrels and ordinations and associations names keep reappearing, now in one role, now in another. Robert Breck was attacked in a pamphlet ascribed to Jonathan Edwards, Breck may have cast the deciding vote in the dismissal of Edwards, and, by time's whirligig, Breck preached the funeral sermon of the first pastor and joined in the ordination of the second in Amherst. Some of the quarrels can be seen as historically interesting, where parties and causes and principles seem to point toward both the past and the future. The history of the town of Amherst, however, does not seem to offer anything of special interest, except for the founding of the academy and then of the college. The ministers, David Parsons, Jr., and his son David Parsons, are described simply as "strict Calvinists," as if all the literature from Edwards on had never been written and all degrees, so important to councils and associations and sermons, on the Calvinist thermometer, to use an old metaphor, had never been marked off with excruciating exactness. It is surprising how little there is available in the record to locate just where in theological terms Amherst College was to stand in its beginnings, especially since everyone supposes that the prime motive of the founders was something vaguely called religious idealism. Of course these men who established the academy and then the college were Calvinists and Trinitarians, but so in their professions were most of the inhabitants of the town and valley. They were also men who knew well what could be accomplished on this earth, where money was to be had—the village squire, the enthusiastic promoter, the dignified pastor of his flock, the austere unattached minister pulling all the political wires within reach, they do seem a worldly lot.

If we do not know what the issues and principles and differing articles of faith were, the bitter quarreling that did go on in Amherst seems senseless, only more evidence of the deep-rooted universal disease of human depravity. Yet the intensity of personal animosities can obscure the fact that there really were large events taking place to divide men one from another—the Revolution, Shays's Rebellion, the War of 1812. As for this last there is not much more to say than that the town voted against it, but as for the first two it is hard to imagine how anyone's life could have gone untouched by what was happening in the immediate neighborhood. Of course the bare record of what went on in town meeting leaves nearly everything we want to know unsaid, and the formal language of motions made and carried conceals the nervous excitement of partisan feelings. But the voters themselves were well aware of what was really at stake and for whom. From the records of the town we would never know, for example, that there had ever been any difficulty in procuring from the legislature a charter for the new college, though the issue must have controlled the way many votes were cast for several years, finally deciding the election of the governor of the state. The way parties divided must have had a long history, composed of local and national events, which would be unique for every single person, and given a bias by individual temperament, corrected by a vision of self-interest, and in such terms almost irrecoverable. But why people voted as they did may at least be suggested by placing one event against another in a simple narrative. Motives can then be guessed at.

The first minister of Amherst was named David Parsons, Jr. He was a good example of the old, aristocratic, colonial clergy, wellborn, a descendant of the founders of Hartford, a grandson of Judge Parsons of Northampton, a kinsman of the Chauncys, and married to a Welles of Connecticut. His father before him had been a minister, and one who cared so little for whatever good will there remained in his parish that he actually sued for the arrears of his salary. As a student at Harvard in the class of 1727, David Parsons, Jr., was said to have been "a quite disorderly undergraduate." It is hard to know just what at this period the limits of disorder might be because they seem sometimes shockingly wide and then ludicrously confined. Like his almost exact contemporary at Oxford he may have done nothing worse than lounge about entertaining his friends or sliding on the ice. Once established in the ministry, however, he is described as grave and solemn in his deportment. His father's experience with his parish seems to have taught him something, for he was very slow in accepting the call to what became the First Church of Amherst, and only after dickering for four years did he accept what was by going rates a good salary, a house, some lots for farming, and a most extraordinary yearly supply of firewood, something up to 120 loads or about 90 cords. Apparently his wife brought with her from Connecticut a black slave, for whose apprehension on his running away a reward was offered of three dollars. Amherst plainly had a minister its people could be proud of, and at church councils, as at the dismissal of Jonathan Edwards, he could play his part, whatever that may have been, with dignity. Parsons also seems to have been something of a scholar and, according to the custom of those days, prepared boys for college, among them his own son and one Nathaniel Dickinson.

The first sign of real trouble in the parish occurred when both the north and south ends of the town tried to be set off as separate parishes, an act that would surely have ruined the First Church. But this attempted separation came to nothing, for it took place just before the outbreak of the Revolution and was probably the result of feelings that soon found more direct expression. Although the political consequences of Congregationalism were profoundly in support of freedom and independence, Parsons, like a good many in his congregation and some other ministers, was loyal to the King. This was not an unusual situation, for the minister and part of his church to be on one side, while the majority of the town was on the other. Shutesbury provides a notorious example, where the church was finally reduced to the minister and exactly one loyal occupant of the pews. There the Reverend Abraham Hill was aggressive and dictatorial. Daring to lecture a group of young men including Daniel Shays, he told them that the King's arm stretched to that hilltop and he would take off their heads. He called them rebels and ordered them to disperse, whereupon "one Cody took him and threw him a rod." The young men then shut him up in a kind of pound and tossed over to him salt fish to eat. So it is said. Certainly the town of Amherst voted to exclude him from the pulpit of the First Church. The town also voted to correct the behavior of one Chauncy. And another vote reads: "That the conduct of the Revd David Parsons is not friendly with regard to the Common Cause, To choose a Committee to inform Mr Parsons of the preceeding vote." What happened next the record does not say.

Behind these political differences there was much that was personal, individual, private. To David Parsons, a man proud of his name and family, accustomed to think of himself as an Englishman and a loyal subject of the King, and almost isolated in the community by his superior education and knowledge of the world, it would have seemed incredible that his neighbors—and men like them—could resist with any success the King's authority and the might of his arms. Even his Most Catholic Majesty, the King of France, could not maintain his rule in Canada against the power of Britain—this had been demonstrated for all the world to see. On the 18th of April 1776, a letter was addressed to the Committee of Correspondence in Amherst by Moses Smith, Elisha Ingram, and Noah Dickinson, accusing the Reverend David Parsons of being unfriendly to the colonies and making a number of specific charges. He neglected to pray "to the sovering disposer of all things" that he would stir up the hearts of the people to defend the rights of their country. He neglected to pray for "the Unity of the several Collines." He neglected to pray for the success of our army and for our "captivated" friends. He did not show by the word of God whether the people "were Right or Rong." He treated public orders in a different manner than they used to be "by adding and neglecting. . . ." A story survives to support one of these accusations against a wilful man. When he read aloud in church a proclamation ending with the new formula, "God save the Commonwealth of Massachusetts," he added, "And I say, God save the King." At this a young man named Nathaniel Dickinson rose from his place in the congregation and answered, "And *I* say, you are a damned rascal."

Such a moment contains within it all the complexity of life in a small town where everybody knew everything about everybody else. This minister, now denounced in his own pulpit, had prepared this Nathaniel Dickinson, along with his own son, also named David Parsons, for college. They both graduated in the class of 1771 at Harvard. During their four years of study occurred the Boston Massacre, the General Court had been moved to Cambridge, and the commencement of 1771 is called by Morison "the last great ceremony of the old regime." Their class was one of the last in which students were listed according to the precedence of their parents. Of a total of sixty, young Parsons was in eleventh place, almost exactly where forty years earlier his own father had been ranked, while Dickinson, whose father kept a tavern, was forty-eighth. Since no one any longer knows the exact basis on which these distinctions were made, though it was probably no more or no less rational than the seating arrangements in a meetinghouse as made by a committee, who can now say what it meant to two boys brought up together in a small town? But whatever their youthful relations may have been, there is no question about what they felt as grown men. Dickinson studied law with Joseph Hawley, the leading Whig in the western part of the state, and became the political leader of the town of Amherst. Next to Ebenezer Matoon, Jr., who said of himself, "I studied no profession except that of arms," and who fought at Saratoga, he was most active in revolutionary affairs, as delegate of the Provincial Congress and as a member of the Amherst Committee of Correspondence. David Parsons the younger studied theology with his father, was licensed to preach, and then because of the unsettled times and his own weak health—he was to die in his seventy-fourth year—engaged in what are vaguely called mercantile pursuits. This is not an enlightening way to describe ten years of a man's life and at such a period of history. He was like his father, a Tory, and he somehow survived and then prospered. He was to give the land on which the Amherst Academy building was constructed, and he became the first chairman of the Board of Trustees of Amherst College. Dickinson became a Justice of the Peace, was known as "Squire Nat," and succeeded his father as tavern keeper. Matoon, the man of arms, became town moderator, county sheriff, and in his old age and blindness was supported by the charity of Abbott Lawrence the philanthropist.

When in 1782 David Parsons succeeded his father as minister of the First Church, there was immediately trouble. After one morning service the congregation divided, as in a trial of strength, and stood face to face. Twenty members, including Nathaniel Dickinson and Ebenezer Matoon, withdrew and formed the Second or East Street Church. This separation in 1782 engendered feuds that were to endure, stated someone who knew what he was talking about, for three generations.

In a New England town where nearly everyone seems to be named Dickinson or Kellogg, where nearly everyone seems to be related by blood to nearly everyone else, the lines drawn by old animosities must have been the very essence of one's individuality, as plain as the landmarks picked up by the selectmen perambulating the line between Amherst and Hadley. Indeed much of the business of town meeting was concerned with running lines, laying out a road from Ebenezer Eastman's to Kellogg's mill, as if differences, distinctions, boundaries, stone walls, were the heart of a community's life. Of course a person's position on the map continually altered, while lines were redrawn by circumstances and the lapse of time, when boundary trees fell down and decayed. Even the broad distinctions of political parties, Whig and Tory, Federalist and Republican (or Democratic, words meaning much the same) could be crossed if something was at stake locally, particularly. This was to happen in a notable instance where the new college was concerned.

There were roughly two groups of people in conservative Western Massachusetts or conservative Hampshire County: those who supported the rights of property and those who felt deprived and put upon, those who resented the hardships they had to endure, those who were troublemaking, rebellious, against Boston and shipowners and merchants, hostile to the very forms of government, in the true Puritan tradition hating lawyers, complaining about the high salary paid a local judge, and comparing how little he worked with the toil of a Pelham farmer. All of these people or nearly all of them were Calvinists, and they could fight bitterly, with conviction, over articles of faith or the choice of a minister. What is most difficult to comprehend when particular men are seen acting at that level called local history is that a person's animosities, antagonisms, prejudices, partisan feelings, loyalties, beliefs, do not fit together in such a way that we can see a single reasonable intelligent consistently organized man. It is not always possible to see him acting according to what was evidently his own self-interest. No simple explanation will ever explain his inconsistencies and inner contradictions.

When on June 1, 1782 the parish voted to extend an invitation to David Parsons (the son) to settle in the ministry of the First Church of Amherst, other events that had provoked intense excitement had been taking place in the immediate neighborhood. The past year had seen the assembling of conventions on the model of the conventions of committees of safety so useful a few years earlier at the beginning of the Revolution, and they had been held in Northampton and Hadley and Shutesbury, but not apparently in Amherst. All this was the first stirrings of what became Shays's Rebellion. Rioters had only recently shut down the courts in Northampton and some of them had been apprehended and jailed. A mob gathered in Hatfield, and, when the release of the prisoners was demanded, the prisoners were given up. This happened two days before the parish meeting in Amherst. The parishioners who voted for and against David Parsons were doing more than choosing or rejecting a particular man with certain religious convictions. About those convictions little can be made out. The report of his preaching does not tell us much, his sermons were said to be "sensible and instructive," and there is no suggestion anywhere that there was any disagreement over the Trinity or baptism or the terms of church membership, the usual occasions for argument. Parsons' position must have been self-evident to all who knew him, a matter of character and social attitude and personal pride. These were times that tried men's souls. To be sure Parsons won the support of the majority of his church, and this would seem to be a victory for one side, yet within a few years the majority of the town voted that a petition be presented to the General Court stating their grievances and ending with the threat of establishing a new state composed of the western counties. This was carrying one step further the movement that began when the Third Precinct or New Swamp petitioned to be set off from Hadley. And it shows how deep the spirit of resistance and independence ran.

It is hard to imagine the kind of strictly Calvinist minister who could have brought together the irritable inhabitants of Amherst for a joint enterprise, like founding a college. Or even for maintaining for very long a single parish. Certainly it was recognized that this David Parsons had had his enemies, and on his dismissal in 1819 the First Church made overtures to those who had, calling themselves the aggrieved brethren, gathered at East Street, as if now there could be no reason for grievance. This attempt at reconciliation failed, and divisions continued. In 1824 the Third or South Congregational Church was set off, and so began a history of spectacular divisions: at one time one part of the congregation worshipped on the ground floor while the other part worshipped above them. Two years later, in 1826, the North Church or Amherst North Parish was set off. In the same year because of general dissatisfaction with the arrangement, the faculty and students of Amherst College withdrew from the First Church to form the Church of Christ in Amherst College. The Baptists were organized a few years later. But the Universalists who to the horror and disgust of the orthodox flourished in other parts of the state did not appear in Amherst till many years later. The town of Amherst seems to have been Calvinist and Trinitarian, independent, contentious, and even rebellious. When General Lincoln had reached Amherst in pursuit of Shays and his army, most of the male inhabitants, it was said, were out with the rebels. Over 100 men in Amherst were to take the oath of allegiance according to the terms of amnesty. Yet, all things considered, Amherst remained a conservative community. There is no other way to explain the founding of Amherst College.

Tyler tells the story briefly, as if the granting by the legislature of a charter for the charitable institution at Amherst "for the giving a classical education to pious young men" were but a part of the first chapter in a heroic narrative, and the hostility aroused and the difficulties overcome were to be expected in the beginning of any noble enterprise. Viewed from a safe distance, the campaign for the charter, extending for two years, with its humiliating defeats and final victory, can seem only one more illustration of the extreme contentiousness and general wrongheadedness of our ancestors, for it is hard to see how anyone could reasonably oppose the idea of a free education for those who needed and desired it or could oppose the ideal of an educated clergy or any other class of men. Meanness of mind and spirit, jealousy, theological odium, a contempt for learning, must have operated on those who resisted so bitterly the proposed new college in the Connecticut Valley. And victory when it did come was not overwhelming: the vote for granting the charter was 114 for and 95 against.

The alliances, once clear to everybody, that go to make up an opposition party that finally loses are after the event especially hard to locate. So it is with the vigorous resistance coming from different parts of the state and composed of disparate elements in the population to the establishment of Amherst College. First of all and most naturally there was Williams College and, it was said, all of Berkshire

AMHERST COLLEGE IN 1821, AFTER AN OIL PAINTING
BY MRS. ORRA WHITE HITCHCOCK.

County. Self-interest, self-preservation are explanation enough. Williamstown was remote, hard to reach over Hoosac Mountain, really facing westward toward the Hudson. The number of possible students seeking an education beyond the writing and grammar schools was much smaller than might now be supposed, for it was estimated that in 1823 there were from Massachusetts not more than 569 young men attending the half dozen colleges in New England, either within or without the state. Only a few years before when some students discharged a cannon in order to destroy a partition they did not like in their common room and were expelled, Dartmouth College had all but disappeared from the map, and it was then felt that this would be no great loss since Williams and Bowdoin could easily absorb any students who were displaced. Then there was the objection that Amherst was offering what amounted to unfair competition. Indigent pious young men were to have their term bills paid, first at Amherst Academy, then at Amherst College, and finally at the Theological Seminary at Andover. The Charity Fund, so called, would guarantee, in effect, both a supply of students and an income for the college. To help pay board bills and incidental expenses there

were already in existence organizations like the Hampshire Education Society and the American Education Society. No wonder Williams made remonstrance, since her resources were limited to funds
misappropriated from the estate of Colonel Ephraim Williams. In
their selective account of the early days Amherst writers include in
their list of enemies Harvard College, and now Morison denies the
justice of the charge. Yet, as Morison himself shows in a paper
contained in the *Publications of The Colonial Society of Massachusetts,*
the debate over the charter occurred at the very time when nearly the
entire senior class was expelled, when the attempts at reform proposed by George Ticknor, and the attacks on the administration of
President Kirkland made the minds of Harvard men unusually irritable. To men of ordinary judgment and good sense, those who had
found the whole idea of the Andover Seminary repellent, there could
have been nothing attractive about the proposed college at Amherst.
Opposition might also come from some Baptists, who had their own
college in Providence, Brown University. There at a commencement
speech making a witty senior held up to everyone's mocking laughter Amherst's declared intentions of "civilizing and evengelizing the
world," an ideal preserved to this day in the college motto *Terras
irradient.* At the cornerstone laying of South College Noah Webster
had spoken, not it would seem with the approval of everyone, of the
time not far distant when through the efforts of Amherst men a
church of Christ would be planted "on the burning sands of Africa,
or in the cheerless wilds of Siberia." This was the way people talked,
and it was not hard to find fault with it. Then there was still another
sect that had no reason to love the orthodox, the Universalists, and
they cared nothing for the idea of an educated clergy. Behind these
conflicting and competing forms of dissent there must also have been
wide class differences, for the Baptists and the Universalists appealed
chiefly to those least favored with goods of this world, and for them
formal education was an unimaginable extravagance and totally useless. Interestingly it was in the immediate neighborhood of Amherst
that the most vehement opposition was to be found, this, on the
great principle that familiarity breeds contempt. Northampton, after
all, had just failed in persuading the trustees of Williams to move to
that town, and Hadley, which contributed all of $11 to the Charity
Fund, spoke of the new college as Amherst's Folly, if such words
were actually ever said. Implacable opposition, a continuation of

hatred generated a good forty years earlier between the First and Second Parishes, came from East Street and its friends. For this there was good reason, since the chairman of the board of trustees who presided at the ceremonies when work began on South College was none other than the Reverend David Parsons, and the Charity Fund, as Tyler gratefully acknowledged many years later, was so largely contributed by members of the First Church that they should be considered the real founders of Amherst College. Certainly whatever was going forward, being created, provided occasion for active resistance. Combined with all the obscure motives in what amounted to a family feud, there were Dickinsons and Kelloggs on both sides, wide political differences must also have existed, and for a long time, going back to Tory vs. Patriot, creditor vs. debtor, those who stayed at home and those who were out with Shays, and more recently Federalist vs. Republican or Democrat. The political lines seem specially tangled. This part of the state was said to be the last stronghold of Federalism, and many loyal Federalists who were also Calvinist and Trinitarian and active supporters of the new college must have felt aggrieved when members of their own party in the State House joined with the opposition to vote down by an overwhelming vote the original petition for a charter for the college. What did party loyalty, loyalty to religious principles, amount to, then?

In the legislature itself when the charter came before it for debate there was some talk about the theological position of the proposed college and its harmony with the new seminary at Andover and the American Board of Commissioners for Foreign Missions and the American Education Society. The attempt to incorporate the Charitable Institution as Amherst College was described as an "extension of illiberal, aspiring, and dogmatical orthodoxy," and the whole enterprise was said to have begun "in bigotted sectarianism" and to have been nursed by "over-heated zeal." It is certainly true that by this date colleges already in existence had relaxed whatever religious tests they had ever insisted upon, and for a few such tests had never even existed. The entire movement, composed of the recently established seminary, the missionary and education societies, and now this proposed new college looked toward the past or an imagined past, toward the so-called primitive religion of our fathers, when church and state were—or were at least said to have been—identical, when the clergy were watchmen on the towers of the New Jerusalem, when all joined in worshipping the same Triune God. Furthermore many of the Calvinist clergy were once more trying to gain strength and authority over the often dissident parishes by gathering representatives of local associations into a large annual convention. There seemed to be favorable signs of widespread support, for the attempt of 1820 to revise the state constitution by separating church and state had failed, and parish taxes for the support of the ministers of the standing order were maintained. And just to show how complex, dizzyingly complex, the situation had become, many of these ministers now supported by the law of the state were Unitarians. When debate arose over the charter for Amherst College in the legislature, the theological issues could only be alluded to, though a theological bias must have operated powerfully in men's minds. The strict Calvinists of the First Church were also Federalists, but Federalists elsewhere gave them little support.

The ground of argument in the debate shifted to dollars and cents. What was this Charity Fund said to amount in subscriptions, pledges, notes in hand, to a total of $50,000? It had been raised and was to be administered by the Trustees of the Amherst Academy, an institution only three or four years old. The original intention, plainly copied from an arrangement already at work in Phillips Academy, Andover, was to support the studies of candidates for the ministry as part of the functioning of the Amherst Academy, but this plan came to nothing because the money could not be raised for such a project. It was then proposed to raise a fund of $50,000 as a basis of a charitable institution, a college, distinct from the Academy, a fund which would pay the tuition of candidates for the ministry and so give them the advantages of a classical education. Land was obtained, and South College, a President's House, and North College were built. A president was obtained from Williams, faculty and students assembled, and so the college was in operation, but without a charter and so unable to grant degrees. Finally after rejecting the petition to recognize that a college had really been established in Amherst, the legislature selected a committee to look into the financial state of the petitioners, a committee composed, it was said, of Unitarians to a man. They were directed "to inquire into the state of the funds" and to discover "what means had been resorted to by persons wishing a College at Amherst to procure funds. . . ." The intention was plain enough.

Yet there could have been few surprises. Affidavits had been collected and then printed, by an agent of Williams, it was believed, in which various people gave their version of how their pledges had been obtained and with what promises. The Reverend Samuel Austin of Worcester declared that his pledge of $1,000, which he now repudiated, had been made on the assurance that Williams College would certainly move to Amherst. There were other complaints: one solicitor—Colonel Graves, the money raiser, must finally have shown himself as unreliable even to his friends—promised free tuition for a son, then at sea, in return for a pledge. Others claimed that they had been told only their names were needed and no one would ever expect them to pay up. Much was made of the fact that women and children had been imposed upon. There had been many, many promises of small sums, and it was even stated (though this does seem unlikely) that the average subscription for the total amount worked out as only $15. Women, "Christ's female friends," had subscribed a dollar or two, hoping to accumulate that much by giving up coffee or by making some such personal sacrifice. Small children promised 12½ or 10 cents. And until such ridiculous amounts were paid, the interest on these trifling obligations was supposed to be kept up. It was easy to make fun of such financial arrangements, easy to question the integrity of the trustees. Indeed one sarcastic member of the legislature proposed that Amherst engage a professor to instruct in what he called ordinary commercial honesty. Yet if the intention was to ridicule those who having almost nothing hoped against all appearances to find something, however small, to give to the cause of education and true religion, that intention must surely have failed. Whatever this society was it was generous. In time of loss or catastrophe neighbors were accustomed to collect sometimes surprisingly large amounts for immediate relief, and yet the individual contribution might be small indeed. The very support of the minister might depend ultimately on someone paying more or less cheerfully a tax of, say, $1.27. Odd amounts were the rule. One entry in the records of the Hampshire Education Society reads: "To avails of peas, beans and millet seed from Cummington, $4.20," and this went for several weeks board (at 75 cents a week) to some ministerial student at Williams or Dartmouth. There is nothing ludicrous here. It was a world of small beginnings, and the Concord fight within living memory proved that.

Now with the appearance of the hostile Legislative Committee in Amherst occurs the dramatic scene where the strength of the First Church was displayed. President Heman Humphrey tells the story with gusto: the tables were turned. When the Committee met at Boltwood's Hotel, "Every subscription was carefully examined. . . . The trial lasted a fortnight. Were we to live or die?" When a note was questioned a trustee would pull out of his pocket a roll of bills and say, "I will cash that." Then a number of the trustees, including David Parsons, drew up an obligation, assuming the amount of $15,000. So the Committee reported that none of the remonstrants' charges—agents from Williams and Northampton and East Street had worked in collecting and presenting evidence to that effect— implicated the trustees, and they recommended that any further delay would "very much increase the excitement which exists in the community on this subject," and the college, they said, should be chartered at once. The excitement was natural enough. After all the college had at that time 150 students already enrolled.

Now the narrative becomes obscure, and only two or three versions of what happened are available. (The records of the trustees of the college were destroyed by fire in 1838.)

Someone who joined the Amherst faculty in 1824 and must have known what he was talking about, namely, Jacob Abbott, makes a surprising comment on these early days. If, he says, some future generation should conceive the idea of erecting a statue to commemorate the founders of Amherst College, "the man most deserving of the honor would be Austin Dickinson." And it is his story, impossible to recapture, that would today make interesting reading. Those more usually mentioned as founders are all recognizable types: the warm members of the First Church with their rolls of bills, like Samuel Fowler Dickinson, a deacon at twenty-one, or the Reverend David Parsons, a minister able to join in signing an instrument by which he acknowledged responsibility for paying a large sum of money, or Colonel Graves of Sunderland who never seems to have succeeded in anything except as a solicitor for the Charity Fund.

As for the possibilities of the ministerial character, the vagaries of the Calvinist imagination combined with the eccentricity of the Yankee, these seem completely illustrated in the pages of Hawthorne or in the eight volumes of Sprague's *Annals of the American Pulpit*. Austin Dickinson is a rather different sort of man, about whom we know almost nothing, a man who combined the convictions that the world is dying and human nature is utterly corrupt with the faith that creating a human institution called a college may help redeem the unredeemable. Even in a bare account of outward events Austin Dickinson remains more than a little mysterious. Abbott described him as "the most grave and austere man I ever saw." When his work was done," says Tyler, "he disappeared from the scene. . . . He was one of those men who love to do their work out of sight." On the college records his name is not to be found, except for a scholarship founded in his memory by a member of the class of 1904. This is strange, because in the years remaining to him of life the college did confer the doctor's degree, in divinity, in laws, an honor much relished by the otherwise unworldly clergy. And apparently he had no claim to be made a member of the board of trustees, which still contained other influential ministers in the neighborhood, Theophilus Packard, Joseph Lyman. Perhaps there was something about the whole episode, the soliciting of subscriptions and then the difficulty of obtaining payment, the maneuvering in state politics, the lobbying in the State House, that those who knew most preferred not to recall. Or was it that with the successful compromise, no one was really satisfied, least of all those trustees who may have felt that in the bargaining everything unique about Amherst had been sacrificed. Perhaps the lack of recognition was nothing more than an institution's brutally short span of memory, the beginning of a long history of benefits forgot. However this may have been, when his work was done and the Collegiate Institution was in business as Amherst College, Austin Dickinson moved to New York, where he edited a religious newspaper and conducted a kind of press bureau for the distribution of news about Congregational churches and ministers. On his death his body was brought back to Amherst and buried in West Cemetery, a monument in his memory was erected by friends of the college, and now the inscription on that monument is so worn by the weather that it is illegible. It may well be that Austin, the grandson of Samuel Fowler Dickinson and the brother of Emily, was named for him.

Austin Dickinson's career raises many questions, and although they have no certain answers simply asking them helps define the kind of person he must have been. How did he deal with the other ministers with their varying shades of Calvinism—an attempt at harmonizing different parties had been the major issue in establishing the Andover Seminary—so that they would agree to support the new college? How much of his own belief—whatever that may have been—did he sacrifice for the sake of the new institution? Was the newly awakened faith in the future of foreign missions so great that it would make the foundation of the college necessary at any price? How seriously did he believe that this struggling institution should take upon itself the task of civilizing and evangelizing and lighting the world? Or was this only a way of talking? What did he understand by the phrase, classical education, and how would he account for its value? What of his own everyday moral standards? How scrupulous was he about money matters, and what did he think of the child's pledge of 12½ cents or of crediting the Charity Fund with $3,000 for a gift of some acres in Maine that no one had even tried to locate? It would be an insult to his memory and to our own sense of the noble past to suppose he was purely an organizer, an administrator, a money raiser for a college in Tennessee, in Massachusetts, no matter where, a man concerned with making something work, no matter what. Or, even more degrading, that he was doing something simply for the prosperity of the town of Amherst because a college would provide a market for farm and garden and store. Whatever his motives may have been and however mixed, Austin Dickinson did carry through to success his purpose, and against overwhelming odds. A few men held his memory in high regard, and among them Tyler. The worst thing that could be said about him, just to keep the balance even, was that he was the perfect example of the Calvinist minister about whom as a term of abuse his enemies would use the word Jesuit.

Austin Dickinson was born in Amherst, graduated in 1813 at Dartmouth, where he had lived in the family of Professor Zephaniah Swift Moore, tried the profession of law in the office of Samuel Fowler Dickinson, then studied theology and was licensed to preach. He visited the south for reasons of health and there started a religious paper, and without further explanation in the record he is said to have raised $20,000 for a college in Tennessee. Apparently he was never settled in a church of his own. He represents a new and special kind of evangelist, the man who works behind the scenes, as promoter, as public relations man, as administrator, campaign manager, politician, and lobbyist, what, in the old language was called a religious projector.

As for his influence in establishing Amherst College the most extraordinary claim is made for him: it is said that he planned and controlled every decision and every move made by the trustees, and this from the founding of the academy. It was he who selected its first preceptor. He was deeply interested in raising the Charity Fund, and as a solicitor he adopted special and surprisingly modern techniques in money raising or acquiring property, such as addressing an audience limited exclusively to women and proposing that they make themselves responsible for furnishing a particular room in, say, North College which was to be occupied by a candidate for the ministry. It was he, we are told, who persuaded President Moore on leaving Williams to come to Amherst, and on Moore's sudden death he persuaded Heman Humphrey, then a minister comfortably settled in Pittsfield, which was enemy territory, to succeed to the presidency of a charterless college. He chose and more remarkably secured the services of most of the faculty, including the Reverend Edward Hitchcock of Conway, and the Reverend Samuel Melancthon Worcester, the son of the late Samuel Worcester of the Tabernacle, Salem, and the first teacher at Amherst of what we call English. It was Austin Dickinson who prepared for the visit of the Legislative Committee and planned the strategy that frustrated the hostile efforts of agents employed by both Williams College and members of the East Street Church.

Most remarkable of all it was Austin Dickinson who after repeated failures and against the hostility of the majority of the legislature finally secured a favorable vote for the charter of Amherst College. Here he moves on to a larger stage, while yet remaining a shadowy figure in the background. The little that can now be made out about the bargaining that went on suggests new and surprising alignments in what was an extremely complicated political situation. The matter of Amherst College deserves no more than a paragraph or two in the long and involved history of religious freedom in Massachusetts, and then Amherst's place in this struggle cannot easily be made the occasion for more mindless complacency about the good intentions of our ancestors. Amherst as conceived by its founders looked to the past or a dream of the past, toward control and repression, toward creeds and their observance by force of law. This college, founded on the strictest principles of orthodoxy, found itself unwanted, undesired, actively discouraged by the establishment which it would seem to be a part of, which it certainly proposed to support. How such a state of affairs could come about, how the establishment had shifted its center of power, can be read in the remarkable study by William McLoughlin, *New England Dissent.*

The first application for a charter was made in January 1823. Much that had happened in the immediate past proved relevant to this matter. A couple of years before, in 1820, there had been a constitutional convention in which another unsuccessful attempt had been made to revise the system by which members of certain religious societies under certain defined circumstances were taxed by the law of the Commonwealth for the support of their minister. So, with many modifications, was preserved the system centuries old. A year later occurred the celebrated Dedham case by which the right of the parish, as opposed to that of the church, to choose a minister, and to claim the meetinghouse and other property as its own, was sustained. The minds of the legislators and of the public were perplexed and confused, and well they might be when the established church, the church supported by taxes imposed by law, turned out to be Unitarian, while the Orthodox Trinitarian Congregationalists found themselves in a minority, a dissenting sect, allied in interest with other dissenting sects, most notably with the Antipaedobaptists. The world was turned upside down. The Calvinist, Trinitarian clergy had been, with rare exceptions, loyal supporters of the Federalist party. Especially in the Connecticut Valley were they famous for their political sermons in which they had used the most outrageous language about the opposition: Jefferson had been called Jeroboam and, worst of all, Beelzebub, his followers were atheists and jacobins, and Tom Paine was a toad. And now their own Federalist party was actively opposing the very idea of this new college in Amherst as a stronghold of orthodoxy.

Austin Dickinson went to work, becoming a "Lobby member . . . ubiquitous by his personal influence." He "ascertained"—that is the word used—that the Republican candidate for governor, first William T. Eustis and then Levi Lincoln, would "favour" the college, a characteristically bland way of putting it. In 1823 as a result of the combination of Trinitarian Congregationalists and the Republican party, Eustis defeated Harrison Gray Otis by a comfortable margin, and so the power of the Federalists in Massachusetts was finally broken. Otis's biographer, Samuel Eliot Morison, says that after Austin Dickinson extracted from Eustis a promise to support

Amherst College he carried on in the newspapers a "mendacious" campaign, and Tyler apologetically saying it belongs to another age prints one of these articles in which Otis is described as an immoral character, guilty of habitual profane swearing, a Sabbath breaker, an aristocrat, a Harvard man. By such arguments as these, presumably, the members of the First Church of Amherst were persuaded to join with East Street in the support of the party of Jefferson, atheism, and equality. In 1825 Levi Lincoln received every vote cast in Amherst save one, and his election throughout the state was almost unanimous. Austin Dickinson could claim some reward, if only in helping align the Orthodox Trinitarians with the inevitably victorious Republicans. When the bill for the proposed charter was brought to a vote for the third time, it was amended and then carried by a margin of 19 out of a total of 209 votes cast.

The final evidence of Austin Dickinson's maneuvering, of his bargaining and compromise, is in the form the charter took when voted. Amherst College was not going to be the unique institution originally dreamed of, "a fountain pouring forth its streams to fertilize the boundless wastes of a miserable world. . . ." It was not going to be allowed to become an exclusively Calvinist college. Guarantees to this effect were written into the charter, guarantees that were, Tyler concedes, peculiar to Amherst. The legislature was to elect five out of the seventeen trustees. The trustees were to be composed of seven clergymen and ten laymen. And as if this were not enough to show the world where the college must be made to stand, the legislature was empowered to appoint overseers or visitors for the college. (This right has never been exercised.) And of course there were to be no religious tests for students or faculty. By such concessions, felt by some, perhaps, to be humiliating, Austin Dickinson won the necessary votes.

When the news reached Amherst that now they had a college legally empowered to grant degrees, the college buildings and certain buildings in town were illuminated as an expression of joy. Noah Webster exclaimed, "What hath God wrought."

For as many as a dozen years after receiving its charter Amherst College flourished mightily, so that by 1836–37 the number of students enrolled amounted to 259, making it in size second only to Yale. This was for a number of reasons a dull moment in the history of Harvard. Tyler accounts for the amazing growth of Amherst, abnormal he called it and not altogether healthy, by ascribing it to the enthusiasm generated by the many revivals in the years 1815–1835, or the Second Great Awakening. These revivals nourished the college with "a copious supply of young men recently converted," full of zeal for the ministry, eager to serve as missionaries to the unnumbered heathen, and so prepare for the Second Coming. In its first twenty-five years and of its 765 graduates 501 had been aided by the Charity Fund and the American Education Society, and almost all of this number had entered the ministry, mostly as orthodox Trinitarian Congregationalists, a good many as Presbyterians, a few as Baptists, a very few as Episcopalians, and there was an occasional Unitarian. Most remarkably there were two Roman Catholic converts, both of whom achieved high position in their church, one as Archbishop of Baltimore, the other as Superior of the Paulist Fathers. There seems not to have been one Universalist. The flow of students from Amherst to Andover was constant, and almost every member of the college faculty had studied at the seminary. Amherst also had had its own frequent revivals, and the early presidents gave the exact figures of those added to the college church, as later presidents were to boast of new buildings and increased endowment. We are told that one Newhall, said to have been an elegant scholar, "talked straight to everyone about his soul. He could not spare time to eat." This is the language of approval. Another way of speaking would be to say that all the worst forebodings of Amherst's worst enemies had come true.

Even though the final score is not to be kept in numbers of souls saved or ministers—or priests—ordained, much in the day-by-day life of this college commands respect and admiration. It retains some of the ordered simplicity of colonial New England. Our dream of the past seems reality, here was a gathering of individuals, most of whom had the quirks and eccentricities of the Yankee character, brought together to form a community or society. Every student on enrolling in the college had willingly signed a statement that he would comply with all the stated rules and regulations as drawn up by the faculty. But more than this there was an active, powerful source of energy at work to make them all, faculty and students, a band of brothers, namely, the Church of Christ in Amherst College. This was a nondenominational church with strictly Calvinist articles of faith. On every individual every pressure was brought to bear, despite the profession of religious freedom in the charter, to join that church. There were regular religious exercises in church and chapel at which attendance was required, evening lectures and prayer meetings, and the extraordinary concentration of revivals, when all other activities, like attending classes, were suspended, when there was a noise and shaking among the dry bones. Yet if religious experience existed within the individual's breast, there was also the church, as a gathering of mortal men. Other people did exist. Morality did matter. The covenant of this church explicitly states that all its members shall live in love and harmony, "watching, reproving, exhorting, and comforting each other." The Statement of the Church Discipline explains what steps should be taken when one member sins against another "or seems to be . . . neglecting Christian duties," leading up to the terrible threat of a public statement of the case before the whole Church, which in its turn would "seek by prayer, sympathy, and exhortation to reclaim the erring disciple," and when all else fails "there follows the painful duty of excision. . . ." This meant, in the old language, to be "surrendered to the buffetings of the devil." Belonging to a society or community or congregation carried with it such fearful responsibilities balanced by threats of such immediate and eternal shame and punishment that it is hard to see why there should ever be backsliders, why evil doers at all. This college, this church, combining with a course of classical study (modeled on that of Yale) a way of life determined by the conveniences and hardships of a New England town demonstrated that at one time in our history men really lived together happily, with dignity, in the pursuit of knowledge and truth, sharing together their highest aspirations.

What did happen in these early days can be described in quite different language. During these years of noble achievement the college was in a desperate situation. It had no money, no endowment, it was almost entirely dependent on the Charity Fund, and it was badly in debt. Its repeated appeals to the legislature for assistance from the state had only resulted in more attacks on its theological bias and disreputable financial dealings. (There actually was owing the sum of $12,000, about which Tyler makes the astonishing comment, "No one seems to have known just what it was.") Furthermore both students and recent graduates were what Tyler calls disaffected, so much so that in 1844 the entering freshman class amounted to no more than thirty-four students. This was the year President Heman

Humphrey was forced to resign. It took the combined efforts of his successor, President Hitchcock, and the faculty plus the benefactions of Samuel Williston and others to save the college from utter collapse.

President Humphrey was the first of a number of Amherst presidents whose reign was troubled, unhappy, and seemingly the cause of much dissension. When he resigned, his enemies called him "stern, severe, unsympathizing, unprogressive, and even in his dotage." Against this last charge President Hitchcock defended him by saying he was as well qualified for the position when he resigned as he had ever been, and Tyler in a couple of obscure pages compares his valedictory with the death of Socrates.

Any narrative of battles long ago between students and what is now called the administration soon becomes as complicated and unintelligible as an account of the origins of the War of 1812 and about as interesting. The actors in these silly dramas do not appear quite human. The students, at best raw country lads, at worst rough, coarse, and brutal, the faculty *in loco parentis,* suspicious busybodies, opening students' doors without knocking, trying to find fault, demanding confessions, taking every advantage of their victims, praying with them, punishing them, how can these people with their immediate, their repeated, their absurd appeals to conscience be taken seriously? The story reads much the same at any college of the period, with variations only in the degree of violence and destruction. Nor was Amherst peculiar in that its very virtues seemed to attract vice. Well-to-do and pious parents of unruly sons saw this college as a place where, sanctioned by a religion which recognized that man had suffered the entire loss of divine favor, the hope of repentance was yet held out, where strict discipline was enforced and where on every hand, one might suppose, there should be good examples. New England colleges had the way of attracting certain southerners. Henry Adams describes in a couple of venomous pages his classmates, Roony Lee and his friends, as little fitted, he says, for the relative complexity of a school as Sioux Indians for a treadmill. They at least had Boston as a place to escape to for the practice of their low vices, but the town of Amherst was isolated, and for the seven mile trip to Northampton—and whatever it had to offer in the way of corruption—permission had to be sought from the president of the college. The faculty minutes of this period contain page after page dealing with disciplinary problems, some silly, some shocking by any standard. A goose was found fastened to the pulpit of the Chapel, and as the students filed out after service they were carefully scrutinized by alert members of the faculty looking for a feather still attached to someone's clothes. One Robert McNairy of Nashville, a member of "the chivalry" as the southerners were sarcastically called, beat over the head with a heavy cane, quite in the classic style, a New Hampshire boy who had condemned the peculiar institution of slavery, injuring him severely. The Yankees, too, made plenty of trouble. An Anti-Slavery Society was established with much excitement. After debate the faculty decreed that it must be disbanded, taking the high ground that "the college was not formed to be a school of moral and political reform." The students argued and resisted, making the unanswerable appeal to conscience. But this decision was not taken in a vacuum. Much had been happening in recent months in the larger world. There had just occurred the anti-abolitionist riots in New York, when Lewis Tappan's house had been wrecked, and in Boston there had just been made the outrageous attack on William Lloyd Garrison, and plainly it was felt that college students here and elsewhere should not be encouraged to indulge their sense of indignation or their passion for justice. Then, since everyone shared the feeling that language adds dignity to the most trifling event, there was Gorham's Rebellion. One Gorham, believing that distinctions were invidious, bringing praise to some, to others shame, refused on the grounds of conscience to take part in certain customary rites of public speaking for which the faculty made the appointments. And for a while it looked as if the entire class of 1838 would withdraw from college. Of more serious consequence was the fact that the graduates of the college organized the Society of Alumni, plainly for the purpose of driving President Humphrey from office. These were dark days for the college, says Tyler. For some the bitterness engendered was carried in their hearts to their dying days. So it is said.

Yet at his last commencement, when Heman Humphrey said farewell to an audience who knew he had failed and that he was leaving the college in a desperate situation, he nonetheless used the same hopeful language that had been on everyone's lips at the laying of the cornerstone of the first building. Once more an audience was told of "the yearnings of Christian benevolence over the moral

wastes of our own land and the great world of pagan darkness."
Speaking of how those yearnings brought into being Amherst College, he said, "It was the religious impulse that opened these rich
mines of science and literature." And so he goes on to tell his version
of the story, from the founding of the academy, the building of
South College ("[T]he timber was in the forest. . . ."), the appointment of Zephaniah Swift Moore as president and his death, the granting of the charter, the founding of the Church of Christ in
Amherst College, to his own administration—and its seven revivals.
It was, this whole history, "a noble Christian enterprise." There was
not a word about his troubles with the students, the disaffection of
the alumni, the desperate financial situation. Nor did he speak of
himself as one who had suffered persecution and final crucifixion
because of his own belief.

Narratives like these can be matched by anyone who looks at the
material nearest at hand in the history of a New England town, and
when they are presented in a form as balanced as may be contrived
these scenes from provincial life can be raised to a new level of
interest by making certain general questions about the nature of man
and the problem of evil. What possessed these people? Why this
neverending contentiousness?

It is not always easy to see who won. Everywhere forces of
resistance, opposition to making something where nothing had been,
seemed almost, but not quite, overwhelmingly powerful. In a situation where so little had been created, where a town, a state, and a
federal government were barely in operation, where organizations of
all kinds, such as the Congregational Church or Amherst College,
were held together by the force of individual character, the marvel is
how much was to survive and grow and change and become institutionalized and so come to possess a life of its own. As soon as a
college was actually put in motion, and this through the generosity
and sacrifice of plain people who deeply believed that there was a
need to be filled, a desire to be satisfied, subsequent events can be
read as showing that really there was almost no such need, no such
desire. The president and professors and tutors had to spend an ex-
travagant amount of time in this already highly defined world trying
to define just what should be ordinary decent behavior. There was
the student who put asafetida in a classroom stove. There were students guilty of playing ball and shouting in a dormitory or of pour-

ing water from a window on the heads of respectable townspeople of just the sort who by contributing to the new college had made this conduct possible. Then there were students guilty of cardplaying or of giving a convivial entertainment or of stealing or of fornication. Then there were students suffering from some constitutional defect that made it difficult for them to rise in the morning and once on their feet impossible for them to do anything on time. There were students who given the chance to read the *Iliad* in the original Greek preferred to spend their time in idleness. At Andover Seminary, the apex of a religious and educational system, where everyone had made a personal and public confession declaring God's manner of working upon his soul, the whole community was for a while divided over the question whether there should be served in the commons coffee, tea, and sugar, since these were indulgences. At the same institution when the trustees proposed that along with the students the professors should be required to attend morning chapel, the faculty actually resisted. What a spectacle human behavior presents. Why should all the extraordinary goodness of these people be marred by such ordinary selfishness? Why in spite of the high aspirations and real sacrifice should human life also be lived at this level of triviality and meanness?

Answers to such questions are not usually articulated in words, yet they can be discerned as supporting certain attitudes toward the past as expressed in tones of voice. Nowadays the ironic, the sardonic, place values on human behavior as mean-spirited, selfish, deliberately destructive, self-deceiving, and so on. In this manner, and most unfairly, all life in the past is reduced to the level of a family quarrel, where years of the closest association make possible the cruelest blows, where nothing discreditable is ever forgotten, and the language of love is distorted to convey hatred. From such a spectacle of motiveless malignity one turns in pure disgust to the larger trends and tendencies and cycles and movements and immense destruction of formal history. Names like Darius the son of Hystaspes or Cyrus or Alexander seem to suggest larger possibilities, a larger life, than Samuel Worcester, say, or Austin Dickinson. Certainly human nature exhibited in particular instances in particular places, at least in small New England towns, does not always present an entirely edifying spectacle. And yet even there—?

Once upon a time and for these very people who acted parts in these minor, forgotten dramas, so useful still as illustrations of human frailty, there was no problem at all. A college faculty had no doubts about what it was doing when it disciplined a student. These highminded men began with prayer their deliberations as to the exact degree of punishment to be inflicted, and they used prayer as their final and utmost means for reaching the heart of another person. For that heart was by nature corrupt. Mankind was from earliest history diseased. This is the language of the Professor of Christian Theology at the Andover Seminary, by name, Leonard Woods, obviously what was called a very fine man. He could in the same even tone of voice say that no fact of science is more conclusive than the mere depravity of man. "The appearances of human nature from infancy to old age, and from the fall of Adam to the present time, prove a deeprooted and universal disease. . . . The existence of this moral disease is practically acknowledged by all, who have any concern in the education of children and youth. . . . This disorder of our nature is indicated by as clear, as various, and as uniform symptoms as ever indicated the evidence of a fever or a consumption. . . ." And this calm, scientific language is benign compared with the echoing thunder of the Westminster Confession of Faith. By eating of the forbidden fruit our first parents fell from their original righteousness and communion with God. "They being the root of all mankind, the guilt of this sin was imputed, and the same death in sin and corrupted nature conveyed to all their posterity descending from them by ordinary generation. From this original corruption, whereby we are utterly indisposed, disabled, and made opposite to all good, and wholly inclined to evil, do proceed all actual transgression." But even here in determining the ultimate source and exact degree of man's moral sickness there was the same endless disagreement. Leonard Woods and the Hopkinsians drew back from the proposition that the sin of Adam was imputed—that is the key term—to all his posterity. There does exist the possibility of the renewed agency of the Holy Spirit. Hence the energy that founded colleges and seminaries and sustained home and foreign missions and all other good works.

Even with the grand hope of civilizing and evangelizing this miserable world, as the earlier generations of Puritans had prayed for the converting of the Jews, such conceptions of human nature struck many people as narrow, bleak, and dreary, to choose three adjectives from the many that were used. John Lowell's question was not at the time, as it may now seem, partly witty, "Are you a Christian or a Calvinist?" At stake were two questions: was it not possible that God might be more generous than even a highminded Yankee professor of theology? and was not man also capable of spontaneous acts of generosity because his heart was good? Henry Ware, whose appointment to the chair of theology at Harvard helped set off the conservative reaction which contributed powerfully to the early success of Amherst College, had this to say in reply to Leonard Woods: "Man is by nature . . . as he comes from the hands of the Creator, innocent and pure; free from all moral corruption, as well as destitute of all positive holiness; and, until he has, by the exercise of his faculties, actually formed a character either good or bad, an object of divine complacency and favour." In support of this view, which, as it now seems, would most of all encourage the growth of an educational institution, since it placed the responsibility for the forming of character upon society and environment, he presents arguments drawn from observation and experience, from the Scriptures. Both Unitarians and Calvinists found that education served a useful purpose.

Time, history, political change, the literary tradition, theology, proved to be on the side of an increasing confidence in the goodness of the human heart, and the days of Calvinism were numbered. How its final struggles appear in the history of a New England college is told with brilliant clarity by Thomas Le Duc in *Piety and Intellect at Amherst College, 1865–1912,* published in 1946, and now out of print. This excellent book any college might be supposed to value, since it makes sense out of a kind of experience as intractable as it is muddy, the chronicles of local history. Like most existence, what happens in a college year by year is routine, going to classes, studying, playing games, waiting on table, sleeping and eating, and all the rest of it. No one has ever succeeded in transforming this dreariness into a good novel, and it is the rare person who looking back has very much to say for himself of the slightest interest to anyone else in speaking of these years. With the passage of time and for some people nostalgia keeps something alive about youth and college days, while others as long as they live carry the scars of hatred of themselves when young and the detestation of their alma mater. Le Duc rises above all this and connects what was happening at a small New England college with matters that perplexed acute minds elsewhere, and those who are after all not very large figures, speaking comparatively, in world history, however gigantic they loomed in their small world, Seelye and Emerson and Garman and so on, receive a moment's respectful consideration for the positions they took and the language they used in defining the purposes not only of an education but of a good life. Did a college exist to bring its students—and the whole of the rest of the world—to Christ? Or was it to combine somehow (but how?) Christian faith with scholarship and learning and science? Or should it develop well-rounded men for the world as it is, however that may be? Or create citizens who because of their educated social consciences know how it must be reformed and are determined to bring that about? Or, here the tone often changes to contempt, to train students for graduate schools and the learned professions? At least one of these questions, according to Le Duc, was finally answered: when President Gates brought a professional evangelist to the campus to conduct a revival, the Church of Christ in Amherst College, though it did not go so far as to propose that all classes should be suspended, did ask the faculty to relax for the period of a week their demands upon the students. The faculty, some of whom were already conscious of how slight these had become, refused. The date was 1895.

As reported in Le Duc, the administrations of Gates (1890–1895) and Harris (1895–1912) make dismal reading. When Gates was forced to resign—there had been an event called in the rhetoric of the past Gates' Rebellion, led by a future Chief Justice of the United States—he slipped off to Europe without the normal theatricality of a farewell appearance. Harris was said to have been a man of polished manners, and his administration was described, uniquely in the history of the college, as an era of good feeling, and toward this happy state of affairs his blandness of mind must have contributed largely. He wrote an entire book demonstrating that in inequality there is really equality and in variety uniformity, or the other way round, for he was adept in reconciling the irreconcilable by the fluency of his sentences with the aid of the metaphor of wholeness. Curiously, inexplicably, unless it was a burst of energy in the last flickering of the horrid, penal flames of Calvinism, Amherst produced during these years, or at least graduated, a disproportionately large number of men who distinguished themselves in public service or who accumulated money and power, proving once again that how education works remains forever a mystery.

Le Duc does not go on to deal with the administration of Alexander Meiklejohn, for the good reason that the documents were not available, nor are they now. An agreement seems to have been reached among the principals and lived up to, that neither Meiklejohn nor the trustees would reopen the case in public. And even at this late date, when all the major participants are dead, there are those who remember and in whom loyalties and hatreds still burn bright. No single sentence could ever be framed to satisfy those who think they understand what was really happening, whatever that was. No single word can be used, as "rebellion" had been in the past, to fit this event in June 1923, when the trustees drove—if that is the metaphor—Meiklejohn from the presidency. The Meiklejohn episode, affair, fracas, mess, outrage, ordeal, martyrdom, sacrifice, crucifixion, defeat, victory, all say too little or too much about a complicated situation in which many people took part and deep feelings were engaged, and all this in a past the records of which are beyond our reach.

The literary view, suggesting that this action was really like a play, does have its attractions. Of course certain decisions would have to be made, according to one's sense of how drama works best, given the sketchy materials. Then it must be decided just what role the star performer is to assume, the innocent idealistic man ahead of his time destroyed by the stupid people around him, an Ibsen character, or is he the flawed hero who in his pride and self-will and arrogance and unyielding self-righteousness brings himself and his friends to destruction, a modern Coriolanus. The antagonists as persons in a drama are easy to locate. The opponents of the hero, his virulent and implacable enemies on the faculty, appear as small-minded men in a small place, motivated by wounded pride, hurt feelings, jealousy, envy, and a love of the second-rate, almost figures of fun. Easily typed also are the trustees, rich men, orthodox ministers, men devoted to preserving the injustices of the past, ignorant of the present, the blind leading the blind. It is hard to imagine how anything might be revealed from the now closed record that could alter the story in any essential, except in some slight variation in interpreting the leading roles. Both faculty and trustees were wrong in trying to resist the wave of the future. That time has proved. And in education the nay-sayer has the least claim on anyone's attention since as a general rule change must always be for the better. Certainly in real life, in the public mind, and over the years Alexander Meiklejohn came to stand for something admirable, and in 1966, in his ninety-fourth year, he received from President Johnson the Presidential Medal of Freedom.

Today no one can read Meiklejohn's speeches at that Commencement in 1923 without admiration, a lifting of the heart for his expression of defiant courage. The painful situation of saying farewell in the face of triumphant enemies, a genuinely literary situation if there ever was one, was not new for a college president or for a minister. No wonder, then, that Meiklejohn spoke at moments in the same way others before him had spoken, referring to others who had been in his position, to Socrates slain by the Athenians yet forming the mind of our civilization, to Jesus who "wanted life affirmed . . . men to be themselves . . . life fulfilled with its own beauty and significance . . . whose enemy was the Pharisee . . . the man who makes and keeps intact the social order of the time." These quoted words are from Meiklejohn's final Baccalaureate Sermon, addressed to the seniors and their families. Then, at the alumni luncheon, in the presence of his enemies and of his friends too, Meiklejohn's tone changed to one of defiance. He set himself off from everyone present and stood up alone, self-assured, a single mind, a single conscience. The trustees, he said, must be abolished because they were men "who do not understand." As for the alumni, not only did they know what is going on in their college but also they "know so many things that are not going on." As for the faculty, teachers do not like to improve themselves and "find it most objectionable if someone attempts to make them better." The older professors, to put it quite simply, hate their younger colleagues. Speaking then for himself, he said, "I am, perforce, a minority man. I want to change existing institutions." Almost invariably "I am against the larger number. . . . I am quite willing to take my medicine. . . . I am usually in the minority; and institutions must inevitably be in the hands of the majority." Then his last moving words: "Now you go your way— and I go mine. I shall try to keep fair in spirit toward you, as I have tried before, as you have tried to do with me. And we will, I trust, keep honest with one another. I differ from you on most of the issues of life—and I shall keep it up."

In 1957 at the invitation of the trustees, Alexander Meiklejohn, then in his eighty-sixth year, returned to an Amherst commencement to conduct once more a chapel service. It had been in this role many years before that he had most effectively reached the students. He read from the old favorites, Epictetus and Tagore. He spoke of his old friend James Stephens, who had but lately died in poverty in London, and said, "In all my wanderings I have not found a wiser man." Then, incorrigibly, as if he had learned nothing, he read a poem ending with the assertion that as men we are "equal to the peaks of our desire." In closing he told his audience that however much they had ever differed in opinions they were still friends. He received a standing ovation.

It may be doubted that anyone could then have said exactly what these differences of opinion were or had been. Now everyone was on Meiklejohn's side. Everyone was now in the minority. This is a possible interpretation of what happened. Another might be that after all everything came out all right in the end for the reason that this was Amherst College, where differences of opinion were merely intellectual and did not matter and where the normal emotional tone is one of good feeling. Against this is the fact that for decades after 1923 the atmosphere of the college had been poisoned. Lines had been drawn, often factitiously, parties did exist, memories were long and were handed down, ways of talking became customary, and between all parties, students and faculty, faculty and president, faculty and trustees, alumni and the college, the normal relation was, to put it mildly, irritable suspicion.

These quarrels, so insignificant, so localized, as to seem the feuding of families in an isolated valley in the mountains, remain detached from the important sweep of history with its large-scale warfare and immense armaments, its compulsory beliefs and demands for unconditional surrender, its gigantic heroes, and its complex of social, political, and economic factors in which all individuality is blurred in the statistical man. Yet even at the level of the parish meeting or college commencement one common element with the great world persists and is highly visible, namely, the surging energy of the human will. A single agent, with the support of those who more or less share his determination, strives with all his might to impose his will on others, and he does this for their own good so that they will conform to his idea of what they ought to be and are not.

Immediately, as if by the release of a spring, other wills are set in opposition.

This is the stuff of drama, though it is little regarded. The very smallness of the setting seems to suggest that the actors, too, must be small men, even though life as lived in Fitchburg or Deerfield or Amherst was lifted by Samuel Worcester or Samuel Willard or Heman Humphrey far above the level of subsistence into a world where tradition and principles and courage were expressed in word and deed and can still be distinguished by anyone who cares to glance backwards. Certainly as usually written local history fails to endow these backwoods characters with the interest the arts of style and our own prepossessions have given to many a despicable brute living in a vaguely distant age and indistinctly defined land. The long and memorable quarrel of Iran and Touran, says Gibbon, is still the theme of history or romance, and the reader does not pause over this remark with incredulous astonishment. Yet when an attempt is made to revive the past nearest at hand in New England and find in it materials to be raised to a similar dignity of phrase, the examples do not seem large enough or important enough to stir the imagination. This is hard to understand. They do remain a little pathetic, these ministers and their congregations, and when engaged in a struggle of wills a good deal less than heroic. It is not easy to say why this should be so, why against a background of dreary mediocrity the surging desire to do good to others seems in this setting to exceed all reasonable limits of egotism. The farewell speech does not always say the last word, and tears and pity and applause and standing ovations are not the only response to these puny monsters of egotism at their moments of greatest self-assertion. As for the opposition in these squabbles, the will to resist the will to do good, that seems utterly perverse in its obstinacy. Why did these people care? They must have seen that in fighting their losing battles they were making life more unhappy than at worst it had to be. It may be as simple as this: the devil was in them. They liked to fight. They had to fight.

Such judgments of those who have honorably preceded us and on the same ground are discouraging. They obscure the real and persisting problem of what ails man in general by treating certain periods in time as it elapsed in certain neighborhoods with what amounts to condescension and contempt. In this manner, the past which has to be dealt with somehow, can be disposed of. But it is grossly unfair.

Those who preceded us were men, after all. Their quarrels were real, full of pain and exultation.

Since it takes two to make a quarrel both sides deserve attention, though this proposition is hardest of all to accept and do anything about. One way to express this two-sidedness is to put together compound sentences, where equal statements are balanced, action and reaction, and the subject of one clause becomes in the next the object. The effect is curious. A minister insists that his congregation, grown lax in their belief, should return to the faith of the fathers, and the parish after four years of bitter fighting drives him from the pulpit. A candidate for ordination claims the right to confess only to those beliefs he genuinely holds at that moment, and the church council knowing that whatever words he may use his beliefs are really heretical refuses him the right of fellowship. A college faculty draws up a set of rules by which the behavior of students could be defined as decent, considerate of others, Christian, and the students behaving in various outrageous manners confront that faculty in rebellion. For the first time in decades the president of a college tries to engage the intelligence of its students in a direction toward the world they are going to live in, and the trustees whose only concern is with the welfare of the institution and its relation to the rest of society dismiss this president from office. These are short versions of situations so complex, so obscure, that we know they can never be completely and justly recovered from the past. The conjunction *and* joining the two clauses, the two opposing parties, leaves them loosely bound together with cause and effect unexplained. Furthermore this construction discourages the natural inclination to take sides. The phrasing may be altered, but the effect on a reader is the same, that this is a partly crazy world. The flat conclusion seems to be that, when some people think they know how other people should behave, other people actively resist. This is inane, pointless. In such a world people do not act even according to their own interest.

One clear, completely satisfactory explanation for man's wrong-headed, inexplicable behavior, an explanation that turns mere conflict of wills into high drama, can be found in those repulsive Calvinist articles of faith. It was said, "[M]en loved darkness rather than light, because their deeds were evil." By the fall, man is made opposite to all good, is wholly inclined to evil and yet those who know a saving grace are predestined to be among the elect. The belief that many are called and few chosen could be terribly depressing to some sensitive and fearful souls, but to others, who might in any particular quarrel be on one side or another, unpredictably, it gave their wills a supremely careless sense of urgency. Added to this inner conviction there were also the explicit rules of Calvinist discipline by which duties were imposed. It was the minister's duty to reprehend, admonish, and censure. It was the duty of every member of the church to watch, reprove, exhort, and comfort everybody else, including the minister. It was no extraordinary thing, for example, for a member of the congregation to tell the minister that his sermons were too long. It was this kind of world, of open exchange, everybody was his brother's keeper. The elect had ready at hand an immense vocabulary of vituperation by which enemies could be classified with apparent exactness by calling them atheists, infidels, deists, Arians, Pelagians, Antinomians, Socinians, Antipaedobaptists, Sabellians, Papists, Unitarians, Pharisees, and so on and on.

Men with bad beliefs were bad men, and some held that even the prayers of the unregenerate were addressed really to the devil. So it was that the punishment and sufferings of the condemned could be viewed without a trace of pity, and good and kindly men could see without a tremor their unfortunate victims beaten and hanged. And here is a paradox. Election could also act as a consolation and assurance for the victims, so that it was an ordinary event for men and women to go to their death unflinching, with an exactly phrased confession of faith on their lips. Severus, as the slow fire rose about him, made his heresy clear to his persecutors and did justice to his own claims of conscience by the defiant position of a single adjective. In the horrors of such a world, where every man faced every other man with a determined and sanctioned will, where it was a duty to make others suffer, a duty and a privilege to endure that suffering, all yet agreed that there was still the day of doom when all should be judged by a power greater than man. It was the constant awareness of this last thing that reinforced the individual will, making it uncompromising, implacable, hateful, selfless.

Fortunately this world is in the past, and no sensible person can yearn for its revival. Our ancestors were wrong in one important article of faith: the human heart is not, as they had supposed, depraved. Despite the overwhelming evidence of the past, it has been redefined as good, or, if not exactly entirely good, then as capable of being formed one way or the other by education, environment, this very world. Such had been the assertion of the Reverend Henry Ware. To be sure, this faith makes the history of these small New England towns simply unintelligible, impossible to write except as anecdote or gossip, appealing to easy laughter, with the consolation added of cant. Any embarrassment felt over a history so poor, so simple and earnest, so passionately wrong, can be removed by saying, this, like the old-fashioned furniture and utensils so lovingly collected, is our heritage. This is what museums are made of. And when these old times have to be alluded to in an occasional volume celebrating the anniversary of church or college or town, all these differences by which men once valued themselves can be fumbled up in some smooth and easy phrase: these men, it will be said, were men of deep religious convictions. Of course they were, and this goes for both the First and Second Parishes of Amherst. Or more pretentiously the words *conscience* and *principle* can be used, as if such terms belonged only to the side later proved right, as if they did not belong as well to the enemies, the losers, those who were certainly wrong. All these are simple devices by which the past is made bearable, comfortable, reassuring. Better, more to be respected because more honest, is the careless ignorance of the illiterate barbarian who knows nothing of the conquests of his ancestors or of their defeats.

CHAPTER FIVE

THE GROWTH OF CIVIC CONSCIOUSNESS

POLLY LONGSWORTH

Polly Longsworth has written a book on Emily Dickinson and is currently engaged on a biography of Austin Dickinson. She has served as president of the Amherst Historical Society

In the Spring of 1870 the trustees of Amherst College consulted prominent New York landscape architect Frederick Law Olmsted concerning the placement of Stearns Church. It was a significant request. The college was a monument to the self-sufficiency of Amherst townspeople and its own alumni. Although Olmsted had received an honorary degree in 1867, he was an outsider, and outsiders were rarely called upon for advice.

Mr. Olmsted's response to President Stearns, preserved in the Library of Congress, proposed a new vision for Amherst College:

Accept the necessity of a change of the old idea of a single front on the main street of the village and towards the Connecticut River, and a back yard on the other side. . . . I strongly advise that all idea of a front toward the west or the main street, or toward the north or the village, be abandoned, that the college cut loose from the village wholly, and form a center for itself. . . .

Amherst College subsequently adopted Olmsted's plan for a quadrangle, recognizing that the world now approached the college from the east (via the railroad) as well as from the traditional west and north. Instead of trying to face outward in several directions, the academic institution might better look in. Placing its temple of God on the east side of the grounds, adjacent to the brand new temple of

FROM BURLEIGH, L. R., AMHERST, MASS. 1886

THE AMHERST COLLEGE CAMPUS, FROM AN 1886 LITHOGRAPH.

science, Walker Hall, on the north, the college faced inward, mark-
ing a new sense of apartness from the town which gave it birth and
breath. But never, either figuratively or literally, did Amherst "cut
loose from the village wholly."

The emerging self-consciousness suggested by the process of the
fifty-year-old college centering upon itself was slowly discernible
within the larger corporation of the town in the years following the
Civil War. For some seventy-five years Amherst had focused about
several separate geographic centers, a fracturing that emerged acci-
dentally. Originally, settlers of the precinct strung their autonomous
households along several broad intersecting highways in the same
one-dimensional, front door-back yard spirit remarked upon by
Olmsted. Even when they were blacksmiths or lawyers, the settlers
were also independent farmers whose loosely structured commonal-
ity lay in their orthodox Congregationalism, their educational wants,
and their need for decent roads.

At the time of narrowing and selling off the wide town ways for
home lots in 1788, breadths of the original highway were held apart
at intersections in Amherst center, East Amherst, South Amherst,
and North Amherst City (today Cushman) to provide public use and
grazing land for the most clustered areas of the precinct. Neglected in
appearance except when mown for their annual haycrops, these

commons became the hubs about which stores, schools, churches, and some manufacturing accumulated. By mid-nineteenth century there were five separate villages within the town, those four with commons, and a large settlement at commonless North Amherst. Although the center village dominated the town, the outlying communities each contained a hundred or more families, most of them farmers who devoted their energies to wresting food and shelter from the land by steady and hard labor.

Jones Library owns the diaries of Charles Eliot Hayward, a South Amherst farmer and cooper who recorded his daily routine during the 1880s and 1890s. The pages reveal long hours of toil by all members of his family to produce the food and small sums of money that kept his household going. Social life revolved around the church. News was illness, death, and the weather. There were political ties to the center of town, as men came in to vote, to participate in town meeting, and to elect the necessary fence viewers, field drivers, constables, measurers of wood and bark, and surveyors from their own part of town. There were economic and social ties, too—the occasional excursion into the center by wagon or buggy for staples or to East Amherst for the doings of the Agricultural Society. But probably Mr. Hayward was typical of Amherst dwellers. His was a circumscribed existence, tuned not to the outside world, but to the small community of South Amherst, whose every family, with its personalities and problems, was known to him.

If a strong sense of identity with the section of Amherst in which one lived, rather than with Amherst as a whole, characterized nineteenth century townspeople, there existed, too, a sense of kinship with the environment that is remote to us today. Because residents, whether farmer or tavern keeper, housewife or student or child, worked in the heat and the cold, the wet and the dry of the climate, handled the earth, hauled through the mud, brushed the dust from their skirts, pumped their water, chopped their fuel, fed and cared for barnyard animals, and grew their own fruits and vegetables, they were intimate with the landscape. By extension, there was a kinship felt among the people who shared one landscape, who worshipped at one church, who embraced a common set of values, and among whom change occurred slowly. This is not to suggest that the people within the community were of one mind. Even a cursory reading of town meeting records or the newspaper uncovers strongly differing opinions, cantankerous argument. And anyone familiar with a small town would concur with the assessment of its limitations made by Mrs. John Jameson, wife of the postmaster, when she wrote her son Franklin in 1883: "What an abominal place a village is for defamation of character—and how easily the worst will be believed of folks."

But it was the sense of belonging to and caring for their villages, together with what George F. Whicher termed "a surplus of moral energy," that led a group of devout, like-minded men who believed in the worth of Christian education to found Amherst Academy and Amherst College early in the century, acts which set the character of the town and reinforced the preeminence of Amherst center. Other men like them later brought in the railroad because they believed industrial progress was good for their village.

When Amherst was settled, town and parish were one. At meetings held in the meetinghouse, problems of both civic and religious nature were treated together. Although political and religious concerns diverged late in the eighteenth century, until the Civil War the spirit of caring about the town almost as an extension of piety was still evident. In addition, the gradual shift during the nineteenth century away from strict and consuming adherence to Calvinist doctrine spoke of a shift in attention among Congregationalists. While revivals continued right up through the 1880s to remind townspeople, and especially students, of their moral direction, focus on the world to come was replaced by stronger emphasis on the world that was here to be lived in. These two strains, moral concern for the town and a new focusing on immediate life, developed into recognizable civic self-consciousness after the Civil War, a civic consciousness that culminated in 1896 in proud publication of *A History of Amherst* by newspaper editors Edward Carpenter and Charles Morehouse.

Among the many, many projects of civic improvement undertaken by Amherst people between 1865 and 1900 there were some failures and some near failures. It took the town a long time to come to grips with its most destructive enemy, fire. For too many years expense and factionalism stood in the way of bold, essential solutions as the local fire companies experimented with halfway measures involving men and equipment. After the Civil War ten major conflagrations, including the burning of Phoenix Row in 1872, Merchants Row in 1879, the Hills Hat Factory in 1880, and Walker Hall in 1882, occurred before water, equipment, fire fighters, and sufficient insurance were adequately organized to cope with the frequent disaster. The Phoenix Row fire led Emily Dickinson, down the street, to observe: "The fire-bells are oftener now, almost than the Church bells. Thoreau would wonder which did the most harm."

Amherst proved no exception to the general failure of nineteenth century America to cope with the problems of the poor, for the puritan conscience was out of sympathy with those who did not work. Like other communities round about, Amherst had a poor farm on the South Amherst common where paupers were lumped with vagrants and madmen, all categories considered but a step above the criminal. The three Amherst selectmen acted as overseers to the poor, awarding annual contracts to the lowest bidding warden, doctor, and parson. Records for the Amherst poor are typically scanty, although town meeting expenditures for the last three decades of the century show between two and three thousand dollars appropriated annually to care for numbers that varied from five to fifty, some of them transient and some regular inmates. Additional funds came from the sale of the poor farm's crops and individual support provided by some guardians.

The overseers appear harassed by the cost and bother of the indigent, particularly by an unexpected expense of $692 in 1864 for doctor fees during a smallpox epidemic and the need to rebuild the poor farm in 1882 for $4,700, after an inmate burned it down. An aura of shame surrounded the poor farm, making it a useful threat for errant children and undoubtedly causing aged or ill persons who entertained fears of ending their days there to prefer the grave.

Civic-mindedness was slow to take hold in some areas, but it did survive and eventually flourish. Shortly before the Civil War the common at the center of Amherst became the object of an attempt at beautification. The effort to improve the green was modest, prolonged, and faltering, but it sounded the *leitmotif* for this era of accelerated change and challenge to the shared life within and among the villages of Amherst. To early inhabitants of Amherst, Carpenter and Morehouse remind us, "beauty of utility appealed more forcibly than the utility of beauty." The shy emergence of the aesthetic came not in the generation of Samuel Fowler Dickinson, Noah Webster, David Parsons, Hezekiah W. Strong, and those others who founded Amherst Academy and Amherst College, nor in the generation of

Edward Dickinson, Luke Sweetser, Ithamar Conkey, Leonard Hills and those who brought in the railroad, but in the generation of their children, Austin Dickinson, I. F. Conkey, Henry Hills, and Edward Hitchcock, Jr.

In particular Austin Dickinson, a rising young lawyer, had developed what a later admirer identified as "an intense and cultivated knowledge of nature, a passionate joy in the landscapes seen from Amherst hill-tops, and in the trees and blossoming shrubs all about him." As a boy Austin Dickinson helped plant young pine trees in the burial ground and cultivated fruit trees on the adjoining property where his family then lived. His interest in landscape gardening flourished with the building of his Italian-style home on Main Street in the mid-1850s, next door to his father's reacquired, remodeled Dickinson homestead. Austin oversaw the planting of trees and shrubs on both estates and later extended his lavish devotion to the property of Amherst College. He was perhaps the first to stand apart and look at the Amherst landscape with which he lived intimately, to appreciate, and also to improve. How long his eye had been troubled by the unsightly, marshy green at the center of town is not known, but certainly he stimulated the group who undertook in 1857 to fix it up.

That year, in September, Austin Dickinson, I. F. Conkey, and Edward Hitchcock, Jr. were among twenty-two petitioners who applied for permission to form an association to beautify the public grounds of Amherst under an 1853 General Court Act. A dozen of the petitioners organized the Ornamental Tree Association with the object of "laying out and ornamenting the common, improving and adorning of public walks by grading, graveling and lining with trees, and doing anything to render public grounds and ways of the village more attractive and beautiful."

That Amherst was already attractive and beautiful much testimony exists. Young William Gardiner Hammond wrote in his journal upon seeing the town for the first time in the fall of 1847 when he entered Amherst College: "This village, which is probably to be my home for the next three years, stands upon a hill, almost in the center of a huge amphitheatre formed by the hills or mountains which bound the horizon. The prospect is splendid, and the village itself a neat, pretty place."

The hill upon which Amherst stood deserves a pause, for the twentieth century has lost some sense of it. Beginning in 1870 the hill was slowly reduced as the town reset the grades of the roads leading through the center from the south, west, and north. Before that time anyone entering the village experienced considerable hill, as the high banks still lining the roads attest, and loaded wagons approaching from South Amherst had to circumvent the last steep pitch on which Amherst College stood by taking Park Street (now Snell Street) around to the west.

In mid-nineteenth century the south end of the common was much higher than the north end, and the west side considerably higher than the east side, so that the expanse sloped dramatically to the north and east, ending in a marshy, fenced section along the east side, about opposite Spring Street. There geese and frogs and peepers held sway. One long-time resident recalled from his boyhood the "nightly screaming of the dulcet voices of those geese." In spring the streets at the center of town were heavy in mud. In summer the dust rose thickly and suffocatingly around the wagon wheels and horses' hoofs. The common collected refuse. Weeds grew up around the water pump and the hay scales.

What the Ornamental Tree Association proposed to do was to fill the lowest sections of common, lower the grade along the west side, and plant trees in the open expanse. As a first step the group decided to secure permission at the November 1857 town meeting for the OTA to use and control the public common. Lawyer I. F. Conkey, the new vice president of the Association, was regularly chosen town meeting moderator and could help the matter along. Town meeting records indicate no opposition to the Ornamental Tree Association's novel request. Permission to control the common was granted, subject to approval by the selectmen. The Association collected forty dollars among its small membership. William W. Smith of the executive committee took charge of filling and grading during the following summer, doing enough work that he parted with the organization after disagreement over his payment for extra expenses. Austin Dickinson, Professor William Clark, Lucius Boltwood, and others of the executive committee located and transplanted trees from the surrounding countryside during the fall of 1858.★

★"Today that seems like an easy thing, with so many trees available in all the fields going rapidly back to woods. But 120 years ago all fields were cleared—and kept clear—and even most of the acreage on the Pelham Hills was agricultural fields. Furthermore, woodlots were depended upon heavily for fuel and lumber, so that all trees there were precious. And there were no nurseries to provide trees for the common." Philip Ives

In mid-century the Amherst common hosted two annual celebra-
tions. Amherst College Commencement, held the second Thursday
in August, was a day of widespread rejoicing which brought alumni
and prominent out-of-town guests to participate in parading and
speechmaking with the faculty and students, brought also peddlers
and tradespeople who set up booths and tents on the green and
brought wagonloads of people from the area roundabout to join the
general festivity. Catching the carnival atmosphere in August 1857,
the *Springfield Republican* reported: "We have had the usual accom-
paniments of commencement—crowds of boys, plenty of ancient
oysters in the tents . . . . girls combing their lover's hair in the sitting
rooms of the hotels, and a rumor that Gov. Gardner, with brass
buttons and a cockade, was present."

The other celebration on the common was the Hampshire Agricultural Society's autumn Cattle Show, an increasingly popular
event. Amherst citizens were committee members, judges, and
competitors for ribbons and prizes for the best vegetables, fruits,
flowers, bread, jellies, and animals. Participants came from Leverett,
Pelham, Belchertown, Hadley, and spaces between and beyond,
overflowing the common, several display halls, and the Amherst
House, where a big dinner with speechmaking took place.

By 1854 Cattle Show was a two-day affair, attracting several
hundred yoke of cattle and several thousand people to the common,
as well as the tents and booths of the perennial hawkers. To the
members of the Ornamental Tree Association, who were concerned
about the appearance of the common and who had just set out a lot of
tender young trees, the wear and tear produced by Commencement
and Cattle Show was disturbing, particularly the trampling of live-
stock and jostling of teams. Asserting its power for the first time, the
OTA in 1859 forced the Hampshire Agricultural Society to find a
new location for Cattle Show, and in so doing inadvertently pushed
the farming interests out of the center of town. After considerable
controversy the Agricultural Society built fairgrounds and a hall near
the East Amherst common.

The Civil War soon changed the complexion of Commencement,
for the date was moved back into July, and eventually to late June,
while festivities were curbed in deference to the seriousness of the
times. After the war Commencement blossomed into a more sophisticated social and intellectual event, confined to the college grounds

and college constituencies. The common was left in peace to weeds and grass and wildflowers, and its sprinkling of new trees.

Town meeting records show that until 1860, except in wartime, town government concerned itself almost exclusively with selecting necessary officials and raising monies to support a parson, schools, highways, and the poor. Until 1860 the town of Amherst had no bonded debt. But beginning in that year, and increasingly through-out the decade, the financial demands Amherst made upon itself for new graded schools, for military expenses (primarily bounties to volunteers), and to secure the presence of the Massachusetts Agricul-tural College ($50,000) necessitated repeated borrowing of money at up to 6 percent interest. Town expenditures continued to increase through the century. During the 1850s Amherst had spent an average of $11,000 annually. During the 1860s it jumped to an average of $48,000; in the 1870s to $73,000; in the 1880s it was $63,000; and in the 1890s $91,000.

Other changes marked Amherst soon after the Civil War. Be-tween 1865 and 1870 the population increased by 620 people, the largest gain in any half decade of the century, bringing the total number of residents to 4,035. Since local statistics for the period indicate that births declined and deaths increased, the population growth can be attributed to newcomers, including foreign immi-grants. The local newspaper commented in April 1867: "Never has Amherst shown such unmistakable signs of prosperity and growth as this spring. The contemplated buildings, both public and private, must give employment to a large number of workmen, and cause the disbursement and circulation of a large amount of money among our tradesmen. The influx of newcomers is very large, and tenements and boarding places are quite scarce."

Among the new buildings were Walker Hall at Amherst College, the new Congregational Church on Main Street, the new Episcopal Church along the common, a new post office, and the first buildings of the Agricultural College. These attracted outsiders and provided continuing work for Irishmen who had come near the end of the war to lay the north-south tracks of the New London Northern Railroad. The Irish settled with their families in houses along Railroad Street and around the Hills Hat Factory. As their numbers swelled and they found employment as servants and handymen in private homes in Amherst, Irish families clustered in two other locations in town, one in the area to the east of Mount Pleasant, termed Irish Hill, and the other at the northern end of what was later laid out as Sunset Avenue, a section nicknamed "the curragh."

The population of blacks, designated "colored people" at the time and settled principally in homes south of Northampton Road near the Hadley line, also increased from the ninety-one persons counted at the end of the Civil War, as Amherst College prospered and employment opportunities there and at the student boarding houses expanded.

Amherst College, under President William A. Stearns, was prospering. The number of students was growing, and the nature of the student body was becoming sharply secular. For over forty years most of the graduates of Amherst had become ministers or missionaries. Although Amherst continued for a time to prepare more theologians than any other American college, by 1871, 75 percent of the graduating class went into other professions—law, teaching, medicine, journalism, or business. Fraternities had evolved into social rather than literary centers during the 1860s, although they were not yet residences. The more than 300 students lived either in the college dormitories or in one of dozens of boarding houses or rooms kept for them by Amherst families. Student boisterousness was on the increase, however, and contributed to a growing concern with law and order in the town.

Except for a small Baptist congregation, the five Congregational churches in Amherst maintained a religious monopoly until near the end of the Civil War. But by 1870 Grace Episcopal Church, the Wesley Methodist Church, St. Brigid's Roman Catholic Church, and Zion Chapel were all built or underway. With so many indicated changes in the populace, perhaps it is not surprising that by 1868 the town felt the need to adopt a code of by-laws, for the first time setting spoken guidelines for a way of life within the village.

At the annual town meeting in March 1868 Enos F. Cook, I. F. Conkey, and Austin Dickinson were appointed a committee to "report a code of bye-laws . . . for directing and managing [Amherst's] prudential affairs and preserving peace and good order and maintaining the internal police of such town." The seventeen rules in the code adopted later that spring advocated the arrest and fining of truants (ages seven to sixteen); imposed a fine for wandering animals; forbade bonfires and gunpowder explosions in the streets without approval of the selectmen; forbade also indecent exposure while swimming near a public way, the posting of signs and handbills on private property, mutilation of public fruit or ornamental trees by posting signs or tying animals; prohibited ball playing, kite flying, and stone throwing within a mile radius of the center of town; restricted sliding to designated streets and sidewalks; banned horses and other animals from the sidewalks and garbage and refuse from the streets; and prohibited the malicious unfastening of horses. In addition, several regulations controlled turning in false alarms of fire and condemned refusal to assist at fighting a fire.

The By-law for Amherst, copied into the Town Meeting Record in the clear spencerian hand of Town Clerk Samuel Carter, is a noticeably different kind of entry from the customary listings of elected officials, appropriated monies, and recorded votes. Implicit in the very need for by-laws is recognition that mutually held values, certain understood ways of behaving heretofore generally accepted by residents of the village, were undergoing change, were no longer known to all. The inherent concern for the quality of life in Amherst seems a suitable prelude to an increasingly complicated era of town government, when such needs as new schools, new highways and sidewalks, public water, public lighting, public sewage, better public transportation, even another cemetery, and eventually a town hall crowded upon its citizens, raising their taxes, and subtly forcing them to recognize and meet their own requirements and those of the diverse others with whom they shared Amherst.

Between 1860 and 1873 the minutes of the Ornamental Tree Association reveal only sporadic, sparsely attended meetings. A core group kept its eye on repairs to the common and supported any improvements through sale of the grass and increase of membership. Although items in the *Hampshire Express* (later the *Amherst Record*) during the 1860s indicate that efforts continued on filling the low sections, work must have languished, for the editor complained at the end of March 1867 about "neglected roads and sidewalks, and the common growing up to weeds, many places dirty and uncared for." Over a year later a disgruntled resident queried the paper: "Will the Ornamental Tree Association, or somebody else, now that the frog pond on the common is filled up, properly drain and level off the ground, sow it with grass seed, and make the common look at least respectable."

THE AMHERST COMMON AFTER THE 1860s, VIEWED FROM
THE AMHERST CHAPEL TOWER.

During the decade following 1873, however, the concept of village improvement took hold. In 1873, after several attempts, the Ornamental Tree Association won the right at town meeting to enlarge the common to the north by enclosing with fence a new section beyond the old pond, in the process protecting some shade trees across from the Kellogg block. Strong opposition to this and to an attempt to extend Spring Street westward across the common was voiced by local merchants who feared that fences and new roads replacing traditional paths and cart tracks would hurt their businesses. The opposition tried but failed to rescind the vote that sixteen years earlier placed the common in the hands of the Ornamental Tree Association.

With new acreage in hand, Austin Dickinson seems to have reasserted leadership, though not yet president of the association. By now Dickinson was acquainted and impressed with the plans and insights of Frederick Law Olmsted, who had advised Amherst College in 1870 and had earlier drawn a detailed design for the new Agricultural College grounds, a plan rejected by the institution's trustees after considerable controversy, although it was well-suited to the educational goals and the rural setting. Now, in 1875, at Austin Dickinson's request, the designer of New York's Central

Park made a plan for the Amherst common. It is sad that that plan and Olmsted's accompanying letter were burned with so many other historic Amherst documents the night the Dickinson-Cooper law office caught fire during the blizzard of March 1888. From a number of sources, including a satirical article in *The Amherst Record,* and from subsequent actions, we know Olmsted sketched new traffic patterns, suggested sidewalks and curbings, approved tree plantings, and recommended the removal of telegraph poles and the old hay scales, a perennial eyesore. The latter promptly became a bone of contention and did not vanish from the common for three years.

Inspired by Olmsted's plan, the OTA gathered new strength. It changed its name to the Village Improvement Society in 1877, suggesting an enlarged scope of concern. Ladies were invited to join and were placed on the executive committee. As membership and subscriptions swelled in response to repeated efforts, committees of one or two prominent persons were appointed annually to keep an eye on the principal streets of the village, to keep them tidy and attractive and their trees in good repair. The society urged residents to take down their white picket fences, which created a higgledy-piggledy appearance, and to plant flowers and shrubs. By 1883 village improvement had made such an obvious difference to the center of town that East Amherst and South Amherst founded societies in emulation, and a few years later North Amherst and North Amherst City did the same.

The center of Amherst was described by Mabel Loomis Todd when she and her professor husband arrived in town in September 1881. Mrs. Todd wrote her first impressions in a letter to her parents: "There are some very nice buildings, shops, etc., and many dignified houses. There is a sort of park or green running through the principal street, full of elms and nicely kept grass. It makes the whole town lovely. It is much more than an average pleasant country village."

More specifically, the *Springfield Republican* reported in June of 1883, after Amherst College's Baccalaureate Sunday: "Five years have done much for the village of Amherst. She has during this time removed her ash-heap [from the 1879 fire]—thanks to the vigilance of the village improvement society—built a sidewalk, taken to herself gas and water, and secured a street sprinkler. . . . The common which used to net the town $7 a season in hay and thistles, is now well sodded, cropped and curbed. . . ."

Gathered together in the village improvement effort and in many other town enterprises of the late nineteenth century were some men of remarkable character, ability, and feeling. Winthrop Dakin has pointed out in his *Historical Sketch of the Amherst Savings Bank* that "over and over again these same men would be found associated in one combination or another to execute some beneficial project." They were men born and brought up in Amherst, who either stayed in town or who, if they left for a time, came back to focus their talents and devotion, to spend their lives, here.

Ithamar Francis Conkey, charter member of the OTA, died in 1875 at age fifty-two. His obituary characterized him as "prominent in every enterprise and every question in which the town or any portion of it was interested, expressing his opinion on all subjects promptly and emphatically, and though often opposed to some of our citizens on public matters, his honesty was never questioned, and he was almost uniformly in the right." Mr. Conkey led in establishing the Amherst Savings Bank in 1864, and he was annual town meeting moderator for twenty-six years, the longest span in the town's history.

Conkey's death, and the death the preceding year of Edward Dickinson, left a void into which Austin Dickinson stepped. Not only did he succeed his father as Treasurer of Amherst College, changing the nature of that office from an accountancy to responsibility for supervising the financial planning and investments of the college, but he also oversaw the building programs and the beautifying of the college grounds for the next twenty years. Although few activities in the town went forward without his participation, or at least his counsel, his chief contributions beyond village improvement were the building of the new First Congregational Church, the bringing in of Pelham water after the disastrous 1879 fire, and the laying out of Wildwood Cemetery, on which he spent his finest and most intrinsic creative energies, again in consultation with Frederick Law Olmsted.

Austin Dickinson served as town meeting moderator for the fifteen years before he died in 1895. Commenting upon his death *The Amherst Record* noted: "He was a strong man, strong in his convictions, strong in loyalty to his ideals, strong in his likes and dislikes, strong in words and in action. He was frank and outspoken. . . . There was no misunderstanding his attitude on any matter of public or private interest. . . . He looked upon the town of Amherst as one of the most beautiful places in the world and was ever seeking to add to its natural beauty and alert to combat anything that might menace it." The *Springfield Republican* mentioned: "He had an open, frank and vigorous way of speaking to and looking out at the world that commanded respect and confidence from the moment that he appeared on any scene. But his nature was all gentleness and refinement, and there were a shyness and reserve in his composition, coupled with an intensity of feeling that were almost pathetic at times. He led the town of Amherst and he largely moulded the interests of Amherst College. . . ."

Probably his friend Mrs. Todd touched most closely on Austin Dickinson's indispensability when she wrote: "I suppose nobody in the town could be born or married or buried, or make an investment, or buy a house-lot, or a cemetery-lot, or sell a newspaper, or build a house, or choose a profession, without you close at hand." In truth, it was more accurately Austin Dickinson than his poet sister, Emily, who might have used as signature, "Amherst."

Two other prominent Amherst men whose lives closed within that same year of 1895–96, the year of publication of Carpenter's and Morehouse's history, the year the century, in retrospect, seems to have culminated for Amherst, were Julius H. Seelye and Henry F. Hills. Larger than life in build and temperament, Seelye was theologian, philosopher, teacher, president of Amherst College from 1876 to 1890, and a man of great orthodoxy and conviction. Under his leadership Amherst College acquired potent new teachers and prospered materially.

Seelye represented the tenth district in Congress for a term in the 1870s and was active thereafter in Amherst's town government. In 1876 he inspired the town program of building public concrete sidewalks by anonymously offering $500 if Amherst would put up an equal sum and abuttors would pay half the cost. Thereafter appropriations for sidewalks were a regular part of the town budget until, by century's end, Amherst pedestrians were released from seasonal annoyances caused by snow, dust, and mud. In 1870 Julius Seelye headed a six-man study on ways to bring water into Amherst for domestic and fire-fighting purposes. His proposal to build a reservoir and pipe in Pelham spring water was tabled until after the disastrous fire of July 4, 1879 gutted the center of town. Then, largely under Seelye's direction, the Amherst Water Company was formed, and the town began the long, complicated process of putting in hydrants and water pipes (which broke frequently enough to cause regular flooding and highway repair problems) and sewers.

Eulogies at Seelye's death (or, to use his own term, his translation), were many and eloquent, but perhaps none more succinct than one which stated simply: "The oak has fallen!"

Henry F. Hills, son of Leonard M. Hills who founded the Hills Manufacturing Company, makers of straw hats and shaker hoods and largest employer in Amherst, had a part in numerous civic enterprises begun in the 1870s and 1880s. An early participant in efforts to bring in an east-west railroad, he helped persuade the town in 1870 to subscribe for stock in the Massachusetts Central Railroad, of which he was a director, and thus open Amherst to the west. Plagued with problems, the line did not begin service until late 1887, and by then Hills had abandoned his original dream of having its depot located close to the straw hat factory.

Another of his keen interests was the Amherst Gas Company, which he founded with Julius Seelye, Austin Dickinson, and others. Until 1873 Amherst had no street lights. Then sixteen oil lamps, lighted and extinguished by the night policeman, brought the first illumination to the center of town. The Amherst Gas Company began service in 1877 with a "grand illumination" of the straw hat factories to proclaim the functioning of the first mile of pipe, and by 1882 the town changed to gas street lights. Eventually the company purchased electrical power, and Amherst switched to arc lights. Austin Dickinson left his directorship at that point, objecting to disfiguring the center of town with poles and wires.

Henry Hills was instrumental in purchasing the land that became Wildwood Cemetery, a project which, like others of the period, endured an embattled town meeting history between 1880 and 1889 as one group vied with another over the location. Determining at last upon a rise of ground Edward Hitchcock had once dubbed "Mount Pleasanter," Amherst entered late upon the rural cemetery movement, that cultural uplifting of the burial ground from simple graveyard to landscaped park to accommodate the emotional and aesthetic tenor of an age which spent considerable of its leisure moments at the graveside.

One vision of these three men, Dickinson, Seelye, and Hills, never became reality. They had hopes during the early 1890s of creating a new central avenue for the town, a broad, tree-lined street

PHOTOGRAPH BY CARLTON BROSE

WILDWOOD CEMETERY.

that would begin at the north face of Walker Hall (establishing a grand entrance to Amherst College), cut north across faculty properties, utilize Churchill Street, cross Lessey Street and the Tyler property, cross Triangle Street, and pass through fields owned by Henry Hills to reach the gates of Wildwood Cemetery. Frederick Law Olmsted mapped out the avenue, three rods wide. The Amherst College trustees in 1894 authorized purchase of the right of way to Spring Street. Hills was willing. Only the stubbornness of John Tyler in refusing to give up his side yard and garden kept the plan from becoming reality. And, of course, the deaths of Dickinson, Seelye, and Hills.

Other names than these appear persistently in the public record of late nineteenth century Amherst. There is Amherst House and stage line owner and Savings Bank president, Enos Foster Cook, for example; and Town Clerk Edward D. Bangs; lawyer Dwight W. Palmer; President William S. Clark of the Agricultural College who brought Amherst and the Orient in touch and who later lost money of many Amherst residents in a gold mine fraud; and Clark's ubiquitous right-hand man who ran constantly for public office, Professor Levi Stockbridge. There is beloved minister of the First Congregational Church, Jonathan L. Jenkins. The list could go on, but perhaps it is time to take stock of the names that never appeared. Only one woman is mentioned in the town meeting records during the century, and she is Mrs. Mary E. Stearns, widowed daughter-in-law of the former Amherst College president, who conducted in the President's House a school for girls known familiarly as The Convent. Widely respected and admired for her courage, ability, and high-mindedness, Mrs. Stearns was voted onto the school board in 1880 by the first female voters to intrude themselves upon an Amherst town meeting. She declined to serve because she was busy running her school and raising her seven children and because she disapproved of women voting and holding office.

What were women in Amherst doing during the last decades of the nineteenth century? How did they live their lives and manage their households, and what impact had they on the history of the town? The record is scanty. Women surface briefly in published vignettes of Mrs. Luke Sweetser, whose purple kid gloves flapped at the fingertips as her stubby hand passed a peppermint across a pew, and of charismatic Mrs. Lucius Boltwood, able to prompt her husband into recollections of everything that ever occurred. Mary Adele Allen, in *Round a Village Green,* provides the fullest record with her memories of cultured maiden ladies and gracious Amherst hostesses.

For the rest we must piece together letters, diaries, reminiscences, and the counsel and advice supplied in the local newspaper to recreate an existence centered upon home and family—the *Christian* home and family—and the work involved in keeping both running: cooking, cleaning, washing, sewing, training servants, caring for children, and taking responsibility for the moral tone of the family. To appreciate why young Millicent Todd was embarrassed that her mother was so different from other Amherst mothers when she sang and lectured in public, got up art exhibits, and only went into her kitchen under protest, we must realize that it was socially unacceptable then for women in Amherst to engage in any activities outside the home save teaching and missionary work, home and abroad. Men alone got involved in public activities. Mabel Loomis Todd was an exception. During the 1890s she edited three volumes of Emily Dickinson's poetry, collected and edited the poet's letters, and wrote two other books of her own. She also, during that decade, founded the Amherst DAR and the Historical Society and led in organizing the Woman's Club. In so doing she risked the village's social disapprobation for using her time to the assumed neglect of her home and husband and child.

The tasks Mrs. Todd shied away from, the housecleaning that prompted Emily Dickinson to declare she preferred pestilence, were very real drudgery. They were the "jobs that didn't stay done," and few women liked them any better than Mrs. Todd and Miss Dickinson, though the majority accepted women's traditional duties, resignedly wielding needle and dustmop in Christian spirit. To examine one—that of providing clothes for a family—is to appreciate the skills and industry needed by a housewife to select patterns, fabrics, and notions for all the many undergarments and most of the overgarments worn by men, women, children, and babies in the family. Most of the sewing and mending a woman did herself, and her work basket was a fixture in the household, but in addition a seamstress might come to the home for several days at a time to help cut, fit, baste, sew, and remodel, while for fancier dresses, suits, and coats a tailor or dressmaker would be sought at his or her shop. Once made, a garment must be cared for. Washing was done by hand in tubs of water pumped by hand and heated on a wood-burning stove. After drying came starching and ironing with flatirons heated on the stove or by the fire, winter and summer. Nonwashable garments were brushed and aired and put away or gotten out according to the season. Help for these chores was plentiful and cheap in town, but help must be properly trained and managed, a responsibility in itself.

It is a wonder, in fact, that there was time for social activity, and yet a constant round of calling, the preparing and carrying of "attentions," not to mention picnics and sleighing parties, church-centered activities, and lectures, kept people in touch with one another. The plain living and high thinking of an earlier day merged into quietly elegant forms of entertainment. Dancing, card playing, musicales, and even delivery of the *Springfield Republican* on Sunday (though some would not read it until Monday) gradually became part of Amherst during the last two decades of the century.

A darker side of life, reminders of which were spread across the front page of the local paper week after week in poetry, prose, and fantasy, was very much the province of the woman in Amherst. Illness and death were constant and prolonged worries, and steadfast religious faith was a necessary supplement to the insufficiencies of medicine and medical knowledge. Mrs. Stearns's life was prime example of the kind of tragedy to which so many families fell victim. In 1880 she took into her struggling boarding school a girl so sick with consumption that she was confined to her room, and her lessons had to be provided privately by Ethel Stearns, eldest daughter of the Stearns family. At that time tuberculosis was not known to be a communicable disease. The sick student stayed only three months, long enough to pass the disease to William, the eldest Stearns son, who was buried on his twenty-first birthday in 1881, to Ethel, who died at seventeen in 1882, to younger Annie, who died in 1885, and to second son Harold, who fought the illness on and off for a decade before dying in 1890. Perhaps the public record of women's lives in late nineteenth century Amherst lies among the bolts of crepe purchased at Mr. Cutler's store, and is graven in the granite of West Cemetery.

Woven into the history of late nineteenth century Amherst is the founding of the Massachusetts Agricultural College. The detailed account of its birth and infancy supplied by Carpenter and Morehouse suffers the tedium of too recent hindsight but exhibits the

THE MASSACHUSETTS AGRICULTURAL COLLEGE
AFTER THE CIVIL WAR.

pride and high expectations Amherst citizens had in encouraging the fledgling institution to take root where Amherst College already flourished. The state college was finally located in Amherst because local taxpayers appreciated and enthusiastically endorsed the relatively new concept of scientific agriculture, because they were able to compete successfully against other communities who desired the prize, and were willing to pay in taxes and raise by subscription $75,000 to secure its presence. Judging by the space allotted to both subjects in the Amherst newspaper, the Civil War was less dear a cause than the battle between 1863 and 1865 to secure the Agricultural College.

Soon after passage of the Morrill Act, which in 1862 provided public land grants to establish educational institutions, Massachusetts determined to found an Agricultural College, following the guidelines of a germinal report on agricultural education written in 1855 by former Amherst College president, Edward Hitchcock. At Hitchcock's suggestion the Amherst College trustees petitioned the Massachusetts General Court to found the state's agricultural college in association with Amherst College, but the General Court refused the request in favor of a completely independent institution, finally, however, selecting Amherst among communities competing to be the site. Interestingly enough, seventeen years later when the General Court was fed up with increasing debt and regular requests for appropriations from the growing Agricultural College, it tried briefly to abandon responsibility completely by giving the institution to Amherst College, but by then the idea had lost its appeal.

Hitchcock had educated the Amherst region to an appreciation for science, the emerging god whose principles and experiments enabled nineteenth century man to pump water and illuminate the dark. He communicated, too, the advantages of scientific farming, although ironically the concept was applied in Massachusetts about the time that agricultural prosperity peaked in New England. More fertile lands to the west and western extension of the railroad caused a shift from the small, less productive farms of the northeast, where generations of farmers had pitted muscle against the soil and where, until mid-nineteenth century, "brawn, not brain, cultivated the most acres and raised the largest crops," as Messrs. Carpenter and Morehouse acknowledge. Turning, as usual, to Europe as its model, America determined to set up schools where future farmers could be educated in botany, chemistry, practical agriculture, veterinary medicine, and other applicable subjects. Included would be facilities for experimentation with better methods and strains of plant and animal production. Since America was at war during the years the state agricultural colleges were being built, it is not surprising that military training was also included in the educational program. And at least in the college at Amherst there was an English course, an attempt to uplift the agricultural life.

The struggle to found a new institution, with its contests among General Court, trustees, and a succession of presidents, the problems of finding enough money and enough good students, of getting buildings built, of establishing standards and procedures, and of satisfying differing opinions on how a school of scientific agriculture ought to be organized and managed, must have seemed an eternity of trouble to townspeople for whom memories of the early and not unsimilar exertions to found Amherst College had pleasantly dimmed. Yet by 1892 when the Board of Trade issued a pamphlet, *Amherst, the Village Beautiful,* which called attention in vaulting prose to the natural, physical, and cultural charms of the town, the civic pride in the influence of the Agricultural College was evident: "The Amherst farmer of today works with his head as well as his hands, his business being not so much farming as scientific soil-culture. He plants the crops that are best adapted to the soil, uses the fertilizers that soil and crops require, and if the returns are poor he knows the reason. He does not wait for certain phases of the moon to do his planting, and the old superstitions have no hold upon him."

Civic pride. The public speeches and writings of the 1890s sing rhapsodically of the beauties nature bestowed upon this particular New England town and of the further enhancements made by its industrious natives. The *History of Amherst, Amherst, the Village Beautiful,* and *The Handbook of Amherst* all advertise for the world to look upon the perfection achieved by one self-centered, contained village, or rather cluster of villages, for the civic history of the town in the nineteenth century is largely the history of the center of town, with the benefits enacted there eventually extending to North and South and East Amherst, usually after a little kicking and screaming. But the nagging question was put by Austin Dickinson, who mused at the First Congregational Church's one hundred fiftieth anniversary celebration in 1889: "Those independent, strong characters— men of mark—who used to be scattered over our hills—ministers, lawyers, doctors—are not to be found there now. They are in the cities—in the struggle for wealth and power and fame. . . . While it is [so], the town or parish of this size that holds its own is the exception, and must be surrounded by most favoring circumstances."

The dominant note of the late nineteenth century was uplift, improvement, a belief that mankind, and Amherst in the bargain, was on the threshold of a better world of its own making. Was Amherst truly better than, more perfect than, other small New England villages? And if so, what was requisite for the continuing beauty and prosperity of the town? The inhabitants of nineteenth century Amherst expressed little doubt that their industry and commitment would carry them successfully into the twentieth century.

CHAPTER SIX

AN AMHERST NEIGHBORHOOD IN 1870

HELEN VON SCHMIDT

These essays are being published just at a time when "the new social history" is learning to use census records and other demographic data in sophisticated ways to suggest more completely how the patterns of family life, household composition, community relationships, and the stages of life from childhood to old age have been changing in the last two centuries. Probably the next versions of Amherst's history to be published will draw upon these new methods of social history far more fully than this present volume does. We do include here, however, a brief, simple example of what can be learned about life in a small neighborhood of Amherst in 1870.

Helen von Schmidt, a member of the class of 1977 at Amherst College, is one of the first women to have graduated from the college. She is also the first person to have completed a full program of studies at Amherst while actively mothering two teenaged children of her own. This essay was originally written for a class on Family and Community in America.

The anonymous author of the *1869 Business Directory for Amherst* commends the town for "the facilities of approach, the beauty of its surroundings, the tone of its morals, and the religious and educational advantages" that it offers. He thus presents, in the typical booster spirit of the era, the picture of an ideal community. Close to the center of this model town was located the neighborhood of ten unpretentious houses outlined on the accompanying detailed map of Amherst center in 1870. Many of the ten dwellings still stand; their exteriors seem as attractive today as they were 100 years ago. Yet it is highly unlikely that in any one of them could one find today the variety of life they contained in 1870. From the remaining records of

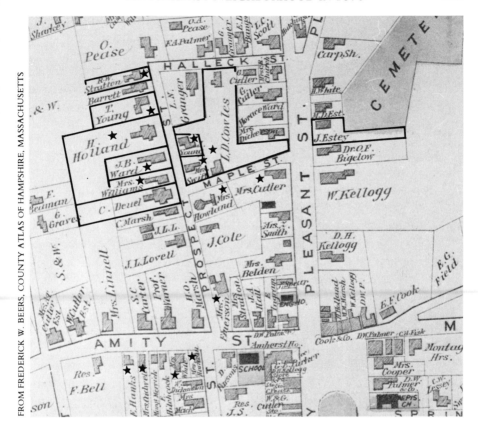

AN AMHERST NEIGHBORHOOD IN 1870.

the census and the town directory, however, it is possible to recapture some sense of the patterns of life within these ten Amherst households a century ago.

In 1870, not one of the dwellings contained only a single nuclear family. Seneca Holland's home contained three generations of Hollands—grandfather, two grown sons, and the family of the elder son. In addition, it housed a servant and one of Holland's employees. At seventy-nine, Seneca still retained the management of his grocery store; the home, though, is listed on the map in the name of the elder, married son. Since the financial data for the family is omitted in the census, we cannot know who actually owned the property. A glance at the map shows that they held a lot considerably larger than most of their neighbors. The store itself was on the common, only a few minutes walk from home. Like many of their neighbors, the Hollands' lives seem to have been contained in a very small circle.

The residents on the block were far from uniformly prosperous. J. B. Ward, right next door, was a fifty-seven-year-old retired farmer. His home was on a lot one quarter the size of the Holland's; his family was servantless. Listed as having a personal estate of $4,500 as well as real estate valued at $4,000, he and his wife were joined in their home by two boarders, a laborer and one of the local school teachers, as well as a widow and her two daughters. We do not know if the Wards were childless, but they were certainly in no danger of feeling lonely. Nor can we assume that the taking in of boarders was based simply on economic grounds.

Across Prospect Street, Mrs. Martha Swift, a widow with a total wealth of $60,000, was also boarding one of the teachers. Her children and the others on the block were more likely than their modern day counterparts to know their teachers outside the confines of the classroom. There were at least three teachers living in the neighborhood. Mrs. Swift herself had been born in Massachusetts, but her children are all listed as having been born in New York. It may be that the town's educational advantages brought her back to Amherst. Mrs. Swift's children in all likelihood were enrolled in Amherst's progressive graded school system, an innovation of 1861. In the same neighborhood school would be found the children of the widow at the Ward house—a family which according to the census had no financial holdings at all. Amherst had also in this era an ungraded school "to meet the wants of that class of the young, of either sex, who desire school privileges, but who are employed in various avocations through a part of the year." This school met in the winter months only. In this neighborhood, it was the only sign of social differentiation based on economic class. John Donahue, the illiterate fourteen-year-old farm laborer at the Cowles's house, would be enrolled here. Such a school would prevent that adult illiteracy which could be found in some of the older servants, but the school probably did little to enable John to rise in the world.

The outside world impinged far more on the town than it had in 1770. Sleds and doll carriages were manufactured here for the "New York trade." The irons for the plane factory came up from Connecticut. An examination of the census data shows that the heads of households for the most part continued to be natives. On the lower level of the social scale, however, there were immigrants. Mrs. Swift had one servant who had been born in Ireland, another born in New York with an Irish name. The Deuels had a fourteen-year-old black servant from South Carolina. The Cowles family had a Canadian farm laborer. Mr. Deuel himself was the only one of the ten heads of households who was not from Massachusetts. He was a New Yorker who married a native girl and began a business here. Several of the boarders in the neighborhood were students from out of state; it may be that Mr. Deuel met his wife while at school here. (The "beauty of the surroundings" still induces students to settle in the valley, and it may never have been entirely the beauty of the scenery alone.)

The outer areas of the town, North and South Amherst, were still in great part farm areas, but in this center neighborhood most of the men were merchants or artisans. There had been sufficient growth to insure a good deal of competition. Mr. Deuel was one of five druggists, Mr. Holland one of twelve grocers. Without exception, they lived close to their business establishments. While a great deal of property was held by women, few of them were working for pay. Those who were employed were in traditional women's work, teaching, seamstressing, or domestic work. Mrs. Barron was the only one who worked outside the home or school. Since she boarded at the Esty's, it may have been at her landlord's request that "Mme. Barron" had a piano studio downtown. Judging by these families, it was still common for the son to continue in the father's business and not uncommon for more than one of the sons to join the firm.

The only one of the men listed as still a farmer was Len Cowles. Progress, however, had changed his work. Although he still had a large piece of property for a town resident, most of his farmland had recently been sold to become the site of Massachusetts Agricultural College. Atypically, he had a large family of five children. His seeming persistent effort to get a son, successful after four daughters, did not provide for a successor on the family farm. Though the neighborhood was economically heterogeneous, it was becoming exclusively "town" people rather than "country."

Proximity to the center of town may have been one factor that made the neighborhood desirable to boarders. Each of the ten dwellings contained at least one person who does not appear to have been a relation. The boarders do not seem to have followed any single pattern. Single women and men might predominate, but there were also at least two young married couples. The men appear to have been establishing themselves in their trades; both were in their early thirties, and it is possible that they were veterans making a delayed entrance into the labor market. Clearly, they did not feel the need to be in their own home before starting a family.

The single most noticeable quality of residence in this neighborhood is that no person was alone. Aging parents, unmarried siblings, bachelors, spinsters, widows, retired men—all were living in a family-like situation. No fatherless child lived in a household without a male. The Young family was the clearest example of nearby residence based on kinship. The two brothers had homes on the same street; one of them cared for the grandfather. Without knowing for certain the maiden names of the women, one cannot determine some of the other possible connections. Eliza Buckland, for example, a seventeen-year-old female who as "at home" in the Williams residence, may have been a cousin or sister-in-law, rather than an unrelated boarder.

Whatever the unseen patterns, some patterns are clear. The recent war had apparently created a number of fatherless families. Excluding servants and nonresident students, there were six single females compared to two single men between the ages of twenty and thirty. Two women married men at least ten years older than themselves. If this neighborhood was typical, perhaps the war meant that some of the women of this generation would never marry. The war may also have helped to place much property into women's hands. The houses on the map outside this neighborhood seem to follow this pattern. (Widows' homes are starred.) Significantly, they seemed to be controlling the property even where there were mature males in the family.

Perhaps the recent war had skewed the patterns of Amherst life sufficiently so that these data are atypical of long-standing patterns. Yet they demonstrate clearly that the town seems to have had a system of adjusting to human needs, to social upheaval. Looking backward from the 1970s, the pattern of extended family and unrelated boarders seems to provide answers to a number of contemporary problems. There would have been no need for many of the social institutions that have arisen in our time—the Senior Citizens, Parents Without Partners, "singles" organizations, and others. With the exception of the teenaged servants and the Irish help, the neighborhood seems to have provided a supportive living situation for most of its residents. No generation was cut off from any other. Kin and surrogate kin must have provided the children on the block with an intimate knowledge of the whole life cycle, from birth to death. Grandparents could watch their grandchildren grow. Grandchildren could see their elders die.

We cannot determine what different strains these households had. Six of the ten had seven members, none less; one had thirteen. While the houses were sizable, such diversity while it solved some problems may have raised others. Remembering my own household of eleven (with one bathroom), both extended family and nonkin, I would hazard a guess that whatever the strains might have been, the variety of life there might have provided a richer, fuller awareness of the patterns of a whole life, that the children growing up on Prospect Street were in many ways more privileged than their modern counterparts. The educational advantages of life in Amherst were not confined to the school system.

CHAPTER SEVEN

TWO GENERATIONS OF AMHERST SOCIETY

SUSAN H. DICKINSON

Susan H. Dickinson, wife of Austin Dickinson, was born Susan Huntington Gilbert in Deerfield, Massachusetts on December 19, 1830, a few days
after her future sister-in-law Emily, whose close friend and intellectual companion she became. Susan was the youngest of seven children of Harriet Arms
and Thomas Gilbert. Her father was proprietor of a series of taverns in the
valley, including The Mansion House on Main Street in Amherst from
1832–1836. Orphaned early, Susan lived for varying periods of time with an
aunt in Geneva, New York and with her married sister, Harriet Gilbert Cutler, on Amity Street, Amherst. Though she was in and out of Amherst during
her girlhood, she attended Amherst Academy several terms and considered
Amherst her home. In 1856 she married Austin Dickinson and moved into the
newly built Evergreens on Main Street, next door to the Dickinson Homestead. Sue and Austin had three children, and The Evergreens was a social
center of the village during the eighteen sixties, seventies, and eighties. Susan
lived there until her death in 1913. This manuscript, never before published,
was probably written about 1900.

Turning over the pages recently of *Northampton the Meadow City,*
I was freshly impressed by the chapter on their past social life written
by Mrs. Annette Hopkins Emerson of Amherst, who by her temperament, talent, ancestry, and social gift was especially fitted to draw
the fascinating picture.

The social life at Amherst two generations and more ago was no
less unique in grace and charm, although differing markedly from
her rival across the river in certain social habits held contraband by
piety and conscience in Amherst, usages quite natural to a "shire"

town with its wider association and more cosmopolitan traditions. The harmless bores of cards and dancing, common there, were not even so much as mentioned in Amherst as suitable, nay possible occupations for immortal beings, until a quite recent day.

Northampton—how jealous we were of her! As our men trooped to her banks while for years we had none, and our ladies pressed to her dressmakers or hung over the counter at "Stoddard and Lathrops" in hope of some more distinctive elegance than Sweetser and Cutler could afford from their standard repertoire of sober merinos and a good quality of black silk. A few of them, fired to a more fastidious taste, bought their best bonnets at Mrs. Osborne's in Northampton too, sometimes venturing as high a price as six dollars, enamoured by the foreign touch to a momentary forgetfulness of the missionaries. These works of art were carefully packed in really huge band-boxes of those days, made of high-colored paper and ornamented with the most tropical scenes and exaggerated flowers, unknown to any botany. These treasures were anxiously committed to the sincerest protection of Brown, the always driver of the daily four-horse-stage coach that ran between Amherst and Northampton, which left us early in the morning and brought up with cracking whip in front of the post office promptly at five in the afternoon. Brown delivered these boxes with a positively tender hand, unrewarded by the scenes that followed behind closed doors—the tilting and trying of this alien bit of millinery, so tragically disturbing to any woman of taste and ambition!

In time we felt sure that the college was more than bank or court house and gradually forgave Northampton her smartness and praised her beauty. O scimitar of Fate! She has now more colleges than she can manage, but they are only women's colleges and we are still amiable. Bless Northampton! If there was jealousy between us in past ages, we all boasted of her when we got far enough away from home. Fifty years ago or more I could have shown you, dear moderns, in the small circle of Amherst—for there was but one in those days—as beautiful girls, or young ladies, as they were then called, as ever graced any drawing room. There were as handsome and accomplished young men, nay men both old and young, as full of high purpose and generous achievement as could be found in any town, either university or commercial.

Under President Humphrey and also under President Hitchcock, society was one. The village, being smaller than now, was fully represented at all the college levees, as the receptions were then called, and entered warmly into all the college affairs, lectures, and literary occasions.

My recollections of the hospitality of President Humphrey are limited to the children's games in the big kitchen and dining room of the original President's house. Such wild, exciting games of blind-man's buff as were played there! The high mantel in the kitchen was the rather perilous retreat for the taller boys of the party. There they were safe from the nervous clutches of the blind-fold girls, who suddenly recognizing a great shrinkage in numbers would sometimes pull up their blinders and bring the culprits of the mantel-piece speedily down to justice.

President Humphrey! When was there ever such gently though firmly anchored conscientiousness as his? How wholesomely Beecher's tribute at a long time ago Alumni dinner lingers in the mind! "The impression he made on me unconsciously of deep, strong manhood, when I was a student at Amherst, has never for a day of my life left me." What an epitaph for a man! It was on this same occasion that Beecher spoke of Professor Fisk, saying, "Professor Fisk, too, clear and pure as the light on Mt. Holyoke—how I admired him! But how his brain chilled him." Then with a whimsical smile to himself he added, "I can't remember that he ever put his arms around me!" Continuing this reminiscent strain, he spoke of Professor Worcester, calling him "a really great man, mentally," rather sadly concluding, "long since gone to his reward." But a faint reminding voice from the audience was heard. "Mr. Beecher, Professor Worcester is still living!" All the fun and ingenuousness in Beecher's nature flashed to the surface, as rallying quickly, he replied, "Well, if he is alive, and wants to be, I am glad of it!"

I well remember that this levity was too much for some of our serious folk, who associated prayer more naturally than laughter with the college of those days. Mrs. Deacon Sweetser, bowing stiffly in passing out of the hall, was heard to remark by some of us who were chuckling over a little natural fun amid obituary records and missionary reports, that "she did not care for Mr. Beecher's remarks. It was highly improper to ridicule such good men as Professor Fisk and Professor Worcester!"

The Senior Levee given by the President to the graduating class was the social event of the year, occurring in August at the close of the term. To this the villagers and all friends of the Seniors were invited. Weeks before-hand the young ladies were in a little agitation over it, arranging becoming gowns with a charming refinement of economy. As the Summer was so nearly over, to these same young ladies, at least, there was a sort of collapse after the party and a slight feeling of gloom in the earliest drawing in of evening with its sad-voiced crickets, and a rather pensive waiting for the return of the students. But never was the slightest utterance given to that effect, lest maiden modesty might blush to own dependence upon those naturally fascinating comrades.

These levees were held in the ample parlors of the President's house, only recently remodeled, and well adapted for the unusual number of guests in the hall, stairs, and study and the rural side-walks in front of the house, as well as the narrow porch on the north side, offered abundant room for the strolling couples who wished to escape, ostensibly, the modest glare of the astral lamps within. There was never dancing, never vaudeville of any sort. I confess there were flirtations—whatever that might have been—entirely un-French of course, in odd corners, especially under the stairs in the front hall, where a Puritan-backed sofa, covered with horse hair, sans pillow of any sort, was converted into a rather stiff Arcadia. I do not re-member that any one was bored by these simple affairs. There was music in a modest way, with the piano, and I can hear now, most plainly, the artistic rendering of the charming "O Summer Night!" as sung in a strikingly clear voice by Miss Gridley, daughter of the notable Doctor Gridley, the medical genius of the village and the region round about. Her metropolitan grace and culture lent a pecu-liar impressiveness to the staccato motive. In effective contrast was the sweet, winsome, "Wert thou in the cauld blast," as sung by Miss Fowler, a wizard in person and power. Everywhere at her ease, she was intellectually and socially a rich leaven, both in the village and at the head of her father's household, where she entertained her own and her father's friends with a rare fascination quite her own.

Of course there was the diversion of refreshments, with a "re-freshment table," as it was then called. This was usually a most simple but tasteful affair, a pyramid of wild flowers in the centre often attracting the most attention, leaving the actual repast to somewhat secondary importance. The matter of one's escort to the table was distinguishing; one felt honored for the year if the President, or one of the Honor-men among the Seniors, complimented one in this signal manner, these Honor-men being the monitors of the four classes and those of high appointments for Commencement Day.

President Hitchcock was strongly in favor of early hours, so that we all felt like intruders if we lingered long after ten o'clock at his parties, though our gentle host on this festive occasion seemed to ignore his hygienic principles, still greeting his guests with unaffected cordiality and blandly tolerant of the late, mad hour!

Mrs. Hitchcock impressed her sweet vivacious nature upon every one. Her smiles were revelations, not masks. Her dainty caps, trimmed in pink, and, according to the fashion of the day, quite large, and half concealing her soft curls, lent a deeper color to her own fresh cheeks and heightened an impression of youthfulness in her appearance, unbelievable to a present day woman, who would flee a cap as she would her first wrinkle, and mount any device instead in the mode of puff or cushion. Mrs. Hitchcock was mentally alert upon every topic of the time. She drew and painted with a natural ease and freedom, in an untrained way, beside closely following every pursuit and interest of her distinguished husband. She was a woman not only sweet but stimulating, earnestly recognizing life and its meaning, yet undaunted by its possibilities. I must speak of an amusing little incident in a lecture course of the President's as characteristic of his chivalric devotion to her. He was lecturing upon the bird tracks of the Connecticut Valley, now so well known. These lectures were given in a bare but decent hall in the third story of Sweetser's block—now Jackson and Cutler's—a cheerless place, lighted with whale oil lamps, and furnished forth with wooden benches of racking discomfort. As the fascinating lecturer stretched out his enormous maps and stated his theories of those monster petrifactions, a little gasp of unbelief ran through the audience. President Hitchcock smiled, saying, "If you doubt this, ask my wife about it, for she loves the truth better than she loves me." How everybody laughed and looked at her, blushing with a charming modesty!

For many years the dress that satisfied feminine taste and vanity among us was of the simplest, and would but oddly adorn the pages of the "Bon-Ton's" programme of fickle modes, or even those of Harper's Bazaar. Soft merino dresses of equally soft color were worn entirely for ordinary visiting; black silk for larger occasions. The young ladies in summer wore muslins, white or sprigged, not too prudish in cut at the throat. As the season grew chilly, sashes of scarlet ribbon were added, with knots of red berries festooned on the shoulders and drooping gracefully from the hair. Often quite heavy wreathes of myrtle leaves were bound about the head, giving a perhaps too classic touch, as if of filleted martyrs or Parnassian victims.

No one smiled over the simplicity or enforced economy of these toilets, or coveted richer or more elaborate effects. The girls were so pretty and winsome, they dominated their externals. I am sure I do not lend them the enchantment of distance. It comes to me how fully I am confirmed in this memory by some world-famous savants from Europe—I think Lyall the geologist was one of them—who were taken by President Hitchcock to the wedding reception of Mrs. Davis, then our beloved saint in the flesh. These stony-hearted scientists were enthusiastic over the beautiful party, and spoke most warmly of the unusual number of handsome girls and attractive women present.

President Stearns coming among us as a stranger, and not an alumnus of the college, was never so closely allied as his predecessors with the village people. His invitations were a little less general than those of President Hitchcock had been, although he welcomed warmly all friends of the Senior Class and the few families whom he knew to be in various ways connected with the college at the annual Senior Levee. Few are still left in these present days to remember the grace and distinction with which President and Mrs. Stearns received their guests on these occasions. Theirs was the perfection of manner, because no manner at all. There was a cheeriness and warm individuality in their hand-grasp quite away from the blasé, limp formula of modern fashionable usage. As the present is not in reality as far removed as the annals of Dolly Madison, and as Mrs. Stearns still graces the village with genial hospitality, I ought not perhaps to dwell upon personalities, but her shy manner, and beautiful old pearls, did well complete the youthful beauty of the President, with his fairly celestial smile. In this there was no trace of a simper, no hint of approbativeness. I think it came straight from a rift in heaven. The gallantries of the crude Seniors seemed trite after his invitation to promenade in the grounds in the moon light.

With their administration came a touch of the world in the general appearance of the house, always before so plain and simple. Very rich odd cabinets and carven chairs, unique bric-a-brac, from the son then living in India, as well as the inherited silver of aristocratic pattern, brought by Mrs. Stearns, lent an air of elegance quite agreeable and suitable. The early hours were however long kept; the inherited ten-o'clock-President-Hitchcock-bed-hour I believe still lingers rather banefully in our social atmosphere. For the witchery of mere lateness, the mellow glow of the advancing night, the foam of the beaker, has alas! to this day, no potent charm for our rather heavily balanced folk.

Sometimes funny episodes might have been chronicled as a result of our early bed-time, as when a wife of one of our Professors, coming uninitiated into our simplicities, lost several of her guests at her first party before the leisurely and elaborate supper, served after the manner and hour of her own gay city. We could not blame her as she laughingly asked, "Had they to meet a train?" The fascinating aroma of the last drop in the glass, of the after-supper wit and glow, never seemed to entrance our good, busy, practical folk, whose duties began in early dawn with family prayers.

There was little social variety fifty years ago; never dinners; rarely an evening party, perhaps, for some college class; and sometimes the small friendly suppers or tea parties. When these were too large in number to permit of seating the guests about a table, a bountiful homely supper would be handed around on large trays, every one being comfortably seated, with little tables for the tea cups, for which the gentlemen, with no lap and no tact, were as thankful as beggars! The stately parlors of Deacon Luke Sweetser struck rather the grand note in these affairs. There was more light, more elegance, more inherited silver, more inherited boarding-school-manner on the part of the hostess. Mrs. Sweetser, a most happy, genial hostess, though of a certain pomposity, always received us in gloves, usually of a light purple shade, with a rather flippant hand-shake and the long, low backward dipping curtsey, a relic of her gay education. Mr. Sweetser was a picturesque looking person, with a profusion of grey hair and a full beard. And although in ordinary daily life he bore himself with the traditional severity of the at-that-time accepted Old-Testament doctrines, at those tea parties he was literally wreathed in smiles of friendly welcome and approval. Mrs. Sweetser

DEACON LUKE SWEETSER.

never sat down at supper, but moved about among us, lest there should be an empty cup or an unfilled plate that escaped the derelict eye of the servants, all the time waving aloft a remarkable feather fan sent her from a thousand miles up the Nile by an old friend, she gaily affirmed. Tea and coffee with delicious cream, very high raised biscuit, sliced tongue red and tender, escalloped oysters, with many kinds of home made cakes, was the repast. After this hospitality was disposed of, Mrs. Sweetser revelled in the proud handing about of curios and Syrian relics sent over to her by her niece, now the wife of the Reverend Daniel Bliss, the President of the Protestant College at Beirut, Syria. Our own bijouterie seemed familiar to stupidity, and commonplace indeed, beside these musky specimens of Arabs and Turks—inlaid coffee cups, exquisite scent bottles holding attar of rose, fans of peacock feathers, lentils, and husks, "Such as the swine did eat!" according to the enthusiastic description of our faithful hostess. Friendly talk was the only entertainment offered, except perhaps just at the end of the evening the open piano suggested a little music as desirable, and voices somewhat decadent sang sweetly, though with a timid tremulo, "Are we almost there? Said the dying girl," "Coming through the rye," etc., or a resident basso of solemn mien, with a tone really below any pitch known to musical necessity, was prevailed upon after the habitual prolonged urging to give us, "Rocked in the cradle of the deep," the refrain being held with such sustained power I am sure the glasses in the corner cupboards tinkled from the jar.

By this time music was in the air, and aroused to an almost vivacious gaiety, all stood about the piano and sang together, "Lest auld acquaintance be forgot," "America," and "Scotland's burning!" We were all in a glow when we went out for our wraps at last. I can never forget Deacon Sweetser's final beaming gallantry, as he stood at the top of his high terrace steps, holding an oil lantern in the air for our safety, at that time the only beacon of the night known in all Amherst. Those lanterns, and lantern-bearers! What chapters could be written of them! Stevenson alone could hope to do them justice!

After such an experience as this, as a young girl I used to wonder, as I removed my simple adornments, why in the many noon hours of a Sabbath I had sat through a deadly monotonous Bible class under our host's leadership, he had never by word or smile lent a relaxed beam of cheer or hope to the simplicities of the New Testament. As he unfolded them via Barnes Notes, he weighed down my youthful spirit every Sunday with his picture of myself as a rebellious sinner in the hands of an avenging God, with possible death before another dawn staring me full in the face. I suppose I got used to it, for I did not express my own religious life with this sacredest of old churches until some years later. What a loss of days of natural, gentle adoring love of God the Father, whose very Spirit was within me, and whose world was my splendor! They were indeed queer good men in those days, and as some one has said of them, "They believed like fury!"

The pallid pleasures of half a century ago were diversions few and tame, leading almost invariably back to the religious activities of the church. There was an occasional lecture, there were also the Wednesday evening prayer-meetings in town and college, and the Ladies Sewing Society, where once a fortnight the minister and husbands came in for tea. In this, the college and village were one. There was tea drinking among neighbors, knitting in hand, varied only by the serious entertainments I have mentioned. One might call any day in the week in those primitive times without disturbing a club of any sort, a fact hardly credible at present, when men, women and children are so listed in federations of every kind that the command to "enter into thy closet and shut the door" seems but an old time irony!

In mid-winter there were usually four and more weeks of religious "protracted meetings" held, at which, according to the habits of those days, all clergymen in the region preached and held prayer meetings, resulting in many admissions to the church. As the snow lay two or three feet on the level in those wintry days, Amherst, with no street lighting, no trolleys, no railroads, seemed to my youthful and perverse mind, animal spirits and vigorous habits, a staring, lonely, hopeless place, enough to make angels homesick. The lugubrious sound of the church bell still rings in my winter dreams. Emily Dickinson, when a girl, used to say it reverberated to her solely of the judgment day!

There was all of a sudden an innovation upon the routine of unbroken evenings one winter. How it came about I know not, but we were bidden to an exclusively college affair once a fortnight dubbed a "Conversatzione!" It was, in spite of its foreign title, just a literary club, with papers and talk and light supper, or refreshments as it was called. Was it dull? Or was I stupid? I remember only one given at Professor Waner's, rather brilliant in effect but memorable chiefly for an astute paper given by that shining intellect, Professor Smith, who merged his power in the New York Theological Seminary soon after, a loss irreparable to Amherst College. The affair was short lived and some plain folk said it died of its imported name. Conversatzione to be sure! A queer frill for this Plymouth Rock college!

There are not many now living in the village who remember the unstinted hospitality of the Tyler home. Home indeed it was for the stranger, the foreigner, rich and poor, Savants, Missionaries, Statesmen and Scholars. How, with the usual stipend of six or eight hundred a year, and an expensive growing family, the door could be always open and the welcome spread, is a modern marvel. Mrs. Tyler, over-burdened with cares domestic, social and public, always kept a free mind for all written thought as well, whether of memoir, history or fiction. When a certain other dear woman among us was refusing to read *Adam Bede* at the time of its publication, on the score of the author's ungodliness, Mrs. Tyler was reading it aloud to her husband and both were filled with its charm and moral power. Indeed they were for a long time the only persons in the village who knew anything of George Eliot or her work.

When Sumner was in Amherst, he found with them the only welcome the village afforded an abolitionist. The aristocratic tone and salvation of our nation, as then held, lay in the voice of the old Whig party, who so long and so obstinately resisted any stirring of the slavery cause as disloyalty to the constitution and a menace to the national safety. How slowly they yielded, those handsome stubborn gentlemen in velvet collars and stiff beaver hats, to the emancipating chariots of the God of battle and Abraham Lincoln!

Professor Tyler, in these days, believed in the best and worst of human nature, which furnished him with the double equipment of genial sympathy and the relentlessness of a two-edged sword in his eloquent denunciation of sin and the sinner. There must be some few living, who, like myself, recall his famous sermon preached from the text, "When will the Sabbath be gone, that we may sell corn?" in which he took the opportunity to lash the students for all their violations of the then strictly-observed Puritan Sabbath. What force and genius must there be in another sermon of his from the text, "Whoso drinketh of the water that I shall give him, shall never thirst," that it has lingered with a compelling power in the mind and soul of one past the prescribed physical boundary, whose life too has been rich and diverting, crowded with associations of European color? This same nature of Professor Tyler's yielded, as years went by, to human timidity and modified distrust of some of the old finalities, for he told me once, in an informal call of sympathy, "When I find myself getting dusky in doubt and depression I get to work to help somebody."

Even in those far off days stolen pleasures were sweet. Emily Fowler, whose overflowing nature was ever diffusing itself, used to bid us to her home for an evening of impromptu dancing, if our floundering attempts to get through a plain quadrille and Virginia Reel, to the sharp voice of a superannuated piano, could be called dancing. It was great fun and seemed real; besides it was contraband. The lines of right and wrong, how queerly they ran and do run, and perhaps always will! Just across the river good people danced and played cards and loved God and tried to obey his will, innocent as children of any wrong in their soul's service, or violation of the humanities. While this side that same river, such harmless recreations were as wicked as idols or juggernaut! For secrecy's sake, these occasions were always alluded to between times as "P.O.M. Meetings." Poetry of Motion, to be sure!

Once only were we invited to surreptitiously gather at the home of a dignified pair who were to be away for the night, and would therefore remain in blest ignorance of this departure on the part of their young people from the stern and fossil moral code of those days. All went merry as a marriage bell. We danced late, with something not unlike abandon. But trifles light as air are time-proven betrayers—attest, the slight scarlet thread of Jezebel, Newton's apple, Fulton's tea kettle! "Great oaks from little acorns grow!" It was the lion's tail on the hearth-rug in the parlor of this staid home that convulsed domesticity for twenty-four hours, and led to discovery at last. Taken up to relieve the dancing toes from clumsy entanglement in the fringe, it was put back in the flurry of righting up in the morning before the return of the parents, regardless of the lion's anatomy and jungle grace. He was a big brown fellow, set off by a vague green background of some appropriate sort. The silly, half-frightened young folks had replaced him, but completely reversed, so that his majestic tail turned up where, by precedent, it should have turned down, and all his members were accordingly topsy turvy! Only too soon after the return, the maternal shriek, "Why girls! Girls! What *has* happened? The lion's tail is upside down!" proved the fore-runner of a little private judgment day. Eventually the mother was "managed" and recommended not to trouble Father about it! I should have explained, of course, that this best-parlor rug was never taken up except at the change of solstice.

Watching with the sick would hardly be included in nocturnal

pleasures, but it was considered, as I look back upon it, too natural a
duty to even speak of, much less question as a suitable dissipation.
Young and old took the place of night watchers in all emergencies.
Quite early in life I showed a knack with the sick and tried my
powers somewhat enthusiastically. A night of length and stillness
passed in the sick room of Mrs. Moore, the widow of the first
President of the college, is cut upon my memory like a steel engraving. She lived in what came to be known as the Bentley house, but
was then the residence of the President, standing where now the
Alpha Delta Phi house displays its unbroken lawn. In the manner of
the time, the plan of it was four square rooms and a wide, long hall,
unwarmed and uncarpeted. As my vigil began at eight o'clock and
"the hired girl" was entirely banished at that early hour, the solitude
of the lonely May night, both within and without, began to tell upon
my nerves before midnight. My patient was comfortably convales-
cent so that I was not braced by anxiety for her case. I will own I was
habitually called a "fraid cat" by my own family, who sharply chid
me, "for my good" doubtless, after the Puritan recipe, urging "What
are you afraid of?" To which, in disdain, I shot back, as any mystic,
"Oh, I dont know! If I did I would not care!"

Such being my temperament, I was chilled to the marrow to find
I must go down to the kitchen for broth for my patient. With a sickly
oil lamp in my hand I made my journey down the long black hall
and stairway, which together with the lower halls were furnished
with a narrow width of striped carpeting, the stairs being painted in
wild grey scrawls and the walls papered in landscape designs with
strange animals, so that the shadows cast by my half dying lamp
distorted everything frightfully. I somehow lived through this, and
reached my sick woman's bed with the broth. As she sat propped up
in bed to take it, her shadow on the wall would have entranced an
impressionist's brush, out-mastered Hogarth! A much beruffled
night cap set off a quite masculine head with large solemn features,
and all unsoftened by any least tendency toward French lingerie. A
narrow waspish figure, bent and cracked, she did not, to my
sixteen-year-old soul, radiate any atmosphere that I loved. But I
softened in every emotion when she spoke of her possible demise. As
I heard her say, "My dear girl, the habiliments of the grave assume
an aspect of terror to me," I rallied, out of sheer girlish pity, and
talked glibly of the joys and certainty of heaven, and her own per-

sonal crown, quoting the scriptures to the point, until I was so fascinated with my theme I felt ready to fly away to the better world
myself! When morning had come and my patient had fallen into a
gentle sleep, I softly made my escape out into the dawn. What a sight
was mine for a life time! Not a person, not a sound was abroad. The
sun was not yet visible, but the whole circuit of Pelham hills was
suffused with a deep wine color, hardly transparent, yet hardly a
mist. I forgot sick old women and every bogy, even the heaven I had
conjured up, and just adored, saying over to myself Mrs. Brown-
ing's lines from *Sunrise at Sea,*

> I oft had seen the dawn light run
> like red wine through the hills.

Only once more I watched and was so scared I withdrew from
the ministering angels of that day, forever. It was a dreary setting,
that last night of watching. A large old fashioned kitchen with an
enormous fireplace, and two small bed rooms opening off, was my
arena. My charge was a very old woman slowly recovering from a
long illness, whom I had never seen before, who was comfortably
fixed in one of the bed rooms. If one wants to make a sensitive
computation of time, let him try my position only from eight to
twelve on a still summer night in the country fifty years ago, when
all human life gradually withdraws, and dies utterly away, and the
tricks of darkness begin their antics. The steady talk of the clock of
time and eternity, the wild scramble of the rats in the wall, the
cracking and snapping of the old house itself, the soft scurry in the
grass outside the open window of things I could not name but worse
did imagine. And in between, such stillness! Suddenly a series of
curdling shrieks pierced the darkness and filled the house. It was
murder of course, and frozen with terror I stiffened. But the sick
woman faintly whispered, "It is my daughter. She is subject to
nightmare. You must wake her quickly." There was only a thin
partition between me and those hellish yells. I could not do it—but I
must! My reputation as a watcher was at stake. Shaking with fright I
grasped the iron candlestick—the tallow dripping over my fingers—
and fled to clutch the poor victim, who with wide staring eyes was
fast in the grip of her horror. She blessed me for delivering her, but
alas! nobody saved me from the most awful night of my life! I never
watched again.

There were lectures in those days. How we loved them, and throve on them, though now we cry enough, and draw nearer to the fire with our books, almost abhoring a lecture, for are we not lectured to death? We did not have many, but the professors in turn gave us of their best, and wise men from Europe now and then, and sometimes John Lord with his wizardry of style and manner, who could pursuade one against one's better reason. But we were young then, and Professor Shepard's lectures on botany, given in the basement of the old chapel on summer mornings, were graceful in style and manner, and the "young ladies" liked them because it was a pleasant pastime to attend them, escorted by some attractive Senior before whose class they were delivered. The walk and the escort and the lecture had a refinement of morning-glow quite fascinating to remember. Though a blur of values clouded my young brain when I found, toward the last of the course, that our charming beaux mostly got out of the window and took their botany au naturel gracefully disposed on the grass under sky and trees. As the years have passed and I have been often bored by instructive utterances and could not get out, their habit has seemed to me increasingly enviable and delightful.

The poet Dana, father of Richard Dana, gave a course of six lectures on poetry in the old college chapel way back in the fifties. They were exquisite, subtle, most poetic, but rather over the heads of sweet-sixteen and the college boys. But these, as all our lectures not strictly in the college course, were given in the evening, affording a delightful sort of time as we were invited by our gentlemen friends, strolling slowly up the long hill under their escort, and even more slowly back, under the stars when the lecture was over. "And no chaperone!" I hear the conventional modern exclaim. No such order was ever heard of in those days. Poor chaperones! They earn their honors protecting the budding beauties of today's ball rooms and happy times. My experience of it in my later society years found it a tedious service, amusing only by its contrast to our earlier freedoms.

One of the present day only can scarcely realize the importance and interest of the two great occasions as fete days of Amherst back in the mid-century. These were of course Commencement Day in August and the annual Cattle Show in October. Both took place all over the common, which was mown only once a year, becoming a wild jungle of every known weed from thistle to burdock, and becoming the very marshy, happy home of countless frogs and all sorts of batrachians. From early morning on Commencement Day, it was the camping ground of fakir's tents, peddler's carts, every imaginable sort of vender, and most delightful of all, lads and lassies in their Sunday best, from Shutesbury and Pelham and all the hills and valley about us. These last, hand in hand, or even with arms entwined, enjoyed with unsated appetite the joys of the common, and the wonderful, if to them meaningless, array in the old village church, now College Hall. Very green, they were, or as the French say "insouciant," and unattractive, with white dresses limp before noon—but was it not Commencement Day at Amherst! And everybody was there, and wonderful young men were declaiming even more wonderful pieces on a big stage, where all the Trustees in stiff collars and stiffer dignity were sitting with other important men and women of the valley, listening in compact rows to the eloquence displayed and sizing up its quality. I must not omit the place and deference always bespoken on this stage for the returned missionaries, the idolized children of the college, for whose sacred and brave ideals the college was prayed into being. Alas! Let any one attempt to report from Zion now, at a Commencement dinner, and they are soon drowned out by a new college yell, or ushered to a speedy close by a half-ribald song or ridiculous applause. One sometimes feels that Mahomet might teach ethics and manners better than Amherst College, such an impetuous flare has there been in these new generations towards young might and right.

The Cattle Show, in the beginning of its existence, was an affair of genuine bucolic sweetness and simplicity. The procession formed at the Amherst House, an inspiring band leading the way, while mounted escorts, with a military hint in their dress and style, curveted hither and thither about it. An address of almost religious seriousness, given by some notable person in the village church, was followed by a prayer of thanks for the in-gathering of the harvest. The plowing match was always of intense interest, held just west of the church on the Hadley road. Draft matches were held on the west side of the common, now in the front of the Psi Upsilon property. The exhibition of horses included the entire space of the common and Main street. Luke Sweetser, Edward Dickinson and Seth Nims (post-master many years, and father of the Savings Bank) were invariably owners of the finest horses in the county, and one would always note the style of the two latter, as they drove through the village streets at any time, sitting very erect, reins taut, with the high showy heads of their steeds refusing the senseless check or a careless hand. I never failed to turn and look after these horsemen, whenever they passed me in the street. If not irreverent, I should exclaim, "Where are the chariots and the horsemen thereof?" in these latter days. Something of the strong chivalric stuff must have departed from a man who can relinquish a live breathing horse drawing on and stimulating his vitality for a pondrous, ill-smelling machine that tears through the sweet hill and dale about us, as if Satan himself were let loose. What would dear George Herbert say to it all?

Architecture was never thought of or mentioned in those days, except by Professor Snell in an accidental way in a stiff lecture. The old village church, with its Grecian pillars late in its life, was a target for any lazy wit. But the fact that it survived beheading once and lived bravely on in defiance of jests, and with little external change stands today, rather Grecian in effect in spite of its malefactors, bespeaks its original integrity of composition. The original interior was truly an odd picture. There were high pews painted white, with doors fastened securely by a brass button, affording something of a sense of tribal ownership and comfort in one's sentiment of worship. They were too often carelessly slammed, but that only set off the noise made by Mr. Armstrong, the sexton, just as the sermon ended, when it was his habit to throw open the doors of the two cast-iron box stoves that stood near the doors with violence, and hurl some strange looking geometrical wood called "felly wood" into the Satanic depths, so that the farmers and their families who remained for afternoon service at one o'clock might warm their half frozen members and re-fill their foot stoves. As they sat about on the circular seats round the red hot stove, neighborly visiting was indulged in, in low sad tones. A meagre chilling lunch was drawn from the large yellow muffs to stay them up for the long afternoon service, while small soap-stones, drawn from the same capacious quarter, were re-heated for the cold drive home in the early winter dusk.

The light, weather-stained walls, patched and cracked, were brought into bold relief by the heavy mahogany pulpit and the really immense red damask curtain draped for a background. Whoever conceived and executed the plan of that end of the meeting house must have been fresh from a mince-pie-dream of Solomon's temple! The pulpit was so high the minister was obliged to chiefly infer the effect of his sermon from the tops of the heads and bonnets before him, to the exclusion of the more normal and favorable angles for sympathetic observation of human expression.

I have often wondered what became of all those ramparts of rich old mahogany forming the sides of the pulpit. The chairs I think are in the pulpit of the present college church. What became of that pulpit? I am not an idol worshipper, but that or any other pulpit must be a sacred thing, from which was preached a certain sermon by Dr. Swift of South Hadley, from the text, "I heard thy voice in the garden and was afraid." His pronounced spirituelle physique and solemn manner emphasized the supernatural awe of the text. Adam's apology—not then dissected by a short process of *reductio ad absurdam,* or through minute German scholarship pronounced a mere careless rejoinder—became, through his interpretation, the shrinking experience of every listening soul from the white ineffable, eternal God. There was left only a wide, cold planetary space, void of all save sin and its consequences at his close. The stillness and the sobs must have been mingled proof of the power and excitement of his impassioned delineation of his text. . . .

When Dr. Dwight, a nephew of President Dwight of Yale College, accepted a call to the church in 1850 on condition of a few practical changes, there was a slight softening modification in the revered old building. The concessions he begged were that the tin kettles hung from the long high stove pipes that ran from the stoves by the doors down the side aisles to the chimneys in the opposite walls—kettles set to catch the black creosote that dripped from the pipe joints—might be abolished by some ingenuity. And that the big iron catches on the front doors, of more than Eastlake boldness of design, be replaced by some device compelling less racket in the opening and closing. Also, that the hanging of some green baize doors be effected, to be drawn when "the house" as everybody called it then, was filling. Most people were, on the whole, not displeased with the changes. But one or two persons exclaimed against such iconoclasm, remarking in hope of repetition, that we were "getting most too refined!"

In his quiet way Dr. Dwight influenced the congregation to remain seated during the last hymn, instead of rising and turning round to face the choir, in which habit there seemed to be neither worship, ethics or esthetics. There was certainly little to see in our village choir. Only the men and women of one's daily round in farm or shop, some bald heads, and the tip top of Josiah Ayres' bass viol. There was no reason for the custom, but it was an old habit, and such things die hard in a New England village. They may be willing to die, but simply can't! There was a good deal of smiling among the youngsters the first Sunday it was tried, as the ice cracked under the new force. There was a little relaxing of muscles among the older Saints too, but Deacon Leland, and such men as Deacon Mack and Deacon Sweetser, who did not dare be "good and natural too," preserved their John Calvin sternness. Afterward, when a small organ had supplanted the bass viol, a large woman singer, by whom the accident of key was seldom noted, ruffled by some gentle suggestion as to harmony, left the choir to resume her place in her own family pew near the pulpit, always reserving to herself the right to turn and face her singing comrades of yore. This she continued to accomplish, in face of the entire congregation, till she passed on to heavenly choirs. The organ was resisted and deplored. It was pronounced "a step toward Romanism." It was called "a wicked outlay of money." Deacon Leland, although of musical repute, objected stoutly on the ground that "it made his wife's head ache!" And besides, the organist was a young and handsome girl. Sins easily outgrown! Later when Dr. Parkhurst was in college and took the place of organist, his strong sympathetic playing and skillful renderings converted all sorts of opposition to the new heavenly aid.

Even in those days of old fashioned conviction and conversion, sin must have lingered in the heart-corners of those good folks, breaking out into violent expressions not retailed as the fruits of the Spirit. A land boundary, that never-dying cause of quarrel and litigation, was the bottom cause of one most vivid happening I remember. The Deacon in the case was vindicated by law. It followed that the routed adversary was recommended to withdraw from the church, after certain inquisitory steps had been duly taken. On the following Sabbath, the sacrament of the Lord's Supper being served, he was accordingly passed by when the holy bread was offered, this being cruelly hard to bear, as the victorious Deacon was bearer of the denied plate. The victim was passed by. Everyone winced and waited. After the Deacons had tasted their share of the emblem, standing in a decorous row in front of the communion table, and sat down, there was a sudden sound of scuffling with a door. We were all buttoned into our pews with a strong brass button and the sides were too high for any escape save by thought. And then, terrible to relate, and more to see, the victim of his sin strode to the sacred table, clutched his bread and returned to his own pew, where with bowed head he ate the forbidden symbol. The wine was partaken of in the same manner. What a riot of emotions followed as we rose to sing,

> Blest be the tie that binds
> Our hearts in Christian love!

The saints were horrified. The very young folks, who all stayed to this service in those old days, were somewhat scared, but on the whole liked the variety in so solemn a season, and some few whose carnalities were not wholly over-come by grace, were obliged to cover their red and smiling faces in their hymn books. But the angels must have wept. Had our good old church never read the echo from Judea, "let them grow together till the harvest?"

Somehow there crept into the college life certain tendencies to modernism quite irrepressible. The most obvious of these was the decision of the graduating class of '74 to finish their year with a public ball! As I remember, those who were on the committee to accomplish this found it a difficult task and had a pretty tedious and trying time of it. Only a few of the men really wanted it, so besides all the practical details involved in putting it through, there was the haunting fear of final failure in charm and éclat. Palmer's hall, in the top of the small block where the town hall now stands, was scrubbed up for the event and in evening light, subdued by necessity of oil lamps, was quite festive in appearance with its rural decorations of daisies and evergreen.

When the evening came an interesting dinner party of men at our house caught the spirit of the wicked precedent about to be established, and insisted upon strolling up to over-look the dancing from the gallery that ran across the end of the hall. The young Seniors looked very attractive as they made the grand promenade, and I remember very distinctly that our present Congressman Gillett led, with the beautiful Miss Foote of New Haven, a niece of Reverend Dr. Jenkins. The ball grew merrier and less stiff as the hours grew small, till these novices must have been fully satisfied with their wicked experiment of the first ball ever given at Amherst College, and I think the first ever known in the village. As this happened also to be the night of the President's reception, is it strange that there were wonderings with aspersions cast on the distinguished men who failed to appear on that honorable occasion? And why not? Who would not lament the loss of such guests as Honorable Edward Gillett, Whitelaw Reid of the New York Tribune, Samuel Bowles of the Republican, Dr. Storrs of Brooklyn, and Judge Spofford of New Orleans? It was indeed a gallant row to be missed and longed for by any host. The year after, as no seismic convulsion followed this departure from venerable custom, there was another ball, and a few years later one given in College Hall, the former village church, with finer music and a little more of everything fascinating to youthful blood. There were even later hours—and so good bye to tradition!

It was relished as a funny happening at the time that the impressive portrait of Professor Tyler, hung over the stage to lend dignity to the Alumni dinner held earlier on the same day in the same place, was left by accident in its temporary place of honor, and proved to be the sole adornment of that end of the building, from which it stared benignly down upon the "pretty pairs" circling so madly in the waltz under his conservative gaze, literally lending his countenance to the whole festivity.

But why contrast our present with the older days, or why attempt to anticipate or fore-tell? . . . We cannot over-estimate this earth of ours, or fear as to how, or to what extent, the devices of coming man may mar it in the rolling years.

PART THREE

The Self-Conscious
Small Town
1900–1945

CHAPTER EIGHT

VERSIONS OF COMMUNITY

DORIS E. ABRAMSON
ROBERT C. TOWNSEND

Doris Abramson has lived in Amherst for most of her life and is a senior member of the Theater department at the University of Massachusetts. She wrote the sections of this essay on the town's attitudes towards the two black men, on Indians, and on Warren R. Brown and contributed other items and perspectives throughout.

Kim Townsend is a member of the English department at Amherst College. For a number of years he taught a course on Community in which students interviewed many Amherst residents about their lives, their occupations, and their sense of change in the town. This essay draws upon the research of many of those students as well as upon the independent inquiries of Professors Abramson and Townsend.

In the first issue of 1900, Charles Morehouse, editor of the *Amherst Record,* reflected on the previous year's events:

The mighty current of world and national events has hardly disturbed us in the little New England community we call home. Not that we are not alive to the importance of those happenings, but we are remote from the great disturbance, we are not in immediate contact with the disturbing force. But we have a little history of our own which, unimportant as it must appear to the outsider, means to us a great deal.

With a population of just over 5,000, Amherst was not, literally, a little New England community, or even town, but in his summary description Morehouse struck a note that would become characteristic of his and others' writings for years to come. Size was not so important, image was: out there, large and ill-defined forces, mighty currents, great disturbances; here in Amherst, a small community,

191

self-sufficient, strong in its own right, secure in its home. The image was attractive; the town imagined was one in which his readers could take pride and comfort.

It was not hard to make Amherst and its history seem little in this sense, especially in the earlier part of the century. Morehouse's January third issue has all the necessary ingredients. A few factories manufactured straw and palm goods, and in 1899 they had done (and here a note of wit) "a rushing business all season." The educational industry was still small. In that year 124 students entered Amherst College, forty the Massachusetts Agricultural College. A large and lovely ring of farms surrounded both—though they had not had so good a year—and beyond them the hills. It was Amherst's kind of politics as usual: "The business of the town has been conducted in safe and conservative fashion." "The churches and religious societies have carried on their work under favorable conditions." The street railways had petitioned to extend their lines that year. More citizens would have easier access to the center; outings to the Notch or Orient Springs in West Pelham would become possible. The townspeople could come or go off together more. And they would be able, literally, to see each other more: the gas company was being consulted about improved street lighting. Racial strife was unthinkable; in fact, a football game between representatives of the Hills Company and "our colored population proved so successful it will doubtless become an annual event." In the "Local News" column public and private events, social and commercial activities were reported one after another. There were no radical discontinuities; private lives were there for public consumption; in public no one was depersonalized. Professor H. P. Smith gave an informal dance at his home on Lessey Street; the Amherst Grange will install its recently elected officers at its next meeting; E. S. Wikbur has given up his work at the Amherst House and has entered the employ of Burnett and Sons; you can buy trunks and bags and dress-suit cases at less than cost at James F. Page's closing-out sale.

Amherst was set apart from the world, and within its confines, as Morehouse often said in his yearly summaries, no startling events occurred. The year 1908 could have been almost any year during the period: "Amherst as a town has gone along in its customary respectable and methodical way, with few experiences of interest to others than its citizens." There could be disturbing news, as Morehouse reported in his summary of 1899 when a seventeen-year-old South Amherst girl was murdered. Another year there was a fight and then a fatal shooting, in still another a "cutting affray." But the murder was the work of an Indian farmhand who then committed suicide; the fights were among "fellow countrymen," Italians or, more commonly, Poles. They and the events they caused seemed Other. Amherst—the real Amherst—was basically a peaceable kingdom.

It became more difficult, but for many years Morehouse and other writers could create the image of a small, respectable, idyllic Amherst. There was enough to go on. In thirty years the population increased by only 1,000; by 1945 it barely reached 7,000. As for the confusion of the 1912 election, say, or the Lawrence strikes of the same year, the suffragette movement in England or the impending conflict in Europe: "None of the happenings of large importance have touched Amherst very closely," Morehouse wrote in 1913. "The turkey we had Thanksgiving-day wasn't raised in Europe. Our suffragettes are quiet and peaceful." Wars would agitate the population and the Great Depression would be felt. After 1917 it was harder to think of Amherst as a place blissfully set apart, but the town was never "in immediate contact with the disturbing force."

Amherst took an interest in national politics, but it was not strongly influenced by fluctuations in national opinion: about 90 percent of those registered voted in presidential elections, but they voted Republican every single time. Voting Republican had always worked at the local level. As Lyman Thompson put it: "Small town like this, you take a good man, will hold his office year after year. Folks will vote for him. Course you know the rule when you're playing cards, 'Doubt lead trumps.' Come election time, if you don't know, vote Republican." So the town's voters supported McKinley by a five to one margin over Bryan, Taft by four to one. Harding received three times as many votes as Cox in 1920, Hoover had the same over Smith in 1928 and over Roosevelt in 1932. They supported Landon and Wilkie two to one. "They were staunch Republicans," Jean Elder remembers. "There was hardly a Democrat. Democrats were scarce as hen's teeth then. This was straight Republican—they just couldn't imagine anything but a Republican. . . . I suppose they thought Democrats were riffraff, and they didn't have riffraff in Amherst. It was years after I'd been out earning my living, for a long time, before I ever dared admit that I would vote Democrat. But it was just unheard of, at least in my circle."

In fiscal matters the town was equally conservative. By Morehouse's rendering, the country would go on overextending itself financially, spending more and saving less than it should, but throughout the years the town would conduct its business "in safe and conservative fashion." In the January third issue, for example, Morehouse reported that there had been talk of the need for a new high school building. In March he reproduced a plan to add on to the old one, but nothing was heard of the school's needs for three years. Then the town meeting voted to erect an entirely new building instead, only to refuse to appropriate the necessary funds at a special meeting a month later. Eight years after that nothing had been accomplished, and Morehouse concluded: "There doesn't seem any reasonable prospect of a solution of the high school problem for a good many years to come." Finally, in the fall of 1915, construction of a new building began, fifteen years after the need for space was first expressed. Similarly, the subject of the town's purchasing the Amherst Water Company was first broached in 1916, but it was not until 1941, after numerous exposures to town meeting, that the idea was realized.

It was in Amherst College, the college under George Harris at any rate (1899–1912), that one could see the ideals of the little community of Amherst most clearly and influentially embodied. Everyone looked up to "the college on the hill," and there "no great issues arose," Claude Fuess writes, "nor did anyone care to have them raised. . . . In [Harris's] hands the college was safe because it was stable." As was the case at the Massachusetts Agricultural College, athletics were gaining the prestige they have never lost, fraternity life was flourishing, and clubs grew up on the basis of every conceivable interest and hobby. Classroom activities did not intrude. Harris specifically said that the college aimed at producing gentlemen and not scholars:

The purpose is to turn out refined, honorable men. . . . The educated man is the all-round man, the symmetrical man. The one-sided man is not liberally educated. The aim of a college is not to make scholars. The aim is to make broad, cultivated men, physically sound, intellectually awake, socially refined, and gentlemanly, with appreciation of art, music, literature, and with sane, simple religion, all in proportion, not athletics [sic] simply, not scholars simply, not dilettantes, not society men, not pietists, but all-round men.

Harris himself exemplified his ideal. He was an immaculate, aristocratic, well-traveled man, his home as much of a cultural and social center as Amherst could boast. He was a theologian, but his theology was liberal, unobtrusive. His credo was not as fatuous as that of Bruce Barton who, as President of the student Christian Association, welcomed "any man who believes that God is always on the side of the right, that Amherst is the greatest college in the world, and who is trying to do the square thing by his fellows," but it too served essentially to create a sense of well-being in his all-round men. What he preached to his students was a doctrine of good works, an inclination, at least, to serve one's fellow men, but adherence to that ideal was not taxing. Some students worked in the boy's clubs in Amherst and the hill towns. One year others tried to set up night classes for foreigners. (When that failed Morehouse wrote: "There are many illiterate farmers in town but only a few of them show ambition to get an education.") Study groups read Rauschenbusch's *Christianity and Social Crisis,* but in a book on *Inequality and Progress* Harris himself argued that the former was the condition of the latter and that criticism of the status quo sprung from envy, so it is not surprising that what prevailed at Amherst College was mostly earnest and sincere talk about crises, that more than half of the students in Harris's time went on to business, and that under him the endowment doubled. Amherst students, like Amherst citizens, gave some attention to the great world outside, but like the townspeople, they did not worry overmuch. They were secure in their fraternal societies and in their relative prosperity. It was, one Professor Nitze wrote, "a Golden Age in American college life."

Morehouse projected the image of a small New England community onto the pages of his *Record,* and for a time the college seemed to be a rarified image of the same. One naturally suspects the accuracy of the image, but looking back, many Amherst residents have a similar picture in mind.

In idealizations of small New England towns, town meetings play a prominent part. Morehouse's praise of the system which supposedly provided each citizen with an equal voice in deciding how his community should function knew no limits: "There isn't any other institution like it in the world, and, come to think of it, nowhere in the world are there any other people like New Englanders." He would wax lyrical in describing an annual meeting: "From an early hour in the morning a constant procession of teams wended their way from the outlying districts toward the center village. . . ." But looking back, so do others:

We used to run a town meeting, instead of having a representative form of meeting like you got now. You'd have a town meeting, fourth of March I think it was. Vote in the morning for the town officers, and then in the afternoon they'd fill up the auditorium in the Town Hall for appropriations. Most everybody attended. Town meeting was like a big holiday really in town. Everybody could get up and express their views. No microphones, you'd just get up and start hollering.

And this man's brother agreed:

I think typically it was an all day affair, and the farmers drove in, the wives prepared a meal. They'd have a session in the morning and have a community meal together and then finish up in the afternoon and go home in time for chores.

As Morehouse reported, town meeting did little more than elect officials and approve a budget that increased yet remained, proportionately, the same year after year. But more than assure the town of its political stability, it reflected its social and domestic tranquility as well. The day was neatly split, everybody was there and spoke and was heard, political and domestic tasks were apportioned along traditional lines, and after having fulfilled his civic duties everyone returned to take care of his personal ones. In memory, the town meeting is proof that Amherst was united in its devotion to communal ideals.

In memory, the town was not crassly materialistic. It was no place for financiers or fortune hunters. Everyone made a living. In every issue of the *Record* the same businesses inserted their ads— Mason Dickinson's Grange Store, E. R. Bennett the Jeweller, E. M. Bolles's Shoe Store, C. R. Elder, Henry Adams's Drugstore—as much to remind readers of their existence, their place in the community, as to foist goods on them.

A former factory worker told of working seven to five, Monday through Saturday, getting paid by the number of hats she made. She earned about ten dollars a week, $7.20 of which went to her boardinghouse for room and board, but she never complained. She was proud of the living she was making: "You see, one thing us older people were brought up to believe, you shouldn't get anything unless you earn it." Warren Witt, head mechanic at the Hills factory, did not complain either, not then anyway:

In those days you got maybe $8 a week or if you were lucky $9 or $10 or $12, and it was just subsistence, nothing more than that. Some of us were paid by the hour, and if you were two minutes late they docked you 15. . . . It was slave labor, and the workers were slaves—I was one of them. But subsistence was all that anyone was getting so we learned to live with what we had because what else could we do?

There was no thought of getting ahead. Earning, really earning a living, had to be and was enough.

There was not much money in farming either, but here, more obviously and acceptably, making money was not the point. The point was that with a very little money and a few animals one could get by, be outdoors, share:

Some of the neighbors had a team of horses, made a living teaming horses when they weren't farming. Men didn't have to have a whole lot of cows in those days. It was ten, twelve cows, and you take a man now, can't make a living with a pair of horses like he used to. Other neighbors specialize in berries, began to have some small one-man orchards in South Amherst.

Everybody was well known in those days. Father used to be pretty well versed because of the garbage route. Neighbors used to swap work a little bit, you know, like filling silos, getting in ice.

There was no cutthroat competition, no competition of any sort. One swapped work, and if one got into trouble there were friends and neighbors, as Bill Ives relates:

When Mr. Schoomaker was down with something at the time his apple trees needed spraying, Mr. Atkins sent his crew over to do the spraying for several weeks. When Harold Wentworth had a heart attack at the start of haying season, the neighbors pitched in and did his haying that summer. No money was exchanged.

I've never helped a barn raising; I've helped several times in cleaning up. Take across the road here, the big place; lightning struck there one time and burned it. They had a big set of buildings there and burnt the barn. The lightning struck and it burned all of the barn down, and they put it out just at the end of the house. We went in there, we went in, I guess we worked a week with horses and dumpcarts, and some of the rest of us went in with shovels and cleaned up the debris so you could start building a new barn.

One time a fella over here, well went dry in the middle of the summer. He wanted town water. Well, the town said, you can have town water, but you better dig the ditch and lay the pipe. It was just about the end of haying time, and so the work slackened up a little bit and so farmers around, we went in there with men and horses, and plows, and dug a ditch, and the plowers came down and put the pipe in, and then they went back another day and covered it up for him, so he had water down there.

Friends and neighbors helped on the farm. In the harsher world of the factory they made life not only bearable but pleasurable. They came first. Talking to them, you drowned out the noise of the machines, and you escaped with them, no matter what the cost:

The noise from the machines was loud [Catherine Blodgett remembers], but we could always talk over it. Oh, did we talk—you could walk by the hat factory when it was running, and you could hear the din of people talking. We'd tell jokes, stories to each other and have a real good time. We used to fool around a good bit. I remember one morning it was real nice out so we took off and went for a walk—of course we didn't get any pay that morning but when you know you're never going to have much you don't mind missing a little sometimes. I wasn't like that as much as some of them, though. There were quite a few of them who didn't really care how much time they missed so long as they kept going. It was, as I said, the other girls that made the job fun. We used to have a lot of fun, the group of us. We were always taking walks, that was a big thing.

Working at the Knickerbocker Leather and Novelty Co. one woman tells of allegiances that have lasted up to the present day. Out of the monotony of work that her narration emulates, there arose these relationships:

Quite a lot of machines there. I worked on a sewing machine. It was a branch from New York, and our boss informed us that there was a big order coming and that it was going to be black leather bags to hold safety razors and they can't do them in New York so they sent them up here to see if we can do them. Well, so many girls got sore fingers, the leather was so stiff and you had to turn that leather over and get it under the foot of your machine to sew it and I got, look, two crooked fingers bending that over, so I have arthritis in my fingers now, very hard work. Another girl cried one day. She was a young girl and I felt sorry for her. See her all the time on the street now, and she rides a bike. So, she had her fingers bleeding—they had to turn them over, I forgot what they done with them because somebody else put the snaps on, and so on and so on, but we had to fold them over and hold them together and put them under the foot of the machine and stick them. The stiffest hardest leather and they couldn't do it in New York and they sent it to us. When I first was working there it was I think twelve dollars a week.

The boss, the head man, Mr. McCarty, was lovely, he was a lovely man. Then he died, and he was so nice, but the foreman, he was then the boss, he wasn't. And when he picked on some of the girls and everything else, and he'd keep at them and keep at them, and I'd just told him once, two, three times, I told him I says "Stop picking on them," I says. "It isn't their fault." He blamed a deaf and dumb girl. I saw her yesterday. I was so kind to her in there and stuck up for her, and she couldn't talk but she'd make a noise when she'd want to say something to the boss when he was blaming her for the bad work she stitched. I knew who it was, but it wasn't up to me to tell him who it was, it was up to him to find out. . . . He'd have looked at everybody's work. And you know, everytime she sees me she pulls me nearer, and she kisses me. She's so grateful. I felt sorry for her. He was blaming her, so I says, "Look here, don't blame her," I says. "It's up to you to find out." Well, I know all the time but I wouldn't squeal on the other ladies.

In the Amherst of many recollections, time seems so well spent. Drudgery it may have been, but in thinking back canning, bread, or ice cream making or just dressing seem enjoyable:

We had so many clothes to wear at one time. My mother was always ironing and starching my petticoats. If you could see an outline or touch a leg, you had to put on still another petticoat. We had corsets, too, that laced up with steel wires around them. Underneath them we wore a shirt, and a corset slip. Bloomers were tied to the waist along with the petticoat. We also had a sticky tape which we glued to the hems of all our skirts so that as we walked the skirt would stick to our shoes and not drag in mud or snow. They still did and only tangled our feet in folds of sticky material, making girls stumble all over the place. So you know that even dressing took a much longer time after all that. Everything took more time, and everything was necessary.

It took days to prepare for a party, and the preparation seems to have been as engrossing and as challenging as the party itself:

We had parties, too, although not as often, and ate doughnuts and drank hot chocolate. It took a lot of preparation, but parties were fun, and we were always thinking of games to play. Once I remember I cut out the shapes of all the states and pinned them on the walls around the parlor. I numbered them, and everyone had to walk around and write the names of each they knew. Some didn't know too many actually, and the one who knew all of them won. We always had to think of games such as that. We had coffees and teas, too, but usually hot chocolate was better, as far as I could see.

Catherine Blodgett could afford little more than a walk, but the pleasures of wealthier girls were almost as simple, in large part because of parental strictness. Katherine Cowles was taught "ethics and social codes" by her parents. "Read any book of etiquette and you'll find me right there!"

There were not many things one could do with their leisure around Amherst. Or should I correct myself to say that there were not many things that I was allowed to do. When the winter came, wherever there were hills, you could rest assured that my girlfriends and I went down them on our little sleighs. Also as a child and as a young lady my friends and I used to ice skate on Pratt Football Field. Sometimes my girlfriends and I would walk up past the center to catch a ride on the barges, carrying lumber to the lumberyard. The lumberman never objected. He knew us. The trolleys were always fun. On those terribly hot, humid summer nights when the air was still, we could always depend on the trolleys to shower us with cool, refreshing air.

Katherine was not allowed to go on sleigh rides with boys "because father thought that sitting snuggled up against the opposite sex was promiscuous." He need not have worried. Those who were allowed to go were models of good behavior. Mildred White went to church socials and went sleigh riding:

I went with a boy once who had a pair of horses. He'd take me sleigh riding in the wintertime, me with a heated stone at my feet and a muff for my hands to keep me warm. After the ride we'd go inside and have a cocoa and pears. But we really didn't go out much.

Sally Sheppard was a sophomore in high school before she was alone with a young man:

There was a grove of trees outside Amherst where there were a good number of natural springs and a candy store, and once that year a boy in my class walked out to the house and asked me if I wanted to go and get some candy. I said I did, and was telling my mother about it and asking if I could go, and I remember she said that she and father thought it would be a good idea if I was home by dusk. They never mentioned it again, but I did always come home just before dusk.

Peering through the haze of years, it seems that life really was better then. The pace was slower, the rules were clear, pleasures were simpler and more easily come by, people were closer to each other. No one depended on gadgetry and expense, on keeping up with or getting ahead of others. Out of the simple chores and settings at hand they seemed to be able to find activities and relationships that passed the time and passed it richly. Even Marion Fisher, who made nine dollars a week in 1909 for fifty-eight hours of work and who spent a good deal of her time killing cockroaches in her family's apartment above one of the town's two Chinese laundries, prefers the past:

Now I'm not saying we were all-privileged, Lord help us. People were damn mean about a lot of things. But I think people were more friendly years ago. Like you'd go outdoors, and you'd hang up your clothes, and your neighbor would be talking, but now they go to their washers and everything and that neighborliness is all gone now.

Another woman looks back with even more regret:

People were concerned and involved in other people's lives. They were there to help you, to take you in and comfort you when you most needed it. They acted in love and faith and cooperation. But today people are too busy with themselves to even cast you a friendly smile as they rush down the sidewalk attending to their business. I think back to the times when I was younger, before the war and the loss of the last of my family and how people used to be so friendly to you, when they knew your name and asked how you were. Today people greet one another—if they bother to at all— with hardly more than a mechanical toot on their car horns as they race past each other on the street.

And who does not seek love and faith and cooperation? If there was an Amherst—or in this case South Amherst—such as Bill Ives here describes, who can blame Morehouse for celebrating it or average residents for looking back on it longingly?

If a person had a fire and burned down a barn, why they all got together and had what they called a barn raising, and they would build a barn for him. If a neighbor died, why they'd get around and take up a collection, buy flowers, or help him out. The woman folks would get together and bake and make sandwiches and so forth to feed the people who came to the funeral. We also took up a collection if anyone died on this street. They'd go a mile or so each side of the person that died taking up a collection, and if it happened to be at the wrong time of the year and you didn't have much money, if you didn't have more than ten cents, then you put it in. Everything was appreciated.

Everybody used to burn wood in the stove, and so you got up in the morning, and you looked and didn't see smoke coming out of somebody's chimney, why immediately somebody went there to find out why there wasn't smoke coming out of the chimney. That was generally the first thing people did in the morning when they got up, they started looking around and see if the smoke was coming out of the neighbor's chimney, see if the neighbor was all right. The minute you didn't see a house that wasn't smoke coming out of the chimney, why you paddled right off to find out why there wasn't smoke coming.

In 1920 Morehouse wrote on "The Community Spirit," saying: "Amherst is a live town. Whatever community spirit is, this one is alive." He said that there was more cooperation than there had been a generation ago, that the trolleys had put an end to sectionalism, that cooperation between the college and the town had increased. Listening to his and other voices from the past, one tends to believe that there was such a thing as community spirit. Certainly one wants to. Whatever community spirit is, it involves commitment to others on the basis of something other than contractual agreement; it involves a sense of oneself and of others as more than economic or physical beings; it involves a commitment to something beyond the personal in the light of which differences can be resolved; and it involves maintaining and experiencing this commitment over an extended period of time. If there was a sharing of political responsibility, a downplaying of economic ties in favor of richer relationships among individuals, if there was such order and stability and good fellowship, then Amherst may indeed have been an ideal little New England community.

One wants to believe this. The more unlikely it is that community spirit can be created or maintained the more one yearns for it. Having so little experience of communal life ourselves, we in the present would love to know it was once available. But even when Morehouse started to praise Amherst as a community, signs that a community existed were fading. Trolley traffic was decreasing. In 1924 Morehouse warned: "The public has gotten used to the trolleys, would hate to do without them, but it must patronize them or they will vanish." By 1932 they had, replaced by smaller machines that enclosed and carried many fewer people, people usually bound by ties no more extended than those of a family. In 1927 the Central Vermont Railroad passed into the hands of receivers, and Morehouse wrote:

Gone are the days when the road carried passengers by the hundred on excursions to New London, thence by boat to Watch Hill and Block Island, when thousands were carried to the Valley fair at Brattleboro, the cattle shows at Stafford Springs and Belchertown, the Saturday night festivities at Lake Pleasant. Those were brave days and nights, that some have not yet forgotten.

In 1920 Morehouse began a campaign to encourage townspeople to ignore mail order houses and to buy at home, to patronize local businesses, but in his pages out-of-town merchants were already taking out the largest ads. Town meeting attendance declined, and when a representative form of government was proposed the *Record* supported the idea enthusiastically. In 1929 and again in 1930 Morehouse wrote passionately about what he thought was an increasing lawlessness in town, petty thievery, insulting female passers-by, gangs of toughs destroying property: "The keynote of the new freedom is an utter selfishness. When it wants anything it goes after it, regardless of ownership or consequences. Its motto is, What the hell do we care?" The *Record* itself, after Morehouse's death in 1933, made a sad attempt to speak for the community. The "Local News" column was replaced by a "Tid-Bits" and then by a kind of "Talk of the Town" that was intended to be a "community round table" but carried notes about Mrs. Churchill's garden and W. R. Brown's fishing or asked, "Where's Doc Nugent been lately? He hasn't cadged a cigarette from us since the library froze over," and only showed that there was no longer a voice that could even pretend to speak for Amherst.

The *Record* tried to name a spirit and then to scold or coax it into existence. Looking at the present, Marion Fisher and others can point nostalgically to a friendlier time. But the fact is that in this century Amherst has always been too big, too diverse to support intense community spirit; no belief or ritual or activity could bring all its citizens together. "I can't think of any real project or goal or idea that carried the town successfully," Harold Elder said, "any project that everybody would get behind. I can't think what it might have been." Amherst never was Oneida or a Shaker Village or a kibbutz or a commune and never aspired to be. At best it was a large town made up of small communities tolerant, or ignorant, of each other.

A couple of times adverse circumstances may have led the people of Amherst to believe that there was something more compelling in their lives than their work, their particular church or organization, their families or their selves. The Hurricane of '38, for example.

Walter Dyer may have been right when he wrote in the *Record:*

The spirit of the people has been an inspiration. Nature's catastrophes bring us close together in friendliness and neighborliness, and we are much the gainers because of it. Many a person during the past two weeks has had the pleasure of doing a neighborly act to people who had never before been in need, and many another has had his heart warmed because of some unexpected kindness rendered.

There may have been similar feelings two years before when the Connecticut flowed over Hadley and Sunderland, and a thousand refugees were brought into town.

When Amherst had entered the Great War, it certainly sounded united. When the first home boys were drafted, Madame Bianchi asked on behalf of the Red Cross:

Is Amherst worth fighting for? Is Amherst worth dying for? This is what it amounts to now. Is Amherst, our own home town, the part of all united America we know best, worth dying for?

"No offering is too precious for the altar of our country," Morehouse wrote. About 375 townspeople served, and eleven died, while at home a Safety Committee was set up to insure and increase food resources, relief funds were established, nearly two million dollars worth of Liberty Bonds were sold, German was banned from the school curriculum, and a lot of knitting was done. ("I remember the First World War as mostly socks," one woman said.) But for all their good intentions, Amherst people could not be thrown together as a community. They were too far from the disturbing forces, even from the Great Depression.

Between 1928 and 1932 the town's welfare bill went from five to twenty thousand dollars, and all town employees took between a 5 and 10 percent salary cut. When Winifred Cowles went in to offer the bank his farm because he could not meet a payment, he was told they already had too many farms left to them. The Depression, like the war, had its effects, but by then Amherst's industry was education and, as the *Record* said in reference to the State College:

A state-supported institution in the town is probably the safest asset a town can possibly have. It is only slightly affected by depression, brings into town an enormous purchasing power. It is almost the exact opposite of a factory which may fail and throw hundreds of employees on the relief rolls of the town. . . . Amherst has barely felt the depression because of the steady income enjoyed through college employees and students.

Amherst was safe, safely apart and relatively safe within. It was a town made up of factory workers and farmers and educators, foreign and native born, black and white, permanent and transient residents out of which a community might be imagined but which was in fact cut up into very distinct units.

To Harold Elder the town was a three-ring circus:

I've always felt the structure of Amherst was like a three-ring circus: the two colleges and the town. I've always sensed that people were so busy doing what they had to do that they tend to revolve in their own orbits. My feeling's been that Amherst College has always felt superior to the University, and maybe rightly so, over the years. Amherst College always, in our time anyway, had status and was influential and all that sort of thing. So that they were right, I think, to feel that they had some superiority. But aside from this factor that you had these three rings, I don't think there was any kind of antagonism.

Of course there were more than three, but the point is that no matter how many there were, everyone just went around in his or her circle. Nobody remembers any antagonism. There was the college, always the college at the top, but, according to Sally Sheppard:

People didn't go up to the college much at all that I can remember. They never publicized lecturers who were speaking for the general public's benefit, if they ever had any, that is. No one felt any need or want to go up there, and I doubt if anyone felt welcome—it was a private, a classically private college. There was little mixing between the townspeople and faculty socially. I would say that the faculty of Amherst College was a very tightly knit community in itself, at least as much so as was the black population of the town. And there was, if anything, much more distinction between faculty and factory workers than between the townspeople and the colored in many ways.

Sometimes the lines are subtly drawn but are no less sharp for that.

The impossibility of there being any contact between the factory and academic worlds is clear in Catherine Blodgett's recollection: "One of the things we used to do was go watch the girls from Smith and Mt. Holyoke come over on the trolley for their dates all decked out." It is fairly clear in Lyman Thompson's version of town meeting:

They'd vote in the morning, and then in the afternoon they'd have the town meeting, and everybody who was interested in it, and almost everybody was, would come. One farmer down below, he wasn't too good with his speaking abilities, the professors thought he sounded kind of funny. In those days, the farmers in South Amherst used to go to the town meeting, speak on different problems, keep the old college professors in line a little bit. The farmers, they wanted to keep taxes down. You don't think a man in South Amherst wanted to build a sewer way up in North Amherst when he didn't have any down his way, do you? Raising taxes. They didn't want school too fancy for what they thought they could afford. A lot of people at the meeting, they didn't have to pay taxes directly, lived in college-owned housing. They used to want gold-plated schools, the farmers didn't want them gold-plated.

Along later in the evening, after the farmers would have to go home to milk the cows and so forth, after that, some of the big, some of the people from the town, they didn't have any chores, want to bring the articles up again, put it back up, after the farmers who'd voted against it had gone home.

Had to vote with a paper ballot, a yes or no ballot, and that would take a long time with some of those things. Town Hall used to be full, course, town got too big for that, so they got this modern town meeting form of government. I didn't approve of it myself, just a way for the college people to get rid of the farmers. Some of the farmers were laughed at when they took the stand and got up to speak on an article, the farmers they wouldn't be used to public speaking much. The professors, they let them talk, but they thought it was funny.

Recalling earlier accounts, one might be tempted to argue that differences were worked out in town meeting, that conflicts were resolved and that an enriched sense of community emerged, but that is not what Thompson is describing. He is describing a process of exclusion that has resulted in there being few farms in Amherst at the present time. If a community was evolving, it gained strength as it excluded. Even Morehouse could become impatient with the divisions: "It is a fair proposal that one half of the people in Amherst do not know how the other half works," he wrote in 1924. "Some of the hardest workers are regarded as idlers by the unknowing."

Sometimes the lines were obscured for a while. Several people think back to their school days, when they studied with people of different backgrounds: "In this town it was different than being in a big city, cause you see, a colored fellow, you know, see him in school, and the Jewish. . . ." Marion Fisher used to play with a factory owner's daughter. But after school all that changed. The economic and social differences between Marion and the boss's daughter soon put an end to that friendship. One girl was nice in school, but her religion disqualified her: "She was a Catholic and didn't live in the neighborhood, so she didn't get invited much to parties." Another man would not say "that there was *no* association" between Catholics and Protestants, "because, say in our school circles, there were bound to be Catholics, and this didn't trouble us too much. But if anybody had suggested any kind of an ecumenical service amongst all of us, it was out of the question."

Towards blacks there seems to have been not so much prejudice as downright indifference. That football game between representatives of the Hills Company and "our colored population" did not become an annual event: another factory fielded a team the next year, then bachelors played married men. By the same token, there was contact in school, but after school the blacks returned to "Nigger Heaven." "No, there was little prejudice—no problem at all. There was just a separation then that was complete." Three others remember it the same way.

We weren't scared of the coloreds. They were just different, you know? We never had any trouble with the colored people, down Northampton Road and Snell Street. That used to be called Nigger Heaven.

There was a small number of black families here in town, and I believe that most of them came here as servants in some category or another. And we didn't—I think we were like everybody else. We didn't dislike Negroes, but we didn't associate with them. I'm sure these people were just about a 100 percent ignored, although this brings to mind there were on the football team at least two blacks and maybe three. I don't think we disliked them, we kind of admired them, but after they got off the football field, I don't believe that we had one iota to do with them.

They were treated with, I think with stiff kindness, but they stayed in their place. I'm afraid in Amherst there was a bit of a barway there. It wasn't violence really, it was just a bit of indifference to hobnob, just as we didn't hobnob with the Slavic people. They never worked in stores except, perhaps, as janitors. They rode the trolley, of course, but I don't know that we would sit with them, though we should have for we went to school with them.

Nigger Heaven was really in behind the golf links, but it included Hazel Avenue and part of Snell Street. I would say some evenings years ago, two things would have happened on a warm spring day. With the wind coming from the south we'd have heard accordians playing Polish folk songs and dance. There were backyard picnics, you see, and maybe a fiddle but definitely an accordion. And on a west wind day, say in June, some evening over the hill came spirituals in part harmony.

There was a black community. It was cut off, but it was there, and it had been there for a long time.

To look at documents of the period brings one closer to the black experience, but it serves also to sharpen one's awareness of black exclusion from white society. In Amherst in 1902 two black men had their stories told for them by local white writers, to such different ends that it is worth looking at the accounts to try to discover what we can about white guessing at black at the turn of the century. One of the men was Charles Thompson, eighty-two years old, the subject of a little book called *Prof. Charley* by A. E. L. (identified on the title page as daughter of the Rev. William A. Stearns, D.D., late president of Amherst College). The other, Henry Jackson, was dead at eighty-three and being honored in *The Amherst Record* with a front-page obituary signed C. O. P. (Charles O. Parmenter). These two men must have known each other, being the same age and black. In this small town their paths surely crossed frequently. Neither of these accounts, nor any other available to us at the moment, tells us anything about that probability. The two pieces do tell us a great deal about the authors and their town on the brink of the twentieth century. The pull of one piece is toward the nineteenth, the other toward the twentieth century.

A. E. L.'s sketch of Charles Thompson, commonly (and, we are told, affectionately) known as Prof. Charley, was designed to get help for an old black man who had for the past forty years been janitor or handyman on the Amherst College campus. The author's tone is patronizing, but the purpose of the book is to patronize, to benefit Charley. She writes to remind Amherst alumni of a debt owed to a man who was part of their daily life during their college years.

It is to Charley's "boys" that the following sketch is written, by one who has always known and loved him, with the hope that for his faithful work in the past he may, with their help, be kept from the Almshouse.

Long before pension plans and retirement benefits, an appeal has to be made to charitable impulses. A. E. L. suggests that, having shoveled walks and tended boilers, having made fires and swept halls, Charley has a claim upon those he has served.

She tells his story from the special perspective of one who as a child and young woman knew him in her home, first in Boston, then in Amherst.

Charles Thompson was born in Portland, Maine. It was in December, 1838, when he was about fifteen years old, that he came to live with my father. It was at the height of the abolition excitement. My father had given some offense by refusing to countenance the extreme measures that were generally desired. Nevertheless, when the leading abolitionists were unwilling to keep the boy, he took him in and made him one of his family.

Who those leading abolitionists were and what opportunity they were given to help the boy we never learn. We do hear her father's words:

I said: "Send the colored boy to me, and we will see what next." In about half an hour Charley came in. His clothing was scant and in a very dilapidated condition. We looked him over, talked with, liked him, and concluded to keep him.

There follow sentimentalized stories of Charley's youth within the Stearns's household, of his brief career as a fireman in Cambridge, and of the decision to send him to sea—a decision made by the Reverend Stearns, who "must have felt that his companions were not altogether desirable ones, and that my brothers would now be better with friends of their own age and station." By the time Charley returned to the household after three long voyages around the world on a whaling ship, his beloved Mr. Stearns was president of Amherst College.

Many instances are cited of the black servant's devotion to the Stearns family. When Frazer Stearns fell in battle in 1862, it was Charley who was "sent to attend to everything needful" and who "sat up all night in the cold hall of the library, 'so he shouldn't be left alone.'" It was Charley who walked at the head of the long procession when relays of students carried President Stearns' casket in 1876.

The details of these and other stories in this little book are affecting, well chosen to arouse the sympathy of white readers who had it within their power to help Charley in his old age. That help is needed, we learn, because he has spent all his savings to pay debts incurred when his wife Eliza (described as an attractive mulatto woman who faithfully attended the college church with him) was ill with a "sickness worse than death," namely, insanity.

Anyone who has read *Uncle Tom's Cabin* or the special pleadings

CHARLES THOMPSON (PROF. CHARLEY).

of nineteenth century missionary tracts recognizes the kind of book that *Prof. Charley* is. It is possible to accept, even in our seemingly enlightened period, the use of pietistic sentimentality for a good cause. It is impossible, however, for us to read the penultimate paragraph of this book without wincing. After telling of Charley's loving care of Eliza and of his present condition, A. E. L. speculates:

Perhaps it would have been wiser if he had allowed her to be taken to an asylum and cared for there. But Charley was not wise. It is a "happy-go-lucky" race, and if it has bread for to-day, it seldom takes thought for the morrow.

If we are startled to come upon this generalization, it is only because we have forgotten that side of the nineteenth century's view of "the negro race." The picture of Charley is complete only when we know that in addition to being hard-working, devoted, and simple, he is also happy-go-lucky—not thrifty like the sensible men whose charity can give him a home for "a few years longer."

It would be interesting to know Charles Thompson's view of himself and of Amherst, what he thought about the patronage he enjoyed or endured (perhaps both) in order to survive. We have only the words of a white woman who knew him and loved him but could not really speak for him. In the case of Henry Jackson, his contemporary, we have a more detailed account of his life, again from the pens of others, but without the attendant air of condescension.

Henry Jackson's obituary in the *Amherst Record* of January 29, 1902 was three full columns long, beginning on page 1 and continued to page 8, the back page of the newspaper. It replaced the usual columns for those pages, "Concerning Passing Events." The obituary's title was "An Honored Citizen Dead," and a photoengraving of the black man was the only picture on the front page. The engraving, taken from a photograph made in C. R. Kenfield's Palmer studio, is the same one used on his business cards which announced, "Henry Jackson/Truckman/Amherst, Mass./Orders Solicited." The tribute to Jackson was written by Charles O. Parmenter, the Pelham historian. It was a careful consideration of this black man's contributions to Amherst. It begins:

By the death of Henry Jackson on last Wednesday evening the town loses one of its oldest and one of its most respected citizens; one who held the

HENRY JACKSON,

TRUCKMAN,

AMHERST, MASS.

ORDERS SOLICITED.

HENRY JACKSON.

respect and esteem of the business men for a long term of years. Henry Jackson was born at North Amherst in 1818, being 83 years old in October last as he informed the writer, though many believed him many years older. After coming to this part of Amherst to live, he attended school at East Amherst during the winter for several terms being obliged to work the rest of the year, but he picked up education in this way that was of great assistance to him in his long business career.

During the old staging days when Sheriff Henry Frink was interested in stage lines he worked in the stables caring for horses, and later started for himself as a teamster and freight handler for the merchants and business men of the town and vicinity, beginning the work long before there was any railroad in town, hauling goods from Springfield, Northampton, Millers Falls, and other places for the merchants, and taking palm leaf hats and other finished manufactured products to the various points for shipment upon trains to market. For more than 60 years up to the time of his death he had drawn the freight for certain stores during all the changes of proprietors. Mr. Jackson also did a large part of the banking business for Amherst people for many years before there was any bank nearer than Northampton or Greenfield, when large sums of money were entrusted to his keeping with orders to make deposits, obtain checks and drafts for the business men of the town, and there never was a dollar lost or unaccounted for during his long career.

Claiming that "any account of Henry Jackson's life would not be complete without the story of his connection with the abduction of Angeline Palmer in 1840," Parmenter recounts in detail the story of Henry Jackson, William Jennings, and Lewis Frazier—"young, active, athletic colored men of Amherst"—who prevented Angeline Palmer's being sold into slavery by the Shaw family with whom she was living in Belchertown. The three men had to kidnap the "active colored girl 10 or 12 years of age" in order to save her. When brought to court on charges of abduction (Angeline had been spirited away to a trusted black family in Colrain), the men declined to state her whereabouts and were sentenced to three months in the county jail in Northampton. Parmenter makes it clear that they had the support of the community, though that community could not save them from serving time. Perhaps these observations show best why the story is included in Jackson's obituary:

To have saved a fellow being from the possibility of being sold into slavery as they believed they had done, was their sufficient reward; and when they came from the jail in June, 1841, they were met by the congratulations of all classes, coupled with commendations for their display of pluck in taking Angeline from possible harm to a safe place, and for resisting in a manly way all overtures that might restore her to those from whom they had taken her. It is more than 60 years since the occurrence above related took place; the court, the jury, the jailer, the sheriffs and all connected with the so-called abduction have passed on and are at rest, Henry Jackson being the last, and no one is left to tell the story of Angeline Palmer's escape from possible enslavement. Mr. Jackson's long career in the capacity of a public servant of the business and professional men of the town gave an opportunity for an extended and personal acquaintance with all of the prominent men that have lived and moved and had their being in town for two generations or more, he knew them all, and all knew him.

Parmenter's account ends with a description of the well-attended funeral at which the Reverend John F. Genung, Amherst's distinguished professor of rhetoric, officiated, and at which he read lines from William Cullen Bryant, ending: "For when his hand grew palsied, and his eye/ Dark with the mists of age, it was his time to die."

The editor of *The Amherst Record* ended his note on the death of Henry Jackson, "the patriarch of [Amherst's] colored population," with: "He was a negro, but a whiter man than Henry Jackson ne'er drew breath." Here is the almost obligatory condescension that Parmenter happily avoided.

A touring company presented *Uncle Tom's Cabin* at the Amherst town hall the very evening on which Henry Jackson died. The company was advertised as "one of the largest organizations of white and colored artists ever gathered together in one combination." In the advance publicity references were made to the thrilling floating ice scene and the plantation by moonlight, "genuine Siberian bloodhounds," trick donkeys, and Shetland ponies. Amherst was treated in the morning to a free street parade with two bands, chariots, and tableaux. On page 4 of the paper that contained tributes to Jackson was the statement that "Stetson's *Uncle Tom's Cabin* Company attracted, as usual, a large audience to the town hall last Wednesday evening. The entertainment was of the time-honored kind and was well received."

It is not difficult to find racial ironies in a small-town newspaper. Dr. Charles A. Eastman (Ohiyesa until he took his maternal grandfather's name), a Sioux Indian who made his home in Amherst for

CHARLES EASTMAN (OHIYESA).

the first two decades of this century, published his first book, *Indian Boyhood,* in 1902. There were many more to follow, most of them on the subject of the strength and wisdom of his people. Two years earlier, in the April 11, 1900 issue of the *Record,* there had been a front-page headline, "The Red Men In Amherst." The occasion for the article that followed was the founding of a fraternal group, the Improved Order of Red Men. It is difficult to imagine what went through Charles Eastman's mind if he ever read the article. Of the red men (not once called Indians) who 150 years earlier had "possessed all rights of original residence and ownership in Amherst and neighboring communities," the journalist says that they were "not held in very high repute by the palefaces who had come to settle in their midst, and, in one way and another secure possession of their heritage." Not only does he call the red men "ignorant, lazy, with little moral sense," but he charges that civilization brought to the surface all that was "selfish, cruel and barbarous" in these original residents.

Then, just before the announcement of the formation of a lodge to perpetuate "all that is best and noblest in the history and traditions of the aboriginal inhabitants of America," there is this statement about them: "The primitive red men have departed from the Connecticut Valley, gone to the happy hunting grounds where game is ever plentiful and labor there is none." Now, in 1900, in place of the primitives will be the Improved Order of Red Men. In March Norwottuck Tribe No. 128 had been instituted in Amherst, with sixty-six names on the charter list.

Patriotic and fraternal and historical societies abounded, so many that Morehouse used to report about their doings with impatience:

For some reason unknown and entirely unregretted, the year 1913 brought no new additions to the long list of society organizations in the town. The fact seems to be that Amherst is about as fully organized today as the inhabitants can stand and any further attempt to add to the list must, to be successful, show reasons far out of the ordinary.

In the tercentenary parade in 1930 the American Legion, the Disabled Veterans, the Sons of Union Veterans, the D.A.R. marched. There were Scouts and the Norwottuck Tribe of the I.O.R.M., the Daughters of Pocahontas and the Order of the Eastern Star, the Massachusetts Catholic Order of Foresters, the Pacific Lodge A.F.

and A.M., and many more. And in each of these one can imagine something that could be called communal spirit, some life in which people were committed to each other and to a common sense of purpose. But of course each served too to cut off its members from others in town—as did the churches, the neighborhoods, and the educational institutions. With some justification one can speak of South Amherst as a community, South Amherst with its economic life focussed on its own farmland, its social and religious life centered in the Congregational Church; but in Amherst at large, people went to their churches and their organizations, and the lines did not usually cross. Whites did not go to that church, blacks did not join that club, faculty did not go to one church or join another club, people from one neighborhood seldom went to church in another.

Most people, I think, went in to church and then felt better when they came out in Amherst. I did, and there were other ways to socialize than through solely the church. There were the Women's and Men's clubs in Amherst and the Masons—many groups like that. They pulled the town together the same way that the churches did. You see, there were so many churches that they divided the town into almost smaller towns of one denomination.

And who would have thought otherwise? As we have seen—and will go on to see—many have, if not with good reason, *for* good reasons. Amherst was a relatively small town; it did retain the town meeting form of government; it did not have extremes of wealth or poverty; the life in it did seem to be lived in the light of higher ideals—work with nature, work with books, caring for others. There were many who lived in it or who came to it (and they were not necessarily academics) because it seemed to hold out the responsibility of realizing the virtues of communal life. It even inspired some to imagine a whole country dedicated to communal ideals.

No one expressed this catalytic power of Amherst better than the proletarian novelist Mary Heaton Vorse. Looking back on her youth in Amherst at the end of the nineteenth century, she saw its idyllic qualities but she did not, as did so many, overlook the life-denying aspects of what was idyllic. Her father had retired to Amherst to read and tend his garden. Her mother had a social conscience, and

life, she felt, should be everywhere as it was in Amherst, where poverty was an accident and great fortunes unknown. We lived so far from industry that we didn't know the industrial revolution had happened. Yet within a few miles of us were the manufacturing towns of Holyoke, Chicopee, and Springfield. Chicopee had and still has one of the worst infant death rates of the country. There was overcrowding; there was frightful poverty; social conditions were bad.

We in Amherst knew so little about these things that we might have been the original dwellers in the garden of Eden. We sat on our shady porches, reading indignantly about the suffering of the Siberian exiles. Almost everyone voted the Republican ticket, went to the Congregational or the Episcopal church. Life was removed from the great forces that were forging America in workshops and steel mills. It was a little like living without the knowledge that there was such a thing as pain or death.

Writing in 1935, Mary Heaton Vorse noted a great difference: Amherst now "discusses these social problems and asks to know about them. Today Amherst studies conditions in Holyoke and Chicopee." And they did, a little. But even if they did not, Amherst was a place where such conditions and their causes were contemplated and where means for improving them were considered:

If in Amherst we knew nothing about the conditions under which cloth was woven or coal or steel made, yet it was in the quiet of Amherst that my mind was prepared for thought. Like many New England families of that day, we combined a speculative and inquiring habit of mind with a conservative manner of living. My early training taught me not to fear the "pain of a new idea." It gave me the inclination toward a questioning and scientific attitude of mind. It taught me to value life and to hate injustice; to prefer warmth and simplicity in human relations to intellectual attainments. . . . There was a lively interest in thought everywhere. It was the prelude toward a wide questioning of a system which placed profits above people.

And this was not because she attended one of the colleges. She did not. By the time of her writing Amherst was a college town but her final tribute is to Amherst people generally. "Amherst bred people of personality and character. They had a precious quality, hard to grasp, which we call American: simplicity and candor combined with shrewdness and integrity."

Mary Heaton Vorse describes the most that one can ask of Amherst thinkers and talkers and writers about their own and America's social conditions. Amherst would always be removed from the worst, even from very bad, social conditions, but the best observers in town were those who would not overlook the less than

Utopian conditions of their own surroundings and those who, if they chose to contemplate a larger social situation, would not confuse it with their own relatively simple one at home. We have seen and heard many people on Amherst itself and tried to understand what kind of community they imagined they lived in. It remains to examine the work of several men who considered Amherst and, in the light of what they saw, tried to envision a better social order for the country as a whole.

Poets might but in this case they do not count. They seldom turned their attention to Amherst itself. If David Morton had Amherst in mind in "New England Summer" or "Petrified Idyl" or "To the Hill Back of Town," one would never know it, so ethereal are his lines:

> On this green acre where the heart kneels down,
> Not sure that heaven, itself, could be more fair:
> The green of fields invading the white town. . . .

> For the perverted sake
> Of what mistaken honor
> Did this green country take
> The gray of Towns upon her? . . .

> If nought ends utterly, if each thing passes
> To other forms and hours, and nothing dies,
> I must believe your tall and thrusting grasses
> And burning flowers, and wandering butterflies
> —And those two, in the summer of their year—
> Bear the flown sparks of what had hurled you here. . . .

If they looked more closely they could find themselves on dangerous ground, as was George Whicher whose "Amity Street" was printed in the *Record* twice and then in the *New York Herald Tribune*. It began:

> Many a gleaming ingle-fire
> Lights the Land of Heart's Desire.
> Oh! a harbor safe, a glad retreat,
> Is an Amherst home in Amity Street.

A few months later he produced "Poverty Row."

> Poverty Row goes gurgling down
>   Half-way to China. Her chief renown
> Is her liquid assets, now at their best.
>   Come on down and give 'em a test.

Robert Francis came to the area and found the two things he wanted:

Being with plain people, and being by myself. . . . I had friends, music, poetry. I had a sundeck and a fireplace. I had the work and all the time needed for it. The natural world around me was mine to enjoy in perfect freedom. Above all, I had my thoughts, a world of them.

His thoughts were not particularly about Amherst or the implications of its communal or noncommunal life. Nor were Robert Frost's, who also came to get away. "What I am after is detachment and long times alone rather than money," he wrote George Roy Elliott, as he prepared to leave Michigan and return to Amherst. Amherst might remind him of the farmlands of New Hampshire and Vermont, and he might draw on some spirit of neighborliness, but, as Elliott pointed out, that spirit as Frost conceived of it was pretty grim: "The burdens and limitations of the neighborhood keep the poet from being very glad; but his faith in the latent value of the neighboring spirit prevents him from being very sad." No one ever accused Frost of being a communard.

Two visionary college presidents, one man of the world who settled in town, and a Yankee businessman tell us much more about the processes by which creative residents could imagine a world that would be like Amherst. The first, Alexander Meiklejohn, focussed almost exclusively on Amherst College, and not the town, as a model community:

A college must be a good place in which to live as well as a good place in which to study. For this reason we have our chapel and church, our fraternity houses and dormitories, our athletic games and other student activities, our friendships of pupils and teachers each with his fellows and each with the members of the other group. Taking them all in all, I doubt if there are better communities in all our social schemes than are our colleges.

During his eleven years as president Meiklejohn not only preached the good communal life but he actually tried to have some of what he preached practiced.

ALEXANDER MEIKLEJOHN, PRESIDENT OF AMHERST COLLEGE.

First of all, he envisioned a college in which the diverse elements one saw in town could be brought together:

And so I cast my Anglo-Saxon vote for Pure Democracy. We Anglo-Saxons have the upper hand. How shall we use it? According to the principles on which the country's life by us was founded . . . , if we are not to have a racial aristocracy, democracy must have a dwelling-place within our college, If here, where thought is free and men are young, we dare not let our Anglo-Saxon culture take its chance, no other men or institutions will take the risk. . . . [W]e must welcome boys of other stocks. And if they do not come, we must go out and bring them in.

Next, though he was not in intimate touch with his own community, nor was he very good at holding his community of scholars together, he was intent upon directing the college community's attention to problems of American society. "We must send forth more ministers and teachers," he said, and Amherst College did. But he was not satisfied with the old doctrine of service, of helping one's fellows. He wanted students to know more about the situations they supposedly were going to help improve. In 1914 he reported to the trustees on a new course for freshmen on social and economic institutions: "We wish if possible to make students, at the very beginning of the college course, aware of the moral, social, and economic scheme—the society—of which they are members." He wanted them to know and evaluate just what it was they were going to offer up as improvement, he wanted to see more than their consciences salved:

Service, as such, is not a term of value at all. To give to another is valuable only in a secondary and derivative sense, never in a final one. There is nothing gained by giving to another something which is not worth giving. To serve one's fellows is to give to them what they need, what they enjoy, what is worth while. And if one is in search of the final term by which all our activities and all our teaching are to be justified we must find it among those things the having of which is good and the lack of which robs human living of its value. . . . Much of the teaching and preaching which our students hear is far too self-centered in its emphasis upon social justice and upon the duty of service.

Meiklejohn thought that an essential "measure of a college," to use the title of an article he wrote for the *Amherst Graduates' Quarterly,* was the extent to which it reached out beyond itself. In 1920 the

British social and economic historian R. H. Tawney served on the college faculty, and soon Classes for Workers were set up in Springfield and Holyoke along the lines of adult education ventures in England. "The aim," the catalogue said, "is to assist in the promotion of liberal culture among mature men and women engulfed in various industrial occupations in the surrounding communities." The director, F. Stacey May, echoed Meiklejohn: "A college is not for the purpose of training men to live in small college communities. It must make them aware of the problems of life, of the problems of the cities." So for about five years Amherst teachers gave courses or led discussions on economic and political issues in the industrial communities to the south, and in 1931 Professor Willard Thorp led a class in surveying unemployment patterns in Holyoke, thereby giving rise to Mary Heaton Vorse's optimistic comment. But after that the college's sense of community shriveled, shrank back to normalcy.

Meiklejohn himself went on to establish the Experimental College at the University of Wisconsin. There too he wanted to make the institution itself an ideal community and also to have its members go out into other communities to learn. "The college must be small enough and coherent enough to be in a vital and dominating sense, a community which will bind together all of its teachers and all its pupils in the carrying on of their common enterprise." Students and teachers studied and ate and lived together, tutorials replaced lectures, required courses on Greek and American civilization replaced electives. Having tried to understand how Periclean Athens ordered itself, in their first year, students were required to go out into communities of their own choosing over the summer in order to begin at firsthand their inquiry into what could make for individual and social welfare in America.

Meiklejohn was continually trying to extend his idea of the ideal college community out to include and apply to the country as a whole—and the reverse. When he came to ask the question "What Does America Mean?" he imagined it would mean most if it resembled an ideal college community.

In an English-speaking democracy, every man and woman among us must know and delight in Shakespeare and the Bible. Every normal person must have some understanding of what Darwin and Galileo were doing. Music, drama, and the other arts must, at their highest levels, be made matters of common delight. All of us must study Plato and Augustine and Marx and Henry Adams and Emily Dickinson. The permanent recurring problems of a social order must be, for each member of society, objects of vital and lively study. The life of the community must be shot through with the activities of inquiry, of taste, of creation, of interpretation. The sharing of the most significant human experiences must bring us all together into spiritual unity.

Some of the experience of Amherst as a town must have rubbed off.

Characteristically Meiklejohn projected his vision of communal life onto larger sites. He tried to prevent the college community from becoming isolated and contented, to make sure that it was diverse and in touch with the realities of the problems under study. His was not a simple, idyllic idea of community, but having tried to realize it on the hill, he took on the country. The town of Amherst hardly figured in his plans.

Indeed, he did not make a good impression in town. When Meiklejohn was fired in 1923, Morehouse put only a small announcement in the *Record* and underneath it, in large letters, "Cheer for Old Amherst!" Meiklejohn made no effort to carry on Harris's work, was brought in not to, and he was bound to offend. He had tried to deemphasize athletics, downplay the role of coaches. "Give the game back to the boys," he said. His political views were leftish; he counselled students to complete their college courses rather than to run off to war. He was a philosopher by training, more interested in sharpening intelligences than making life comfortable for all-round men. A town taken up with athletics at the two colleges, inspired by the war effort, and conservative in business affairs was not going to be enthusiastic. Two months after the firing Morehouse wrote: "In dispensing with the services of Dr. Meiklejohn, the college has taken the first step in a return to normalcy."

Kenyon Butterfield paid much more attention to Amherst. He was a member of the town's finance committee, helped establish its planning board, and presided over the committee that wrestled with the problem of the new high school building. When he retired in 1924, after eighteen years at the head of the Massachusetts Agricultural College, editor Morehouse treated him to a rather different send-off than he had Meiklejohn.

Amherst citizenship will suffer a real loss with the departure of President and Mrs. Butterfield, honored in a community where good citizenship is the rule rather than the exception.

KENYON L. BUTTERFIELD, PRESIDENT OF
THE MASSACHUSETTS AGRICULTURAL COLLEGE.

Butterfield's own institution and its relation to the nonacademic world differed from Meiklejohn's. Meiklejohn had wanted Amherst College to be "in all genuine meanings of the term . . . a people's college" by admitting boys from varying backgrounds; in the more common sense of the term, the Massachusetts Agricultural College already was one. When Butterfield took over, three-fifths of the students were from rural communities in Massachusetts, the fathers of many being farmers or wage earners in industry. The composition of his student body was different, so was Butterfield's sense of mission. Imagining in 1916 what the two institutions would look like in forty years, he paid tribute to his neighbors' lofty idealism. He saw Amherst men "treading upward into the mountains of God," helping bring about progress in business, in education, in statesmanship, and "in the redemption of mankind from ignorance, sin, and folly." He was not less effusive about his own institution's mission but he stuck closer to home.

Serving the cause of the people of the furrow, she preserves her strength through actual contact with that soil which furnishes food for human kind. . . . Her outlook is still toward the summit of an ongoing and up-reaching rural civilization.

Yet like Meiklejohn, Butterfield was intent upon making his educational community attend to the actual problems of society in both what and how it studied. He was impatient with the pursuit of theoretical knowledge, and he looked forward to a time

when students will choose the agricultural course because it forms for them the best foundation for a lifework even though they may not follow rural pursuits. . . . The time has come when the farm problem is not only a question of scientific agriculture, but also even more a question of economics, sociology, civics.

In the same inaugural address he asserted: "The college lives not merely because it teaches students; it lives permanently only as it clasps hands with the farmer himself." His policy was not one, he said, of "shutting up the college for the benefit of a few students, and damming up the great fountains of agricultural knowledge, permitting them to trickle out of faucets reserved for the elect." The result was an ever-expanding extension service, a continuing process of bringing people on to the campus for meetings and courses throughout the year and in turn sending demonstration agents out into the country.

Of course, however much (or little) these two men may have been influenced by the town in which they found themselves and however much (or little) they may have contributed to the life of the town, their visions of the ideal community were necessarily grounded in the educational institutions they had to administer. They had to watch over and, if possible, improve their college communities; in terms more adventurous than those of most educators, they sought to broadcast the virtues of the life of the communities they led. But they worked in the town's most important industries, not in the town itself. Meanwhile, Ray Stannard Baker was shaping the town in his imagination and thereby creating an ideal community for untold thousands within and outside the town limits.

Baker came to Amherst in 1910, his muckraking days behind him. He had grown up in the small town of St. Croix Falls, Wisconsin and just before coming to Amherst spent several years in the then small town of East Lansing, Michigan. He came to Amherst with the encouragement of his friend and former classmate at Michigan Agricultural College, Kenyon Butterfield; and he came already convinced that in experiencing and analyzing small town life one could learn (what he said over and over again was the most important thing Americans had to learn) "the art of living together in a crowded world." After college, St. Croix seemed dull, but he soon learned that if he talked with men and women about what interested them that he could find as many riches of character and experience as he was likely to find anywhere else. In East Lansing he helped plan and then build the first schoolhouse and then a nondenominational people's church, and from these experiences he concluded:

If *understanding* was what I wished most to achieve, where could I find a better laboratory than I had in my own small community? Or how better discover "the art of living in a crowded world"? One thing I came to believe more firmly than ever before was that the primary need in curing the ills of our body politic was not new mechanisms or a new system of government, however inciting they appeared to sanguine reformers, but more knowledge, more understanding, more sense of obligation on the part of all the people, more willingness to sacrifice immediate profit for future welfare.

Amherst turned out to be an all too congenial place for the furthering of his understanding.

Baker had been exposed to more of what we loosely call reality than had Butterfield's or Meiklejohn's students or than had the average Amherst citizen. For a start, he was relatively down-and-out in

RAY STANNARD BAKER, ALIAS DAVID GRAYSON.

Chicago, reporting on its labor and political situation; he marched with Coxey's Army and covered the Pullman strike; he wrote a book on the racial question and another on his travels in Germany; he was head of the press corps at Versailles and was to write voluminously on Wilson. Yet from the start there was a part of Baker that held back, that always saw the world from the safe confines of the small town. Robert Bannister, in the most thorough work on Baker we have, says that Baker gravitated toward the picturesque and positively enjoyed himself amidst the misery of Coxey's men; that he imagined the worker as a liberally educated man and the people as the educated, public-spirited middle class who had organized and set up chambers of commerce and civic improvement associations; and that he gave little thought to the dynamics of industrialism. Baker had a simple notion of government as an introducer, a maker of understandings; it is primarily an expression of brotherhood, not a form of force. Baker was a defender of Meiklejohn, but only in his journal, where he also confessed, being outside the college family, he preferred "to try really to understand this instructive clash of new ideas with an old institution. . . ."

That side of Baker soon found expression in the writings of "David Grayson," the name Baker chose for his nine volumes of "adventures of contentment." It was through Grayson, he said, that he expressed his "deepest and truest thoughts and feelings, which I considered—I saw afterwards how mistakenly—to be wholly different from what other people felt or thought."

Only the first, *Adventures in Contentment,* was not written in Amherst, but in it are many of the notions that might go into the making of an ideally imagined little New England community. There is the notion that in the country you find "real self-government," real politics, "the voluntary surrender of some private good for the upbuilding of some community good."

The real motive power of this democracy lies back in the little country neighborhoods like ours where men gather in dim schoolhouses and practice the invisible patriotism of surrender and service.

There is the notion that the country assimilates foreigners better than the city, that it "encourages differentiation, it loves new types," both notions based on the myth of the restorative power of the soil.

Bring out your social remedies! They will fail, they will fail, every one, until each man has his feet somewhere upon the soil!

Or, as he was to put it thirty years later in his *Autobiography:*

I firmly believe that if everyone could get his feet, somewhere, somehow, down upon the soil, he could live a richer and a more interesting life. Not field-farming necessarily, but at least a little plot of ground, a garden, an apple tree or two, bees, flowers—a pot of tulips in the window! It is not a panacea, it will not of itself make men happy—but it will help, it will provide the soil in which contentment may easily grow. For it somehow links the soul of man with the creative spirit.

These sentiments were hardly different from what other people thought and felt. Looking back, Baker said:

If David Grayson was only a "mood," as one commentator long ago called it, it was a mood that was life-giving and life-saving for me. When the world seemed wholly out of joint, it was a rebound into the deep, quiet places of the spirit.

The sale of two million copies of *Adventures in Contentment* testifies to the fact that others were saved, or found refuge, too. And who is not susceptible to the vagaries and languorous rhythms of this kind of prose?

I soon found it so pleasant there on my own land, even though the snow was deep, that I brought out a pruning saw and shears and set to work on my favourite McIntosh tree. I worked for some time entirely absorbed, thinking only of the task in hand, but presently, as I stood high up in the tree, I looked about me, across the snowy countryside with all the farms about, and smoke rising from many a friendly chimney—and the cattle calling in the yards—and the hens cackling—and in the town road the jingle of sleigh bells—and it came over me with a sudden glow how much I loved it all! It was something also, I thought vaingloriously, to stand up thus in a sturdy tree which I had planted with my own hands, so short a time ago (it seemed), and cultivated and pruned and sprayed. It gives such a sense of reward and possession as nothing else I know.

The adventures volumes—*Adventures in Contentment, in Friendship, in Understanding, in Solitude*—are filled with depictions of such pristine landscapes and solitary pleasures, and they all contain soft and casual line drawings by Thomas Fogarty, often featuring Grayson, pipe in mouth, in worn-out tweeds. Roaming through such pages, one might well grow impatient with the complexities of international politics or domestic economic or racial issues. One might well conclude that there was little that could be done and ascend into the ideal community that was there at the end of *Adventures in Understanding.*

So I am home again, and think it will take an earthquake in addition to a war to get me away again. Here I live. After wandering, this valley is my home, this very hillside, these green acres. Here about me are friends I love; friends living and friends in old books. This is my progress, the process of the seasons: this is my reward, the product of the earth and work of my own hand and brain. I want no other. Here may I be quiet, and think and love and work. Here, when I lift up my eyes, I can see the fire smouldering in the Bush; I can hear from the clouds a Voice.

Finally, that is what Baker did, he entered Grayson's world. At times he resisted. In 1914, considering how little Wilson had done in the area of social justice, he wavered in his support. "I ought to be on the firing line. I am giving very little for the faith I have. I am too much at ease in my garden," he wrote in his journal. But he did not voice his doubts. The next year he called *Hempfield,* his idealized version of Amherst and St. Croix Falls, an "absurd narrative" and wondered, again in his journal: "How can a man remain smugly contented; and bear to write pretty things, when all the guarantees of civilization and Christianity have gone overboard?" More openly, in *The Countryman's Year,* he has Grayson say: "It is one of the tragedies of our times that so many of us think our rebellious thoughts in private, leading two lives. If only we could have been disgraced, ostracized, defeated, we might have dared."

But he stuck to his garden. He was in Amherst during the Depression, and he would write in *The Countryman's Year:*

Everywhere I go I hear people groaning over the hard times—financial loss, profitless business, falling wages. But when I walk down through my meadow and along the old road into the woods and by the brook, I find no depression. The brown fields lie there waiting, expectant; the sun shines; the water glistens; the birds sing. . . . So much is wrong, but not in my hills.

His view of the "coloured" in *Adventures in Understanding* is a familiar one.

> "You appear to be happy," I said.
> "Oh, Ah'm happy. Nobody ain't happier than I am."
> "You've got plenty of hard work," I said.
> "Ah don' min' that."
> "But what is it that makes you happy?" I asked.
> She laughed as though this were an odd question.
> "Oh," said she. "Ise got lots o' good frien's—and it don' matter whether white or black."

I thought I would sound her a little on the problem of the colour line.

"Oh, that don't trouble me!" She laughed. "I know my place; an' I know who my frien's is."

(How many people, I thought, white and black, lack this wisdom; how few knew their place!)

As he said in his journal in 1933: "I believe I should meet the new problems as I met the old, by turning inward, and at the same time using my ingenuity to the utmost to bring in the necessary living. With a small piece of land, and a few colonies of bees, etc., I could at least live."

In 1906, in the *Springfield Sunday Republican*—for which he wrote a column for nearly twenty years, beginning in 1905—Warren R. Brown stated what he saw as the great advantage of living in Amherst:

On the one hand we can enjoy, near by, the hills and mountains, with the game dear to the sportsman, and with innumerable charms to the Nature lover; and, on the other hand, easily reached, is the city, and we can see something of its elegance and feel its stir. In our midst there is an academic culture that in a measure benefits all.

He lived in Amherst from the time of his graduation from Dartmouth in 1901 until his death in 1957. He provided through his newspaper columns, correspondence, and talks, not only subjects of interest concerning a place and a period, but evidence of the play of a lively mind over those subjects. He made Amherst's every homely event the object of his concern and the basis of speculation about wider worlds. Unlike Meiklejohn and Butterfield and Baker, he did not often move outside the sphere of Amherst, but he valued as much as they did books, countryside, and the workings of men's minds.

W. R. Brown was not to be counted among Amherst's aesthetes, and though he admired Thoreau above all other writers and enjoyed gardening and fishing, he was not a nature lover for nature's sake only. When he went for a drive in the country, it was usually to look at property. Nor did he crave culture only for the enrichment or refreshment of his personal life. He was a businessman, and so he recommended concerts because, if Amherst were to gain a reputation as a music center, "this would be sure to impress upon music-loving

WARREN R. BROWN, CA. 1934.

and literary people the advantages of this place for a residence." He sold real estate, and so the subtitle of a brochure put together by him in 1914, *Amherst, Massachusetts* (published by local merchants, with their own best interests in mind) was "a beautiful, rapidly growing, prosperous Massachusetts community of learning and homes." It was not just a question of his selling the town so that he could sell his houses. He simply never forgot to do what his good friend Robert Frost advocated—"provide, provide."

Higher education made accessible to those who could not afford it but who could profit by receiving it was of great interest to W. R. Brown. Born poor, in a little hill town in New Hampshire, he had started working on farms for his room and board when he was nine years old. He was twenty-five when he graduated from New Hampton Literary Institution and thirty-five when he graduated from Dartmouth, having worked hard to earn his way through both institutions. He valued an education, though he often said that college "came within a hair's breadth of making a fool of me." He also said that too many people used not going to college as an excuse for not having succeeded. He went, and he succeeded, but he never forgot his boyhood poverty.

In 1907 Brown wrote approvingly about a cooperative business experiment, the Mutual Plumbing and Heating Company of Amherst.

It is a cooperative undertaking of working men that is well worth the attention of all who are interested in the solution of the problems presented by the antagonism of labor and capital. . . . By the complete identification of the interests of labor and capital strikes and kindred labor troubles are here obviously rendered impossible. . . . Everything depends on the character of the men who unite.

He reassured readers that these men, uniting in what must have seemed a radical departure from other businesses in Amherst, were "reliable and steady," for they were married, and all but one owned his own house. One feels sure that the communal aspect of this company's cooperation was of less interest to Brown than the good business that might (and did) result from such an arrangement.

In the autumn of 1908, as he did at the beginning of every academic season, Brown listed Amherst's schedule of club activities:

All the literary, musical, social, educational, fraternal, and benevolent societies, clubs and other organizations of like nature will start the season in full swing this month. The official Amherst women's club, which is unquestionably the acme of the social organizations of the town, has just issued its year book. . . . There will be 15 regular club meetings this year and the literature, music, art, home-making, and history sections will each have from six to eight meetings. The first meeting of the club will be held Monday afternoon at Unity Church. Prof. George D. Olds of Amherst

College will give a talk on "Reminiscences of interesting people I met at the recent mathematical congress held in Rome." . . . Some of the other interesting features of the year which have been announced are as follows: October 19, illustrated lecture on "Santa Sophia and San Marco," by Prof. Randolph of Mt. Holyoke College; Nov. 2, illustrated lecture .on "Comets," by Prof. David P. Todd of Amherst College; 16, a piano recital and a travel talk by Miss Fannie L. Story of Boston; 30, talks on "Indian wit and poetry," by Dr. and Mrs. Charles A. Eastman. December 21 will be observed as gentlemen's night and a dramatic entertainment will be given by the club members.

The remainder of the column was given over to the less elaborate but still impressive plans of the Orient Club, the Thursday Club, the Tuesday Club, and the quarterly meeting of the Amherst Club, "composed of just ordinary men, and it makes no pretense of studying art, history, science, or music." Culture is a fine thing, he seemed to suggest, but so is a quiet game of cards, pool, or billiards. The ever-popular Grange received separate mention of its annual harvest supper, fair, and ball.

When Kenyon Butterfield was granted a five-weeks' leave of absence that same autumn in order to work with an industrial commission appointed by President Theodore Roosevelt to study conditions of country life, Brown wrote:

[H]e will devote practically all of his time during the remainder of the year at work with the industrial commission appointed by President Roosevelt to investigate the conditions of country life. The town and college both feel honored by President Butterfield's appointment to this important place, and will take special interest in the work of the commission. Whatever opinion one may hold as to the propriety or even possibility of the national government doing anything to better the bad conditions that may be found in various sections, excepting in the way of reducing the tariff, all will agree that the data that the commission will doubtless collect will be of invaluable aid to all social workers who are endeavoring to improve rural conditions.

Brown had his doubts concerning the benefits of government assistance, but such was his admiration for the ruralist that he could look for benefits from Butterfield's appointment to a federal commission.

In March of 1909 Brown's entire column was given over to the consideration of the history of Amherst's "colored" churches. Over the years he expressed an admiration for this particular community. That there were so many Negroes in a town the size of Amherst—

176 in 1900—was attributed by him and others largely to the need for servants in the homes of well-to-do Amherst College faculty.

For some time the colored people of Amherst have been displaying remarkable church activity. They have had 18 months of linked revival, long drawn out. With a corresponding amount of religious zeal and fervor on the part of the other inhabitants, Amherst could be readily turned into another modern Shiloh or Zion's city. . . . For over 40 years Zion chapel has been maintained as the mission for the colored people by Amherst college. In 1906 some of the good chapel brothers and sisters concluded that the old organization had got into a rut. At this age of progress, according to one of their number, it was at a standstill. All attempts to reform and instil new life into it were fruitless. It was like putting new wine into old bottles. Accordingly in June Moses Goodwin, Robert Till, Albert Bias, and seven others of the pillars of Zion asked for letters of dismissal. On August 7 of the same year, they, with others, were organized by the assistance of Rev. J. P. Manwell of North Amherst into a separate society and took the name of Union Church.

Today Bessie E. (Davis) Taylor, who was twenty-three at the time of this split, remembers that "the first colored minister Rev. Barrows wanted the people to leave the college and become Methodist. . . , wanted his people to pull out from under the white people." Moses Goodwin's daughter Amy recalled: "About 1905, when the college church became less active, some of the older members of the little chapel felt that it was time to become more independent and called a meeting to bring that idea before the whole body."

In 1910 Brown announced that "the new house of worship of the African Methodist Episcopal Zion church of Amherst will be dedicated to-morrow with due solemnity." After mentioning that George E. Bosworth and his crew had started a new building for Hope Congregational, "another colored church society," he observed that 'it is certainly remarkable for such a small number of people . . . to build and dedicate within a year two substantial churches."

The dedication of Hope Church actually took place in 1912. Professor W. E. B. DuBois of New York, editor of *The Crisis,* gave a lecture in College Hall in May of that year for the benefit of the new church. The presence of the two churches was and is remarkable—and very much in keeping with an American pattern by which black churches asserted their independence from white-dominated churches, then divided further to express denominational differences among their own ranks.

By 1915 W. R. Brown was writing a column that was progressive and quite unsentimental, countrified and uncommonly literate. He welcomed an evening school for Poles and Butterfield's taking steps to get acquainted with the local farmers, encouraged such community efforts as amateur theater groups and band concerts on the common, praised the agricultural college for establishing probably the only chair of pomology in the United States, noted that Amherst would welcome M.I.T. if it had to leave Boston for cheaper maintenance, and continually urged gardening in town ("Woe to the land, to hastening ills a prey, where automobiles accumulate, and gardens decay").

In 1920 Robert Frost referred to the real estate agent, without calling him by name, as "the wisest and so one of his best friends." Brown took Frost's poem "Good-bye and Keep Cold" to the "apple department of an agricultural college for a judgment on the apple facts it rests on," Frost reported to a *New York Times* interviewer. "Pomologically it got a clean bill, but not poetically. The pomologists . . . proposed to rewrite it, using the same apple facts to make a better poem."

They had much in common, these two men who called each other Old Man Brown and Old Man Frost. Frost distrusted "anything not genuinely rooted in earth." He said that he had "a strong aversion for high-flown language so often mistaken for the substance of poetry." Brown, in his newspaper columns, wrote clear, never fancy, prose about homely subjects "genuinely rooted in earth." He wrote for *The Amherst Record* throughout the forties, though he declined an invitation in 1945 to write for the *Springfield Union,* telling his daughter in a letter: "I haven't any ideas big and grand to write about."

One piece in the *Record* prompted a letter from one Old Man to another. Brown had listed and briefly commented on Amherst's 1945 literary crop, which included Ray Stannard Baker's *American Chronicle* (Brown praises the chapter on peace conferences); *Bolts of Melody,* new poems by Emily Dickinson, edited by Mabel Loomis Todd and Millicent Todd Bingham, and its companion volume, *Ancestor's Brocades* by Mrs. Bingham (Brown wonders why she bothers with the Dickinson-Todd lawsuit that cannot, he suggests, be of any interest except to a few old Amherst natives); *Walden Revisited* by George F. Whicher (an interesting though "sententious book"); *David Morton Poems, 1920–1945* ("beautiful little poems"); *Church Symbolism* by Harriet Whicher; *Church, College and Nation* by George R. Elliott; and *Heart O' Town* by Frank Prentice Rand ("he hit the mark at which he aimed"). Frost wrote to him from Florida:

Dear Brown

You wonder if there is a town of the size of Amherst that can beat its record in literature for the year. I wonder if there is a town twenty times the size that could beat its record or do its own criticizing as well as Amherst does in the editorial signed by you.

What a sad sad book Elliott gives us. He didn't dare send it to me for all our great friendship. He knows I think the greatest thing human is enterprise, and enterprise is just another name for departure. The reformation was one departure. The United States was another. And what a burst of enterprise it was and still is. You and I keep from getting blue. That's why I'm ever yours

Robert Frost

W. R. Brown was an avowed pacifist, though occasionally he did say, "You can underline *fist.*" He was a pacifist, he said, by dictionary definition, possessing "an attitude of mind opposing all war and advocating settlement of international disputes by arbitration." Here he is on the subject of war:

I doubt if there is another man that can read, this side of the Pacific Ocean, that has read less than I have done about *the war* here or abroad. However, I know about it enough to form my own opinion and to govern my own actions.

If I sit down to my breakfast table and crack open an egg and find it is rotten I do not need to eat the whole egg to know it is rotten and unfit for food. One whiff is enough. And just a little knowledge of war and what it does directly and indirectly to the countries engaged in it, satisfies me that we should keep out of it.

I am a pacifist, an appeaser.

Why—I can't say—I just couldn't be anything else. . . . People cannot be made better by punishing them for their wrong doing. And "All revenge is crime." (Whittier)

Our college presidents, our historians, who know more fully than the rest of us the results of all the great wars of the past, our philosophers and psychologists who know the workings of the human mind, how can they believe that we can make this world better in which to live with cannon, torches, and bombs. It can't be done. They're going in the wrong direction.

These sentiments were expressed by the private man in his journal. In letters too he was outspoken. He wrote to a minister in 1940 to say: "As I feel now, I would rather be killed than to live after I have done my best directly or indirectly to kill others that are as good or better than I am." And in 1945 he wrote to his daughter Alma, "War don't pay." "We should have learned that from World War I. . . . I had a long talk this morning with Ray Stannard Baker. He don't expect much to come out of the San Francisco Conference that will be of lasting value."

In the *Record,* with war news surrounding his words, Brown wrote about "Professor Smith's Peony Garden," "Ferns in Amherst," "Rare Specimens of Trees," about hunting wild bees, about pumpkins. He wrote very little about the subjects he talked about endlessly in his office: pacifism, Mormonism, prison reform, the abolition of the death penalty—and the history of Amherst. These were also the subjects of talks he gave to clubs in the forties and fifties, when he was in his seventies and eighties. A church group asked him to speak, and he accepted, prefacing his remarks with this disclaimer: "I am not as most of you know a church man. I have not attended a regular church service in Amherst for over 30 years and I am not going to begin now." On one occasion he wrote in a letter: "I preach tonight to the guest night entertainment of the Pelham Women's Club." The following week it was the Corn Beef and Cabbage Club, and the next a meeting of the Hampshire County Real Estate Board. "I kinder like it," he wrote, "and yet I don't. Too much effort for an old man."

"His comments were quoted," Eli Marsh says of W. R. Brown. "He was a remarkable person in the community." He was, by all reports—even his own—a character. He agreed with Thoreau that patched clothes were no crime and that cursing was a valuable rhetorical device. He had books of poems (Dickinson, Frost, and Whitman among them) on top of the rolltop desk in his office, and he kept a Bible in his lower right hand drawer, ready to be pulled out in case of a theological dispute. (Margot Rand can remember his taking out the Bible and waving it in the air to make a point in a discussion with her.) Feet on the desk, ear trumpet (later replaced by a hearing aid) adjusted, he told stories and listened to them. Many epitaphs were composed for W. R. Brown (at his urging and playfully), one of the best being:

> Heaven was in an awful din
> When Warren Brown confessed his sin
> A heathen! but because he was a pacifist
> St. Peter put his name upon the list.
>
> The pearly gate was opened wide
> Angels all did step aside
> Old Man Brown with all his sin
> To heavenly home was ushered in.

Writing in 1941, Ray Stannard Baker tried to sum up his life's work:

I have never been a reformer, nor desired to be. I have never accepted any cut-and-dried program for social reorganization, I have never been a Socialist, nor a Communist, nor a Single Taxer. I have never belonged to a political party, nor, since my boyhood, to any church. I am suspicious of those who would change institutions without changing the understandings upon which they rest. What I have wished most, if it can be expressed in a phrase, was to be an introducer of human beings to one another, to be a maker of understandings—those deep understandings which must underlie any social change that is effective and permanent. When men come really to understand one another—if that time ever comes—war will end, poverty will end, tyranny will end, and this under almost any sort of government, almost any economic system.

It was the kind of goal an Amherst resident could aim at. Alexander Meiklejohn and Kenyon Butterfield pointed their students toward it, countless teachers have. All wanted their students to understand their fellows and then somehow to understand them to the point of transcending the differences they discerned. Charles Morehouse could be said to have been trying to create such an understanding, certainly to have been applauding it when he thought he had found it. W. R. Brown, a quintessential Yankee, close in his thinking to Baker (even to David Grayson, though less sentimental about town and country) troubled himself less than Meiklejohn and Butterfield did with a wider world beyond Amherst, but he was glad to have them do so. For Amherst he wanted peace and prosperity and knew how much they depended on the cooperation of men and women with a sense of community. Those who looked back to an earlier time were often trying to retrieve an Amherst in which people seemed to have understood each other better than they do now. And it is an admirable goal, that of establishing a human community freed from strife and domination.

But one has to remember that it is relatively easy to keep such a goal in sight in a place where political and economic and social differences are not marked. We have seen how easily those differences have been missed, missed by many hopeful and contented citizens, missed by Ray Stannard Baker when he turned away from them, turned inward. No community is possible when they are dwelt upon, but no community is worth establishing that ignores them.

NOTE: Quotations from Amherst men and women are from interviews conducted by students in a course on communities given at Amherst College. W. R. Brown's personal papers were made available by his daughter Alma.

CHAPTER NINE

A HALF CENTURY OF CHANGE IN TOWN GOVERNMENT

DAVID A. BOOTH

David A. Booth is Professor of Political Science at the University of Massachusetts.

The year 1900 ushered in a half century of profound change in the town of Amherst. A small, introspective, provincial village, preoccupied mainly with such local matters as police protection, became by 1951 a cosmopolitan community concerned about national and international issues, including the Korean conflict and the Cold War. Many important changes occurred during this period, while the population of the town nearly doubled. This essay focuses on three of them: the change from open to representative town meeting, the introduction of town planning, and the birth of community-organized recreation.

STRUCTURAL EVOLUTION AND CHANGE

In 1900 Amherst was a town of just over 5,000, whose political structure and processes evidenced growing pains. In the preceding fifty years, the electorate had gradually expanded from a group of propertied heads of households to include nearly the entire adult male population. But as the electorate grew, interest and participation in politics declined, causing the *Amherst Record* to comment unhappily on the lack of interest and participation in local politics. On February 14, 1900 it noted that the town caucus for the nomination of candidates was near, and "as always, there are many complaints," mainly from those "who never attend town meeting." Actually, over 300

voters, "besides many spectators," turned out, leading C. O. Parmenter, who presided, to call attention to the law which prescribes
penalties to those who vote in a caucus without the legal right to do
so.

The annual town meetings were conducted according to specific
rules and regulations which were printed in the town report. The
warrant usually contained about thirty articles, but many of them
were of a routine and repetitive character. Some articles were
trivial—should the town vote to install a street light on the corner of
Main and Spalding Streets? Should a hydrant be installed at the
corner of Lincoln Avenue and Fearing Street? In all of this, very little
fiscal or physical planning is discernible; nevertheless, improvements
in town government were steadily implemented. The town by-laws,
which had first been adopted on April 25, 1868, were periodically
revised and new ones were regularly adopted after 1900. Among the
key changes introduced were the establishment of a seven-member
finance committee in 1914 and a nine-member planning board in
1915.

As the years passed, warrants became longer and the articles more
complex. The essential premise of town government—that all citizens should participate in town affairs—was increasingly questioned,
partly because its fulfillment would mean that power would pass into
new and presumably less responsible hands. In the years that followed, several expedients were proposed to adapt the traditional
structures in order to meet new needs. Then as now, a frequent
reaction was a request for a study or report by an *ad hoc* or standing
committee. In 1915 the newly established finance committee was
instructed to prepare a report on "the desirability of adopting the
town manager plan." In due course, the committee reported that
since only one Massachusetts town, Norwood, had the town manager plan in operation, "it would be wise for us to wait until a more
careful judgment can be formed of its merits. . . ." The proposal did
not surface again until the late forties.

Various alterations were also proposed to make the open town
meeting a more workable institution. The first fundamental change
took place in 1916: the town voted to accept the provisions of Chapter 284 of the Acts of 1915, which served to separate the election of
officers from the other portions of the warrant. For the next three
years, until the action was rescinded in 1919, the elections were

scheduled one week after the town meeting. Eventually a limited separation was reinstituted in 1939, when it was decided that town elections would precede the business portion of the town meeting.

A less obvious change was the increasing use of special town meetings which the selectmen frequently called at very short notice. In Amherst, as elsewhere, these sessions were often called to take insignificant actions, where town authorization was legally required. They almost invariably lured fewer voters from their hearths and homes than the annual meetings. Procedure was more informal too, and business was often swiftly dispatched. This caused concern and some adverse press comment, and various expedients were suggested to remedy the situation. One was that warrants for special town meetings should be posted in five or more places at least seven days before the meeting was to take place. Nothing came of it.

Even though it gradually evolved and became more sophisticated, the essential fabric of traditional town government survived and continued to be the chosen preference of a majority of Amherst voters who presumably ascribed to it many, if not all, the virtues that in earlier and simpler times had been mentioned by Jefferson and de Toqueville. But to a small group, that most democratic of legislative assemblies—the open town meeting—was increasingly viewed with disfavor. On the one hand it might be subverted by a mass of uneducated and uninformed people, acting on impulse; on the other, it might become an instrument of potential tyranny by a tiny minority. In the early 1930s, this group spearheaded a systematic effort to change the most cherished institution of local self-government.

Although change had been advocated before, it did not become feasible until 1935, when the town reached the constitutional population requirement of 6,000 needed to establish a representative form of town government.

But, given the strong allegiance that New Englanders normally have for traditional local institutions, it is unlikely that much would have happened had it not been for the determined efforts of Clarence W. Eastman and one or two other dedicated advocates, including the editor of the *Amherst Record*. Eastman, a professor of German at Amherst College from 1907 to 1943 and Major in command of the Army ROTC unit at the college, had served the town as a member of the finance committee from 1920 to 1925 before being elected moderator in 1926, in which post he served continuously until 1948.

Eastman's one-man crusade for change was fought on several fronts. It included fierce oral attacks on the present system of town government, initially delivered before the Amherst Rotary Club; participation in several other meetings sponsored by other groups including the Thursday Club; and the preparation of several letters to the editor and numerous articles for diverse newspapers, including the *Amherst Record,* the *Springfield Sunday Republican,* and the *Amherst Merchant's News.*

The arguments in support of representative town government were developed in a long series of highly biased *Record* articles and editorials that were initiated in April 1935. First, and often reiterated, was the argument that although the town numbered over 3,000 voters, the town hall would seat only 650. Even though there was no evidence that voters were ever turned away from a town meeting, the problem of the hall's capacity was alleged automatically to preclude individual representation. The second argument was that, under the open town meeting, too many important matters were passed by a small number of voters. The third, even more contradictory, point related to the increase in population and suffrage; now that the town had grown, "we no longer have an intelligent group of citizens, but mob rule by sentiment and emotion." The adoption or defeat of warrant articles "purely on emotion [sic] grounds" was viewed as a serious defect of the present system.

A fourth reason mentioned was the "jump in the tax rate" which was inexplicably related to the form of the town meeting. Representative town meeting was claimed to be "the only way to control appropriations," because economy in town government could best be achieved by electing "capable men" to a representative town meeting "where people would solve problems unemotionally." This would be in sharp contrast to the open town meeting where "no real economy" had ever been achieved. The present town meeting, the *Record* alleged, was "composed almost exclusively of people who want something, and that something is invariably something that will add to the tax rate."

A fifth argument asserted that Amherst was already operating under a *de facto* form of limited town meeting, although those who participated were not representative *de jure,* since the meetings were merely made up of those who came to "see and hear the show." Hence the present system was "grossly unfair and scarcely legal."

THE NORTH AMHERST POST OFFICE, 1934.

The use of standing votes was also mentioned as a severe indictment, because on some occasions, when counted votes were requested, less than half of those in attendance were willing "to stand up and vote."

Seventh was the familiar plaint that a small group of determined voters could "pack" a meeting and impose their will on the town by merely making a special effort to attend a particular meeting. This argument was occasioned by a special town meeting, held on July 1, 1935, when forty voters had precipitately dispatched an article dealing with "macadam construction on Pleasant Street." The *Record* editorial noted that, had the issue been more important, a group could have packed the meeting with forty or fifty voters to "enforce their particular sectional views upon all the citizens of the town."

The extreme brevity of some special town meetings and the lack of sustained or serious debate on some issues that the *Record* deemed important comprised the final argument. These points regularly surfaced after some particularly short special town meeting. In one case, it had taken the fifty voters in attendance only four minutes to authorize the transfer of a sum of money. The editorial complained that no reasons had been given to explain the transfer of money, no one had asked any questions, and no one had cared to discuss the issue. Such a thing, the editorial continued, "could not happen" under the representative town meeting, because "a quorum is required for the legal transaction of business at all meetings, whether annual or special."

These eight basic arguments were articulated at various meetings and repeatedly ventilated in the press in the form of articles, editorials, and letters to the editor. The initial phase of the campaign for change culminated in the inclusion of a warrant article for a special town meeting, called November 4, 1935. It proposed to instruct the selectmen to petition the General Court for a special act that would establish a representative town meeting in Amherst and to establish an *ad hoc* committee to draw up the act. A pamphlet urging a "yes" vote on the article was distributed.

The committee proposed in the warrant article, and voted by the assembly, consisted of the town's political establishment; it included the selectmen, the assessors, the finance committee, the representative from the district to the General Court, the town clerk, and the moderator. Its only action, when it met on November 10, was to designate a subcommittee to which it delegated the task of drawing up the act. Appointed with Eastman were Charles Andrews, treasurer of Amherst College and chairman of the finance committee; F. Civille Pray, chairman of the board of selectmen and an employee of Massachusetts State College; Mrs. Elizabeth W. Hooker who was simultaneously town clerk, treasurer, and collector; and Edward L. Spear, chairman of the board of assessors.

The act which Eastman drew up for the committee was closely modeled on Chapter 43A of the General Laws; it was promptly presented to the General Court through Representative Gerald D. Jones of North Amherst. After a perfunctory hearing in Boston on April 15, 1936, attended by the selectmen and Moderator Eastman, House Bill No. 188 was enacted as Chapter 10 of the Acts of 1936. The act provided that, upon its acceptance by the voters, the open town meeting then in existence would be replaced by an assembly, composed of one elected town meeting member for every twenty registered voters, plus a number of members-at-large.

The second phase of the campaign for change began on Sunday, January 5, 1936, when on a cold and bitter day 150 persons went to the Jones Library to hear Charles Andrews summarize the reasons for adopting the representative town meeting. When he turned to the seating capacity of the town hall, Andrews claimed that further curtailment of the hall's capacity was imminent. He stated that representatives of the Commonwealth's Department of Public Safety had recently investigated safety conditions existing at the town hall in Amherst and that they would soon request the selectmen to keep the aisles clear. At the same meeting, Eastman sought to assuage the fears of the townspeople over a possible loss of control over town finances.

An article in the *Westfield Herald* on February 10, 1936 gave the campaign an unexpected boost, by stating that the representative form was more satisfactory than the old-fashioned town meeting or even a city form of government, for larger communities of up to 30,000 population. The writer conjectured that Westfield, which had incorporated as a city in 1920, should have adopted the representative town meeting instead.

On February 12, the *Amherst Record* published the complete warrant and, in an editorial, stated that there was now "scant excuse" for any resident of Amherst not knowing about the proposed change. The issue, the paper noted, had been well aired at the Amherst Women's Club, at other civic group discussions, and in lectures by various proponents. A week later, the paper again reproduced the full warrant which included the entire text of the special act.

With the exception of a single election (1934), the turnout for the March 2, 1936 election—60.1 percent—was the highest recorded for the period 1927–48. Of the 1,880 ballots cast, 837 voted for the question, 856 voted against, and 187 left their ballots blank. The proposition had failed by a narrow margin of 19 votes. If the *Amherst Record* was disappointed with the result, it wisely and cleverly masked its feelings. The newspaper noted that the vote in favor of change had been "surprisingly large" and that, since the issue had only been before the voters a "short time," the sentiment in favor was remarkable. The paper predicted that the town would eventually adopt the plan and urged those in favor "not to be discouraged because it failed to go through the first year."

In the ensuing months, the *Record* passed up few opportunities to denigrate the open town meeting. In May the specter of "packing" sparsely attended special meetings was revived. An editorial on September 16, 1936 described "Another 2% Town Meeting," in which fewer than 2 percent of the registered voters had authorized expenditures that would affect the tax rate "by nearly a dollar."

The 1937 annual town meeting provided more grist for the advocates' mill. By now there were 3,397 registered voters, so theoretically only 20 percent could be accommodated in the town hall. Although the meeting had gone off well, the recommendations of the finance committee having been closely followed, the *Record* nevertheless noted that "over 200 people in the hall did not vote on the school question . . . and about 300 failed to vote either way on the other two articles." All of this, the paper editorialized on March 10, demonstrated that "a group of people could pass an article not in the interest of the town as a whole." The most practical solution, the editorialist again concluded, was the adoption of representative town government.

This renewed attack was soon buttressed by yet another long, Eastman-authorized article and by a hostile "Communication" signed by H. N. G., criticizing the recent annual meeting. Setting the stage for the reprise, a November 1937 article entitled "Representative Town Meeting" summarized the protagonists' main points and concluded that the present open town meeting system was not conducive to the best interests of the town. On January 5, 1938, a letter to the editor from Joseph O. Thompson, a physics professor at Amherst College, helped the final phase of the second campaign to get off to a good start by providing yet one more attack on the open town meeting. Repeating the rhetoric of earlier articles, Thompson also advanced two new arguments. One was that the educational value of local self-government could best be achieved by a hundred people "to look out for our interests." The other was introduced in the form of a highly personal motive. He stated that in 1914, he had built a house and that the tax bill had then been $123.90. In 1927, it had risen to $295.06. Now in 1937, the tax rate had jumped $4.20. The fault, he continued, belonged to the voters. "A group of one section . . . once flocked to a March meeting and secured an appropriation of $14,000 . . . for constructing a road that is used annually by about one percent of our population." In closing and in contrast, Thompson cited Weymouth, where under representative town government, tax bills had increased less than 5 percent in the last ten years. In the same issue, a long article by an unidentified author led off with the statement, "Our present form of town meeting has ceased to be democratic."

With the reform proposal scheduled to reappear on the March 1938 warrant, a few of the earlier campaign activities were repeated, though at a far lower level of intensity. This time the *Amherst Record* chose to downplay the controversy. Its traditional front page article announcing the annual town meeting did not even mention the issue, although a few lines of its main editorial summarized the arguments in support of the change. A week later the paper published the results of a survey of other towns where a representative town meeting structure had been adopted. The resulting article discussed the situation in two of the towns in the most glowing terms. In West Springfield the adoption was said to have been responsible for improving the town's credit rating; in Easthampton the change had been "very successful," and there had been "very little objection to it." This final issue of the paper before the vote carried one more letter from J. O. Thompson and an endorsement of the proposal, signed by thirty-one prominent citizens.

On March 7, 1938, the citizens of Amherst voted by a margin of 799 to 657 to establish a representative town meeting in their community. The voting data for the two elections are shown in Table 1.

Several aspects of the data deserve comment. First, the result was quite inconclusive. Whereas 44.5 percent of those voting in the election had voted in favor of the change in 1936, an almost identical proportion, 44.9 percent, did so in 1938. The first conclusion, then, is that strong sentiment in favor of the change which manifested itself

TABLE 1. REGISTERED VOTERS, TURNOUT, AND REFERENDUM RESULTS, ANNUAL TOWN ELECTIONS, 1936 AND 1938

	1936		1938	
Number of Registered Voters	3,125		3,319	
Percent Voting	60.1		53.6	
	N	%	N	%
For Representative Town Meeting	837	44.5	799	44.9
Against Representative Town Meeting	856	45.5	657	36.9
Abstentions	187	10.0	323	18.2
Totals	1,880	100.0	1,779	100.0

THE CHASE BLOCK AND AMHERST HOUSE ANNEX, ON THE
CORNER OF AMITY AND NORTH PLEASANT STREETS.

as an affirmative vote at the polls remained virtually constant. The
second campaign apparently won no new converts.

Second, a significant number of voters in 1938 either stayed home
or chose to abstain on the question, in contrast to 1936, when they
had voted against the question. Two quite different interpretations
can be adduced to account for this shift in voter sentiment. On the
one hand, it is possible that both the reduced turnout and the increased abstentions were symptomatic of the lowered salience of the
issue. This interpretation is compatible with the quieter tone of the
second campaign as described above.

On the other hand, the lower turnout at the polls and the higher
abstaining vote may have been the results of skepticism, ambiva-
lence, and cynicism about the proposed change. Although events
since the first vote and some of the campaign rhetoric may have
begun to lead them to question the efficacy of the traditional open
town meeting, Amherst voters may not yet have been quite ready to
embrace the proposed, and quite unfamiliar, alternative. It would be
reasonable to anticipate that such persons would express that cynicism either by staying home, or by abstaining on the issue. In any
event, it is imperative to note that this structural change which was
designed to protect the town from decisions made by a small unrep-
resentative group was itself approved by only 799, or 24 percent of

Amherst's 3,319 registered voters. It was, at best, a half-hearted endorsement.

Although representative town meeting has been a Massachusetts institution since 1915, when the town of Brookline adopted this reform, it has not received much scholarly attention. In the case of Amherst, two general questions need to be addressed. These are: Did the reality after adoption match the rhetoric of the two campaigns; and, Was the change satisfactory to Amherst residents?

Preliminary answers to the first of these questions may be provided by scrutinizing available data. After the change, the percentage of voters who took an active part in local affairs by voting in town elections decreased, even though the number of registered voters continued to climb slowly. In the twelve years prior to the change, turnout in town elections averaged 46.7 percent; in the twelve years after the change, average turnout dropped to 26.6 percent. Obviously, when they lost their opportunity to vote in town meetings, Amherst voters appear to have lost interest in town elections. Although totally unexpected, this was an unfortunate development, since the essence of town government is a high level of popular participation. Thus, Eastman's prediction "that more voters would participate in governmental affairs" did not materialize.

The change greatly reduced the ability of ordinary persons to participate in the discussion of policy. Amherst people loved their town then as they do today, and many valued the opportunity of contributing to debate, discussion, and discourse. They loved to ventilate issues—both large and small. It must, of course, be noted that the "right" of discussion was preserved, but the contemporary accounts of the meetings do not indicate that it was widely exercised.

A temporary negative effect of the change was confusion about where the voters should vote. In the first election, it contributed to the wide discrepancies in the winning totals of town meeting members; H. Chapin Harvey received the most votes, 271, while Michael Filipowicz won his contest with only 24 votes.

One positive effect of the change was the shortening of the annual town meeting. Prior to the change, the average length was nearly five hours; after the change, the average length was reduced to just over three hours. The shortening may be due in part to the fact that the sessions now met in the evening, and because for at least the first decade after the change, the town meeting was made up largely of long-time residents who instinctively knew the difference between routine and nonroutine politics on the warrants. For the most part the members did their homework well, wasted little time on needless debate of routine matters, but gave careful consideration to non-routine matters.

Another unanticipated development was the steady increase in the number of articles in the warrant in the years following 1938. After that year, the town meeting was asked to deal with long and difficult articles. For example, in 1940 the warrant contained several lengthy articles, including the first zoning by-law.

Attendance by members at town meetings did not decline as the novelty of the new meeting format subsided in the years following 1938. Attendance averaged 81.7 percent at the annual town meetings, compared to 59.3 percent at special town meetings after the change. As before, attendance varied greatly with the content of the articles. Generally speaking, controversial articles, for example, those dealing with zoning and those proposing large expenditures such as school bond issues, attracted a larger turnout of members. Attendance at special town meetings remained a problem, despite the change. On nine occasions between 1938 and 1950, a quorum was not present at the designated time for the meeting, causing delays of as long as thirty minutes before the meeting could be called to order. On September 10, 1946, a meeting finally had to be postponed for a week when no quorum materialized, even after a long wait.

The number of special town meetings did not decrease as a result of the adoption of representative town meeting; instead the average increased from 1.67 per year before 1938 to 1.9 per year during 1939–1950. The adoption of the new format stopped the pernicious practice of having a tiny troop of voters (on one very cold night, as few as twelve) adopt an article at a special town meeting. The change introduced the concept of a quorum, which was never less than ninety-two during the period under discussion.

One promise singularly failed to materialize, and Eastman, Thompson, and their friends who had predicted that the adoption of representative town meeting would achieve economies, stabilize expenditures, and slow the escalating tax rate must have been disappointed. The years that followed the change coincided with the recovery from the depression, and the town faced increased relief expenditures. The growing popularity of the automobile forced the town to face steadily increasing car-related expenditures for road and street construction and maintenance, for snow removal, and for parking. The period also witnessed a gradual increase in the number of town boards, each with a mission and mandate, each with its own budget request. In addition, the town faced steadily escalating school budgets, and the cost of running the town gradually increased. All of the proposed expenditures had to be approved by the town meeting, but because of the changed circumstances, it is impossible to tell whether or not the representative town meeting proved more discerning than the open town meeting had been in acting upon budget requests. As before, the advice of the finance committee was closely followed.

The remaining question to be answered deals with the level of general satisfaction with the new format. To this question it is harder to provide a definitive answer, although one may note that in its original form, the representative town meeting act contained a provision allowing any 200 voters to require the submission of an article passed by the representative town meeting to a townwide referendum. Had the voters been displeased or dissatified with the policy decisions of the town meeting, then it may be assumed that efforts would have been made to reverse the results by utilizing the referendum. In fact, only one such attempt was made in 1950, and the result of the referendum essentially vindicated the judgment of the town meeting. It should also be noted that no effort was ever made to revert to the open town meeting.

Nevertheless, it is possible to conclude that the change to representative town meeting was a bit premature. Many of the arguments used to justify the change did not then stand the test of logic, nor now the test of time. Although there was general satisfaction with the new format, the representative town meeting failed to fulfill some of the promises made on its behalf, and it also contributed to lowered popular participation in town affairs. There were then, as there are now, plenty of towns with larger populations where the open town meeting has not only survived but prospered. However the lesser medicine that might have been prescribed was eschewed in favor of major surgery, and it was this change more than any other which changed the essential character of the town's local government.

The choice of major surgery appears to have been influenced by surrounding but larger towns. Neighboring municipalities traditionally tend to emulate each other, particularly with respect to the adoption of "reform" institutions. When representative town meeting was brought before Amherst voters, it had already been established in West Springfield, Greenfield, Ludlow, Easthampton, Adams, and South Hadley. The alleged benefits of the change in some of these towns had been well publicized locally. South Hadley may have been particularly influential, partly because of its contiguity, and also because the two towns shared a common newspaper, the *Daily Hampshire Gazette*.

PLANNING

In 1900 Amherst Center was a village with a spacious common, some stately trees, and a cluster of public, commercial, and religious buildings located near its core. There were other "villages" within the town, each with its own church and separate identity. At that time building lots were indiscriminately sold without apparent reference to the effect on contiguous or neighborhood properties, and the liberty of the individual was still construed to mean that a property owner was beholden to no one for the manner in which he divided his property or what he built thereon. The threat to some local woodlands from creeping urbanization led the *Amherst Record* to urge that an effort be made "to preserve the natural beauties that yet remain." Fifty years later, the town had institutionalized planning through a respected board which helped the town to articulate and implement the principles and methods of sound municipal planning.

The story of planning begins in 1868 when the town adopted a by-law which prohibited the free roaming of farm animals in town streets. In 1902 the board of health summarized the poor sanitary conditions then prevailing in some parts of the community where "the family well is found twelve feet from a nasty sink spout, or equally near the family vault. This, even in gravelly soil, helps form a combination which is detestable from a sanitary point of view." The board reported that it had advised several homes to connect to the public sewer. It also suggested that the town water supply, which was provided and operated privately under limited state public utility supervision, should be more thoroughly cared for and that the water mains should be flushed once a month. This concern for water and sewerage was a recurring theme in subsequent years. The early reports of the board of health, and, later, of the planning board often have a contemporary sound. The following example is from the *Town Report* for the year ending February 1, 1903:

The time draws near when the town will be obliged to make large expenditures for a more complete and sanitary disposal of its sewage. The present capacity of our sewers is insufficient.

This concern for sewerage and water quality led the town to engage in the three essential steps of planning: assessment of present problems, goal setting, and plan making. In 1909 the town adopted the provisions of General Laws Chapter 103, relating to plumbing inspection. In 1913, it accepted Chapter 484 of the Acts of 1912, which authorized the construction of a sewer system at an initial indebtedness of $48,000. Earlier the town had voted to provide for a sanitary and sewerage engineer to make a complete report on conditions, to estimate needs for the next twenty years, and to plan to meet those needs. In 1914 sewerage would be financed by fixing fees for sewer use and connection and by increasing assessments on lands served by public sewers. These developments evidence an increased public awareness of, and responsibility for, providing a sanitary sewer system. By 1915 the town had arrived at the understanding that haphazard individual actions regarding sewerage do not necessarily lead to increased public social well-being and safety and that conscious, coordinated planning would provide a better response to this need.

Acceptance of the need for planning led to the establishment of the planning board in 1915 under the provisions of Chapter 283, Acts of 1914. The board was provided $50 to defray its necessary expenses.

In 1915 the board issued its first report. In an exquisite style, the board asserted that it "must have regard not only for present urgencies and emergencies but for future welfare and improvement, for the stay of undesirable tendencies, and for the avoidance of mistaken or heedless or short-sighted action. Our town has reached the point where its various enterprises, communal and individual, can no longer be trusted to happen; they must needs be thought out beforehand and guided with reference to consequences." Among those issues that the board planned to consider in the future, to be taken up

LOOKING NORTH ON NORTH PLEASANT STREET,
NEAR THE CENTER OF TOWN.

"in their relation to a general scheme for the improvement of the town" were artistic lighting, street signs, playgrounds, shade trees, the laying out of streets, service pipe in new streets, electric wiring, etc.," all to wait "their fitting time."

Requiring "immediate consideration" were "building regulations, maps and lay-outs, and a waiting and comfort station." The next thirty-five years brought steady progress. Some of the more visible results of board activity included (with dates of adoption by the town): the creation of the park commission (1919); traffic and pedestrian safety in the form of automobile regulations (1919); billboard regulations (1924 and 1935); building codes (1925); fire regulations (1928); zoning regulations (1940); recreation commission (1948); long-range planning (1950); and subdivision controls (1951).

Taken together, one may conclude that these planning developments were collectively designed to protect the character of the town, to preserve property values, and to achieve economy and efficiency in the use of land. A sense of order was promoted by sorting out incompatible activities, by setting some limits on build-ing heights and population density, and by protecting established historical and residential areas. It was physical rather than social planning.

The board and its work were occasionally sharply censured. The sharpest attack was in the form of a letter, published in the *Amherst Record* on February 9, 1938, criticizing the composition of the board which was made up almost exclusively of newcomers to the com-munity. More often, it was the board's proposals that were criticized, as its influence steadily increased.

In addition to its ongoing concern with physical planning—projects related to weeds and trees, sidewalks, underground wires, lights, street naming and house numbering, mapmaking, building location, soldiers' memorials, billboard regulation, drainage, snow removal, highway beautification, acquisition of buildings and parks, cemeteries, and street resurfacing and widening—the board gradu-ally came to grips with social problems. Though the goals were becoming social, the plans themselves necessarily related to physical things. Building codes, for example, were aimed at the safety of structures through the control of construction materials and con-struction techniques. But safe buildings built according to specific standards are less apt to become overcrowded and unsanitary. They are also far less likely to deteriorate into slums.

Amherst first became exposed to building codes when the plan-ning board inserted a code into the warrant in 1918. In 1920 the board again stressed the need for building codes to control building setback lines and building zones. The board's report stated that the town must control building operations and define the rights and duties of contractors and builders to help ensure the public safety and welfare. The ultimate goals of the board were to safeguard the town's future and to make it a little better than other towns.

In the following years the planning board continued to press for building regulations. Finally, in 1925, the town adopted what it er-roneously called a zoning by-law, but what was in effect a building code. (Its name, in fact, was corrected in 1926.) This by-law specified the building materials to be used in two types of construction—ordinary and mill construction; it applied only to the central part of the town; and it attempted to provide adequate spacing between buildings and the construction of "fireproof" buildings. By gradual amendment, this by-law eventually became a *bona fide* building code.

The planning board also became concerned with land use and population density controls. In 1925, at virtually the same time as it was submitting the so-called building by-law, the board requested $300 for the preparation of a zoning study and town plan. The warrant also included an article which attempted to define zoning and its future role in town affairs. In part it said:

Zoning is the restricting of certain uses to certain areas and is done to preserve present values against the encroachment of objectionable conditions. It is a preventive rather than a curative measure. It should be studied always from the standpoint of community benefit—that is of the greatest good to the greatest number. In such a [zoning] study the several town boards or commissions—School, Park, Sewer, etc.—which have to do with land areas should be consulted and should cooperate, and all public interests in respect to these matters, to health, etc., should be considered. Private interests should be fully respected and restrictions should be suggested only after thorough consultation and discussion.

During the early thirties, the board was preoccupied with physical or capital improvement projects, financed in part by the federal government to stimulate the ailing economy by creating blue-collar jobs. In 1937, the board again advocated a zoning by-law, partly as a means of controlling trailers, what the *Amherst Record* called "The Trailer Invasion" which, it said, was threatening "our fair town" as well as the economic fabric of the community. The board accordingly proposed a by-law. The next year the board met with the state planning board which approved of the town planning board's tentative zoning by-law. This proposal was then mailed to one hundred local voters. The respondents to these letters either approved the proposed by-law or made suggestions for its improvement. The suggestions were incorporated into a final draft which included a map; this final package was distributed late in 1938. The year 1939 was utilized to perfect the by-law before it was presented to the town. Finally, in 1940, the amended zoning by-law was adopted. The preamble stated that its social purpose was the promotion of "the health, safety, convenience, and welfare of the inhabitants of the Town of Amherst."

The planning board's first report (1915) had evidenced an interest in traffic. The report cited the corner of North Prospect and Hallock Streets as "a notorious example of the kind of tangle and inconve-

SOUTH PLEASANT STREET AND THE TOWN COMMON,
LOOKING NORTH TOWARD MAIN AND AMITY STREET.

nience that we ought to avoid." In 1922 a study and plan were developed for Pleasant Street, Amity Street, and Lincoln Avenue dealing with the location of buildings, plantings, setbacks, and the like to
guide future construction and traffic. To the board's concern for
adequate parking and improved traffic was added, in 1933, a new
concern—the safety of pedestrians, especially children. The town
implemented many of the planning board's traffic, parking, and
pedestrian suggestions: stop signs were erected (1934); blind intersections were eliminated (1937); parking was improved (1934, 1945, and
1947); pedestrian safety was improved by the addition of railroad
crossing lights (1942) and by the painting of white crosswalks. A
bicycle regulation by-law was adopted (1946), and, in the same year,

a traffic beacon was installed at Main and North Pleasant Streets.

For the first time the planning board's 1949 report indicated a growing awareness of the interdependence of all the issues it had been dealing with in past years. There was an increased tendency to deal with problems together by fashioning a single, concerted attack on a long-range basis. This report considered the use of parking meters as one way of providing for an overall review of traffic flow, pedestrian safety, and off-street parking. At the same time the report recognized the need for a study of the entire traffic problem. By 1949 the board also had begun work on a proposed long-range program designed to guide the growth of the town through control of sub-divisions, layout of streets, and a study of traffic. The town was thus beginning to realize that subdivisions, traffic, and land use are all interrelated and that all affect the quantitative and qualitative aspects of town growth. The realization that all the problems were related and could not be attacked successfully in isolation was an important step in the direction of true comprehensive (or master) planning.

In its 1950 report the planning board gave further consideration to a long-range plan for the town in anticipation of future growth. Several references were made to a possible ten-year program to provide for the orderly development of the town, and the board recommended that the town manager plan be adopted to facilitate such a ten-year plan. The board also recommended that it be reestablished under provisions of a new state act, "Improved Method of Municipal Planning," Chapter 41, Section 81A–Y, to give subdivision control to the board. This change was effected in 1951. A final recommendation was that the board begin meeting with other town officers to discuss common problems. This was renewed evidence that action must be coordinated to handle the complex social problems of the town; the day had passed when town problems were simple and straightforward. Actions aimed at physical, rather than social problems no longer sufficed—Amherst had become an urban place.

The period 1900–1950 almost perfectly coincides with the birth and institutionalization of planning in Amherst. The planning board's annual reports show a definite shift from physical to social planning. At the outset, planning meant concern with water supply and sewage disposal. This concern was articulated by the board of health, which spearheaded the adoption of various town by-laws designed to improve sanitary conditions. By 1915 the town acknowledged the need for planning *per se* and established a planning board. The board immediately asserted itself and became involved in the improvement of the town's physical and social environment. In the next thirty-five years, the board steadily increased its visibility and involvement in town affairs. Many of what were at first isolated attacks on different problems gradually became integrated into the concept of overall, coordinated planning aimed at more effectively controlling the total physical and social environment of the community, and by 1950 Amherst was beginning to consider comprehensive or master planning. It would be eighteen years before the concept was formally accepted, but by 1950, the planning board had paved the way for its adoption.

During this first half century, Amherst drew some of its planning cues from the nation, but in one respect at least, it was ahead of its time. The board's original mandate required it to be at all times concerned with questions of "decency and beauty." It is only now that such aesthetic values are gaining widespread acceptance. What is equally remarkable is that the board's advice was seriously heeded, in contrast to other towns where planning advice is often treated cavalierly. It was fortunate that, in a town so favored by nature, planning should be regarded as a legitimate activity. Although the passing of time required some "shaded streets and quaint irregularities" to be sacrificed in the name of progress, much of the charm of the town center has been preserved to this day.

RECREATION

At the turn of the century, there was virtually no community-organized recreation, although local transportation in the form of the four-direction trolley facilitated access to well loved hiking and picnic areas such as the Notch or Mount Toby, and the modest athletic facilities at the colleges were made available for community use. Providing recreation was the responsibility of the individual, the family, or informal small groups.

The changes in recreation illustrate several characteristics typical of Amherst in the period under discussion. These are: the development of civic awareness of societal needs; the effective use of committees to develop solutions; the cooperation of the local colleges; the conscientious work and generous contributions of volunteers, and the munificence of local persons; the eventual establishment of a formal group on a permanent basis; and the retention of paid professionals to administer the program.

Amherst was first exposed to organized sport as a form of recreation in 1859, when Amherst College began to require physical exercise as organized by Dr. Edward Hitchcock. The college was victorious against Williams College in the world's first intercollegiate baseball game in that same year. Local residents enjoyed the games at both Amherst College and the Massachusetts Agricultural College. The word *organized* was less specific then than it is now, however, for game schedules were tentative, the umpires were often partisan, and violence was not uncommon. After a high school football game between Amherst and South Hadley in 1901, a local editor wrote that, although they had not won, "the Amherst boys were lucky to escape with their lives." At the turn of the century, both colleges emphasized the importance of physical exercise and the use of athletics as a complementary and essential part of education.

From the beginning, interest in recreation in the town was fostered by the colleges. In 1911 Dr. Percy Reynolds of the Massachusetts Agricultural College conducted a summer playground program. Eighty-six children enrolled. Young children and girls came in the morning, and the boys came in the afternoons. The only apparatus available was a large sandbox, but MAC supplied baseball equipment and allowed the use of its swimming pool. The experiment was praised by school superintendent Audubon L. Hardy, who stated that it showed what "might be done if a playground location could be provided near the center of town."

The following year, the school committee rented land adjoining the East Street School for a playground, but it proved of limited value because it was too wet. Hardy again expressed the need for land near the schoolhouse which could be used "not only for the children, but also for a recreation centre for the young people in this part of town." With the coming of World War I, physical training programs in the school were emphasized and accelerated. Girls and boys were involved in the "Health Crusade." Suddenly, the high school gymnasium and the athletic fields at Amherst College were in heavy demand, and the need for more town facilities became evident. Nevertheless, despite a request for funds in the early 1920s, the recommended playground and athletic field near the High School and Kellogg Avenue School never materialized. Throughout this period, recommendations were made for a playfield at Kellogg Avenue School, and faraway Hitchcock and Blake fields continued to be used for outdoor activities.

After World War I, the emphasis on physical education levelled off, and no discernible progress was made for several years. George Williams, the high school athletics director, supervised a summer baseball program at Hitchcock Field in 1926, but interest waned, and the program ended with only about one-third of the boys who had originally registered. The 1931 summer program expanded its activities beyond baseball to other games, including horseshoe pitching, swimming, and picnics. The Rotary Club donated $35 for equipment.

Meantime, the park commission was making progress. In 1918 two farmers, George F. Hobart and William H. Atkins, and an influential coal dealer, Cady R. Elder, had been appointed the town's first park commissioners. In 1925, the commission accepted its first gift of land from J. Howard Sweetser. The town appropriated $600 for improvements of Sweetser Park, located near the center of town, which were matched by funds from the Garden Club of America. In 1932, the planning board started to plan for additional park areas in view of the probable growth of Amherst. Two years later, Ulysses G. Groff presented the town with a splendid fourteen-acre plot on the Freshman River, which presented an ideal site for a park.

Although these generous gifts served to stimulate interest in recreation, they were not the only factors. For several consecutive years, the Massachusetts State College sponsored a major recreation conference that was well publicized in the local press. Some well-known local persons regularly promoted recreation activities: "Kid" Gore helped to develop scouting; "Tug" Kennedy ran the Boys' Club, while Ernest Whitcomb of the First National Bank played the principal supporting role; and Larry Briggs and Kenneth Cuddeback helped to promote interest in skiing. Local churches also sponsored various activities, and public interest was stimulated by the *Amherst Record*. In June 1935 it praised Look Park in Northampton and wished for "something comparable in Amherst." A few weeks later it was urging the establishment of a "Recreational Council" which, it said, should be given appropriate financial support to enable it "to pursue a program of study and development to meet our recreational needs." Two years later an editorial, "A Playground for Amherst," urged the planning board to give more attention to recreation.

The planning board began to consider the subject seriously, and, in due course, the town's first playground committee was established. The committee, comprised of F. Civille Pray, William H. Atkins, and John R. Lannon, recommended the purchase of the Elder and Pratt properties on Triangle Street for $5,300, which was accomplished in 1939. In 1940, Stephen Puffer, the superintendent of streets, L. Leland Dudley, the superintendent of schools, and Curry Hicks, the director of athletics at Massachusetts State College, were appointed to the playground committee to plan for construction of the Triangle Street Playground. The initial improvements were financed through a $7,000 W.P.A. project. The town spent an additional $1,400 in 1941 to repair rain damage and to improve drainage. The committee, concerned over the control, supervision, and maintenance of the grounds, in 1942 hired George Williams to supervise the use of the field and to plan games.

During World War II, the need for summer supervision decreased "because very few young people were free to make use of the field except on weekends." The colleges became military training camps. Although Amherst was not a battleground, "the community was, to all intents and purposes, a militarized zone." The town made the recreation center available to the military personnel stationed in the community.

After the war, the town showed more interest in recreation, and large sums were appropriated to improve the middle and lower fields. In 1946 a recreation survey committee was appointed, consisting of Mrs. Albert Bergeron, a housewife, Benton P. Cummings, a director of American Youth Hostels and proprietor of Homestead Farms, Dean Eugene Wilson, director of admissions at Amherst College, and Miner Markuson, Lawrence V. Loy, Ruth McIntire, and William G. Vinal, professors at the University of Massachusetts: $150 was appropriated for their use. The mandate of the committee was to:

1. Make a comprehensive survey of the year-round recreational needs of the town of Amherst.
2. Recommend a program which will meet the immediate and long-range recreational needs of this community.
3. Suggest a method of financing capital improvements, leadership services, and other costs of said recreational program.
4. Publish the findings and recommendations of this committee.

Other groups were also concerned with the town's recreation needs. The Parent Teacher Association voted to study recreation possibilities in 1947. The committee on recreation, chaired by Amherst College professor Gail Kennedy, investigated the possibilities of ice skating privileges, ski lessons, bike trips, square dances, weekly recreation nights for youth during the summer, the need for public swimming, and how other communities provide trained recreation leadership. The results all indicated a need for public support of recreation.

That same year, two opposing articles, both relating to the future of Groff Park, appeared on the warrant. Article 28, sponsored by F. Civille Pray, chairman of the board of selectmen, proposed the auction of the unimproved, unused land. Article 29, however, recommended the park's development as a valuable asset. This article, presented by Robert S. Brown, was adopted, and the improvements on Groff Park eventually began in 1950.

The committee on recreation completed its work and presented its report in January 1948. It stressed the need for well-rounded programs and better coordination and cooperative planning of resources. The inventory of facilities revealed that Amherst had no public swimming facility, no public natural areas, and inadequate neighborhood facilities for baseball, skating, swimming, camping, and more.

The committee accordingly made recommendations for the immediate and long-range future, stressing the need for more play centers, fields, programs, a swimming pool, and a town forest. The memorial swimming pool at community field was one major result of the committee's work. It also suggested the establishment of a permanent recreation committee and budget, the continued development of the Triangle Street playground, the beginning of improvements on Groff Park, and the securing of additional recreational area lands.

The town heeded the advice, in part at least, and in 1948 voted to establish a recreation commission, to control and supervise Community Field, as Triangle Street playground was known, and such other public playgrounds and recreational areas as might later be acquired by vote of the town. The proposed budget for the recreation commission was $4,500. This $.65 per capita was far lower than the $3.00 per capita standard set by the National Recreation Association in 1947.

Patrolman Clarence A. Jewett, fruit grower William C. Atkins, director of placement at the University of Massachusetts and chairman of the board of veteran services, Emory E. Grayson, an employee of Delta Upsilon, William F. Casey, and University of Massachusetts professor Lawrence V. Loy, were members of the first recreation commission. They quickly lent their support to different baseball leagues, kept the Community Field in condition, and supported the High School Canteen. The commission used most of its first year to develop immediate and long-range goals in order to maximize leisure opportunities and services. To accomplish this, all resources were necessary, including neighborhood committees. In the following years, recreation made steady progress, following the profession's development. A larger variety of activities were offered, and new age groups began to be served.

For most of the first fifty years of this century, recreation in Amherst was dependent upon indirect agencies, public and private. Schools provided playgrounds and personnel, the park commission secured natural areas, the planning board made plans for recreation. Improvements in the facilities were made in cooperation with the town highway department or the W.P.A., and the colleges provided professional advice and guidance. The recreation commission that was launched on a steady course at the half century was thus one more example of the town's historical ability to overcome potential discord and to act in concert to meet the needs of its people and those of generations yet unborn.

CONCLUSION

During the first half of the twentieth century, Amherst progressed faster and more confidently than other western Massachusetts towns of comparable size. What factors explain this curious but fortunate development?

As the site of two institutions of higher learning, Amherst was the home of an unusually gifted and intelligent population. The two colleges, as they were then, regularly brought new faces to the community, which meant that a rich and steady infusion of new ideas leavened what otherwise might have remained a provincial community. The willingness of some local persons with relevant expertise to participate in the development of planning and recreation added greatly to this; from their inception, both were blessed with the contribution of a few local luminaries who contributed generously of their time and professional competence.

In general, the changes discussed in this essay were spearheaded by groups of influential citizens—formal officeholders, the socially prominent, respected members of the business and farming community, such as C. R. Elder, and several well-known academics, including Andrews and Eastman.

The changes were also promoted by the local newspaper, particularly in the matter of governmental structure. Why the *Amherst Record* so strongly favored a representative town meeting is not clear, but it is evident that by devoting space exclusively to the activities and arguments of one side of the issue, the paper presented, at worst, a biased and, at best, a one-sided account of the controversy. The paper also played a key and catalytic role in the development of planning and recreation by periodically focusing on a particular problem in one or other of these two areas and by suggesting possible solutions that were occasionally implemented. That the newspaper appears to have had a considerable impact upon the community during this period may in part be due to the fact that the population was growing steadily and that political parties played a declining role in community life, as the town moved steadily toward nonpartisan politics, which were adopted in 1947.

One cannot fully explain the record in terms of these internal conditions and personalities. Amherst never was an isolated island, and, after 1900, it was increasingly influenced by the world around it. It has already been noted that the adoption of representative government appears to have been influenced by surrounding towns. While planning was not as universally respected in the thirties and forties as it is today, the need for it in many aspects of political, social, and economic life became increasingly apparent. Planning was being urged more and more at the corporate, municipal, regional, and national levels. Its development in Amherst reflected this basic trend. Similarly, the growing national interest in organized recreation and physical fitness helped to buttress Amherst's modest beginnings in this area.

The interchange between the town and the outside world goes on today. As long as responsible citizens continue to be sensitive to ideas and experience from without, it seems reasonable to assume that the town will neither stand still nor change radically, but that it will gradually continue to adapt itself to a changing world as it seeks and finds solutions to new problems as they emerge.

The author wishes to acknowledge the valuable assistance of several persons in the preparation of his essay, including: Dale A. Berry, Debbie Bickford, Paul C. French, James Hanlon, Jim Machonis, Ruth McIntire, Dwight Salmon, Mary Jane Shaw, George R. Taylor, and Willard L. Thorp.

CHAPTER TEN

AN IMMIGRANT'S BOYHOOD IN AMHERST, 1904–1928

EDWARD LANDIS

Edward Landis came to Amherst as a very young boy, a Jewish immigrant from Russia. His very appreciative memories of his Amherst boyhood offer a particularly interesting perspective on the town. Mr. Landis is now an attorney in Springfield where Kim Townsend recorded these recollections which have been transcribed and edited by Tom Looker.

My parents came from Russia. They were Jewish. My father went to England on his way to the United States. I think he worked in London for a while. He was a tailor and left my mother, my sister, and myself as babies in a little town in Russia. Then he sent for us, and we came through Ellis Island as immigrants in the old-fashioned way. They tell me that we developed chicken-pox—both of us—so that you had the classic picture of a mother and two children who couldn't get out of Ellis Island, who were in quarantine on Ellis Island with the father looking through netting and waiting for them for maybe as much as two weeks to get out.

So far as Amherst is concerned, I distinctly remember riding an open trolley car from Northampton to Amherst when we moved to Amherst. I assume that my father had established himself a bit earlier, perhaps in business. He opened a tailor shop and I think a little store in connection with it, a clothing store. The old classic procedure, immigrant procedure. And my mother, my sister, and I, perhaps with my father, took that trolley ride in an open car, open trolley car. It was a lovely ride as I remember. The tobacco fields of Hadley were tobacco and onion fields at that time, and there were no commercial enterprises of any sort that I remember between North-ampton and Amherst. Well, coming into Amherst I remember where we lived first, right near the center of town, and all of the childish things that happened in those days, and from that point on I grew up as a country boy—barefoot, dusty roads, that kind of thing, unpaved streets. The streets of Amherst were almost wholly un-paved in those days, and I think the only hardtop was right at the center of town at Amity Street and North and South Pleasant Streets and down by the Town Hall on Main Street and down Main Street a way, and then it became dirt roads. And I so remember one of the professors at Amherst College, whom we knew well, trying to get up the paved grade of Main Street coming from the north, heading south to the center of town in a two-cylinder Maxwell and not quite making it. Thompson was his name. Professor Thompson.

If one were to go onto Main Street at the center of town in midsummer in Amherst in nineteen eight, let us say, or nineteen ten, twelve, you could go up to Amity Street, or Main Street and Pleas-ant, and there'd be nobody in sight, not a single human being in sight except Mel Graves, the cop, the policeman—that's all there was. It was that quiet, that dead. Life went on, of course, but at a very very slow, leisurely pace. And the children, of course, had to find some-thing to do.

The jail was in the basement of the Town Hall. And we were always in great awe of that jail and Melvin Graves, a great big corpu-lent man who ambled along the streets and didn't say hello to any-body, or to us, certainly. We were afraid of him. We were really in fear, and we had tremendous respect for the law in those days. And as I say, there was no vandalism, the kids didn't smash anything, there were no broken windows in those days and no broken lights. There might have been petty thievery here and there, it's quite pos-sible. I don't recall it. But there was no such thing as going out and damaging somebody else's property. What we did do, seasonally, was to go up to the orchards at the top of Triangle Street Hill, the old Aggie orchards, a mile or more out of the center of town, in droves. And we used to come away with blouses full of peaches and plums and apples. And nobody bothered us. That was acceptable, appar-ently. Except for once, I remember—and this frightened us—Mel Graves arrested an adult up there in the orchards, and we kids saw him being driven down from the orchard in a horse and buggy, with

EARLY 20TH CENTURY AMHERST. THE STREET CAR IS ON THE
NORTHAMPTON-AMHERST LINE. THE AMHERST STREET
RAILWAY TRACKS TO SUNDERLAND AND HOLYOKE ARE ON
THE LEFT.

Mel Graves holding the reins and his prisoner beside him, going to
the jail. I have no idea why he was arrested, whether he was poach-
ing up there. So were we! And that set us back a little bit.

In those days, the town boys and girls were welcome all over
Amherst College, and at the university too for that matter, but
Amherst had much more to offer boys. For instance, I became a
member of the Amherst Boys Club at a very early age, and we were
given use of all of the facilities of Amherst College—the gymnasium,
we could go into the gymnasium or the swimming pool at any time,
as long as there was somebody there. The Boys Club headquarters
were at the gymnasium. Our directors were students right straight
through the year, volunteer students who became heads of the
Amherst Boys Club. And the interesting thing about the Amherst
Boys Club was that everybody was welcome. It was a conglomerate

of the kids in Amherst. Now the kids in Amherst were divided into the Wasps, of course, with the Yankees predominating. A large number of Irish families in those days. A smaller number of Polish families, although there were many, many Polish families on the outskirts, farming, and a large number, considering the population, of blacks. Everybody mixed at the Amherst Boys Club, and there were no social or color lines in those days at all that I remember. The black boys ate in my house; I ate in their house for lunch or whatever it was. We mixed. There was almost complete mixture. Now the interesting thing from my point of view was that my family was the only Jewish family in Amherst for a fairly large number of years. I don't know how many, but perhaps as many as eight or ten years. And I think back to that phenomenon of a Jewish family moving into a Yankee community which probably had never had any intercourse whatever with Jews up to that time, and here was an immigrant family coming into the community, and I would guess that we were an object of very great curiosity.

There wasn't another darn thing to do in that town for kids

273

except to go swimming which we did all summer long just about every day, without any clothing, down at what we called the Freshman River, which is the Fort River. We built a high diving board there at a little bay. The little black boys, the Irish boys, the Polish boys, myself. I don't know how old I was. I might have been seven or eight years old at that time. When the diving board was built, we used to go swimming there almost every day. And then we also built a dam across a little stream, which may not be flowing now, behind what we called the Cow Barns at the university, at the old Aggie College, down through the dusty fields, across the corn fields, down to that little stream, and there we were totally secluded. We built the dam, we built a diving board, and that's where we spent part of our summers. There wasn't another thing to do in the town. The college facilities were closed. Amherst College was closed during the summer.

There was no disharmony, no serious disharmony, among the young people at all, that I remember. The only lines that were drawn were what probably are natural lines, all things considered, and they were social. They had to do with religion to some extent, with wealth to some extent, with so-called status to some extent. The lines were then drawn as much as they were drawn for many many years after that. You had the Yankee community, which is predominantly self-contained and was the community which was in control of the town, from a voting point of view, from a political point of view. And the Irish community, which centered around St. Brigid's Church and was quite close to the church. It was a believing, practicing Catholic group, quite devout, for the most part. The blacks had two little churches, in my day. At one time my father owned a two-family house in which we lived. One of his tenants was a black minister who had two sons, and we lived side by side for three, four, five years perhaps. No racial friction of any sort, no name calling between blacks and whites, that I remember, at all.

The form those lines took was the same form which has been extant for hundreds of years, perhaps, and that is that you were not invited to certain social events. Let us say the child of a wealthy Yankee family might have had a birthday party. The Irish boy friends, the Polish boy friends, the black boy friends, and this little Jewish fella were not invited, you see. And that remained constant, right straight through my youth, and to a degree, of course, it exists today.

I assume in my case that my mother probably briefed us, you might say, on the overall position which we occupied in the community. I assume that we were infused with that kind of thing by osmosis, by speech, by example, or whatever. So that I think that probably we recognized that there might be some uncontrollable reason for our nonacceptance in certain areas. But we were so busy, there was so much to do, for my family at least, that it really didn't matter much. It mattered some, of course. But as we grew older, our social efforts went off in another direction. I learned to play a mandolin and a banjo at the age of thirteen or fourteen. My brother Mack became an excellent, fine drummer, a great drummer. My sister Rose became a good jazz pianist, and our home became a focal point for the young people of both colleges. We had a ball. We made music, and the house was open, and anybody who played an instrument at either college was welcome to come in and join us. In about nineteen thirteen, I think it was, I started my so-called musical career by sending $4.95 for a mandolin, an extra set of strings and a pick, and an instruction book to Sears Roebuck. And a case. It came, and within three weeks I learned to play it, and in about four or five or six weeks I was in the Amherst High School Orchestra with that mandolin!

Three of us made music in my home. Now, prior to that time, there had been public dances run in Amherst at Masonic Hall and at Odd Fellows Hall. The only music for those dances was a pianist. That's all there was. A person playing the piano, playing the waltzes and the fox-trots and the one-steps of the day. They were Saturday night dances. They were town dances, generally speaking, and the students didn't attend from either college very much. My brother Mack was called Jerry, I don't know why, and it wasn't very long before we drifted into a combo, piano, drums, and banjo, and it began to be known around the town that here's a little orchestra. We began to be hired to play at functions of one sort or another, and we became known as Jerry's Jazz Band. Then I began to run public dances, as an entrepreneur, at Odd Fellows Hall and Masonic Hall, mostly at Odd Fellows Hall on Saturday nights. I must have been— this was late high school for me and during part of my college career. Because we were in college, my sister and I at that time, part of that time anyway, attracted a good many of the college boys from both colleges, and the town girls. So you had a mixture there, and it was great fun, and it went on for several years. I think we did a very good job. No police were needed, there was no rowdyism, no drinking, just a nice, decent lot of young people—dancing. And having fun. That was the temper, the tempo, of that little town at that time.

After we grew up a little the town boys and the college boys used to take the trolleys Friday nights and Saturdays, Saturday nights, to Northampton, to visit Smith, and to go to the Saturday night dances at Carnegie Hall. These were public dances, cost maybe 25 or 35 cents to go into on a Saturday night, and the town girls from Amherst, Northampton, and the areas around Northampton would go, pay their own way in, and the boys from Amherst and North-ampton came, by trolley (nobody had a car), paid their way in, and spent a very pleasant evening together. And again, it was quite polite and nice and not noisy.

There was practically no going out with girls from there. There might have been an occasional liaison, or marriage, it's quite pos-sible. But we had to take the trolley back, you know, and the last trolley left at eleven o'clock. If you weren't on that trolley, you didn't get home. Carnegie Hall was right in the center of town; there wasn't any place to go off into the woods or anything of that sort. There were no automobiles, you see. The boys and girls were not ambulatory. You couldn't get around very far. And you had to get out of town, into the outskirts, if you were going to do any necking or anything of that sort. There was no place, really. Oh, somebody might steal a quick kiss in a doorway—a kiss perhaps. But so far as I know that was about all there was to it. There might have been "I'll take you home," here and there, but not generally. The girls came in groups, paid their own way, and so did the boys. There were no couples to speak of in those days.

I remember the adults, the businessmen, the president of the bank, Mr. Whitcomb, who lived on what was then, what might be called an estate, on Lincoln, South Lincoln Street. Those three or four big houses there. Now these men were countrymen, al-ways available, always "Hello Edward," that kind of thing, if you see them on the street. And I remember them ambling home for lunch, on a hot summer day, from their place of business or from the bank, just walkin' along, in their shirt sleeves, and they'd have lunch, maybe a small nap, and then walk back again, slowly. It was a small, a very small community.

There was not too much competition. Obviously, the population was small. You had the college stores, which catered to the college groups—Tommy Walsh and, later, Golt, Norman Gault, Norman, what was his name, well I've forgotten, it was a partnership of Gault and Southwick. They were in competition. But it was friendly competition. It was friendly. There seemed to be no animosity. There was no point to expanding because there were no more customers.

So far as I know, there wasn't the togetherness in the adult life that there was among the children. There was very little mixture of town-gown in my day. The older population of the town remained pretty much apart from the colleges, and in those days there were not the musical and cultural events which are presently sponsored by both colleges. There were obviously nowhere near as many of them; there probably were very, very few. In the town of Amherst itself, there were no cultural, musical activities as such. There were no concerts, except perhaps an occasional band concert. A band might come in from Northampton. I don't recall that Amherst townspeople had more than just the ordinary interest—no extraordinary interest in world affairs as such, or any great movements. That would be in the colleges, of course. And actually, as I said before, there was very little, almost no, cultural liaison between the townspeople, as such, and the intellectual community of the colleges. There might have been an occasional person like my mother who made contact often, very often, with college people. But she was rare. It was very very different in those days. They were almost separate communities.

Now Amherst, like most small towns, was church oriented. The Episcopal Church was strong. The Congregational Church was strong. The Unitarian Church was strong. And the Catholic Church, of course, embraced the whole Catholic community, quite strongly. The social functions, the card parties and meetings, were church oriented for the most part. There was no common meeting ground for the townspeople in Amherst culturally. The churches had their organizations. They had the women's group, they had whatever group it might be within the church, and there were a lot of church functions. A lot of them. But they were not community-wide functions at all.

There were several fixtures in my day, people. Madame Bianchi and her boyfriend were totally unapproachable. They lived down either in the Emily Dickinson House on Main Street or one of the mansions next to it. There was a big Skillings house down there too, I think, and I knew Mr. Skillings. (By way of a small aside—The first dead man that I saw in my life was a motorcycle rider who collided with the Skillings's automobile down on South Pleasant Street, one evening, and the whole town, practically, turned out to see this dead man lying on the road. These things were events, in my day, you see.) Madame Bianchi had a history of some sort, and it was a sort of, from the boys' point of view, a hush-hush history—we didn't get to know what or why. But she was an extraordinarily interesting figure to be seen out on the streets of a small town. Meticulously dressed, haughtily mannered, totally oblivious, apparently, of everyone in town. But every day she and this . . . count (we called him the Count, he may have been a count, he may not have been—but was a handsome, sort of a Prussian type, with a cane), the two would come up from that part of Main Street, into town, take a walk, and go back. We became quite, totally used to them, but they never said a word to anybody that I know of, they lived their own lives, they were mysterious people, so far as we boys were concerned. It was Madame Bianchi, we never knew the name of the man. We never knew the relationship. I don't know that we were curious, particularly, about the relationship, whatever it may have been; I don't know. But she was a town fixture for a long, long time.

Then of course there was Dean Burns, of whom you may have heard. Dean Burns was a character. He was a character. I knew him for so many years. Dean Burns was a member of a wealthy family, from somewhere in the United States, who had an illusion that he was Dean of Amherst College, and everybody called him Dean. Everybody engaged him in talk, and he always would stop. Now he ambled around the streets alone, every day, all day practically, talking. He was a rather portly, slightly, not too badly, disturbed, not too badly. He was a member of the Herrick Home, was it? Just around the corner from Amity Street, on South Pleasant, big house up on a rise; still there. He was one of perhaps twenty disturbed people, who must have been people from wealthy families, who were sort of just farmed out to live their lives at the Herrick Home, under supervision. They would be taken out for walks, every day, every nice day, a group of anywhere from ten to twenty people, male and female, various ages, ambling along. We became accustomed to them. Nobody ever bothered them, nobody ever hooted at them.

They went their way escorted by two or three teachers or caretakers. But not Dean Burns. He was alone. He spent a great deal of his time around the colleges, in and out of fraternity houses, and consorted with the students, and he was a fixture, both a college and a town fixture, year after year after year. He was a fulminator, he sounded off on many many things. He was an interesting character. Not too often, but too often really, some of the younger children would tease Dean Burns. I've forgotten what form it took. It was never physical, it was taunting. It disturbed him terribly, terribly. Every once in a while some one of the kids, the youngsters, would start hooting at him, or something of that sort. We didn't like it, the rest of the boys didn't like it at all. But occasionally it would happen, and, oh, he would turn on them and start foaming at the mouth and fuming. It, it was not nice, and it did bother Dean, pretty much, the years he was there, the kids, the little guys, would tease him. But they never bothered the rest of the Herrick group. Never.

There was also old man McClellan, who had a little white stubble beard and was a town pauper. He pushed a wheelbarrow. He was disturbed, too, and had no home at all, lived in barns, just pushed that wheelbarrow around town, year after year after year, and then finally he died in a barn somewhere. He was accepted as a town character, never disturbed anybody, nobody bothered him. I don't know that he ever conversed with anybody at any length at all. But there he was, year after year, pushing that wheelbarrow around town.

After the data is all in, you might realize how totally unique and different that little town was, in those days, and still is, from almost every other town in the United States of America. Amherst is an Amherst, all by itself. I don't believe there's another Amherst in the United States. I suppose you have Chapel Hill, which is a small town. You have Williamstown, which is a small town. Bowdoin, Maine, which is a small town. Wesleyan, Middletown, which is a little bigger. But Amherst is Amherst. I don't believe there's another Amherst in the United States which has been comparable in all of its aspects to this unique, different, lovable, wonderful place.

Amherst, so far as I personally am concerned, is still my home town. That's my home town. I love it. And every time I go up there I have a feeling of belonging, of warmness, with the town of Amherst. And I have tremendous affection for it, of course, and a realization that I was privileged to enjoy a unique and totally satisfactory upbringing, which included a free college education, and a good one, which enabled me to go to the Yale Law School, and to be accepted without any question.

Now there's another thing I think that Amherst probably was able to—the tone, the feel, the Amherst feel—was able to instill in people. Robert Frost. Many of the professors. Some of the townspeople. A feeling—of humanness, let us say. That I belong to *here,* and it is my job to help my fellow man, no matter who he is, as much as I can, because this is a small community with common interests. We live for each other. And certainly as children, growing up in Amherst, we did live for each other. The kids did, almost regardless of race, color, or status. Now whether that's unique to Amherst, I don't know. But certainly it's there.

It was a very great privilege to have lived there, to have been, and still to be, emotionally, at least, to be a part of it.

PART FOUR

The Great Change
1946–1976

CHAPTER ELEVEN

THE GOWN OVERWHELMS
THE TOWN

THEODORE P. GREENE

Ted Greene attended Amherst College from 1939 to 1943 and returned to teach there in the history department in 1952. His own impressions of the past generation's changes in the town and in its educational institutions have been greatly assisted here by research and interviews done by students at Amherst. In particular he wishes to express his debt to the thesis by Stephen X. Roberts entitled, "Amherst: If You Can't Do It Here . . . ?"

In one generation—from the close of World War II in 1945 to the nation's bicentennial in 1976—Amherst experienced greater change than it had undergone in any previous resident's lifetime. One way to describe the change would be through numbers. In the first forty-five years after 1900, the population had grown from 5,000 residents to 7,000; the number of students enrolled at Amherst College and the state college had increased from some 650 to about 2,500; the number of new houses constructed each year averaged between six and ten. During the next *thirty* years after 1945, however, the town population grew from 7,000 to about 20,000 off-campus residents; the number of students enrolled at Amherst College, the University of Massachusetts, and Hampshire College increased from 2,500 to about 27,000; the number of new houses constructed every year in the late '60s and early '70s was averaging about 130, not to mention the additional annual increment of 300 apartment units before the sewer ban halted construction. Something of the impact of this tremendously accelerated post-war growth could be seen in the town's school enrollments, which went from 1,179 in 1945 to 3,870 by 1975.

Something of the cost could be dramatized by the annual school budget which multiplied from $164,293 in 1945 to $6,666,570 thirty years later. And something of the changing values and increasing expectations of Amherst citizens can be suggested by the educational cost per pupil which rose from $139 to $1,723 over the same years.

Another way to describe the change is by listening to long-term residents talk about the differences they feel in the Amherst of the 1970s. For an elderly widow, the whole quality of human relationships seems to have altered:

As I changed, so did the town of Amherst, I'm an old woman who has lived alone in this town for 30 years now, and I can tell you that the changes are many. If Amherst was then, at the time of my greatest sorrow and need, as it is today, I don't think I could have survived. I still have many friends here, and I love our town very much. But this place is so different from the Amherst I knew as a girl and a younger woman. Our town has grown colder and more impersonal as it has grown in size, leaving little room for those that need comfort, and old people like me. . . .

Once our community was geared to include all of its citizens, even the old people. But the "new" Amherst, the "growing" Amherst, has no need for such people. We are being phased out by being left to fend for ourselves in a town which has become so big that we cannot move about within it easily, in a town which has become so expensive that we cannot afford to eat properly or live in the homes which we built many years ago.

For a young man, working as the fourth generation on the family farm, the feeling is also one of exclusion from the new Amherst:

My uncle used to own that farm over there. We ran it with a sort of partnership. Taxes got so high two years ago that he sold out and moved to New York State. You know, there he has 250 acres and pays $900 in taxes each year. Here we still have just 100 acres, and we pay over $4,000 in taxes each year on our land. Dad says that we've got to move soon. His grandfather owned this farm and raised chickens. That was back when Harlan Fiske Stone lived down the road. Things sure are a lot different now. It's not for me here; I want to go to New York State to farm.

The situation of the elderly and of the farmers may be special cases. Some long-term residents talk about the new Amherst as a simple extension of the old. The voice of a policeman, interviewed on a street corner, expresses a desire to reaffirm continuity in the face of perceived changes:

I grew up in Amherst, and I've lived here most of my life. I worked in New York City once for a while. But this is my home. My father lived here, and so did his father before him. So I've seen this town grow and change. Even this job isn't like it used to be. . . . When I first started, I knew nine out of ten people that passed me by as I stood in front of the College Drug Store. Now I know only about one out of every twenty people, though I recognize a lot more—well enough to give a hello. But that makes this job a lot easier. It's not so personal. I can keep an eye on things and have a chance to think to myself. Sometimes too much friendly talk can get tiring.

But essentially the work is the same as it was ten years ago. Just that now there's more of it. More windows to close, more complaints to check out, more traffic violations, more drunkenness. It's not the same town it used to be, but there's nothing really bad about it now.

While some saw the change as a radical one, closing off traditional possibilities for communal human relations or rural ways of life, others saw it merely as a moderate extension and enlargement of the older Amherst. Still other longtime residents, however, saw the change as breaking down traditional barriers of discrimination, as opening up to them important new roles within a community which had once kept them on its fringes. Listen to the voice of a fifty-seven-year-old farmer who was chosen as the head of a committee of three farmers to negotiate with the town and the state for tax abatements on farmland:

I grew up on a farm in Northampton. My father was an immigrant, and let me tell you, it was something when these Amherst farmers came around here to ask me to be their spokesman.

Some farmers came to me one night and asked me to act as their spokesman. Well, even when I was a youngster, these guys in Amherst were a gang of cutthroats. That was forty years ago. I told them that I knew they were crooks and clanny and cutthroats and that before I was going to lead them they'd have to agree to do things my way. They'd have to support me, and I'd try to do something. . . . Well, they said that they would stick by me.

The first place that I went was Amherst College. The college owns a lot of land, and they have some influence in town hall. After that I started talking to people in town government. I tried to make them realize that it is good to have farmland in town. . . . I guess that I got through to people because that by-law passed at town meeting by almost a total "yes" vote. . . .

I'm sure that I can stay here in Amherst. . . . We're going to raise more young stock and sell them. Probably we'll milk more cows. I've been lucky in life, I guess, or else I wouldn't be so optimistic.

Even more optimistic is the voice of a long-established leader in Amherst's affairs, the owner of apple orchards, an apple-packing company, a store for farm products, who is now branching out into real estate developments. For several generations his family have been leaders in the economy, the society, and the politics of South Amherst. His father had been one of the town's three selectmen for thirty-five years from 1912 to 1947. He himself has in 1976 been elected to the new five-member board of selectmen as one of the few successful candidates in recent years who has no ties to the university or the colleges. If his roots are firmly in the older Amherst, his vision of change, his view of what Amherst is becoming and should become, is certainly not nostalgic—except perhaps in his desire for the relative conformity and deference upon which the town's earlier leaders could count:

I plan to build a planned unit development for 750 people. Amherst still has a great potential for growth. This is certainly not a small town now, and we can't go back in time. . . . The town consists of a highly variegated population with conflicting thought, and it is difficult to arrive at a consensus on any subject which challenges one of these groups who are vocal. What I mean by vocal is that people talk up a lot more than ten years ago. . . . Today we have more so-called experts who think they have the final sense of that which is correct and that which is harmful. I am not saying this is bad, but it can be bad, especially if they crowd their opinions on others as they stand up and cry out on the soap box. . . .

I have lived in Amherst all my life, as did my ancestors. I am selling some land to those who want to buy, blacks or whites. This is a growing town, it wants to grow. Now I have sold some land my family has farmed for a couple of generations, and it is not a happy occasion when I consider what this land has symbolized for quite a time. But you must remember that events and demands change rapidly, and very few things remain the same year after year after year.

Yes, I am fairly content. You ask what the problems of Amherst are? Well just look in the newspaper, because we experience the same conflicts just like any other suburb. Yes, we are a suburb, although not tangent to a large city. We function just like Longmeadow which is outside of Springfield, and that is a wonderful place to live. There is no reason whatsoever why Amherst cannot grow and preserve the qualities which exist today. What I mean by quality is the safety and beauty of the town, the clean air, and generally a warm feeling among the townspeople. You might not see this because a few loud voices tend to discolor the real situation, but I guarantee you that this town is carefully growing and will continue to be a wonderful place to live.

Wonderful as it might seem to the entrepreneurial spirit, the vision of Amherst as suburbia, as another Longmeadow, was a clear departure from the vision which had inspired Editor Charles Morehouse in 1900. In those earlier years the town had seemed a place apart. It had prided itself on a special identity, "a little history of our own," a unique blend of elements which were not summed up by safety, beauty, clean air, or even warm feelings.

One final voice, that of a professional landscape engineer long involved in the town's planning agencies, tries to reclaim some of that special identity for Amherst, resists seeing it as another city or suburb:

Amherst has changed a hell of a lot since I was a kid, you know. Back then, people would walk down the streets greeting everyone else. Jeez, I lived in Northampton, and I felt like I was from another world—and this is only thirty years ago, mind you. Since I settled here back in the '50s, even, there's a terrific difference.

There is for me something special about Amherst, a feeling that we all belong to something. It's not as strong as it used to be, oh, ten years ago, but a lot of us have still got it. And I'll tell you who hasn't got it: a lot of the faculty families who come out here, those from down at the University and Hampshire especially. They're here for a couple of years before moving along to another job, but they sure do try to stir things up while they're around. . . .

Still and all, the changes have been good ones, I think, for the most part. Strangers have it a lot easier these days, and I think that's good, on the whole. But things can be taken too far. We don't have to turn into a city or a suburb; we can stay a town—a little larger, a little more crowded town, but a town. That's where we town planners come in, you see.

How one felt about the changes obviously depended largely upon one's personal situation and upon one's own values. What seemed to some long-term residents as exclusion from the community impressed others as the creation of a more inclusive community where traditional walls were crumbling. What some welcomed as the transformation of a New England town into the model of American suburbia, others felt as a challenge to preserve some special Amherst identity through conscious decisions and communal planning. What was fundamentally going on, suggested some fashionable academic pundits, was an "identity crisis" for Amherst or its first real encounter with modern man's endemic affliction, the "loss of community."

Faithful readers of this book will have discovered that it took about a century and a half after 1730 for Amherst to become very self-conscious about its identity. They will have learned that Amherst did not begin with any clear communal consciousness, did not undertake any but the most minimal communal tasks until the latter decades of the nineteenth century, and even in the most highly celebrated era of community—the Amherst of Calvin Coolidge and Editor Morehouse and Warren R. Brown during the years from 1890 to 1945—did not fully come to terms with the internal lines of division and indifference and condescension. The fascinating interactions of change and of continuity during the thirty-year generation after 1945 cannot be adequately described simply by comparing numbers, by listening to individual voices, or by imposing fashionable psychological and sociological phrases upon the complex experience of the changing town.

What all these approaches obscure are the very different rates of change during successive periods within these thirty years as well as the really significant changes which developed in the cultural and political styles of the community, in the historic relations between town and gown, and in Amherst's fundamental sense of its relation to the outside world. That story is worth the effort to decipher it.

THE OLD ORDER LINGERS, 1945–1953

Calvin Coolidge could easily have recognized Amherst of the late 1940s as the same town where he had been an undergraduate fifty years before and which had supported him overwhelmingly in the 1920s. The town retained a distinct weight of its own apart from its two colleges, both of which could still be seen in some ways as an extension of the town's own values. Residents outnumbered the student population by almost three to one. Faculty and administrators at the two institutions comprised only 6 percent of the street listing of occupations. The 1,450 cattle in town outnumbered the 210 faculty. The rate of new house construction each year averaged three from 1945 to 1947 and then stabilized at an average of forty-three from 1948 to 1963. In 1946 a traffic light was installed for the first time at the corner of Main and North Pleasant streets, a significant new symbol to mark the center of town where the Hartling Stake had once stood. Yet this new light was simply a blinker, a caution signal, not a red and green and yellow beacon ordering drivers and pedestrians to stop or go.

Politically the established Republican dominance persisted without any significant change. Dewey defeated Truman in Amherst by a margin of 2,453 to 1,043 (Henry Wallace drew 62 votes, Norman Thomas 15). Although town meeting members were elected on a nonpartisan basis, in 1949 the party registrations of town meeting members showed this basic political assembly to be composed of 151 Republicans, 31 Independents, and 22 Democrats. The total voting registration of Amherst in 1948 listed 1,746 as Republicans, 424 as Democrats, and 1,961 as Independents. Amherst's Representative to the Massachusetts General Court (1945–48), Colonel Horace T. Aplington, was a Republican, a man in his sixties, a retired Army officer who had come to Massachusetts State College in the 1930s to head the ROTC program and remained in town after retirement. In the state legislature he firmly opposed a bill calling for an investigation of religious and racial discrimination at private colleges and universities. He voted against a bill which would have mandated that women serve on juries, explaining his opposition by saying, "I would have no woman related to me either by blood or marriage to sit through some of these sordid trials." The town meeting moderator, who served from 1926 to 1949, was Clarence Eastman, an Amherst College professor of German, who had extended his fervent opposition to the New Deal onto the local scene by opposing the town's 1941 purchase of the local water company on the grounds that it was "a risk enterprise and investors had the right to profit." The town's three selectmen, all Republicans, notably represented both Amherst's conservative stability and the persistent identity of separate villages within the town. From South Amherst came William H. Atkins (selectman from 1912–47), from an old North Amherst family came Albert Parsons (selectman from 1939–53), and representing the center as chairman of the selectmen and head of the town's welfare services was F. Civille Pray (selectman from 1934–53) who served essentially as the town's executive. Together the terms of these three men totalled sixty-eight years, for an average of twenty-three years apiece.

In 1949 an Amherst College senior interviewed twenty-two

community leaders in an effort to define the town's power structure and its ideology for his honors thesis in political science. With a recognizable undergraduate tone Edward Barnett concluded:

The influential men have a common ideology. They are staunch conservatives. For them, the Republican Party has a divine mission to save the United States from New Dealism and all that it implies. They believe in individualism and maintenance of the American Way. In other words, they like the way things are. . . . The Democrats are a helpless minority which as a group are not even strong enough to provide a check on majority power.

The one group from whom these community leaders did feel a challenge and for whom they expressed a general resentment was "the academic type." It was not simply farmers and workingmen who found the academics too articulate and persuasive at public meetings. Even the town's own officials, the bank officers, the merchants, the prominent landowners complained that the professors exercised a disproportionate voice in town affairs. According to Barnett's calculations, college and university people comprised only 6 percent of the names on the street list, but made up 32 percent of the town meeting members. Community leaders accused them, especially Amherst College professors who were thought to pay no property taxes on their college houses, of supporting too many measures which would raise taxes.

What seems interesting from the perspective of 1976 about the political context of these early postwar years was not, in fact, how wide a gap existed between town and gown, but actually how firmly the town's affairs remained governed by prudential, conservative guidelines. The town and its community leaders retained a clear identity apart from its educational institutions. Not all those academics who played a role in town affairs were as conservative as Moderator Eastman, but the statistics of party registration for town meeting members support the memory of long-resident professors that the academics who took much part in town affairs were themselves largely Republican and fairly conservative. The more liberal and cosmopolitan members of the local faculties, primarily clustered then at Amherst College, looked upon local politics as a lost cause and concentrated attention upon the national scene. As we shall see, the only issues upon which the most conservative elements of the town found themselves challenged by academics and their allies in town politics were the moderate ones of school construction, recreation facilities, and the appointment of a town manager.

Culturally, the dominant theme of these postwar years in Amherst was also continuity, not change. The eight books published by Amherst authors in 1945 and listed by W. R. Brown in his *Record* article (see Chapter 8) all looked to the past rather than to the present or future. They dramatized Amherst's proud sense of a provincial culture, of being a place apart from the larger world where intense self-cultivation might reveal values which could illumine the earth. Ray Stannard Baker's *American Chronicle* reviewed the experiences of the past generation, hailing the "New Order" which Wilson had tried to impose upon the world in 1919 (while telling W. R. Brown, as we have seen, that little could come from the contemporary United Nations conference in San Francisco). The new poems by Emily Dickinson and the account of old Amherst life and feuds in *Ancestor's Brocades* recaptured the world of nineteenth century Amherst. George Elliott, retired professor of English at Amherst College, in his book *Church, College, and Nation* attempted to reformulate the vision of an organic Christian civilization based upon the church, the community, and the college in a way which reshaped the nineteenth-century hopes of those townsmen who had founded and sustained the college as a bastion of the Congregational order. Harriet Whicher's *Church Symbolism* and George Whicher's *Walden Revisited* testified not only to the cultural energy of one household on Amity Street but also to the belief that one should take one's bearings from the continuing reinterpretation of religious meanings and of the nineteenth century New England individual character. The very title of Frank Prentice Rand's *Heart O'Town* bore witness to the intense feeling of this long-established pillar of liberal culture at the state college (now becoming a university) that this favorite phrase of his combined a geographical reference with an emotional and cultural foundation.

Amid the ferment of postwar changes at the college, George Frisbie Whicher '20 and F. Curtis Canfield '25 made notable efforts to keep an impatient younger generation in touch with the characters, the culture, the ironies, and the conflicts of the nineteenth century college and town. Whicher fulfilled the model of high provincial culture in which Amherst had long taken pride. While publishing regularly his graceful reviews of recent books on American literature and thought in the Sunday edition of metropolitan New York news-papers, he continued in talks and publications to set forth his unparalleled familiarity with the local past. In 1946 he edited for publication the journal of William Gardiner Hammond from the Amherst class of 1849. In 1950 Whicher published *Mornings at 8:50,* a collection of his college chapel talks on the writers, the rogues, and the distinctive characters of this area's previous century, designed, as he said, "to reveal the dimension of time to the most timeless of mortals, the American undergraduate." The cover flap noted: "The *National Geographic Magazine* for March, 1950, reproduced a photograph in color of Professor Whicher examining a letter by Emily Dickinson while reclining on the bosom of Sabrina. What more can a college teacher desire?"

Meanwhile F. Curtis Canfield, founder of the department of dramatic arts at Amherst, in order to celebrate in 1946 the one hundred twenty-fifth anniversary of the college, wrote and produced *The Seed and the Sowers,* dramatizing for a contemporary audience the struggles through which the town had given birth to the college. In 1955 Canfield published the text of this play along with a good number of his own witty, ironic chapel talks on life at the college in its early years. Despite his often humorous style, Canfield represented the serious, sober purpose with which Amherst traditionally approached the arts. Before leaving in 1954 to become Dean of the Yale School of Drama, he delivered a Senior Chapel Address entitled "The Arts and Respectability." In it could be discerned much of his own feelings for Amherst—and of Amherst's attitude toward the arts at that time:

No one leaves the city of Zion without regret. Here we have grown up. Here we have shared the comfortable feeling of belonging and of being a part of something larger and more important than ourselves. And roots sent down in Amherst ground pull out hard. . . .

We shall in the meantime go ahead trying to line ourselves up on the side of good taste, good feeling, and refinement—for that is one of the things that I feel sure Amherst has tried to teach us to do. . . . For one who has spent a long time trying to make his particular field of art a responsible and respectable part of the community, this notion that the man of art cannot be like any normal human being is repugnant. . . . The best poets and playwrights may not only look like farmers, or teachers, or bankers, they behave like them too. . . . If we've had any aim for thirty years it has been to implant the idea that the theater can be respectable without being dull, that it can be serious without being solemn, funny without being cheap. In this we have differed violently from some, like Tennesee Williams, who believe that true theater art can flourish only in an atmosphere of disorder and anarchy, and when it is dedicated to radical causes.

Amherst's cultural style in this early postwar period, like its politics, retained a strong conservative weight and identity of its own. It seemed most clearly reminiscent of the Mugwump tradition, that high-minded, elitist, Protestant New England culture cultivated by the professional classes of the Northeast in the latter nineteenth century. In Amherst one could still understand the tone of the *National Geographic Magazine* where the Grosvenors continued to describe all parts of the globe in ways consonant with the Mugwump perspectives they had known in Amherst. President Stanley King, retiring in 1946 from the leadership of the college, had represented the businessman of this tradition, austere, honorable, dignified, Yankee, interested in cultivating those ideas and those arts which could be considered "cultivated."

In a Senior Chapel Address he had once made clear his conception of "the good life" and of how he felt it was threatened in America both by "a pecuniary ideal" and by egalitarianism:

In the older countries the dominance of this point of view has been contested and its accidence mitigated by the older aristocratic ideal—the ideal of the cultivated gentleman. In America, on the other hand, the democratic concept has canalized our popular thinking into the narrower channel of the pecuniary ideal. I do not decry political democracy. I say, however, that the popular American doctrine that one man is as good as the next, irrespective of breeding, of education, of refinement of taste, of breadth of sympathy, conduces to uniformity, sterility, and dullness; it makes the good life as I have defined it more difficult of attainment.

There was a clear sense of standards in this culture. It was not a culture very congenial to the visual arts. The new permanent buildings constructed at the college and at the new university during these years were of unimaginative Georgian brick design. The town supported only one movie theater and few artists. Professor Canfield's concern for making the arts "respectable" could be understood by many of those who heard him. Respectability was a concept which had meaning and weight.

Socially, the town continued to revolve in the same interlocking pattern of including and excluding circles described in Chapter 8. Of the fifty-eight local clubs and associations listed in Frank Rand's 1958 history, only eight had expired before 1945. The Grand Army of the Republic had been mustered out in 1935. The Village Improvement Association, successor to Austin Dickinson's Ornamental Tree Association, had disbanded in 1917. The Ancient Order of Hibernians dissolved in 1928, possibly testifying to the success of an assimilation process (though the Ancient Order of Hibernians Auxiliary persisted until 1952). The Poultry Association ended in 1925, while some erosion of separate village identities may have been signalled by the closing of the North Amherst Choral Society in 1930 and the North Amherst Current Events Club in 1944. But all the others persisted, the Masons, the Grange, the DAR, the 4–H Clubs, the American Legion, the VFW, the Daughters of Isabella, the Rotary, and at least forty other regular groups which fostered communal ties under one pretext or another.

The churches remained significant centers for mingling and sorting out Amherst's residents. The Congregational churches in North and South Amherst served to cluster residents by old geographical identities, while the variety of center churches (three Congregational, Baptist, Grace Episcopal, Saint Brigid's, Wesley Methodist, Unitarian, and Zion Methodist Episcopal) cut across to some extent and reinforced to a greater extent lines of class, race, and ethnicity within the larger community. Conscious of the historic ties between the First Congregational Church and his institution, conscious also of his own ancestry which included Roger Williams and Jonathan Edwards, Charles Woolsey Cole '27 from the time of his appointment as President of Amherst College in 1946 on through the 1950s attended First Church with some regularity. There he could encounter a few of his own faculty together with two successive presidents of the new university, a large contingent of the more established faculty and administrators from the state institution, and a good proportion of the town's physicians, lawyers, bankers, public officials, and leading businessmen. There and at Grace Episcopal Church (where a somewhat larger number of Amherst College faculty attended), the town's establishment could add another dimension to their sense of some common Amherst identity.

During this early postwar period these churches and others largely followed traditional patterns of church life: Sunday services and Sunday schools; monthly meetings of the Women's Union, the Men's Club, and the Prudential Committee (or Vestry); an annual Church Fair; missionary support; regular calling by the pastor on all members of his parish. First Church, with Roy Pearson as pastor until 1947 and with Chalmers Coe succeeding him until 1954, together with Robert McAfee Brown (Amherst '43) serving for several years as associate minister, and Grace Church, with John Coburn as Rector from 1946 to 1953, were particularly fortunate. These leaders were able, through their preaching and personal qualities, to revitalize the traditional forms and to initiate a resurgence of these older churches which would persist for a decade and more after the departure of these men to larger assignments. In fact the Amherst of this period could point to these ministers as the best exemplars of its early mission to train religious leaders for the larger society. Roy Pearson would go on to head Andover-Newton Seminary, that institution which had been the keystone in the nineteenth century New England Congregational order. John Coburn would move on to head Episcopal Theological Seminary and then spend a year teaching at "street academies" in the ghetto before accepting the responsibilities of a Bishop. Robert M. Brown, while serving on the faculties of Union Seminary and Stanford University, would take such leadership roles in the civil rights movement, the ecumenical movement, and the antiwar movement that by the 1960s his picture would appear on the cover of *Time,* described as America's leading Protestant theologian.

Faculty wives helped to maintain customs of formal gentility. The wearing of evening gowns and tuxedos for dinner parties and opening nights at Kirby Theatre was beginning to fade, but senior faculty and their wives at the college still made formal calls upon new faculty couples, leaving engraved calling cards with the corner turned down to puzzle unsophisticated young instructors who had not been at home to receive the call. The Women's Club maintained a style and a cultural tone appropriate to its elegant Club House—the Victorian mansion on Triangle Street erected by Leonard Hills in 1864 and acquired by the Women's Club in 1921. Founded in 1893 "to encourage the cultural advancement of the town," the club's original membership had included about 400 women out of a total population of somewhat over 2,000 women. In the late 1940s and throughout the 1950s it continued its "culture committees" on Literature, History, Art, Music, Homemaking, Gardening—each with its own chairman and secretary from among the now 200 members. Many women were attracted to it as a way to break through the exclusive circles drawn by their husband's occupations. A university wife recalls her motivation to join: "You're exposed to more than just a small group—you meet people from all over town. If a lady from the university joins, she meets people, uh, ladies from Amherst College and from the community." An Amherst College wife recalls: "This is a very, very stratified town. The university people tend to stay together, the Amherst College people stay together, and the town people stay together. . . . This is why I joined the Women's Club." Yet inevitably this form of seeking inclusiveness seemed also to create its own exclusiveness. A club president later recalled its reputation at this time: "People used to say, 'Oh, you want to join the Amherst Women's Club? You can't do that unless you're the upper class in town.'" The Women's Club testified to a particular lingering conception of "culture," to a persistent desire for an Amherst community, and to a world where women identified their lives with their husband's occupations but cultivated a separate sphere of feminine interests. It was not inconsistent with a town whose schools would not in the late 1940s hire married women as teachers and whose salary scales paid women teachers $300 less than men for equivalent responsibilities and experience.

The lines, the boundaries, the circles were still fairly clear in Amherst's social order and still fairly well accepted as inevitable. Amherst had a larger and more established number of black citizens than any other nonurban community in Massachusetts. In 1953–54 another Amherst senior, David Chaplin, examined the situation of these black residents for his thesis in American studies. What he discovered was that the federal census had listed 199 Negroes in Amherst in 1900, but that this number had been almost cut in half, to 110, by 1950. He concluded that 150 would be a more accurate figure by the early 1950s but that the downward trend indicated by the census was certainly true. Earlier economic opportunities for small scale businesses, cleaning shops, and catering and hauling services had diminished along with the employment of household servants. Most of the blacks still in Amherst were from long-established families. Well over half owned their own homes. The mingling of races in the schools seemed to be relatively easy and without strain, but as younger blacks came of age, it proved difficult for them to find work in Amherst. Potential employers, when interviewed, pointed to the difficulties they would encounter with customers and with fellow employees if they hired Negroes. A director of staff employment at one of the educational institutions asked, "What are you going to do if five of your best workers tell you they won't work with a prospective Negro employee?"

As a result Amherst's black citizens tended to be children or older persons who had found some "place" in the town and who knew where they were and where they were not welcome. They knew the one barber (out of four in town) who was willing to cut their hair. He explained to Chaplin, "I didn't take 'em regular 'til just after the last war—used to cut 'em after hours in the basement." A real estate dealer informed Chaplin that he knew of several dozen restrictive covenants in town, although legally these were not supposed to be enforceable. Only within the last five years had the Lord Jeffery Inn owned by Amherst College dropped its ban against accepting any Negro guests (when a visiting black lecturer, the Reverend James Harvey Robinson, supported by the Amherst Christian Association protested). Chaplin also found that most whites in Amherst refused to believe that any real discrimination existed; as one citizen explained, "I don't know anything about the Negroes here, but I do know that there isn't any discrimination." Meanwhile there were some signs of change. Students rallied to protest exclusion of a black undergraduate from the Quonset Club restaurant and bar. Chaplin found the blacks he interviewed becoming more "touchy" and race conscious. He also noted the recent arrival of three black professionals, two employed as teachers in the Amherst schools and one a woman physician at Smith College.

The social order of Amherst in the late 1940s was established, traditional, and fairly well defined. Newcomers had to find their places within existing circles, and the established residents took considerable pains to recruit likely candidates for what were assumed to be their appropriate affiliations. The Reverend Roy Pearson was jokingly charged with following the moving vans to seek out new members for First Church. Lucy Benson remembers the circumstances under which she first joined the League of Women Voters:

I was pressured into it. I didn't want to join any women's organization. It was about 1950, and my husband had just gotten his teaching position at

Amherst. I wanted to stay away from the Faculty Wives, the Women's Club, and everything of that sort. But the chairman of my husband's department put one hell of a lot of pressure on me, as well as two older faculty wives who were determined to get me involved. From then on I had a meteoric rise in the organization. I was the youngest local president, the youngest state president, and the youngest national president.

The career of Lucy Benson and the advent of the power of the League of Women Voters, however, introduce some of the forces which in the years from 1945 to 1953 were already stimulating change and laying the foundations for a modified Amherst style and order in the years from 1954 to 1962. Numerous conflicts and stalemates over the schools and over proposals for a town manager suggest that the existing town leadership was unable to resolve significant problems. In this situation the young League of Women Voters (founded in 1940 but only now beginning to turn its concerns into effective actions) together with some special town committees dominated by university and college professors pressed for significant changes.

The existing town structures did prove able to take action for meeting postwar needs in two areas, veteran's housing and recreation. Twenty attractive new homes were erected by the town on Memorial Drive and made available for young veterans on terms which eventually returned a small profit of $55,000. Despite some apparent skepticism about the town's recreation needs by F. Civille Pray, chairman of the selectmen (who introduced in 1947 an unsuccessful warrant article for the sale of the still undeveloped Groff Park), the town created a permanent recreation commission with an initial modest annual budget of $4,500.

The schools, however, suffering from both a teacher shortage and a space shortage proved a far more intractable problem. The teacher shortage was aggravated by continuing discrimination against married women and by the salary differentials between men and women. No new elementary school had been constructed in Amherst for four decades, and the postwar baby boom combined with expansion at the university led to double sessions and improvised classrooms in buildings outside the schools. Still the town and its leadership could not agree on any action. Year after year from 1947 through 1952 one plan after another either failed to secure the necessary two-thirds majority in town meeting or was defeated decisively in a town-wide referendum. In 1953 the superintendent of schools resigned. Resolution of the problems would come only when, in that same year, a committee chaired by Professor Arnold Rhodes carefully and persuasively explained the advantages (especially in state financial aid) to be gained by entering into a regional school district for the construction of a new high school.

Meanwhile since 1947 the town, urged strongly by the League of Women Voters and guided by two successive reports of a special committee chaired by Professor George Goodwin from the university's government department, was debating the proposal for a town manager to replace its traditional system of a board of three selectmen and about forty other elective town offices. Again the initial reaction by the town voters in 1951 was decisively negative (715 ayes to 1,055 nays). Again it was not until 1953 that the town could be persuaded to accept change by the slim, skeptical margin of 13 votes (779 ayes, 766 nays, 104 absentions).

Throughout this early postwar period, then, Amherst retained its identity as a prudent, conservative New England town. Not until 1953 did there emerge some clear signs that the community could muster the new leadership and the new forms of organization which might cope with the changes already underway at the college and the university.

During the war years, under the judicious prodding of President King, Amherst College had made more extensive and thoughtful plans for postwar change than any other American college or university. A faculty committee headed by Professor Gail Kennedy had by 1945 laid out specific guidelines to transform the Amherst curriculum, the nature of the student body, and the internal tone of college life. Their vision was for a college which should be more democratic, more intellectual, more national, more secular, and yet more of a community than Amherst had ever been.

Before the war Amherst had enjoyed a good reputation as a small New England college, a member of the Little Three or "Potted Ivy" League, a socially and academically respectable, smaller scale alternative to the Big Three of the Ivy League. President King liked to remind receptive college audiences that a higher proportion of Amherst's graduates had been listed in *Who's Who* than was true for almost any other institution—even the Big Three themselves.

(Amherst, in fact, did rank second nationally—second to Hampden-Sidney in 1929 and second to Harvard in 1939 according to this particular measure of achievement.) He could also point with justifiable pride to the financial strength of the college, an endowment which had grown during his administration from some $9,000,000 in 1932 to almost $13,000,000 in 1946. Despite the years of depression and wartime disruption, Stanley King had even managed to amass a reserve fund of $600,000 from the surplus operating income achieved during thirteen of his fourteen years in office. The faculty's committee on long range policy in 1945 concluded: ". . . [T]here is no danger that so well established an institution as Amherst cannot survive. The real danger is that it will survive merely as 'another good college.' The college has suffered from too much of a certain kind of success."

The faculty committee deplored the prewar composition of Amherst's student body as "too narrowly homogeneous" in both its social and geographical base. They pointed out that only about two applications were usually received for every place in an entering class, that in 1939 about 67 percent of the students came to Amherst from private preparatory schools, that from 39 percent to 51 percent of a class were sons or relatives of previous Amherst graduates, that only about sixteen different states or foreign countries were represented in a class, that only about 2 percent of the students had fathers who were not business managers or professionals, and that even the entrants from high schools came from only about sixty-two different high schools in the affluent urban or suburban areas of the Northeast and Midwest. This narrow selection of students, the committee felt, lowered the intellectual possibilities of the college. The average verbal aptitude scores of the last two prewar classes (1944 and 1945) had been only 521 and 498 (out of a possible 800), while the mathematical aptitude scores had been 533 and 514. The general average of college grades achieved by the entering classes in 1939 through 1941 was 75.03. The gentleman's *c* remained a prevalent measure of appropriate academic aspirations. About one out of every six students at Amherst had ranked in the third or fourth quarter at some private preparatory school and continued at Amherst to perform at levels of *c*− and lower. Only 54 percent of Amherst's students came from the first quarter of their graduating classes in secondary school. Reforms must be made in the recruiting and selection of students, said the committee, if Amherst were to fulfill its proper function in educating an intellectual elite, "a natural aristocracy, one elected, in Jefferson's words, 'for genius and virtue,' to serve our democracy." They urged national scholarships, a larger admissions office to canvass the high schools, and "a proper representation within the student body of different economic, racial, and religious groups." In particular they noted that under Stanley King's administration, the number of Negroes in each entering class had averaged 0.4 instead of the 1.7 Negroes per class in the 1920s. The committee felt confident that there would be no contradiction between their twin goals of a more democratic and a more intellectual student body.

Nor did they, in 1945, feel any contradiction between their desire for a larger, brighter, more diverse pool of applicants and their insistence upon a new curriculum of "general education" courses which was to be more demanding, more rigid in its requirements, and less tolerant of diverse student interests than the program of any competing liberal arts college. The requirement that all students take together at least six newly designed "core" courses during their first two years was a conscious effort to create something of the same sense of community, some of the original serious social purpose which the committee thought had characterized Amherst in its origins. "We believe," they said, "that in some ways it is more significant that the students have a common body of knowledge than it is they have just this particular knowledge as against some other. A common body of knowledge plays an essential part in the creation of an intellectual community." The vision behind Amherst's new curriculum, which the education editor of the *New York Herald Tribune* hailed as "the most important attempt since the war to improve American higher education," was not simply one of cultivating individual intelligences. The vision which Gail Kennedy had imbibed from his mentor John Dewey was the creation of a "socialized intelligence," the conviction that "a man's knowledge and skill are his only to serve the good, public and private, of the community." Such a goal could be achieved only through emphasizing the communal dimensions of the college: "The framing of a curriculum is in a fundamental sense an attempt to make of the college an intellectual community. To do this is to fulfill the deeper religious intent of producing a common faith." The new educational vision, like that of

Vermont's John Dewey who had inspired it, was a twentieth century effort to revitalize and secularize a sense of mission which seemed to be associated with the democratic structures, the communal purposes, and the high-minded intellectual style of some imagined New England town of an earlier era. The committee went on to call for abolition of Amherst's fraternities which seemed most clearly to be undemocratic, anti-intellectual enclaves corrupting this larger vision of a community actively learning how "to control by intelligence a changing world." Here was certainly a heady vision of education and of community to emerge from the rather sleepy, very conservative, not very intelligently managed town of Amherst in 1945.

By 1954 Gail Kennedy published a review of *Education at Amherst* in which he assessed the actual impact of this new program almost a decade after its conception. The new dean of admissions, Eugene S. Wilson '29, together with the attraction of a coherent, rigorous curriculum, had begun to transform Amherst's student body. In 1953–54, almost five candidates applied for every place in the entering class. For the first time in decades, the class admitted that year included a majority (53 percent) who came directly from high schools instead of from private prep schools. Only 15 percent of that class were sons of Amherst alumni, and the earlier classification of "relatives" of Amherst alumni was no longer recorded. This class came from thirty-two different states or foreign countries instead of the sixteen areas represented in the class of 1941. Its official verbal aptitude had climbed to 583 from the 498 of the last prewar class, and its mathematical aptitude to 626 from the earlier 514. Professor Kennedy noted that "a real effort" had been made to recruit more Negro students, but in 1953–54 only eight students (averaging 2 per class or 7/10th of 1 percent of each class) were Negroes, a fact which he attributed simply to the lack of sufficient large scholarship grants.

Amherst's board of trustees had decided against the faculty recommendation to abolish fraternities, but they had insisted upon "radical reform." In 1946 they required each fraternity to "formally advise the Board of Trustees at Amherst College that there is no prohibition or restriction by reason of race, color, or creed affecting the selection of the members of such chapter." Amherst delegations led the way at national fraternity conventions in the effort—sometimes successful, sometimes frustrated—to strike explicit racial and religious restrictions from fraternal covenants and constitutions.

Even where explicit written taboos did not exist, the Amherst chapter of Phi Kappa Psi discovered in 1948 that the initiation of Thomas Gibbs, a Negro freshman, in defiance of instructions from their national headquarters, led to the revocation of their charter. The *New York Times* commented: "In this episode we see the real meaning of a liberal education. An Amherst degree has always been respected. It will be more respected now." By 1953, five of Amherst's thirteen fraternities had broken with their national bodies in order to assure the freedom to select their members without racial or religious discrimination.

These changes at the college attracted national attention, generated complaints from the more conservative alumni, and enlisted the enthusiasm of a new postwar generation of faculty members. Yet from the perspective of 1976, what seems most striking about the immediate postwar college is not the novelty of its new program so much as the fundamental continuity in its institutional ethos. Amherst was seeking more diversity in its student body, but it would strive even more earnestly to mold its students into a single intellectual community, into a common conception of the educated man. Not only would the core curriculum work toward this end; so also would the extracurricular context. More Catholics and many more Jews entered as Amherst freshmen, but President Cole feared that allowing any formal organization of a Newman Club or of an Hillel Society to parallel the official (Protestant) Christian Association would create divisiveness. The administration of the college remained firmly and even exclusively in the hands of men reared in an earlier Amherst. During the academic year 1950–51, the list of officers of administration numbered a mere sixteen posts. Thirteen of these were held by Amherst graduates. "Outsiders" functioned only as superintendent of buildings and grounds or director of dining halls, while the sole woman listed in the administration or the faculty was Gladys Kimball as recorder. Among the faculty of ninety-three men twenty-two members were Amherst graduates (24 percent or one out of every four). Over one-third (36 percent) of the Amherst faculty had received their graduate training at Harvard, and over two thirds (69 percent) had taken their advanced education at an Ivy League university. Four faculty members had no degree beyond an Amherst one. Those who were to administer and to educate a newly diverse student body remained themselves a fairly coherent group embodying the cultural traditions of the northeastern professional class and of Amherst itself.

The new program at Amherst called for a more "democratic" college, for the erosion of prewar lines of race, religion, region, and class in selection of students. It envisioned molding these various minds into a single "intellectual community" which would provide a "natural aristocracy" to show the nation how to "control by intelligence a changing world." But within this vision there was little place for nourishing diversity itself or respecting cultural identities different from the dominant one. Peter Schrag, a 1953 graduate of Amherst, wrote a book in 1970 called *The Decline of the WASP*. In it he displays his own later consciousness of the kind of cultural mold which Amherst in the 1950s imposed upon even such a cosmopolitan student as he was:

I was born a German Jew, moved to Luxembourg when I was four, to Belgium when I was not quite ten. . . . Growing up in Queens in the forties, I regarded myself simply as a New York Jew; thereafter, going to Amherst College, I tried (with less success than I imagined at the time) to become a WASP, an attempt I did not give up until, years later, I began to suspect that there were, for me, other and better ways of being an American.

The immediate postwar years saw Amherst College bring to the Connecticut Valley a much wider sample of the nation's youth. Nothing in the college's new curriculum nor in its extracurricular ethos, however, would significantly challenge the cultural identity—even the cultural complacency—of this established New England town with its remnants of the old Mugwump style.

Up at the other end of town in 1945, far more extensive changes were impending for Massachusetts State College. Yet the existing accounts of that institution's history suggest it had done very little before the end of World War II to plan seriously for the postwar transformation which actually took place. Passage of "the G.I. Bill" for veterans' educational benefits had led in 1944 to creation of a committee headed by Professor Theodore Caldwell to plan for meeting the expected needs of returning veterans. The committee's vision focused primarily upon how to fit these older students into the existing prewar patterns of the institution by offering them refresher courses, remedial training, and credit for varieties of educational experience. It pointed to the established two-year programs in agriculture and horticulture for those veterans who might wish direct vocational training. It emphasized that the standards of the regular four-year program of studies should be maintained. Its one call for any real change in the institution itself was to urge preparations for expanding the program in engineering. Meanwhile the State Emergency Public Works Commission also in 1944 had made proposals for postwar building needs. Its recommendations (for an institution which had with difficulty accommodated its 1,700 students before the war) were limited to three new buildings for engineering, physics, and home economics. Even these facilities, thanks to the lengthy planning and appropriations process, would not be available until late in 1948. The essential story of the emerging University of Massachusetts from 1945 to 1953 was a story of hectic, ingenious, hastily improvised steps to cope with a flood of veterans whose numbers and whose needs had not been clearly envisaged.

Evidence of this improvisation sprang up rapidly on the Amherst campus in 1946: three new dormitories funded by the Alumni Building Corporation, five new simple cinder block dormitories (including accommodations for married couples) authorized by the state legislature, and eighteen wooden residence buildings transferred from military camps. Four more large "temporary" wooden "annexes" were mustered into peacetime service as classrooms, as laboratories, and as dining halls. One of these would burn before completion while the other three actually remained in use into the 1960s. It proved difficult for Massachusetts fully to accept the idea that after World War II a new social order was developing in which over 40 percent of its youth, instead of the prewar level of 15 percent, would expect access to some form of higher education. The persisting presence of wooden annexes and crude cinderblock dormitories on the Amherst campus testified to some continuing reluctance to accept as permanent those changes in society which had initially been accepted as the special and temporary benefits due to veterans of the war.

The most dramatic instance of improvisation as well as the most obvious manifestation of the incapacity of the Amherst campus to accommodate immediately the new scale of things was the creation of the Fort Devens Branch of the Massachusetts State College. By the spring of 1946 returning veterans, unable to find space in the

COURTESY OF THE JONES LIBRARY

THE UNIVERSITY OF MASSACHUSETTS IN 1945.

state's private colleges and universities, were clamoring for state action to provide that higher education which the G.I. Bill had promised. Never in history have politicians and educational administrators
responded as quickly to demands for change as they did at this time.
On April 14, President Baker of MSC wrote the Governor proposing that one of the army camps be converted into a branch of the state
college to provide returning veterans with the first two years of a
college education, after which the veterans could move to the
Amherst campus for their final two years. By May 14, the Governor
had convened an advisory committee consisting of the heads of the
private colleges and universities in Massachusetts. By June 8, under
the chairmanship of Harvard's President Conant, this committee had
endorsed and spelled out procedures to accomplish this plan; on June
14, the legislature enacted the proposal into law. By the end of September over 1,300 veterans assembled at the new college in Fort
Devens to begin their studies. Three years later almost 3,000

graduates emerged from Fort Devens looking for an appropriate institution within which to complete their educations.

It was this pressure, rather than any deliberate, long-range educational planning, which led the state legislature in May of 1947 to transform Massachusetts State College at Amherst into the University of Massachusetts. Neither in its size nor in its emphasis was the prewar MSC suited to meet the needs of these veterans. Few of them wished careers in farming or in agricultural research where the Amherst institution had earned international recognition; many of them desired training in engineering which had previously been slighted; more of them looked for a program in business administration which had been nonexistent. And those undecided on careers expected a liberal arts course of study which had not yet emerged fully from the subordinate role to which President Butterfield had clearly consigned it during the early decades of the twentieth century. The decision to create a state university at Amherst was in 1947 simply a decision to meet the pressure of veterans by hastily expanding the state college in those areas for which there seemed to be the most immediate demands. No one yet could clearly envision the potential size or nature of the future University of Massachusetts.

The years from 1947 through 1953 continued this tale of heroic scrambling and adjustment. Change, ferment, improvisation, and unprecedented expansion seemed to pervade the Amherst campus. Yet from the perspective of 1976 what impresses one is how much more closely the new university still continued to resemble the prewar college than it yet did the institution of the 1960s and 1970s. Ill health forced President Baker to resign in 1947, but his successor, Ralph Van Meter, had spent his entire academic career since 1917 on the Amherst campus and had been head of the Division of Horticulture. Although many retirements did occur around 1950, President Van Meter stressed continuity rather than innovation by appointing existing members of the faculty to head the newly expanded Graduate School and School of Home Economics, the newly reorganized School of Agriculture, and the newly created School of Business Administation. Frank Prentice Rand, longtime head of the English department, became dean of the School of Liberal Arts while Walter Ritchie of the chemistry department became dean of the School of Science. Not until 1955 did it prove possible to merge these two areas into a College of Arts and Sciences. Even the numerical expansion of students during these years did not give Amherst townspeople any very clear sense that the future at the university might be on a radically different scale from the past. After the phasing out of Fort Devens in 1949, total student enrollment at the Amherst campus had grown from the prewar figure of 1,700 to 3,900. Five years later the enrollment had increased only to 4,400, an apparent annual increase of no more than 100. Amherst residents, at the end of this first postwar decade, might well have concluded that the pace of development of the new university would not greatly disturb the traditional balances between town and gown. In any case, the moderate expansion at the north end of town seemed to be well in the hands of familiar figures who had long since been acculturated to the relatively conservative social, political, and cultural patterns of the surrounding Amherst community.

THE WELL-MANAGED COMMUNITY, 1954–1962

What marked the second phase of Amherst's postwar development was the emergence of a remarkable new group of leaders to manage the town's affairs. Again unprecedented change and growth occurred during another eight-year period from 1954 to 1962. But once again the nature and the rate of change within these years did not seriously shatter the town's essential sense of continuity and stability. The competence of its new leadership and a persistent, firm sense of its own cultural identity induced most of Amherst's citizens to share in the confidence expressed by the planning board in 1955 that "most of the questions can be foreseen and properly dealt with if sufficient study and planning is carried out ahead of time." A new note of rationality, a new degree of communal consciousness now flavored the continuing Yankee sense of prudence and the persistent pride in being a rather special "place apart."

The front page of the *Amherst Journal-Record* for April 15, 1954 carried two dramatic stories. One announced a $5 increase in the tax rate; the other described the selection of Allen Torrey to be Amherst's first town manager. Torrey was then a young man of thirty-one years with noticeable traces of a Yankee twang in his speech and a solid record of prudent achievement in such New England towns as Lancaster, New Hampshire and Camden, Maine. The newspaper commented that "his record at Camden shows two years of reduced tax rates while numerous improvements in the services of the town government are noted." To work with the town manager, there was created a new five-member board of selectmen to replace the aged, experienced three-man board with its traditional representatives from North Amherst, South Amherst, and the center. This new board also represented the established, older leadership of the town—its youngest member was twenty years older than Allen Torrey—yet it embodied a recognition that the significant new constituencies in Amherst were not geographical divisions but functional groupings. Two members of the new board were respected leaders of the town's business community; a third was Eunice Mannheim, the first woman ever to serve as selectman, whose election was clear evidence of the central role which the League of Women Voters had played in creating this new form of government and would continue to play in implementing it; a fourth member had been for many years before his retirement treasurer of Massachusetts State College and the new state university; the final member was the longtime comptroller of Amherst College. All of them were registered Republicans. Four of the five might on occasional Sundays see each other in the pews of the First Congregational Church. All this constituted a rational reorganization of town government but not any significant departure in the cultural style or values of the town, except for the larger role of Amherst's women.

Before 1954 most of the secondary town offices, about forty of them, had been elective. Under the new charter of town management only the selectmen, the moderator, and a few other posts were to be filled directly by the voters. It would now be Allen Torrey as town manager and Moderator Winthrop Dakin (to a lesser degree) who would select the persons to serve in the town hall offices, to fill out the town's standing committees, and to comprise those special ad hoc committees and advisory groups to deal with emerging problems. Amherst was fortunate in that both these men had a keen eye for quality and a good knowledge of the more likely candidates for town services. "Toby" Dakin, the Squire of Amherst, the most respected leader among all New England's town moderators, chairman of the Massachusetts board of higher education, author of a wry, witty column in the local paper during these years, brought to the town's service much of the same distinction of style and high dramatic purpose which his brother-in-law Thornton Wilder had cast around the theater's archetype of a New England small town.

Meanwhile Allen Torrey, despite his relative youth, took hold of town affairs with a firm hand and managed to create in town hall both a personal, familial atmosphere and a high degree of efficiency. He spoke his mind without hesitation, but like the good Yankee he was, he also listened to anyone willing to stand up to him. These two men set the tone for a new level of responsibility within Amherst's "establishment." They helped to create an atmosphere within which capable men like Ted Bacon, Arnold Rhodes, and others gladly shouldered heavy burdens of planning for the town's steady, pressing growth.

The style of town leadership during these years was very much that of an enlightened, prudent, confident "establishment." The board of selectmen met regularly on Friday mornings, which was a convenient time for them but which made it impossible for most citizens to attend any meetings if they had wished. Agendas were made up and circulated the night before the meeting with the result that no one outside the board could know when issues would arise for discussion or decision. Under Ted Bacon the planning board also proceeded about its business with little community participation to supplement the high level of technical knowledge and intelligence on the board itself. Even the representative town meeting did not prove a focus for any widespread community interest and participation. In 1952 Amherst was ranked thirty-ninth of forty Massachusetts towns in the number of candidates running for seats in representative town meetings. Amherst's citizens were generally glad to let Allen (or Toby or Ted or Arnold) do it.

This style of leadership seemed to work well in keeping the town abreast of its problems. In 1957–58 new water sources were secured. In 1959 a housing authority was created which soon had built thirty apartments for low-cost rentals to the town's elderly citizens. In 1961 a half million dollars was voted to rebuild the sewage plant. In 1962, with little fanfare, a conservation commission was created to buy up and preserve appropriate areas for the town. All these the town accepted quietly as prudent steps in its gradual, incremental growth. A final symbolic recognition of the dominant role town hall had come to play in town affairs occurred in 1962 when the town hall itself was extensively remodeled. The old second floor auditorium which had served for over seventy years as the scene of open and then representative town meetings was eliminated in order to make room for the growing number of town agencies under one centralized roof.

Only at one point—in 1958—did Amherst's citizens revolt against the establishment's expert management. At that time, Ted Bacon's planning board brought a carefully devised major new zoning law to town meeting. The plan was designed to prevent high-density residential building, a suburban bedroom overflow from Springfield and Holyoke, from arising in the outlying town areas, especially in South Amherst where it would cause high town expenditures for water, sewage, roads, and schools. In order to avoid these expenditures and prevent crowding while still allowing for continuing growth of university faculty housing, the plan called for minimum sizes of one-acre and two-acre lots on which individual wells and septic tanks could be located. The town meeting representatives, after eliminating the two-acre minimums as too severe, passed the proposal with the necessary two-thirds majority and thereby unleashed the most significant debate of this period over the town's sense of its own identity and of its future. Within five days a petition was handed to the town clerk demanding a referendum on the new zoning law. In support of the modified plan were lined up all of the town's official "establishment"—town manager, selectmen, finance committee, town assessor, board of health, League of Women Voters, and newspaper. Opposed to it were a few identifiable figures along with a host of anonymous letter writers in every day's edition of *The Hampshire Gazette*. To them, the issue seemed very clear:

Isn't the one acre lot stipulation an indirect way of keeping fine but relatively poor people out of Amherst? Isn't it a means of discriminating in favor of the well-to-do?

Father of Two

This machine sounds and resembles many Russian tactics I have seen in the last War. Is this another purge? A secret method to ride the working class people out of Amherst? To make Amherst a home exclusively for intellectuals?

Underprivileged Citizen

Fifty-nine percent of the registered voters went to the polls and by a count of 1,606 nay to 1,032 yea gave the planning board and the town's leaders a resounding defeat. Most of Amherst's citizens saw the new zoning proposal as a far more obvious and radical threat to the historic identity and composition of the town than seemed the steady but still very gradual growth of the university in those years.

It was true that the university had in fact begun to break away from seeing itself as a simple expansion of the prewar state college. In 1954 an outsider with considerable experience at other public and private universities, Jean Paul Mather, had been brought in to succeed President Van Meter whose health was failing. Together with an energetic young provost, Shannon McCune, the new president spent six full years trying to enlighten the citizens of Massachusetts, their state legislators, and the Amherst campus as to what would be necessary to create a good state university. Schools of Education, of Nursing, of Physical Education became firmly established. At last the College of Arts and Sciences brought together separate programs into a stronger basic core with a full range of separate academic departments. Mather managed to secure, from 1954 to 1960, almost thirty-eight million dollars in new construction from the state legislature. Before quitting in frustration in 1960 because he had been unable to gain the full fiscal autonomy needed to compete for hiring and retaining first-rate educators to staff those departments and fill those buildings, Mather had nevertheless done much to create a consciousness of the further changes which would be needed. His successor, John W. Lederle, would thus be in a position to preside over the emergence of a full-scale, dynamic new state university.

Yet up to 1962, at least, Amherst had not felt the full nature of the changes such an institution would make upon the town. None of the extensive new building construction under Mather had yet launched into the scale of high-rise structures. Continuing active erection of new dormitories testified to the still prevalent assumption that the new waves of students, like the old ones, would mostly be housed on campus. Mather, in fact, spoke only of a goal of 10,000 students by 1965. When he left in 1960, university enrollments in six years had grown from 4,400 to 6,500 at a rate of about 350 additional students per year. The concomitant expansion of faculty had proceeded at a rate which simply supported the average building in town of about forty-three new houses every year from 1948 through 1962.

At Amherst College, also, the changes between 1954 and 1962 did little to alter the fundamental ethos of the college or of its long relation to the town. A formal decision was made by 1960 to raise college enrollment from a limit of 1,000 to a new level of 1,200, but in practice the college had already often exceeded the lower limit. Even with this modest expansion, the ratio of applicants to spaces in an entering class continued to rise from 5:1 to 6:1 or 7:1. Along with this increase in selectivity went a rise in the statistical measures of intellectual aptitudes and a further range of geographical and religious, but not of racial, diversity. The greater and abler numbers of students, however, continued to be molded into the same curricular and social patterns which had been envisioned with such success in 1945. A new curriculum which would have introduced more variety and choice within the essential framework of the existing core curriculum was strongly urged by a select committee under Professor Koester in 1959, but was rejected in the faculty vote. President Charles W. Cole '27, who had led the postwar revitalization of Amherst, resigned in 1960 after a thirteen-year term. His successor, Calvin H. Plimpton '39, came from an old and particularly distinguished Amherst family. His father, George·A. Plimpton '76, had been an Amherst trustee for forty-one years and had headed the board for twenty-nine years before his death in 1936. The brother of the new president, Francis T. P. Plimpton '22, had already served on the board for fifteen years and had been chairman of the selection committee for the new president. Despite the novelty of appointing as president a man trained in medicine, the new selection seemed to assure continuity far more than change. By 1962 no one could yet foresee very clearly the actual changes in tone and widening of horizons which this urbane, cosmopolitan new president would bring to the administration and atmosphere of the college. Certainly no one could yet imagine the drastic forces for change which would impinge upon Amherst during the second half of Calvin Plimpton's administration.

In the year 1962–63 the administration and faculty of the college still seemed to represent the dominance of past traditions and past identifications. But some evidence of erosion in particular forms of clubbishness, some slight indication that the diversity sought in the student body was also beginning to affect their elders could be discerned. In 1950–51 all administrative posts except those responsible for buildings and grounds, dining halls, and record keeping had been in the hands of Amherst graduates. By 1962–63 the number of listed officers of administration had risen from sixteen to twenty-six, outsiders had been admitted to second-level positions as assistant or associate deans, and the overall proportion of Amherst graduates in the administration had dropped somewhat from 81 percent to 62 percent. Within the faculty Amherst graduates had declined slightly from a proportion of 24 percent (or one out of every four) to 20 percent. Those with graduate training at Harvard had declined in their proportion of the faculty from 36 percent to 27 percent, but the dominance of the Ivy League in the career lines of Amherst's faculty had eased only from 69 percent to 63 percent. Amherst College still retained most of its clubbish, Mugwump, mandarin tone.

Even as late as 1962, then, the gradually growing presence of the gown had not yet changed significantly the traditional political, social, and cultural patterns of the town. In 1956 Amherst gave 3,154 votes to the Republican President Eisenhower and only 1,071 to his Democratic opponent Adlai Stevenson. In 1958 the town listed its registered voters as 2,091 Independents, 1,753 Republicans, 642 Democrats. Even in 1960 Massachusetts's own native son, John F. Kennedy, could draw only 1,789 votes from Amherst compared with Richard Nixon's 2,716 in an election where over 92 percent of the town's voters cast ballots. All of the selectmen continued to be registered Republicans.

Socially the existing lines of clustering persisted. In a delightful column published in the local newspaper, Toby Dakin undertook to explain the particular qualities of Amherst society. His view from the top (a top which he denied even existed) would not have appeared wholly strange to Sue Dickinson, that perceptive raconteur of Amherst's nineteenth century social customs:

Women on settling in Amherst are so often baffled by our social and cultural situation that I gladly undertake to clarify it.

Social tone here is almost imperceptible. Our social structure is not the conventional laminated pyramid in which the ambitious strive for access to the top layers, but rather a cellular diffusion. The town is a jumble of social cells. Any given individual will have access to four or five or fifteen or twenty of them.

There is no distinct feeling that any cell is more desirable than another, although that may often be the case. The feeling, rather, is that they are different: one vapid, one earnest, one gentle, one worldly, one witty, one mental, one salty, one avant-garde, and so on. Some are conglomerate, some nondescript. . . .

Socially Amherst, like the Mediterranean, is 'large enough to hold a varied weather,' and fortunately it is not benumbed by institutional distortion, as by a country club, a '100' club, a yacht club, or the like.

Women will acquire access to some cells through their husband's occupation; and even in the purely distaff zone he matters somewhat. Many of the mentally animated go in for the League of Women Voters, and there each stands pretty much on her own merits. The three or four women's clubs of numerically limited membership tinge social life too faintly to effect institutional distortion. The churches and the Amherst's Women's Club offer a better fare than one might be led to expect from first exposure. . . .

It is appreciated for guests to go home early, for our social functions are diversions, not enterprises. Although conversation is performed acceptably, any improvement wrought by newcomers is warmly welcomed.

A religious census of the town taken in 1957 revealed a number of striking points about the continuing hold of this traditional base for Amherst's culture. First, perhaps, was the rather surprising fact that 4,719 adults (about 200 more than the town's registered voters) actually responded to a questioner at their door who asked about their religious affiliation. Second was the discovery that a full 84 percent of these adults listed themselves as affiliated with one of the following religious groups:

Congregationalists	31%
Roman Catholics	30%
Episcopalians	10%
Methodists	8%
Baptists	3%
Unitarians	2%

Third, then, was the discovery that Congregationalism and Catholicism pretty well divided and dominated the town's religious culture between them—while for some reason these census takers did not even record those who may have announced their ties to Judaism, to the Quakers, or to any other persuasion. Religious activities flourished throughout these years. Both Paul Tillich and Billy Graham drew overflow crowds to the college hilltop during Christian Embassy week. The First Congregational Church had never in its long history drawn so many townspeople and students on Sunday mornings. It had to hold two successive services and build a new wing of classrooms in order to accommodate the throngs of worshippers and of Sunday school children.

All the evidence suggested that the gradually growing numbers of students, of faculty, of administrators at the university and at the college were generally sorting themselves out among the existing political, social and religious institutions of the town. A particularly able group of town officials conveyed the impression that the process of moderate growth was under wise control. No one in 1962 could have foreseen the radical confrontations and drastic transformations which most of Amherst's institutions would experience in the next decade.

THE TRANSFORMING YEARS, 1963–1976

The rather startling fact about this postwar generation of change in Amherst is that most of the significant changes were concentrated into the span of years from 1963 through 1972. This was the decade which transformed Amherst from a recognizable extension of the town Calvin Coolidge had known in the 1890s into a new form of community which no one by the 1970s could clearly categorize. In these years buildings in Amherst rose at amazing rates, reached heights and sizes not previously seen outside major cities, and took on forms which set natives to shaking of heads and clucking of tongues. The buildings were simply the most visible symbols— along with the intensifying traffic and the changing student garb—of transformations in scale and in consciousness which affected the relations of town and gown, upset the old political balances, challenged the established Mugwump culture, and altered Amherst's sense of itself as "a place apart" from the larger world. The abrupt halt to growth by 1973 combined with the financial stringency besetting higher education after that date to leave Amherst citizens somewhat benumbed and bewildered as they faced the last quarter of the twentieth century.

In 1945 the campus pond at Massachusetts State College had served as an impressive, pleasing focus for the two- and three-story buildings and the solid old grey stone chapel which clustered loosely around its placid water. In 1976 this pond remained at the center of the campus of the University of Massachusetts. Its waters were still placid, and the old stone chapel still overlooked the pond. Yet a passing observer had to peer purposefully to make out these old campus landmarks. The delicate quiet of the campus pond was almost obscured by a massive, sprawling, concrete fine arts complex to its south and by a twelve-story Campus Center to its North. The upward thrust of the old chapel spire was dwarfed by the towering dimensions of five twenty-two-story dormitories, the twenty-eight-story library, and the massive proportions of other buildings. By 1976 many people in the town of Amherst could identify with that pond and that old chapel spire. The old Amherst was still there. Many of its longtime residents and most of its institutions retained their original proportions and their own quiet culture. But somehow the new bureaucratic culture of the university and of the chain store shopping centers on Route 9 seemed to have overwhelmed older cultural landmarks.

At the heart of this new bureaucratic culture, the person chiefly responsible for envisioning and effectuating the new scale of things for the University of Massachusetts, was John William Lederle, appointed president of the university in 1960. His skill in the new bureaucratic culture was attested to by his experience as director of the Institute of Public Administration at Michigan State University and as controller of the state of Michigan. His missionary zeal in expanding the bureaucratic culture had been demonstrated by his service as organizer and first director of the Institute of Public Administration at the University of the Philippines. Convinced of the need for creating a "public center for excellence" in this region of great private universities, he saw this small university of 6,500 students in 1960 as "potentially a giant." His first step was to secure from the legislature that fiscal autonomy to allocate educational funds for which his predecessor had fought. His second step was to increase dramatically the annual rate of additional new students from 350 to 1,500 every year after 1961—the maximum rate for which he calculated the university would be able to provide new buildings and new teachers regularly until stability might be achieved (in his estimate) somewhere around an enrollment of 25–30,000. By 1970 when President Lederle resigned after a decade of dynamic expansion the student enrollment had tripled to 21,000, the faculty had kept pace in numbers and improved notably in quality with the doubling of faculty salaries, seventy new buildings had been erected at a cost of $150,000,000, and eight other major buildings including the twenty-eight-story library, the Graduate Research Center, and the massive Fine Arts Center were under way. It had been an exhilarating, hectic, confused period. Ted Bacon recalled the problems of the university's master plan committee: "The ink was barely dry on one plan, and we'd have to draw up another. The specific dimensions of growth and change were that unpredictable."

While the major impetus for changing the scale of things in Amherst came from the university, President Lederle's institution was not the only source for expansion and innovation after 1962. On a warm, misty, dreamlike autumn Saturday late in October of 1963—about three weeks before his fatal motorcade in Dallas—President John F. Kennedy landed by helicopter on the playing fields at Amherst College. At the request of John J. McCloy and Francis T. P. Plimpton, two Amherst trustees who were distinguished appointees in his administration, President Kennedy came to dedicate the ground for a new library, the Robert Frost Library (soon to be known simply as "the Frost"), located at the center of the college. The occasion also helped to launch a major capital funds drive for Amherst. By the time of his resignation in 1971 President Calvin Hastings Plimpton could point to about $40,000,000 added to Amherst's capital assets during his ten-year administration as well as to eight major new buildings and several additions which altogether gave the college during these years more additional building space than had been constructed in all the previous 140 years of its existence.

A further, somewhat unexpected consequence of the Amherst College energies mobilized for this fund drive was the creation in these same years after 1962 of a whole new liberal arts college in South Amherst. Charles R. Longsworth '51 had been brought back to Amherst College as assistant to the president in order to administer the fund drive for his alma mater. In the process of this successful enterprise, he encountered a wealthy Amherst alumnus who was very interested in the *New College Plan* of 1958 which had been conceived by representatives from Amherst, Mount Holyoke, Smith, and the University of Massachusetts. The result was a gift of $6,000,000 from Harold F. Johnson to found a new, innovative liberal arts college on a site of 450 acres in South Amherst. By 1965, with Chuck Longsworth as its vice president (and only officer), Hampshire College had received a charter from the state. By 1966 Franklin Patterson, as its new president, and Chuck Longsworth had published in *The Making of a College*—a full and striking plan "For a

HAMPSHIRE COLLEGE, OPENED IN 1970.

New Departure in Higher Education." By 1971 the first class entered Hampshire, and Longsworth became president of the fledgling institution which he had effectively nurtured.

The founders of a brand new college had to look with a more open eye than did older residents at what was happening to Amherst by the middle of the 1960s. What Patterson and Longsworth described in 1966 was a vision of the four-college area which had only begun to penetrate the consciousness of most Amherst citizens:

Over the Mount Holyoke range to the south . . . a great wave of urbanization is coming to crest. The trapezoid itself is more a part of megalopolis than it knows, and within fifteen miles of Amherst rampant urbanization is in full view, with all of the trappings: exhaust smog, traffic jams, water pollution and water shortage, racial tension, slums, tract housing, industrial blight, and the rest—a dramatic contrast to bucolic Amherst and Hadley.

The fact is that things are not all that bucolic in Amherst and Hadley either. The Hampshire trapezoid is in a stage of incipient urbanization, catalyzed by the rapid development of land that is more available than land to the south, spurred by new roads, and nourished by the rapid, inexorable growth of the University of Massachusetts.

The result in Amherst, where there is the greatest pressure, is a large number of new home starts (many in tract housing of mediocre design), a rising tax rate (already as high as any in the Commonwealth of Massachusetts), and dramatic increases in road traffic, land costs, and the rate of commercial development. Suddenly, within a stone's throw of the University and Amherst College are the evidences of instant Los Angeles transplanted: large shopping centers with enormous parking areas, drive-in theatres, motels, automatic car wash establishments, and similar manifestations.

The Hampshire trapezoid is in the early stages of a cycle of urbanization which can lead to planless sprawl, ugliness, noise, and short-term profit taking which does violence to the priceless land. But the cycle has, if men and institutions are wise enough to make it so, the potential of achieving urbanization without wanton destruction of the essential loveliness of the Valley, even as the order changes. Man here could truly be the architect of his urban environment.

In four short paragraphs this passage testified to even more change in Amherst than it realized. Here was, first of all, the simple assumption that the whole area was to be defined entirely in terms of its educational institutions—a Hampshire trapezoid for which Mount Holyoke, Smith, Amherst, the University of Massachusetts, and the new Hampshire College provided the essential points of orientation and identification. In this vision the gown had overwhelmed the town. Not only did the towns seem to retain no significant separate identities or interests of their own, the Hampshire founders also proposed explicitly that the educational institutions should take a more active part in determining community policies: "The founding of Hampshire College could provide a 'takeoff point' from which it would be possible for the institutions in the Valley to move strongly toward increased and more productive interinstitutional cooperation in academic matters and with equal strength toward playing an active, vital part in helping shape the urban transformation of the Valley now already under way." What this new Hampshire prose primarily raised to consciousness was not so much how urbanization was threatening to inundate Amherst's acres as how the academy, its values, its members, its modes of organization, were already coming to dominate the older mixed cultures and identities of the town.

A second change evident in this Hampshire passage marked a difference in the sense of Amherst's relation to the outside world. No longer did the conception of Editor Morehouse prevail, the notion of

Amherst as "a place apart" with a special history of its own which spared its citizens most of the problems of the larger world. Now the drama lay in how Amherst symbolically contained all the problems, all the tensions, all the issues of modern society. Now one sought out "the evidences of instant Los Angeles transplanted" within the Asparagus Valley.

The third change apparent in the rhetoric of the passage lay even more clearly in the cultural style, the emotional stance of the authors. Their tone was not the ironic detachment of a Mugwump, the calm assurance of a mandarin, the bemused humor of an observer. Theirs was the language of the activist, 1960s style. It pointed to impending cataclysmic disasters ("rampant urbanization," "megalopolis," "instant Los Angeles transplanted")! It countered these with fascinating utopian possibilities ("Man here could truly be the architect of his urban environment"). And the authors went on to suggest rather vaguely that disaster could be averted, utopia might be achieved, if only the active participation of the whole community could somehow be mobilized—and if the special revelations perceived by the young could be honored. The Hampshire authors followed the passage quoted above by themselves noting: "A long time ago St. Benedict set as a rule for his monastery, the following:

As often as any important business has to be done in the monastery, let the abbott call together the whole community and himself set forth the matter. . . . Now the reason why we have said that all should be called to the council is that God often reveals what is better to the younger. . . .

The Making of a College in 1966 not only described the outlines of a radically new form of liberal arts college, it also reflected the new developments which transformed Amherst after 1962—the enormous expansion of higher education through which the gown overwhelmed the town, the change in Amherst's perception of its relation to the outside world, and the youth revolution with its impact on the town's politics, its renewed amorphous search for a sense of "community," and its own versions of counterculture and new cultural styles.

By 1970 evidence abounded that the town was thoroughly enveloped in the folds of the gown. In 1963 the increased pace of expansion at the university produced a drastic jump in the construction of new housing units in town—from an average over the previous fifteen years of about forty-three new units annually to a new average over the eight years after 1962 of 430 units each year, about 130 houses along with 300 new apartments. In 1963 alone permits were granted for four new apartment complexes. By 1970 some 3,000 new housing units had been constructed in Amherst since 1960—a total greater than all previous dwellings built there after 1730. And still permits were outstanding for 3,129 more units. Police Chief Frank Hart pointed out in 1970 that the population served by his department, both on and off the three campuses, had reached 35,000—double the number served only nine years earlier. He reported seventy-five arrests that year for narcotics violations against none in 1961. Even the sewage in 1970 amounted to over one billion gallons, double the amount of 1965.

This expansion transformed the proportion of academics to nonacademics within Amherst. By 1976 a study showed that 58 percent of the children in the elementary schools had at least one parent at the university or the colleges. Even in the regional junior and senior high schools 54 percent of the students also had one or both parents similarly associated. Analysis of the 1976 Amherst Street List, which lists only those residents seventeen years of age or older, reveals that among these adult residents of the town living entirely outside any of the three campuses, a full 48 percent (or 6,868 out of 14,246) listed themselves either as students, teachers, or professors. Such a listing fails to capture all the many administrators, staff workers, and others employed on one of the campuses. Nor does it include the spouses of any of these persons associated with the campuses unless those spouses identified themselves as students, teachers, professors, or educational administrators. What the list may reveal with some accuracy, however, is the small proportion of some other occupations. Only fifty-six persons (or 0.4 percent of the total residents living off campus) list themselves as farmers or farm workers. Only 596 (or 4 percent of the off-campus residents) describe themselves in terms identifiable as blue-collar workers. Amherst has become a town within which farmers and workers are feeling increasingly uncomfortable and out of place. A groundskeeper notes:

Amherst is no place for the laboring man, or for the working class. The professors, instructors, and professional people have taken over, and want us to move elsewhere. . . . Look at the school budget for instance—an increase of 24% over last year. . . . The taxes on my home were $88 in

1947. Taxes on the same property are $900 today. . . . I'll admit I don't like Amherst anymore, and if I could move my property to Hadley, or a place like that, I'd do it on the spot. A lot of my friends feel the same way.

A bank janitor observes:

My Pa owned a thirty-five-acre farm and a small herd of cows, and when his taxes reached $100 a year, he complained he'd have to move. Today, I'm paying $1,200 in taxes on 5 acres and a home. . . . I don't know if I'll be able to stay here much longer.

A barber reflects on change in his occupation and in the town:

This trade used to really flourish. . . . Right now? Forget it. The hair's going to stay longer. You'll never see it turn around and be short again. . . .

Amherst used to be much more closely knit, when it was all Republican. If you mentioned the word Democrat here, you'd be dead. Now the town is all Democratic, and the people are pulling each other apart. We've got problems with the sewers, the land—and everyone's on everyone else's back. We're not pulling together anymore.

It was a delusion, of course, to think that the old Republican Amherst had resolved all its problems in some happy consensus. From 1945 to 1952, in fact, the town had been bitterly divided and unable to resolve issues over the schools and over the proposed town manager form of government. It was no delusion, however, to feel that by 1970 the dominant Republican political culture of Amherst had been overturned by a new Democratic majority. And it was also true that this Democratic revolution was accompanied by a more contentious, activist political style than the town had known perhaps since the days of the revolution against British rule. The new Democrats, moreover, were not particularly congenial allies for workers or farmers. The old minority Democratic party which had served Amherst's workers, Catholics, Irish, and some academics as a minor cultural protest group against the dominant Republican-Congregational culture had by 1970 been taken over by academic liberals and by the new youthful voters now legally able to register at their college address. The irony was that Amherst became Democratic just when the working class became persuaded that Amherst was not a town for them.

As late as March of 1968 the town's list of registered voters had shown about 1,200 Democrats still outnumbered by some 1,700 Republicans and by almost 2,200 Independents. That was the spring, however, when Eugene McCarthy challenged Lyndon Johnson for the presidency over the issue of the war in Vietnam. A group calling themselves "Signatures for McCarthy" canvassed the registered Democrats and Independents in town to secure 976 signatures for McCarthy. Colby Dempsey, the leader of this group and a young physics professor at Amherst College, was struck by how little organized effort the Democrats in Amherst seemed to have been making previously and by how many new Democratic sympathizers seemed to be still unregistered as voters. By fall of 1968 Dempsey and his colleagues had managed to stimulate sufficient new voter registration to reverse Amherst's traditional Republicanism. For the fall election that year the figures showed 2,001 Democrats, 1,956 Independents, and 1,703 Republicans. In Amherst Hubert Humphrey beat Richard Nixon by 2,892 votes to 2,096. In addition Dempsey's group backed for state representative a young liberal Democrat, John Olver, who won his race handily. Olver had resigned as professor of chemistry at the university in order to enter politics. His wife was a professor of psychology at Amherst College. His chief campaign organizer was Colby Dempsey of the Amherst faculty. Not only had the Democrats clearly begun to create a new political establishment for Amherst, but that new leadership seemed to be even more closely linked to academia than were its predecessors.

It remained for the Democrats to take over similarly the local town offices which still were almost exclusively in Republican hands. A few steps were taken in 1969 when Paul Ford, an enterprising young Republican attorney, ran for reelection as town moderator while Frederick Ruder, a long-time Amherst resident and veterinarian, ran as incumbent for the housing authority. Ford was defeated by Harry Allen, professor of business law at the university, and Ruder lost decisively to Bernard Moreau, then director of a preretirement education program at the university. Both victors were strongly supported by Dempsey's Democratic organization, and the *Amherst Record* noted that "although the elections were nonpartisan and party affiliations may have played only a marginal part in the voter's choices, the fact is that the incumbents were Republicans and the challengers were Democrats." What the *Record* did not notice was the fact that the defeated were also independent townsmen while the victors were both associated with the university.

As late as 1970, however, the board of selectmen had never included a registered Democrat, and in that year it numbered only one member with university connections along with four independent townsmen. The total experience of these seasoned town officials amounted to forty-four years for an average of eight and a half years apiece. In 1971 and again in 1972, after very lively campaigns, two fresh faces appeared on the board each year. By 1972, therefore, the Amherst board of selectmen totaled only seven years of experience, or an average of less than one and a half years apiece. At least four of its five members were registered Democrats. And only one member of the new board had no obvious connections with the university. The gown had clearly come to dominate the politics as well as the population of Amherst.

Along with the town's loss of any clear identity separate from its educational institutions went its sense of itself as a place apart from the major conflicts and problems of the larger world. Increasingly after 1962 the political style of the town came to resemble that of the campus. It seemed to be a kind of symbolic politics in which the matters at issue were raised for their larger educational value as much as for any immediate local application. The new style was apparent in its purest form, for example, in the drive to fly the United Nations flag on the town common. For some of the new academic liberals it seemed important to be able to claim that Amherst had become the first town in the United States to fly the flag of the United Nations alongside the American flag as an official town act. Others who opposed the United Nations or symbolic politics in principle combined with some who opposed the specific role of the United Nations in the Middle East to prevent funding of a flag pole by the town meeting. Resolution of this conflict represented the kind of pluralistic compromise toward which Amherst moved more and more frequently in these years. The town meeting voted official approval for flying the United Nations flag on the common provided that the funds for the flag pole should be voluntarily contributed by the supporters of the proposal.

The newer forms of symbolic politics for Amherst took on far more substance and significance in the civil rights movement and in opposition to the Vietnam War. Most of the initial attention went to dramatic efforts by persons from Amherst to assist the struggle for the civil rights of blacks elsewhere, either in the South or at the level of national policy. Shortly after the first sit-ins at segregated lunch counters by black college students in the Carolinas during the early months of 1960, some Amherst College students initiated a demonstration in Washington by New England collegians to support their black colleagues in the South. Over 100 (almost entirely white) students from the Amherst area, dressed in their most respectable coats and ties, carrying signs lettered in the most discreet wording ("We Support Human Dignity"), walked sedately back and forth outside the White House fence on an early spring Saturday in 1960. A similar conservatively dressed, decorously silent group of some fifty faculty and students stood quietly in rows outside Amherst's Alumni Gymnasium to greet President Kennedy in October 1963 as he drove up from his helicopter landing on the playing fields. Their purpose—as their neatly lettered signs attested—was simply to urge the president to support more strongly his own civil rights bill which was bogged down in Congress.

From these most moderate measures Amherst's participation in the growing purpose and tactics of the civil rights movement escalated. Faculty, students, clergy, and townspeople from Amherst were present at the Lincoln Memorial to hear Martin Luther King invoke his dream for America. Another Amherst contingent marched at Selma. Amherst students were clubbed on the beaches of St. Augustine and jailed in Mississippi. An Amherst graduate was in charge of the border state training headquarters for civil rights workers preparing for "the long hot summer" in Mississippi. Amherst clergy, faculty, and townspeople stayed for a week or more at a time with black families in a rural area of North Carolina to support demonstrations at the Court House. The publishers of the *Amherst Record,* the de Sherbinins, covered these events extensively and themselves participated in some of the activities.

Meanwhile, much more quietly, smaller groups of residents turned their attention to the local scene. A fair housing committee formed in the early 1960s to assist blacks in finding housing in Amherst (though a survey conducted by this group showed that most black families in Amherst already owned their own homes). About twenty to forty persons both black and white, both town and gown, collected good neighbor pledges where they could in order to demonstrate to real estate agents and others the possibilities for selling or renting housing to blacks in different areas of town. They negotiated with landlords in the case of specific complaints and assisted some black families to find more desirable housing. By 1964 they had broadened the scope of their concerns and changed their title to the human rights commission but still remained a group of several dozen whose activities were fairly limited. Amherst as late as 1967 was not generally ready to admit that there were any real problems of racism at home. Only in 1968 as a reaction to the assassination of Martin Luther King did the town seriously begin to examine its own posture. Within a month after King's murder the human rights commission had enlisted several hundred members, raised thousands of dollars, and embarked on serious efforts to change existing racism in all areas of Amherst's life from the schools to the economy. Some of the same residents who in 1962 had declined to sign good neighbor pledges even became involved by the early 1970s in supporting strongly the ABC (A Better Chance) program which brought black and Indian high school students selected from all over the country to live in a special house in Amherst, to gain a good secondary education for themselves, and in the process to enrich the lives and educations of all Amherst students. A change was clearly evident within a decade from the early assumption that missionaries would go forth from Amherst to inculcate the town's values elsewhere toward a recognition that Amherst itself was an arena within which both actual and symbolic moral politics should be pursued.

It was the Vietnam War, however, which increasingly led Amherst residents to test the possibilities of symbolic politics by using the local scene to stage their opposition to the war in dramatic forms which might catch national attention. The process began in June of 1966 when Robert McNamara, secretary of defense, came to Amherst College to receive an honorary degree. In a gesture of protest which was pictured and reported on the front page of the next day's *New York Times* about one-tenth of the graduating seniors wore white arm bands as they marched across the platform to receive their diplomas individually, a smaller group rose and walked out as McNamara's honorary degree was awarded, and one graduate conspicuously spurned his diploma as he strode past President Plimpton. A more enduring form of protest began in the same year when some Quakers and other opponents of the war began a weekly Vigil for

Peace on the Amherst Common. For fifty-two Sundays a year over more than six long years this vigil was faithfully and silently kept at the center of Amherst. By the time it ended, the vigil had enlisted participation at one time or another by hundreds of Amherst residents, many students, and numbers of visitors. It had also been reported and pictured in many media. Large-scale teach-ins at the university, picketing of military and corporate recruiters at both institutions, and participation in national protest demonstrations continued periodically as at most colleges and universities.

The more distinctive forms of protest developed in Amherst included the Amherst Letter to Nixon in the spring of 1969. This letter originated during the moratorium at Amherst College—a hectic period when classes were suspended for two days, when groups of students and faculty churned out multifarious proposals for change of the college and of its relation to the larger world, when for two evenings in the Cage mass meetings of "the college community" debated and voted upon resolutions for change. The letter referred to these internal efforts for change and called upon President Nixon to lead in changing national priorities toward peace and social justice. Again the *New York Times* gave this Amherst initiative front-page coverage and editorial commendation. During subsequent months scores of other colleges and universities voted in one way or another to endorse this Amherst Letter. Yet three years later a new president of Amherst, John William Ward, at a moment when the continuing war was escalated still further, expressed his feeling that composing letters to the president was like launching paper airplanes against a wall. He gained further national attention for Amherst's antiwar protest by joining students, faculty, and some townspeople in committing peaceful civil disobedience by sitting down in the entry roads to Westover Air Base from which B 52's were flying to join in the intensified bombing of Hanoi and Haiphong. Symbolic politics had been pushed by accumulating pressures and frustrations to a dramatic act of symbolic civil disobedience. Not since the American Revolution and Shays's Rebellion had Amherst residents been moved to assert themselves so strongly against the larger society.

The major legacy from all the expansion, the tumult, the turmoil of the decade after 1962 seemed to be a new atmosphere of cultural pluralism. It was true that some of the older forms of variety seemed

COURTESY OF THE AMHERST STUDENT

WESTOVER AFB SIT IN.

threatened. Farmers were vanishing. Workers found the town
economically difficult and culturally uncongenial. The academic
style and liberal Democratic ethos in town affairs seemed to be as
pervasive by 1976 as had the old Yankee Republican conservatism in
1950. Inevitably change had produced its own new exclusions and
new orthodoxies, but the fundamental assumptions now were pref-
erences for diversity, for pluralism, for respect and appreciation of
difference.

This new pluralism was evident wherever one looked in Amherst
by 1976. Back in 1800 the town had been bitterly split between two
rival factions—the Center *vs.* East Street, Zion *vs.* Sodom—each
polarized around the First or the Second Congregational Church,
each representing a faction within a single dominant Congregational
culture. In 1976 the old site on top of the hill where in 1800 the First
Congregational Church meetinghouse had stood was occupied by
one of Amherst College's most distinctive buildings, the Octagon,
erected by President Hitchcock in mid-nineteenth century as a "scientific cabinet" to house geological and other specimens sent back to
the college by all those missionaries who had gone forth from
Amherst to evangelize the world with the religion and culture of the
Connecticut Valley. This symbolic location, focus of the town's
central values as those values once shifted from religion to accommodate science, now housed the Gerald Penney Black Cultural
Center. It was a dramatic, visible recognition of the felt need to

create in Amherst some consciousness and some respected place for the values of Afro-American culture. It was also the place where the black students of Amherst College, now forming from 8 to 10 percent of each class, could preserve an identity of their own within the larger cultural community of the college and the town. That diversity in the student body which the faculty committee of 1945 had proposed was by 1976 a greater reality than anyone had envisioned thirty years earlier. In the fall of 1976 one-third of the entering class were, for the first time in the college's history, women. By then about one-tenth of the faculty were women. By 1972–73 many of the earlier remnants of clubbishness at Amherst had diminished greatly. In twenty years the listed administrative officers had grown from sixteen names to forty-eight, while the proportion of Amherst graduates among them had shrunk from 81 to 17 percent. None of the five leading administrators of the college in the 1970s was himself an Amherst graduate. Among the faculty during the same two decades the proportion of Amherst graduates had shrunk from 24 percent (one out of every four) to 9 percent (one out of every eleven), and the proportion of those with graduate training at Harvard had shrunk from 36 percent to 23 percent. Within the extracurricular life of the college an officially recognized Hillel Society and a Newman Club maintained rather more active presences than did the old (Protestant) Christian Association. Within the curriculum of Amherst in 1976 almost complete freedom reigned. In 1971 a faculty committee had pointed to the difficulty of discerning any common body of knowledge appropriate for all persons in a pluralistic society. The faculty had responded by eliminating all requirements except those of four years residence, passage of (almost any) thirty-two courses, and some specialized major. A desire for diversity, pluralism, individuality had replaced the 1950s drive for "the creation of an intellectual community" on the old hilltop near the center of town.

Meanwhile down on East Street, where the only dissenting faction in early Amherst had been located, a similar transformation occurred. The Second Congregational church had dwindled to a small number of old Amherst families. Reluctantly and sadly in 1976 the congregation voted to sell its historic property and buildings. This simple, graceful New England meetinghouse was then purchased as a center for The Jewish Community, a thriving, expanding group which had been seeking a definite place of its own within

COURTESY OF THE AMHERST RECORD

THE STAFF OF THE VEGETARIAN EQUINOX RESTAURANT,
MARCH 1975.

Amherst. The symbolic changes seemed to be clear enough. The old
site of the First Congregational Meetinghouse was now graced by
the Gerald Penney Black Cultural Center. The former structure of
the Second Congregational Church dissenters now provided an identifiable focus in Amherst for the Jewish Community.

In 1945—even as late as 1962—the town of Amherst had still
preserved a definite identity and culture of its own. That dominant
culture had been Republican in politics, Congregational in religion,
and "respectable" in the arts. Both Amherst College and Massachusetts State College (with its remnants of agricultural emphasis)

remained in varying ways and degrees extensions of the town's own values. It was a town which accepted newcomers but which assumed they had come to be fitted into existing institutions and to be educated into the dominant values. Within the space of about a decade after 1962 this older order of things was transformed. The town had become by 1976 largely an extension of its educational institutions. Its politics, its religions, and its arts had achieved a variety and a liveliness which made them far more interesting if nothing else. Above all the town, at its best, had learned a new respect for diverse identities. It had become a place where different races, different religions, different generations, different sexes, different individuals were encouraged to find and assert identities of their own. Whether such a town could also find a renewed sense of that community for which so many of its residents now seemed to be seeking remained a very open question. At least the future promised to be fully as interesting as the past had been in Amherst.

CHAPTER TWELVE

TOWARD RESPONSIVE GOVERNMENT

WINTHROP S. DAKIN

Toby Dakin has for a long while been a moving figure in the town's affairs. Town moderator during much of the period covered by this essay, he has also served as trustee and treasurer for Hampshire College and as chairman of the Massachusetts board of higher education, while continuing to practice as attorney in Northampton.

For twenty years after World War II Amherst town government was molded by circumstance and by a scattering of citizens intent on establishing an efficient and prudently responsive government. Projects germinated in that period came to blossom in the third decade. Then the increasing impingement of government on the expanding population, improved communications, and the spread of personal assertiveness caused citizen initiative to emerge as a new generator of governmental action. Here follows an account of that process, treated as separate subjects more than as a fused chronological flow.

The Town Meeting

The unique virtue of town meeting government is that its legislative body is a fairly random cross-section of the population, with members accountable to no one and free to decide issues without fear of personal consequences. For a period of about fifteen years after World War II Amherst's town meeting was, and was structured to be, one of the finest parliaments in the world. As though the multiplicity of its membership afforded not enough insurance against aberrant behavior, measures were adopted in the 1970s tending to make it a representative body, largely homogenized in social character and with each member accountable to his own electorate. Thus did the members, formerly independent deliberators, become deputies, and minority participation and play of intelligence become curtailed.

In 1938, on its second try, the town adopted a special act of the state legislature to discontinue the New England form of open town meeting—an assembly of all voters in town minded to attend— thereby instituting the more reliable limited town meeting. This new body initially comprised 168 members, electing one for every twenty voters. As voters multiplied, so did the membership. The town meeting is the stomach of the local body politic.

With 195 members in 1950, the town meeting persuaded the state legislature to reduce and stabilize the number at 180, if the voters in town would approve. But on the first test they disapproved, 976 to 600, and likewise the next year, 885 to 504.

By 1958, the elected membership had reached 222, and a move was launched to stop and freeze it at 240. Again the legislature enacted the change, and this time, in 1960, the town approved, 1,315 to 719.

Considerations mentioned as favoring the larger figure were: (1) It promotes the amateur quality. (2) It is less likely to be dominated by a clique or by the *ex officio* members. (3) Its sometimes necessary and unpalatable decisions are more likely to be accepted by the town. (4) It educates a larger nucleus of the population in the affairs of local government. (5) It utilizes Amherst's special asset, its large and willing body of unusually able citizens.

Since its establishment the meeting has had a varying roster of *ex officio* members, called "members-at-large," some specified by state statute, others by town by-law. In 1973, in a move to emphasize the representative character of the meeting, all members at large created by by-law except the town manager were discontinued. So today he and the statutory designees (any resident state legislator, moderator, town clerk, selectmen, school committee members, and chairman of the finance committee) are the only *ex officio* members.

An effort toward accountability developed in 1974 when, by a 100 to 79 vote, the meeting authorized a public recording of the vote of each individual member on any measure when called for by forty town meeting members.

A provision in the original act allowed 200 voters to call for a town-wide referendum on a measure passed by limited town meeting. When that number had become less than 2 percent of the voters, at the request of the meeting a proposal that at least 5 percent of the voters be required for a referendum was submitted to the town voters at the 1974 election, and they made the change effective.

In 1959, the town's bicentennial year, the words spoken at the annual town meeting were recorded on a tape for historical memory. On two other occasions similar tapes were made. From 1969 to 1975 it was a much appreciated practice to broadcast over cable television town meetings, annual and special, but financial considerations prompted a change to local radio.

At annual meetings between 1954 and 1964 attendance averaged 80.9 percent of the full membership; 9.7 percent of those attending entered after the call to order; warrants averaged forty-one articles, each of which averaged six minutes and forty-seven seconds for disposition. At special meetings in that period ten minutes per article was average; latecomers averaged 5.02 percent of those attending who averaged 60.2 percent of the total roster.

Beginning in 1972 free bus tours were provided a few days before town meeting for members to view sites subject to proposed action at the meeting.

Through 1967 annual town meetings completed their agenda in a single evening's session, but thereafter two and sometimes three such sessions were required; the annual 1975 event was so burdened with a revolutionary and unsuccessful zoning proposal and twenty-nine largely notional private proposals, its seventy-seven article warrant took seven evenings to complete. Beginning in 1967 the selectmen have habitually called a special town meeting in October to help dispose of supplemental business.

Nonpartisan Elections

From about the turn of the century until 1948 the ballot for town-wide elections carried political party labels. Nomination of candidates was made by the local caucus of the Republican Party. Only occasionally would the numerically weaker Democrats caucus. Frank P. Toole, seventeen times elected tree warden, was for years the only registered Democrat holding elective town office. He secured nomination by "independent papers" requiring about fifty voter signatures, a device that was later legally barred in Amherst.

In 1940 the national government passed "An Act to Prevent Pernicious political Activities," dubbed The Hatch Act, that forbade a large number of the personnel at the state college—a land grant college—to seek town office while party designations appeared on the ballot. So, in an effort to make our elections nonpartisan, some citizens in 1941 filed a bill in the state legislature forbidding party caucuses here and calling for nomination for town-wide offices to be made by nomination papers signed by twenty-five voters. It was filed late, received no support from the selectmen, and died. The next year a similar bill was filed and was killed in the house. In 1943 another passed the house but died in the senate. In the 1944 annual town meeting an unsuccessful effort was made to achieve nonpartisan elections under the "town caucus" plan allowed by a state statute. On second try in 1947 it passed.

The 1947 plan called for a preliminary election or caucus to be held every year to sift down to two the candidates for each elective post. As enough candidates seldom came forward to make that sifting necessary, the town filed a bill in the state legislature in 1954 calling for nominations to be made by papers with ten voter signatures and a special caucus to be held only if more than two had filed for any office. This proposal was prompted largely by the advent of town manager government that called for fewer town offices to be filled by election. The legislature passed the bill, and in 1956 the town voters approved it, 462 to 75.

Nominations for the 240 elected town meeting members were nonpartisan from the beginning. About one-third are elected every year for a three-year term. Each of the town's eight precincts (originally six) elects its proportionate share. Every aspirant must have taken out a nomination paper bearing the signatures of ten voters of his precinct. Election is by plurality; refined selectivity is neither possible nor desirable. It used to be that, once elected, a member did not have to take out a nomination paper to run again. That was the general rule throughout the state, but in 1972 the town meeting requested the state legislature to pass a special act to require Amherst incumbents to file papers to run again. It was passed and made effective by voter approval in 1973.

State law required names on ballots to be headed by incumbents, with other aspirants following in alphabetical order. The 1974 town meeting, sensing that voter fatigue tended to favor those near the top of the ballot, persuaded the legislature to enact in the following year a law for Amherst by which the order of names on the ballot would be determined by lot both as to town-wide offices and as to town meeting members.

By a close vote in 1975 the town meeting requested a special act allowing public policy questions, at the request of 2 percent of the voters, to be put on a town election ballot in wording approved by the selectmen, but the legislature failed to comply.

Town Manager

In 1947 some in Amherst felt that the town government with forty-four officials elected town-wide was cumbersome, decentralized, inefficient, and expensive. Fry Civille Pray, chairman of the selectmen, then sixty-four years old, and holder of other jobs in the town government, had performed very acceptably as fulltime administrator of the town government, but no one loomed in the offing to succeed him, and a more professional touch seemed desirable. The town meeting voted that year to establish a committee of five to study town management systems. The next year, on the committee's recommendation, a drafting committee was set up to frame a town manager charter. Working on this were Theodore S. Bacon, Jr., George Goodwin, Benjamin M. Ziegler, Eunice L. Mannheim, and Philip H. Smith, the latter having been chairman of the earlier committee. In 1949 this committee, under Mr. Goodwin's chairmanship, submitted a draft and asked for more members, to hold hearings and to perfect the draft. That was voted, and at the 1950 annual meeting the enlarged committee, still chaired by Goodwin, was directed to submit its proposal for enactment at the 1951 session of the state legislature. It was enacted and submitted to the town voters for acceptance, but they rejected it at the 1951 election, 1,055 to 715. So stunning was this defeat that the proponents let a year pass before petitioning to raise the issue again. In 1953 it carried by a thirteen vote margin, the vote, as recounted, being 779 to 766.

Under the town manager act a new five-member board of selectmen displaced the former three-member board. The new selectmen of 1954 were Robert D. Hawley, Harold M. Elder, Herbert G. Johnson, Norman G. MacLeod, and Eunice L. Mannheim, the first woman to be a selectman in Amherst. On May 10, 1954

THE LAST MEETING, IN 1954, OF THE THREE-MAN BOARD OF
SELECTMEN—MESSRS. PARSONS, COLBY, AND PRAY.

Allen L. Torrey took office as the first town manager, and held it
until May 1975 when he resigned to become treasurer of Hampshire
College. He was succeeded that year by A. Louis Hayward at a
yearly salary of $29,000.

The town manager act allows the voters to reconsider once every
three years and return to the old system. In 1957, since enough so
petitioned, the question was put on the ballot, but they chose 1,334
to 812 to retain the new one. It was reagitated in 1960, and again the
voters elected 1,461 to 889 not to turn back. Since then the issue has
lain passive.

In these twenty-one years as manager Mr. Torrey exemplified
what good town manager government can be. In reorganizing the
administrative and protective agencies, he fostered in each a profes-
sionalism in performance, a flexibility for mutual cooperation, a

readiness to drop old and assume new duties, and an extraordinary economy of operation. To a very large extent it can be said that the history of the administrative aspects of Amherst town government over these years has been the story of his influence.

Our town manager act grants very extensive powers to the manager, and experience has shown that, when the selectmen grant a very loose rein to so exceptionally able a manager as was Mr. Torrey, the luster of town government is bright; but when they begin to obstruct his prerogatives a tinge of politics sullies the luster, the smooth efficiency seems to deteriorate, and the pace of progress abates. After about three years of such interference the town voters felt it had gone too far and favored in the 1975 contested election for selectman Diana Romer, an advocate of strict separation of the roles of selectman and manager.

The Recreation Commission

In 1946 the town meeting set up a committee to study the recreational needs of the town. It reported that "Amherst is the center of a recreational desert" and that its greatest need was centrally located outdoor public swimming facilities. It urged the 1947 town meeting either to sell Groff Park in Mill Valley or to develop it. The meeting did neither.

The following year the town voted to elect a five-member recreation commission to have charge of Community Field on Triangle Street. In 1949 it was also given charge of Groff Park. In 1950 $5,500 was voted to develop playing fields there.

In each of the next three years a proposal to develop swimming facilities at Groff Park for $20,000 was defeated, even under the winsome eloquence of the commission chairman, Clarence A. Jewett, Jr. In 1955 he hit upon a new approach. He persuaded Ernest M. Whitcomb, Sanford Keedy, and Winthrop S. Dakin to declare themselves Trustees for the Town Swimming Pool. They would secure pledges from townspeople for contributions to build, with the help of $25,000 in town funds, a War Memorial Pool on Community Field. If the town meeting later favored the scheme, the pledges would be paid by checks payable to the town but delivered to the trustees. If by May 30, 1955 $25,000 or more had been received in contributions, the plan would be executed; if not, the scheme would become void, and the checks would be returned to the donors. The town meeting voted approval, over $30,000 in donations were received, and the pool was built.

It took the commission two tries to persuade the meeting to finance a wading pool at that field, three to get a storage building there, two to get a basketball court there, and one each to erect a comfort station at each location.

As time passed the commission grew in favor. In 1969 and 1970 it was authorized to acquire land long owned by the Puffer family near Mill River in North Amherst, which is now a rather elaborate recreation area. In 1971 it accepted a gift of about six acres in the Orchard Valley region in South Amherst, and in 1974 the town meeting authorized it to acquire twelve acres off Potwine Lane for future development.

At one time it asked that the name of Community Field be changed to Williams Field in honor of George E. Williams, respected and retired high school coach. But for the Amherst College element in town meeting the name Williams associated with athletics activates adrenalin. The name was not adopted, and a letter of consolation was written to Mr. Williams expressing the warm regard of the meeting.

The Conservation Commission

The most constructively successful agency of the town government in the period following World War II was the conservation commission. It was established in 1962 after a study committee had recommended it. The first members were William G. Sheldon, chairman, Ann K. Bain, Charles Chase, Frederick A. McLaughlin, Homer W. Cowles, Bradlee E. Gage, and Janet W. Dakin. Since then it has acquired for the town about 700 acres of pond sites, river bank land, swamps, mountain streams, woodland, beauty spots, and wild life habitats, usually with governmental financial aid, in two instances by eminent domain, and in some cases by gift.

In 1970 it established as its ancillary a private trust for public conservation purposes; called The Kestrel Trust after the town bird. Commission members are trustees. The trust can acquire land in Amherst or in any adjacent town, and in doing so may act more promptly and informally than town procedures would allow. It has been of help on several occasions.

In 1973 the town meeting adopted a policy favoring governmental protection of the Holyoke Range for conservation and recreation purposes. The state had been making timid efforts to this end, and the selectmen had appointed Janet W. Dakin as the town's representative to push for this goal. The town of Hadley and some private landowners opposed such control, but in 1974 the state appropriated $3,250,000 to start acquiring land there for permanent preservation.

The commission's duties became so detailed and onerous that in 1974 the town authorized the employment of a fulltime conservation officer.

Water for the Town

After reports from several successive committees, many town meeting actions, and a favorable test of sentiment at an annual election (853 "to buy" as against 418 "not to") the town bought in 1941 the water works of the privately owned Amherst Water Company for $600,000. Perhaps to induce favorable action, an official proposal had been advanced that the town's new water department would "pay taxes" to the town in the amount that the Amherst Water Company had last been paying them. This peculiar fancy was never executed after the transfer and deserves no further mention.

When so acquired the system had forty-five miles of main in the distribution system, 153 fire hydrants, 1,476 service taps, and an average daily consumption of 628,000 gallons. By 1972 the figures for the same items were 104 miles, 639 hydrants, 4,194 taps, and 3,065,813 gallons.

As consumption increased the reservoirs became inadequate. In 1957 a proposal was made that the town exercise rights it held under a special 1929 legislative act to take water by eminent domain from Leverett. A plea in town meeting that such action would be unfriendly carried the day. So Amherst looked again within her borders and developed her first ground-water supply in the Lawrence Swamp area of South Amherst with a daily output of 1,250,000 gallons. It came into use in 1958, but only after the town suffered a drought so severe in 1957 that it had to transfer water from Orient Springs in Pelham and from Atkins Swamp into its distribution system. Another drought, combined with a pump failure in the Lawrence Swamp well field, necessitated smaller scale pumping in 1968 from the Hadley Water District supply. In 1969 another well, with a capacity of over 1,000,000 gallons daily, was developed in Belchertown near that swamp and the town line. Two new standpipes were constructed: one in 1971 off Bay Road on the range toward Rattlesnake Knob and the other in 1976 off East Pleasant Street near the north line of the Wildwood Cemetery property.

On the initiative of the town's junior chamber of commerce a proposal to fluoridate the water supply was posed to the voters at the 1965 election and met defeat, 1,336 to 702.

A search presently under way discloses that Hadley has water sources sufficient for its needs and the extra expected need of Amherst. This supply has a chemical composition difficult to mix satisfactorily with Amherst water so perhaps it would best be used as the university's sole supply for which its volume is expected to suffice.

Water charges from 1941 were based on quantity units consumed each quarter, a higher rate for the first quantity, and lower by steps for succeeding ones. The schedule for the lower rate changed from time to time with a flattening trend until 1974, when the town meeting voted a single per cubic foot price no matter how great the consumption. The rate for householders today, unchanged since 1941, is cheaper because of currency inflation than it was then.

Public Housing and Boltwood Walk

In 1947 the town meeting authorized a committee to survey the need in town for World War II veterans' housing. Three months later it recommended that the town borrow $195,000 for twenty years, build residences, and rent or sell them to veterans. A project committee of Walter C. Jones, Edward L. Hazen, and Guerard H. Howkins, Jr., borrowed that sum at 1.5 percent, acquired land now known as Memorial Drive, south of the Amherst Golf Club, erected twenty houses for less than the borrowing, rented some, and eventually sold all to veterans at prices fixed by a state board as fair market values. The proceeds were invested at 3 percent, and in 1967, when the original loan was paid, the town was about $55,000 to the good.

In 1959 the town set up under state statutes a five-member housing authority. It proceeded to build and operate a thirty apartment facility for senior citizens at Chestnut Court off East Pleasant Street; in 1974 it constructed for them a considerably larger facility on the south side of Kellogg Avenue.

Sensing that the center of town might benefit by some restructuring, the planning board persuaded the 1963 town meeting to establish a committee on government-aided urban renewal programs. The committee chairman was William E. Aubin, and his group became known as the Aubin Renewal Committee. Two years later it recommended such a program, but the town meeting rejected it.

By 1969 it was apparent that several public school buildings and associated playgrounds in the heart of town between Kellogg Avenue and Lessey Street would soon be abandoned and that care should be taken for the character of the use of the land thereafter. The selectmen appointed a Center School Complex Committee under the chairmanship of Norman G. MacLeod to study the matter. The committee was twice funded by town meeting and in 1971 induced the meeting to adopt approximately what the Aubin committee had proposed. A Redevelopment Authority was set up, comprising originally Raymond A. Werbe, Margaret R. Roberts, David C. Montague, Willard T. Weeks, and Jurgen H. Roetter. It designed and launched the Boltwood Walk complex on the old school grounds and adjacent lands.

The Town and The Jones Library

In 1919 Governor Calvin Coolidge signed into law a special act establishing The Jones Library, Incorporated, pursuant to the will of the late Samuel Minot Jones. It called for three trustees who were to be elected on the town ballot and who, by rare privilege, had power of eminent domain. By various means, narrated in Frank Prentice Rand's *The Jones Library in Amherst* (1969), they became the governing body of town-owned and other corporately owned free library facilities.

Foreseeing that shortly the town would be appropriating for library purposes more in tax monies than the income from The Jones Library endowment and feeling that town-owned library facilities should more properly be under the control of public officers than those of a private corporation, a town meeting in February 1972 requested the state legislature to pass a special act on the subject. They wanted to enlarge the number of trustees and combine the operations of The Jones Library properties with those of the town, which were then the North Amherst library and the library portion of the Munson Memorial building in South Amherst. Five months later the act was passed, and a new regime for public libraries began.

The trustees, still to be elected for three years, were to be trustees of the town's public library rather than as theretofore of The Jones Library, Incorporated. Their number was increased to six. The town library trustees would *ex officio* comprise the trustees of The Jones Library, Inc. That corporation was authorized to turn over to the public library trustees custody of its premises and its tangible personal property, to be operated with the town's library properties as a single library system. Jones Library employees would become employees of the town. Monies from the state, from town taxes, and from The Jones Library, Inc. endowment would be treated as a single fund when the town meeting fixed the annual operating budget for town libraries. Town monies could be used for maintenance of the corporation's property while in the custody of the public library trustees. The future principal role of The Jones Library, Inc. will be to manage its endowment and special trust funds, the net income of which would normally be turned over to the town library trustees.

This new legislation was a tour de force. The system it set up was not easy to operate, but to some extent it preserved the institution that Mr. Jones had established in his will, and it allowed it to work cooperatively with the town government in a single library system for the town.

Problems of Growth

Automobile traffic volume and hazards to pedestrians so increased on that portion of North Pleasant Street traversing the University of Massachusetts campus that university and town officials in the summer of 1969 established a joint task force to study and recommend on the matter. Six town meetings struggled with ways to shut off that portion and to reroute and disperse its traffic away from the town's business center. An excellent committee was appointed operating under the chairmanship of Nancy B. Eddy. Other members were David E. Elder, John M. Foster, Jerome B. King, Stephen E. Keedy, H. Jackson Littlefield, Jr., Nathaniel Reed, Robert B. Whitney, and Jack S. Wolf. That Littlefield was not a resident of Amherst led local jingoes to censure Moderator Dakin for so disloyal an appointment. The state's department of public works patiently bore with the struggle. It had agreed to build the new by-pass highway. By October 1973 plans appeared to have jelled despite lingering pockets of opposition. But before the start of construction the 1976 annual meeting voted 115 to 101 to repeal approval of the project.

Incidental to population growth occurred problems arising from crowding, complexity, and wider impingement of town government on citizens. In 1949 parking meters were installed in the business center. Municipal rubbish and garbage collection was inaugurated in 1958. Pursuant to the blunt aspiration of Governor Furculo that every city and town in Massachusetts opt to have a development and industrial commission, Amherst established its own in 1960.

In 1962 to keep centralized the multiplying government agencies, the town hall was remodelled. The auditorium on the second floor, long the scene of town meetings and the town's first movie theatre, was transformed into offices and increasingly needed committee rooms. Town meetings were held thereafter in one of the regional school auditoriums.

Voting machines and a council on aging were introduced in 1967. Two years later the selectmen set up a citizens advisory committee to reflect and articulate remedial action responding to citizen velleities, and soon afterwards the town meeting set up a landlord–tenant relations committee to cope with matters arising from the explosive growth of residential apartments in town.

That apartment growth, with other demands, precipitated a sudden strain on the town sewer system, and in 1970 plans were made for the enlargement of the sewage treatment plant. The selectmen, responding to a suggestion of the citizens advisory committee, in 1971 appointed a technical committee to advise on sewerage problems; in the meantime the town meeting changed the zoning by-law so as to effect a moratorium on apartment house construction. The technical committee induced a change in the plans and engineers, causing a delay. Early in 1973 the state's division of water pollution control imposed a ban on any additional sewage being introduced into the Amherst system. Much agitation! At a special town meeting in February 1975, $13,300,000, the largest single appropriation ever voted in Amherst, was unanimously approved for a new sewage treatment plant, to be completed in 1977 and the sum to be reimbursed almost in full by state and federal grants.

Also incidental to apartment growth occurred abortive efforts in several town meetings to request of the state legislature a special act for a rent control board in Amherst. After the 145 to 44 defeat in the 1976 fall meeting, proponents procured a referendum but lost again, 2,565 to 1,847.

In 1970 the police and fire departments secured recognition from

TOWN HALL.

PHOTOGRAPH BY MARK KOSARICK

the selectmen of their respective organizations for collective bargaining with the town on salary matters.

In 1971 overhead telephone and electric wires in the business center were removed out of sight and under ground.

In 1972 the town meeting attempted two by-laws both of which were nullified by the state's attorney general: one to favor farmland in local tax assessments, the other to make the town clerk agent for service of process against absentee landlords of apartment units. The following year a by-law, anticipating state law a year later, did pass allowing bicycling on town sidewalks except in the business center, and also a moderate dog control by-law designed by the selectmen in preference to a more stringent one of citizen origin that was defeated. Studies that year were authorized to explore public transportation problems in town, looking perhaps to a free bus system.

Construction of a modern fire station started in 1974, strategically located on land donated by the university along East Pleasant Street near the intersection of Eastman (Lovers') Lane (intended to be the thoroughfare of a new northeast by-pass).

Physical growth in the town can roughly be gauged by the increase in assessed valuation of taxable property (houses and land); in 1944 it was $8,619,850 and in 1975 about $168,000,000. Even with inflation of the dollar and the change in valuation policy in 1963 from 33 percent of full value to 100 percent, the figures are impressive. That the tax rate in town is about average appears from comparing ours with tax rates in other towns on buildings of exactly the same structure and nearly the same age as those in Amherst constructed by the same commercial residential developer in areas of similar social character.

The Schools

After World War II school construction and organization had a turbulent history.

Since 1901 we have had a superintendency union with Pelham, i.e., each town engaged the same person as superintendent of its respective school system. Until 1953 public schooling in Amherst from the earliest stages through high school has been under the control of the town's school committee. In 1953 Amherst and Pelham created a two-town regional school district for junior and senior high school grades. The first proposal for such a district had been defeated

by town meeting in Amherst in 1950. The following year the
Amherst meeting and the Pelham voters favored it, although the
Amherst voters at the polls defeated it 1,276 to 996. Two years after
its founding Leverett and Shutesbury also joined the district. Efforts
were made, one in 1962, the other in 1971, to extend its jurisdiction
to include the elementary grades; Leverett said "no" to the first, and
Amherst and Leverett joined in opposition in 1971. As matters stand
today, each local elementary school is under the jurisdiction of its
respective town school committee, and all junior and senior high
school grades are under the regional school district committee. It is
composed of selected members of the school committees of the
member towns.

The practice has been for the Amherst government to acquire for
school purposes in its own name a particular site and then to convey
it to the district. Only twice has the district directly acquired land
from a private landowner, in one instance by eminent domain. In
1947 the town meeting voted to buy for $16,000 a thirty-acre lot
north of Triangle Street as a site for an elementary school. Part of it is
now district land and the rest town playground.

When in 1961 the meeting voted to acquire future elementary
school sites, the vote was challenged in a referendum which was
hostile, 923 to 883, but as the opposition failed to constitute 20
percent of the voters in town, the action of the meeting was undis-
turbed. Soon afterwards thirteen acres on Sand Hill Road and on
State Street were acquired and are still unused. About sixteen acres
on West Street and Shays Street were also acquired and immediately
used for the Crocker Farm School. "Skillings Pasture," south of
Strong Street, and some nearby lots, aggregating about thirty-nine
acres, were taken by the town in 1965; the southerly portion is being
used by the district and the northerly by the town's school committee for the Wildwood School. In 1971 the town acquired about
thirty-one acres in East Amherst after a warm debate over whether
the site was prone to flooding. Here was soon afterwards constructed
the Fort River School.

Persuading the town meeting to authorize elementary school
buildings was for several years a more difficult matter than it became
in the 1970s. Many felt a queasiness about the plain modern styling
that was always being proposed instead of the normal, pilastered
Georgian.

In 1948 the meeting rejected a proposal to authorize plans for a
$400,000 school of fourteen rooms, but at a special meeting later that
year it voted 83 to 72 by secret printed ballot to supply the funds.
That is the latest use of secret voting in Amherst town meeting; the
process took about thirty minutes. By 1950 the proposal had become
a $600,000 one. It needed a two-thirds town meeting vote that it
failed to secure, 102 favoring it, 92 opposed. The measure was put to
a referendum and was again lost, 939 favoring to 1,764 opposed.
Two years later the proposal was scaled down to $575,000 and sailed
through town meeting 140 to 33. It failed however in the referendum
where, although the vote was favorable, 1,032 to 993, the required
two-thirds was not secured.

A modest victory was achieved in 1953 when town meeting au-
thorized a $60,000 enlargement of the South Amherst Elementary
School while rejecting a $180,000 enlargement of the East Street
School.

Welcome help came in 1961, when the University of Massachusetts constructed and made available to the town a twelve-room
elementary school building in modern styling, known as Mark's
Meadow School, on North Pleasant Street. This facility, by agreement with the university, is run by the town's school department as
one of its schools, but it is also used by the university as a laboratory
for its school of education.

For the Wildwood Elementary School now on the north portion
of Skillings Pasture on Strong Street the 1968 town meeting voted
$2,500,000. The plan of that building was so successful that it was
copied in 1972 when $3,000,000 was voted for the construction of the
Fort River Elementary School.

In the meantime some obsolete school buildings were demolished. After being unused for a year, the ninety-nine-year-old
four-room Amity Street school that stood opposite The Jones Library was razed in 1967, and the site was wrought for automobile
parking, a site on which also stood for over fifty years the private
school building of The Trustees of Amherst Academy. In 1974 the
town high school on Lessey Street and the Kellogg Avenue schools
were demolished to make way for the construction of the Boltwood
Walk complex.

For costs of school buildings belonging to the district by far the
lion's share falls on the Amherst taxpayers. In 1955 our town meet-

ing approved $1,500,000 for the original building. Eight years later it approved a $1,650,000 addition to it, and in 1967 it authorized a new junior high school building on the southern portion of Skillings Pasture north of Chestnut Street costing about $5,000,000.

The organizational efficiency of the town manager government, combined with the pronounced partiality of our people for institutional education accounts for the proportion of our town's annual tax revenues devoted to public schools increasing from about 50 percent in the 1950s to about 70 percent in the 1970s.

Relations with the Colleges and University

The most perpetually restless problem teasing the town government comes in settling its financial and service relationships with the tax-exempt colleges of Amherst and Hampshire and especially with the state-owned University of Massachusetts.

As to the latter the state had undertaken to pay the town an annual sum in lieu of taxes based on the fair cash value of state-owned land in town. The payments seemed meager, and several times the town had filed, in vain, special legislation for a more generous formula. Every five years the state determines the value from which payments are computed. Finally, in 1970, the town carried its appeal from the state's determination to the state's Supreme Judicial Court and won a far-reaching decision. For four years the payments were better, but in 1974 the state, teasing Amherst again, changed its formula, and payments again dropped severely.

In 1958 Amherst College gave the town $4,750 in research monies to study its financial and service relation with such institutions. The study recommended that they pay the town an appropriate share for fire and police protection and some sewer system capital expenses. One or more of these institutions has contributed in the purchase of fire fighting equipment, for a sewerage line of special benefit to it, for the town's sanitary landfill operation, and to ease special situations that arose. The relationship between the town government and these institutions has been unusually cordial.

Wider Participation in Town Government

In the early 1970s the eagerness of citizens to participate in and to be heard on local governmental matters became apparent. The then new and younger group of selectmen, sensing the climate of suspi-

cion of governmental operations engendered by the Watergate dis-
closures, scheduled their meetings in the evenings, and occasionally
in different neighborhoods, to facilitate citizen attendance. They extensively publicized agendas of meetings, records of their actions,
and materials on which decisions were based. In fact they developed
so urgent a sense of obligation to act responsively as at times to
impinge on the role of the manager. By 1974 there were seventeen *ad
hoc* citizen committees appointed by them either to cope with special
situations or to come up with advice. By then the number of permanent boards of control in the town government had grown to nineteen. A few spontaneous private, but short-lived, public interest
groups also emerged, concerned with town growth, environment,
and the like.

Participation of women in official town positions has increased
steadily. When limited town meeting was established in 1939, its
membership was 15.8 percent women. In 1974 it was 26.5 percent.
Of the twenty-five core offices in town (moderator, selectmen,
school and finance committee, and planning board) 12 percent were
held by women in 1954, and 36 percent in 1974, when the last three
were chaired by women. By far the most consistently useful and
politically effective citizen group in town in recent decades has been
the local branch of the League of Women Voters. Its most notable
member, Lucy Wilson Benson, former member of the town finance
committee, and former president, successively, of the local, state,
and national League became in 1977 Under Secretary of State in the
federal government.

A study made in the 1960s disclosed that college faculty and staff
were three times as prone to seek town meeting membership as were
"townies." In the period covered by this essay a trend emerged of
proportionately increased participation of that college element in
other town offices.

With the change in voting age from twenty-one to eighteen the
town adopted a liberal definition of residency to allow students to
register as voters here and set up for them special registering stations
on the university campus. Undergraduates and recent graduates of
local institutions began in 1972 noticeable participation in town government. A few have been elected town meeting members, and
others tried in vain for election as moderator or selectman, one going
unsuccessfully to a federal court charging town discrimination

against student voters in setting the date for town elections in a student vacation period. Among measures they have urged on town meeting are ones favoring unconventional personal lifestyles, favoring apartment tenants, changing the term *selectman* to *selectperson,* and aiding hitchhikers and bicyclists. Most of their proposals failed seemingly less on their merits than because so cast as to be illegal or impossible of effectuation.

Some in town are becoming impatient at the meeting time spent in disposing of callow or ineptly framed measures originating in youthful ardor and urge Amherst to adopt the more callous form of government used in cities. Vulnerable though town meeting government may be to such efflorescences, it is the part of wisdom for our citizens to strain their patience to the utmost to retain the present sensitive form of local government. Possibly youth and age will develop the poise to succeed in this; if so it will be a notable victory for the human spirit.

Another federal court suit was filed early in 1975 also charging the town with discriminating against college students. It alleged that in fixing precinct boundaries for election of town meeting members it relied only on the count of the 10,000 or so registered voters to determine relative equality in numbers per precinct rather than on residents which included also about 24,000 college students, only a few of whom are Amherst voters. This suit illustrates the inappropriateness of applying the U.S. Supreme Court's so-called one man, one vote formula to legislative districts of small population. As we go to press final judgment has not yet ripened. Indeed the case may become moot for, pursuant to a 1975 state law imposing that formula even on municipal governments, the selectmen subsequent to the filing of that case redistricted the town into eight necessarily awkward precincts for the election of town meeting members beginning in 1977.

Amherst's Bicentennial, 1959

For the town's bicentennial observance in 1959 there were numerous activities, among them fireworks, a parade, Earl Amherst's receipt of an honorary degree, an interfaith convocation featuring poems by Robert Frost set to music by Randall Thompson, both men being present, and the dedication of a memorial marker for the late Chief Justice of the United States, Harlan Fiske Stone, who had

COURTESY OF THE AMHERST STUDENT

AMHERST PEACE VIGIL, DECEMBER 1966.

grown up and attended college in the town. The bicentennial symbol designed by Frank Anderson Trapp was so well received that in 1960 it was adopted as the official town seal. His initials are discernible in the design.

National and International Issues

Following five precedents from earlier years, beginning June 17, 1776 the town meeting in the 1970s revived the practice of making utterances on national issues. In 1962 it had declined to adopt a proposed pronouncement that the construction of public or private fall-out shelters against nuclear bombing would not contribute to the public welfare. And in 1970 it had declined, 95 to 87, to condemn the entry of U.S. troops into Cambodia. But the next year it voted, 95 to 85, urging U.S. armed forces to be out of Vietnam by December 31st. In 1973 it passed two votes, one directing that the United Nations flag be flown daily on the town common. It flies. The second authorized the placing on the common of the marker commemorating the Peace Vigil conducted from December 1966 to August 1973 every Sunday from noon to one P.M. by citizens standing silently to protest our participation in the war in Southeast Asia. In 1974 the meeting declined, 109 to 79, to pronounce against nuclear electric power plants until safety factors were assured, but did vote, 91 to 87, to urge the impeachment of President Nixon. The next year it declined to pronounce opposition to funding for Southeast Asia, but in 1976 it instructed our members of Congress to halt construction of the B-1 bomber and to oppose U.S. Senate Bill #1, The Criminal Justice Reform Act.

The role of Amherst in international affairs was signalized in 1957 when it joined the United Town Organization program, *Le Monde Bilingue,* and was twinned with a delightful French town on the Bay of Biscay, Arcachon, which sent to Amherst for our bicentennial, Mlle. Lucienne Boudet, who presented the town with an original letter of Lafayette.

The Select Committee on Goals

The most profoundly and extensively probing survey ever made of the needs of the town that might be met by action of the town government was developed by a group called select committee on goals (SCOG). It was appointed by the selectmen in October 1971 and operated under the chairmanship of Bruce Morgan until he left town in January 1972, and thereafter until its report with recommendations a year later under H. Hills Skillings. Its basic objective was to formulate a plan to preserve the desirable and characteristic qualities of the town while accommodating the increase in population that appeared certain to develop. Details of its report are covered in another essay in this volume, but its dominant theme is the channeling of residential and commercial development into six specified village centers and maintaining relatively open green areas around each. The report was welcomed by the 1973 annual town meeting which voted funds to plan ways to implement it. In May 1975 the first effort to do so by zoning was favored, 133 to 80, but failed of the necessary two-thirds vote, the opposition asserting that farmers would be disadvantaged. A like fate befell a modification of that proposal at the 1975 fall meeting.

CHAPTER THIRTEEN

PUBLIC EDUCATION IN AMHERST

RHODA S. HONIGBERG

Rhoda Honigberg has been actively involved with Amherst's schools
in a number of ways: as a parent of two children who moved through all levels
of the school system, as a president of the Amherst League of Women Voters
who made studies of the town's schools, as a member of two school building
committees (for Crocker Farm and Wildwood schools), and, from 1968 to
1971, as a member and then chairman of the Amherst School Committee.

Educational theories tend to swing within a spectrum ranging
from strict discipline and emphasis on the three Rs to permissiveness
in both style and content of classroom activity, with relatively greater stress on total personal development. During the postwar period,
as town population more than trebled, public education in Amherst
has made the journey from one end to the other, albeit not to either
extreme.

The end of World War II found the schools of Amherst ill staffed
and ill housed. After a series of declines, the numbers of students had
begun to grow as a result of inmigration and birth rate changes. On
October 1, 1945, the date of the annual official head count, there
were 1,179 students, of whom 174 were tuition pupils. The latter,
following a practice of long standing, came from Sunderland,
Leverett, Shutesbury, Pelham; others were wards of the state, of the
City of Boston, or of some private families. The tuition for these
pupils amounted to about 14 percent of the total school budget for
that year, representing an important source of revenue.

Superintendent of Schools Leland Dudley, reporting on the
1944/45 year, summed matters up: Although the total number of
pupils had dropped from the preceding year, there was an increase in

grades 1–6, especially grade 1. October 1 elementary school enrollments had been 532 in 1943, 560 in 1944, and 563 in 1945. Junior and especially senior high school enrollments at the same time were declining: 678, 671, and 616 in the three years.

The town was accommodating these pupils in nine buildings, seven of which were used for grades 1–6. Almost every one of these buildings had serious structural, health, or safety–related difficulties, in addition to lacking enough space to house the children who would soon arrive. Amity Street School was a two-story building, the second floor of which was widely known to be dangerous for any vigorous physical activity by the children.

The general school appropriation for 1945 was $164,293. After deduction of receipts from various other sources, including tuition and state payments, the net cost to the town was $128,513 to be raised by local taxation. This latter figure, net cost to the town, had remained relatively stable over a long period of time. The Superintendent's report for 1941 noted that the budget for that year was only about 2.5 percent greater than that for 1928, while enrollment increased about 6 percent. Annual budgets dipped in the depression years and then began a slow climb. Net cost in 1940 was $104,266, in 1944 $122,161. Annual net cost rose to $153,669 in 1946, the first full postwar year, following a general teacher pay raise and an enrollment increase of forty-five pupils, most of them at the earliest elementary level.

Keeping the schools staffed with teachers was a headache of mi-

TABLE 1. AMHERST SCHOOLS IN 1945

Name of School	Built in	Size
Cushman	1927	4 rooms (wood frame)
North Amherst	1870	4 rooms
South Amherst	1902	2 rooms
East Street	1936	5 rooms
Amity Street	1868	4 rooms
Kellogg West★	1904	3 rooms
Kellogg East★	1911	4 rooms
High School★	1916	22 classrooms
	1936	gymnasium wing
Junior High★	1929	6 classrooms plus 2 shop rooms in basement

★ On one 3.5-acre site in the center of town

THE CUSHMAN SCHOOL, AN OLD WOODEN SCHOOLHOUSE,
CA. 1920.

graine proportions. Each year since 1943 there had been damaging turnover rates among the staff, about 40 percent in 1943 (and again in 1946). Of eighteen resigning teachers in 1943, six went to the military, joining five others already in service. Only substitutes could be hired, since the law required that returning servicemen had to be reemployed if they sought to return to their jobs. Furthermore, in 1941 Amherst's newly adopted salary schedule had a $1,600 maximum for women elementary teachers who were college graduates (not all were) with training in education. Women high school teachers with a master's degree could aspire to $1,800, and men with equivalent training and experience could rise to $2,100. By 1943 teachers with and without college degrees were able to find work in government or industry and have the satisfaction of furthering the war effort joined to that of earning a decent wage. By the end of 1945 the school committee, unable to secure competent teachers, had to raise the salaries by $450.

With the country's emergence from the war, the development of new programs could once again be contemplated, and the school committee planned to initiate kindergartens, the classes to be formed in North Amherst, East Street, and at the Center. Superintendent Dudley cautioned at the time, however, that qualified teachers were scarce and rooms would be very hard to find.

The lack of qualified people to teach had its roots in several sources: the low birthrates of the late twenties and early thirties, mismatched with pupils born during the more fertile late thirties and the war years; the pitifully low salaries and low esteem accorded members of this profession; policies of school boards, which discriminated against women in general and against married women in particular. The Amherst school system paid women $300 per year less than men of precisely equivalent merit, training, and experience and did not hire married women. (This policy sparked formation, in 1947, of a local branch of the League of Women Voters.) Many years earlier, the school committee preferred to hire women because they would accept lower salaries, and it was not until after the war that the Commonwealth of Massachusetts moved toward enforcement of equal pay for equal work for both sexes. At the time, Dr. Dudley opposed this change because he thought it would be impossible to secure men teachers at the lower salaries women were accepting and because raising the women's pay to the men's level would be too expensive.

But the town's school age population was growing very fast, the result both of natural increase and increase in young married consumers of the town's major "industry"—higher education. As a result of pressure from various quarters (returning servicemen, women, increased demand for higher education generally), the Massachusetts State College at Amherst renewed war-suspended efforts to become the University of Massachusetts. Such a change involved something besides a new name; it meant added programs, serving the needs of more, and more varied, students. The growth of the University, as it became in 1947, may be judged by the fact that total enrollment went from 1,773 in 1939 to 24,699 in 1975. To educate this expanding student body, proportionate increases in staff were required, almost invariably young men with young families. To a lesser extent, a similar process was occurring at Amherst College. Total off-campus population in that time is estimated to have risen from 6,410 to 20,713 people. (The population had only increased by 1,300 in the preceding thirty years.)

Scenes being played on larger stages also had local ramifications: by the middle of the 1950's the Cold War was being fought on many different fields of battle. One of these was technology. The Soviets made no secret of their determination to win the battle of technological advancement, and appeared to have done so when Sputnik was launched in 1957. It was widely trumpeted that their education system was geared to the production of scientists and engineers. A chart prepared by the Russian Ministry of Education showed 5,553,000 specialists employed in the Soviet economy in 1955, contrasted with 190,000 in 1913. While domestic Red scourgers sought to achieve ideological purity in the State Department, armed forces, industry, and the universities, other cold warriors urged the latter to enlist in the struggle for scientific supremacy by turning out our own technicians. Soon the high schools, then the elementary schools, were seen to be the incubators of scientists, and it quickly became apparent that the United States simply didn't have enough teachers to staff the classrooms. Hence the colleges had to train many more who, working in the elementary and secondary schools, would send generations of budding scientists and engineers, products of newly enriched curricula, into math, science, and engineering departments of colleges and universities.

Thus Amherst, like towns throughout the country, underwent what was described as explosive growth, the public schools along with all other elements of the community. So severe were the educational problems nationally that a White House Conference on Education was held in Washington, D.C. at the end of 1955, its purpose to make proposals to President Eisenhower aimed at improving the public schools. Six final reports were written, and the major recommendations included proposals for attracting and keeping an adequate supply of good teachers; federal aid for the public schools (this was a bombshell, a stunning departure from conventional thinking about home rule and government interference); a list of goals for the schools that would be acceptable to educators and lay citizens; practices designed to improve efficiency and economy in the operation of school systems; ways to develop greater public interest in education; and—a particular Amherst concern—a list of practices designed to overcome the critical classroom shortage.

Locally, the teacher shortage reached nearly crisis proportions in the fifties, as the rising birthrates were adding to the problem of rapid growth through inmigration. The average number of births per year in the period 1933 to 1939 was eighty-two, compared with 114 in the 1940–1945 period, an increase that owed very little to inmigration.

The White House Conference spawned a nationwide series of Little White House Conferences, one of which was held in the Amherst High School in May 1956. Its focus was on the teacher shortage, because at that time the town had reason to feel it had made a good start toward alleviating its space problem. The only other subject mentioned in the final report was the then controversial one of increasing state and federal aid: fears expressed about loss of home rule were balanced by concern over local taxes. One suggestion was that "a research laboratory or corporation be encouraged to come to Amherst and help relieve the [tax] problem." The final report concentrated on the need to raise salaries, to design incentives to encourage superior teachers, to encourage people to enter the teaching profession, to raise the prestige of teachers, to establish the right of teachers to be free of community surveillance and criticism outside of school hours (this was hedged somewhat: "A teacher can not be expected to balance on a pedestal but should show concern for the impression he or she makes on pupils"). For almost every one of the foregoing problems the solution suggested was better pay.

The second great shortfall—classrooms and other school space—was at once easier and harder to remedy. On the one hand, construction was wholly within the political and economic power of the town, but on the other hand, it proved almost a labor of Hercules to get it done.

Local school committees have virtual autonomy in Massachusetts, subject only to the displeasure of the voters at election. The members, with the advice of the staff and superintendent of schools, make up each year's operating budget, which may be rejected by a municipality only at the risk of having the school committee take the matter to court, where the committee is almost invariably upheld. The community then is forced to raise the amount originally requested and is subject to a penalty of 25 percent of the amount cut. One reason for this is that the authorities trying to cut the school budget may be (and are assumed to be) motivated by pecuniary considerations, while the school committee's motivations are assumed to be purely educational. (In fact, the motivations of each side may be political.) There is, however, one important exception to the above rule: capital expenditures are subject to town meeting approval, and those involving borrowing need a two-thirds vote for passage. Since such expenditures and borrowings are translatable into tax increases, school construction in the town heightens conflict.

In the beginning, 1800, there were six school districts in the town, and by 1838 there were two more. These were quite autonomous, supported by an apportionment from the town and by special assessments levied upon the residents within each district, according to votes taken at district meetings. The town was divided into the following districts: West Centre (1), East Centre (2), South Centre (3), North East or Cushman, sometimes called City (4), North West (5), South West (6), Mill Valley (7), and South East (8). Among these were at one time nineteen "schools," apparently what we now understand as classrooms. In each school (room) children from five years to perhaps eighteen were taught by a single teacher—the ungraded one-room school of sentimental memory. In conformity with a state law of 1851, three of these rooms were set aside as high schools. A written record of the South East School District from February 1828 to March 1862 remains. Its earliest entries include decisions made on improving the schoolhouse, in which, conveniently, all the meetings were held (the following extracts from the 1833 minutes are lightly edited for grammar, punctuation, and spelling and are sometimes paraphrased for clarity).

April 27 – Voted to pass over an article to see what measures if any the District will take to build a new school House. Voted, instead, a committee of three to examining the school House if in their opinnion it is worth repairing.

May 4 – Committee Reported in their opinnion not best to repair the old house.

May 20 – Voted a committee of the whole to examining the old House.

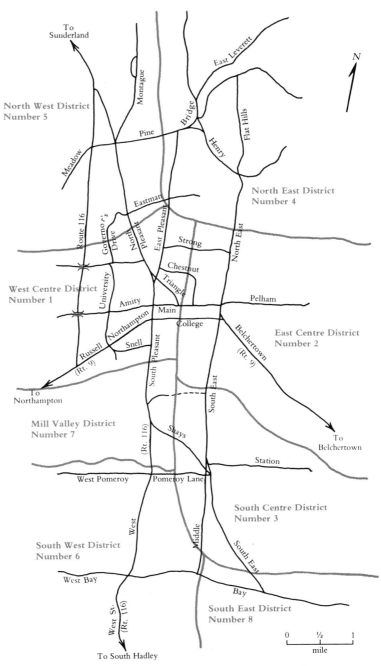

To
Sunderland

North West District
Number 5

Montague

East Leverett

Bridge

Flat Hills

N

Pine

Henry

Meadow

North East District
Number 4

Route 116

Governor's
Drive

North
Pleasant

Eastman

East Pleasant

Strong

North East

Chestnut

West Centre District
Number 1

University

Triangle

Amity

Main

Pelham

Northampton

College

East Centre District
Number 2

Russell
(Rt. 9)

Snell

South Pleasant

Belchertown
(Rt. 9)

To
Northampton

South East

Mill Valley District
Number 7

(Rt. 116)

Shays

South East

To
Belchertown

Station

West Pomeroy

Pomeroy Lane

South Centre District
Number 3

West

Middle

South East

South West District
Number 6

West Bay

Bay

West St.
(Rt. 116)

South East District
Number 8

0   ½   1
mile

To South Hadley

THE SCHOOL DISTRICTS OF AMHERST 1838–1864.

Voted to adjourn fifteen minutes to examining the house. Voted not to repair the house. Voted to Build a new House with Brick. Voted a committee of three to Draft a plan of a school house and lay it before a future meeting.

May 27 – Voted to build according to the plan presented. House to be twenty two feet by twenty feet. Wood [storage] house to be thirteen feet by thirteen feet and no larger. Voted a Committee to let out the Building of the house to the Man that will Build the house for the least sum to the acceptance of the Committee the house to be Built of Brick the wood house of wood the builder to secure the District for his faithful performance of the building of the school house and wood house.

August 26 – Voted all former votes to build a new school House annulled. Voted to Repair the school House and build a wood house and necessary [a privy] and appropriate so much of the District's fund as is necessary to Defray the Expenses.

September 9 – Voted all former votes to build a new school house or Repair the old house Reconsidered. Voted a committee to build a school the next year and sell the old house after the school is out next winter. Voted to build a wood House in addition to the School House. Voted the wood House and school House be of the same Dimensions agreed upon at a former meeting.

Probably the schoolhouse, wood house, and necessary were built; nothing more appears on the subject until 1838, when alterations to the furnishings of the school house were agreed upon, "provided money can be raised to defray the expense of the same by subscription or donation." (Eligible voters were male citizens who paid a poll tax. Only twice were numbers recorded: 17 in 1851 and 37 in 1855.)

A decision to place the students into grades was carried out in 1861, and in 1864 the eight districts were merged into a single town-wide one. In 1839 the districts had considered and rejected joining one another in "Union schools." A high school was built on Spring Street coincident with the grading, and, as the only one in the system, it performed the traditional function of such schools, providing a true community center. Provincials from north, east, west, and south became acquainted; friends could be chosen for congeniality rather than mere propinquity and, on the rather limited town scale, social horizons were widened. Not only was the new high school constructed, but new or reconstructed schoolhouses were provided as needed, apparently with a minimum of strain. A wing for a grammar school (roughly equivalent to today's grades 5, 6, and 7)

THE AMITY STREET GRADE SCHOOL, ON THE SITE OF THE OLD
AMHERST ACADEMY.

was added to the high school building in 1880. In 1905 the South East
School was closed because it did not have enough pupils, and in 1906
crowded conditions at Amity Street led to the decision that no new
classes would be admitted there for the next term. This paradox
demonstrates very well one disadvantage of having many small
neighborhood schools. At the time in question, although Amherst
remained, as it had been from the start, a long, narrow community
with clusters of population density strung out like beads along the
chain of north-south roads, the center had been gaining much faster
than other areas. Hence its schools became crowded, while outlying
ones had to be abandoned.

Only three years after the closing of the South East School, land
was acquired and plans prepared for the erection of Kellogg West.
Amherst's schools changed considerably from 1898 to 1915, the

years of Audubon L. Hardy's service as Superintendent, but perhaps most significant was the trend toward consolidation of school buildings. Each schoolhouse that was constructed contained one more room than the one built before, and children attending the small outlying schools that were closed were transported to another, first' by horse-drawn wagon, later by public street car. The only housing problem Mr. Hardy seemed unable to solve was the high school's. Although he started trying in 1899 and continued throughout his tenure, money for a new high school was not finally authorized until 1915. That must have seemed to him a fitting capstone to his career, because he then retired, living out the remaining twenty years of his life in his big house on Lincoln Avenue.

Under the superintendency of Carroll Reed the new high school was built on Lessey Street, sharing a 3.5 acre site with the two Kellogg Avenue schools, and in 1929 a junior high was built on the same site. That school construction was becoming a passionate affair

COURTESY OF THE JONES LIBRARY

THE SIXTH GRADE AT THE KELLOGG AVENUE ELEMENTARY
SCHOOL, CA. 1930.

AMHERST HIGH SCHOOL (1867–1916) ON SPRING STREET.

can be ascertained from a school committee resolution that was "spread upon the record" in April 1928: "WHEREAS recent controversies in Amherst chiefly relative to proposed new school building [the junior high] have aroused feeling in certain quarters, and WHEREAS the discussions have given rise to a criticism of the management of the schools in general. . . ." the committee affirmed its

TABLE 2. SUPERINTENDENTS OF SCHOOLS★

Superintendents	Years of Service	Superintendents	Years of Service
W. D. Parkinson	1893–1898	L. Leland Dudley	1935–1950
Audubon L. Hardy	1898–1915	Carroll F. Johnson	1950–1952
Carroll R. Reed	1915–1917	Ralph W. Goodrich	1952–1962
John D. Brooks	1917–1920	Ronald J. Fitzgerald	1963–1973
Jason O. Cook	1920–1935	Donald B. Frizzle	1973–

★From 1867 to 1893 a member of the School Committee served as superintendent on a part-time basis. The last one, J. Harry Holden, was paid $500 plus $7.50 per year, the latter fee for serving as one of two truant officers.

support of Mr. Jason Cook, the superintendent, and its "appreciation of his efficiency, industry, wisdom, and devotion."

Because the town was growing, though slowly, the school population continued to expand, as did notions of what constituted education. The high school building had nothing but classrooms, and so in 1936 a wing was added to the original, with nonclassroom space including a gymnasium, the first in an Amherst public school. In that same year a fire at the East Street School necessitated its reconstruction.

Using birth rates and taking into account in- and outmigration patterns, in any given year school authorities can estimate first grade enrollment six years later. This can be done with some accuracy, since long-range plans of major employers and local governments are usually available. The rising birthrate had become evident before the war, and as early as 1943 the superintendent had proposed that a

THE CLASS OF 1868, AMHERST HIGH SCHOOL.

committee be appointed to act with the school committee to study the need for more school space. Although it was widely recognized that, despite the 1936 addition, ours was not a modern or well-equipped high school, that building and the junior high were not overcrowded—yet. Dr. Dudley recommended that the joint committee give serious consideration to a new elementary school. Accordingly in 1944 the town meeting authorized the appointment of such a committee, continuing it in 1945, and authorizing it, further, to seek a proper site for an elementary school. In the next year, a sum of money was appropriated for professional advice. The joint committee employed two outside experts to consider three alternatives: (1) A new senior high school (grades 10–12) on a new site, adapting the old building for other school purposes, probably the junior high. This was eliminated because the elementary schools were older and more worn out than the two secondary school buildings. (2) A new six-year secondary school, economizing by using one large building and infrastructure for all six grades. This was eliminated because, in addition to the reason for dismissing alternative 1, the building itself would be very expensive and the old space poorly adapted to elementary use. (3) A new elementary school for grades 1–6, on a new site. This became the choice of the experts. It was also Dr. Dudley's choice because although he favored alternative 1 he felt it would be very hard to get the town to agree to the expense of either 2 or 1. The joint committee adopted the experts' view, the town meeting voted to purchase the site that had been proposed (the senior high school stands on it now), and a building committee was appointed to plan an elementary school of at least fourteen rooms (the largest then standing had five rooms). Other town meeting action in 1947 specified that the school was to cost no more than $400,000. Subsequently, the building committee, after securing plans, found that the sum stipulated was insufficient—that in fact the school would cost about $600,000—and withdrew its request for the money. By that time some classrooms were being used for double sessions, and the growth of the school-age population was accelerating. Interested citizens began to mobilize (there is no citizen more interested than the parent whose children are going to school on double session) in support of the elementary school, which came to be called, after its architect, the Dirks school. The town meeting in 1949 was asked to raise $571,000 for building the school, but it refused by a vote of 109

WILDWOOD ELEMENTARY SCHOOL.

to 67. Another vote authorized enlargement of the building committee and asked it to submit another, not necessarily different, plan. Significantly, the report later presented by the enlarged group was not supported by all its members, seven proposing the Dirks school and two recommending instead a new high school. Public opinion was polarized between the two positions, effectively halting all action. Despite repeated meetings, referenda, special and regular town meetings, no consensus was reached beyond agreement on the truly desperate need. Students met in basements, attics, the Legion Building, Odd Fellows Hall, Jones Library. Each year a bewildering series of arrangements and rearrangements was made to house the classes. State and local officials sometimes pointed out the inadequacy and occasional hazard of a particular location. Beyond some inevitable public education coincident upon such ferment, the only movement in the direction of increasing school space came in 1953 with approval by the town of a two-room addition to the South Amherst School, doubling its size.

Concurrent with these attempts to build an elementary school, another approach was being made toward the construction of a new school: the town meeting in 1953 approved formation of a Regional School District Planning Board, and this group, together with a similar body from Pelham, proposed formation of a Regional School

District which would build a high school. At least one earlier attempt at regionalization had been defeated by the voters. The issue had been discussed with Pelham, Hadley, Leverett, and Shutesbury, but only Pelham and Amherst, with their long history of the Superintendency Union, committed themselves to the joint venture. Since 1901 the two towns had shared a superintendent of schools, chosen by representatives from their school committees, Amherst accounting for 80 to 90 percent of the Union's expenditures. Pelham's secondary school pupils had long been tuition students in Amherst's schools. Participation in the Region protected Pelham against a future Amherst decision that it could no longer take students from other towns, as well as giving Pelham's school committee a voice in the management of the secondary schools.

Organizing the Region was no incidental side issue in the building struggle: state reimbursement to a community for building a local school was 29 percent of the total. To encourage the formation of larger educational units, 41 percent of the cost of building and equipping a new regional school would be paid by the state. Furthermore, it was much easier to put into effect since only a simple majority, not two thirds, was needed in each town to approve capital expenditure involving indebtedness for a regional school.

In 1954, the town meeting voted 160 to 1 in favor of a plan submitted by the Regional District for a new high school, and in the autumn of 1956, five days late for opening day, the not quite finished building opened with 332 pupils. (Thus Amherst's Little White House Conference on Education could concentrate on the teacher shortage: space problems were on the way to being solved.) Leverett and Shutesbury had joined the Region after its formation. Their tardiness resulted in an apparent inequity which persists to the present day: under the original 1953 agreement, Amherst has five members on the Regional School Committee and Pelham two. Leverett and Shutesbury have one each, although the former is larger than Pelham and sends more pupils to the schools.

The high school's opening resulted in the relocation of grades 7–9 to the old high school on Lessey Street (470 pupils in a 350 pupil building), freeing all but two of its former classrooms for elementary use. Thus ended two years of double sessions for grades 7–12 and even more for several classes in grades 1–6.

Very soon after the high school was built, in response to continued growth in the town, movement began on the elementary school scene. Real help was provided by the University of Massachusetts which, in 1961, turned over to the town the twelve-room Marks Meadow Elementary School to be operated in conjunction with the School of Education as a demonstration school. It represented, except for the necessary reconstruction of the East Street School after the 1936 fire, the first new elementary school in town in fifty years. Thus was Amherst rewarded for its intransigence; but the population was growing so much in size and changing so much in composition that in the next twelve years the old school plant was almost entirely replaced.

Since 1963 Amherst, Pelham, and the four-town Region enjoyed the leadership of Ronald J. Fitzgerald, a young superintendent with a forcefully persuasive manner. While specific proposals encountered spotty resistance, there was no effective rebellion, and educational facilities popped up all over town: the Crocker Farm School and a large addition to the high school (planned at the time of the original construction) in 1966; the Junior High School in 1969; Wildwood in 1970; Fort River in 1973. One by one the small schools were given up, some to the wreckers, others to various uses. In 1975 North Amherst's old building is used by a private day care center, the Amherst Ballet School, and the Alternate Learning Center run by the Advocates Program at the University of Massachusetts. Cushman School is being used as a private day care center. East Street School, across the East Common from Fort River, still belongs to the school system and is used as a curriculum preparation center. The Kellogg Avenue schools and the old high school were torn down in 1974 to make way for parts of Boltwood Walk, and the intermediate building (the original junior high) is expected to be incorporated into that project. Only part of the South Amherst School continues in use among its younger but larger siblings as a kindergarten adjunct to Crocker Farm.

Why did the logjam break so dramatically? In general throughout this period the economy was good. The Russian challenge and the subsequent examination of our education system nationwide created a favorable attitude toward increased expenditures for schools. The eminent Dr. James B. Conant's thorough study of the American high school recommended the consolidation of small high schools, pointing out the impracticality of staffing and equipping the small schools as compared with the larger ones. There were also the undeniable growth in numbers of students; the education of the citizenry that had been a by-product of the frustrations of 1947–1955; and the fact that there had been a change in our population. Many of the newcomers were well-educated men and women with high expectations for their children but, on college teachers' salaries in no position to send them to expensive private schools. They became extremely effective advocates of the public schools.

It would be wrong to write the story of public education in Amherst in the period since 1963 without more mention of Ronald Fitzgerald. He took over the school superintendency following the resignation of Ralph Goodrich. Fitzgerald was twenty-nine years old, a science teacher in the junior high school, and coordinator of science for the whole system. His predecessor had overseen some very important accomplishments, the South Amherst addition and regionalization among them. For many months before Goodrich's resignation, however, the schools were leaderless but for the school committees, while parents were pressing for improvements in the education of their children. The ten years of Mr. Fitzgerald's superintendency saw the greatest growth in the schools in qualitative as well as quantitative terms, and if, by the end of his service, some parents were tired of change, they nonetheless owe him a great deal. In 1963, however, it was as much citizen support that supplied the motive force for the new and well (some thought lavishly) equipped schools, for the hiring and retention of highly competent teachers and administrators, and for expanded curricula.

Adoption of new programs was an immediate concomitant of the newly available space. At the head of the list was kindergarten. The school committee during World War II planned to introduce it immediately after the war but, as we have seen, there was no place to put the classes. The university-donated elementary school had no provision for kindergartens, but the first town-built school in 1966 did. This was a victory for those who realized the value of early childhood education and despaired of finding space in the few private facilities—as well they might, since the existing preschool facilities were insufficient for the demand. To ensure placement in these little schools some of the students had been registered at birth.

The new junior high school had shop classes undreamed of in the old buildings, and secondary school students were able to enroll not only in these, but in courses in television techniques. The TV equipment, run by students, has been available to the community, and a most important result has been the regular televising of town meetings and those of the selectmen and school committee. Because the two new secondary schools were built within a few hundred yards of each other, there has been a complete mingling of their programs and facilities, thus achieving the goal of those in the fifties who fought for the six-year secondary school. The courses are ungraded, meaning that students from grades 7 through 12 may enroll in any, although for the most part seventh and eighth graders do not find themselves in courses with high school seniors.

Taxpayers willingly met the constantly rising costs for such additions as speech and hearing specialists, psychologists, foreign language teachers, curriculum coordinators, summer projects in which teachers rewrote or refined curricula, and the like. It is difficult to compare 1945 and 1975 costs: the consumer price index has trebled, and the number of pupils in both elementary and secondary schools has risen about 230 percent. Cost per pupil, corrected for the rise in the consumer price index, has gone up about 500 percent, but this has been supported by an expanding real estate tax base (the major local revenue source) and significantly increased state and federal aid. The state and federal share of the 1945/46 budget was 6 percent; their share of the 1975/76 budget was almost 20 percent. The school portion of the real estate tax has been kept separately only since the 1950s; in 1975 it was 26 percent higher proportionately than it was in 1955. These figures reflect a willingness at all levels of government to use more of our resources for schooling than was the past practice. Since the White House Conference of 1955 and the ensuing Conant study, such was indeed the conscious decision of government and society.

Not surprisingly, in the face of this large financial commitment to education, the resulting product has come under critical scrutiny. After the upheavals of the 1960s reached our schools, one after another of the nationally felt concerns became manifest among the older students. Race relations, the Vietnam War, long hair (on boys), short skirts, discipline, student rights, academic standards—all took turns on center stage. The earliest adult reaction to each was resistance to change; the next, on the part of some school authorities and some parents, was to yield somewhat. Thus, over time, skirts grew shorter until they practically disappeared, to be supplanted by pants. Male hair trailed down over collars, sometimes billowing, sometimes pony-tailed. Pressure for black studies resulted in reexamination of all curricula for sensitivity to black pride but also for sex stereotyping and similar concerns. "Open campus" addressed the issue of student rights, as did representation of students on a student school committee. Under the open campus plan academically eligible high school students, with their parents' permission, are at liberty to enter and leave the building during free periods, incidentally relieving some of the overcrowding already evident in the school. These students may attend to a variety of personal needs, or they may use library and educational facilities outside the confines of the school.

The secondary school organization and grading system are designed expressly to avoid failure by making it possible for students to take every major subject on a level at which they can succeed. Each student, with teacher and/or parental guidance, chooses one of five levels of difficulty ("phases") for each course. Phasing has been evaluated periodically and is not universally commended. Among its critics are those who believe it encourages able but lazy youngsters to settle for lower phases where they can earn high grades with little effort. In heterogeneous classes, on the other hand, is the undeniable potential for damage that could result when students making a serious effort find themselves always being measured against those of much superior ability. A national decline in academic achievement, as measured by scores in standardized testing programs, has resulted in a renewed concern with teaching basics, and since Amherst usually responds to national concerns, no doubt there will be some changes in this direction locally.

Student behavior seems to each generation of adults to deteriorate. Among children, especially in the young teenage group, disagreements quickly escalate to fights, often provoked but always exacerbated by prejudices brought into the school from home and society. Mischief and even vandalism occur, arousing resentment and anger among taxpayers. Two entries from the minutes of the South East School District of Amherst confirm that this is not unique to our times:

March 28, 1842 – Voted that parrents and gardians shall make good the broken glass and other damages done to the [school] house by their children.

July 24, 1843 – Voted all parrents and gardians in the District A comity to Detect the Rogue or Rogues that Broke the windows in the school house. Voted a five dollar Reward for the Detection of the Rogue or Rogues that Broke the windows in the School house. [At that time, one day's pay for the man who repaired the damage was $1.25.]

Open classrooms built into the Wildwood Elementary School and "humanistic education" (i.e., human relations) both have generated controversy and have, as a result, been somewhat modified. The people objecting to these educational innovations in 1972 often were the same ones who had crusaded for innovations ten and twenty years before. Perhaps the turning point in public opinion came with the Performance Objective Program, one aim of which was to break learning down into a series of units which could be mastered in varying sequences, each child working at his own rate. While the program had many laudable objectives, it raised questions about mechanization of learning and excessive fragmentation of subject matter. Although the program was funded by federal grants and aroused interest among other school systems, it was questioned, criticized, and rejected by many parents. After two years it was modified so that, while its goals have not been abandoned, its most objectionable mechanics have been eliminated.

"Citizen participation" is a phrase often on the lips of government officials and private citizens, perhaps nowhere more than in Amherst. In no instance has the involvement of ordinary citizens been greater than in the struggle for improving the schools. Literally hundreds of people have taken part in efforts to gain approval for one or another plan. Unfortunately, for a long time uncompromising positions were taken (and many old friendships strained) before the formation of the Region provided the way out of the impasse. It was established in 1953 as a secondary school district, but it can be amended at any time, and its extension to include grades K–6 was attempted twice (most recently in 1971). Each time it was turned down by Leverett, the second time by Amherst as well. The emotions engendered by sending the youngest children out of the neighborhood were easily aroused in response to the possibility of sending them out of town. No doubt, however, the last of this issue has not been heard, especially if the state's education authorities are able to make further consolidation of schools economically irresistible.

Underlying the building struggles, of course, had been money, but also involved was a conflict between large centralized versus small neighborhood schools. Those favoring neighborhood schools were put increasingly on the defensive, giving ground before the economic benefits of centralization, which they opposed on emotional (even sentimental) grounds. They conceded first on the upper elementary grades, holding out for the younger children to stay close to home. Events, however, overtook both sides, because as the outlying parts of town opened up to very dense housing developments, what had been outlying became neighborhood for many. To replace the three-room, four-room, and five-room schools, Amherst built 600-pupil buildings and even larger ones for the junior and senior high schools. Nevertheless, the schools on the whole retain an atmosphere of humaneness and freedom from regimentation.

In 1975, at the time of writing these words, it is a source of satisfaction that our modern school plant was built and is being paid for at terms far better than could have been secured had the intransigence and factionalism persisted much longer. We have 1,806 pupils in grades K–6, in schools that were built to accommodate about 2,000. The regional schools, with a capacity of 2,200, currently house 2,017, of whom 1,652 are from Amherst (there were 1,005 Amherst children in grades 1–12 in 1945). It is possible to look forward with some confidence as far as buildings are concerned. Elementary grade enrollments have stopped growing; in fact, there

TABLE 3. CHANGES IN SCHOOL ENROLLMENTS AND EXPENDITURES, 1945–1975

Year	Oct. 1 enrollments[a]	Total budgets[b]	Per pupil	School as % of tax rate	Pork chops[c]	Consumer price index (1967 = 100)
1945	1,179	$ 164,293	$ 139.35	—[d]	$ .37	53.9
1955	1,505	486,387	323.18	51.6	.79	80.2
1965	2,371	1,988,195	838.55	56.5	.97	94.5
1975	3,870	6,666,570	1,722.63	65.2	1.60	162.8

[a] Including tuition and regional pupils
[b] Amherst general (elementary) school appropriation plus the total regional budget, taken from *Amherst Town Reports*
[c] The cost of one pound of pork chops has risen 330 percent since 1945 while the cost per pupil has increased 1,140 percent.
[d] Figure not available

are sixty-two fewer pupils than there were one year ago. The high school is crowded, but it might make it through the next few years, perhaps by adding classrooms as has already been done, until the population peak passes through the schools. The national economic slowdown which brought growth to a halt at the University of Massachusetts and thus in the town is partly responsible for this situation, along with pressures to control population growth worldwide.

A concomitant push to cut back the growth of school budgets may take its toll in curriculum (foreign languages and interscholastic athletics are always candidates for surgery). At the same time, a recurrent deemphasis of academic achievement shows itself as a renewal of interest in vocational (now called career) education. In the town elections of 1975 no one ran for a seat on the school committee who didn't boast of fiscal conservatism. The pendulum swing that began twenty years ago seems to have begun its return journey.

CHAPTER FOURTEEN

PLANNERS AND DEVELOPERS

JAMES A. SMITH

Jim Smith is the Town Engineer of Amherst, and his essay expresses the perspective of one who saw much of the growth in recent years from within the responsibilities and frustrations of town hall. Before turning to a career of public service in engineering, Jim Smith served for a time as a Presbyterian minister.

The myth of the small town and its hold on Amherst's sense of identity has long created problems for town planners. Many people feel that as a small town Amherst is immune to big city problems, that it therefore does not need to adopt the measures of conscious planning and government control over private decisions that may be required elsewhere. Yet Amherst is no longer a small town. Back in 1914 Warren R. Brown wrote:

The growth [of Amherst] during the past five years, and especially in the past three years has been more rapid than ever before in its history. . . . There is room for many more . . . who may wish to locate in a community that unites in a marked degree the advantages of country and city life, without the disagreeable foreign element and vulgar display of wealth common in many suburban towns.

The ethnic antipathy is surely by now outdated, but the idyllic vision of the town is familiar to all of us. Yet by 1948 there were other voices speaking in the town—less idyllic, but more clearly addressed to the reality of our situation. Chairman of selectmen, F. Civille Pray, wrote:

We are suffering from growing pains—growing from a village into a man-sized town and find it hard to readjust ourselves to new viewpoints, needs, and then accept the changes, added expenses, and infringements upon our personal liberties one enjoyed in a neighborhood village but [which are not] feasible in a grown-up town.

It is not even during the most recent decades that Amherst's land has experienced the most drastic periods of change. By far the greatest impact occurred when our European ancestors burned and cut the virgin timber, deforested the land, and allowed the thin soil to wash on down into present-day Hadley. After several generations, many of these early farmers had to move west to the Berkshires, New York, and Ohio. The graves of their young wives and infant children remain, along with the stone walls still to be seen in the young woods of northeast Amherst. Their great grandsons strung barbed wire in Lawrence Swamp when the meadows were still free of trees.

One must not forget the early industrial community of North Amherst with mills (grist and paper), woodworking shops, and tanneries which caused a great deal of air pollution on hot muggy days and continually dirtied the streams. These areas are now pleasant conservation lands, with only bits and pieces left of the old mills. When the two railroads came through Amherst, the ecosystem of Lawrence Swamp suffered a major change due to the massive fill and the interruption of water courses. Certainly the ability to do large scale earth moving cheaply and quickly in Amherst, which began as early as the 1930s, had a major impact upon growth. Coupled with available sewers and water mains, the bulldozers helped to transform former wetlands into housing areas.

Let us look at some of the events and some of the people that affected the growth of Amherst in the years following the First World War to see the legacy of town development which we inherit today.

GRADUAL DEVELOPMENT

The period 1920–1945 was a time of unhurried change in the town. Small mills and factories went out of business, farms changed ownership, and the town adjusted to its second child, the state college. Town government could do little during most of this time to control or direct the change that did occur, for in 1927 town meeting defeated an attempt to pass zoning by-laws, thus supporting the rights and interests of private land owners. All manner of civic improvements were delayed. The Depression altered the hidebound confidence of Amherst's citizens in their principle of allowing private enterprise to solve all their problems, for the federal recovery programs did work. This success eroded Amherst's reluctance to take communal action, to the degree that an unprecedented sequence of town actions took place on the eve of World War II. Not only did the town meeting by 1941 adopt new responsibility for public utilities like water but even adopted a zoning by-law and created a zoning board of appeals.

In the aftermath of World War I, a baby boom occurred in Amherst, with 145 births in 1922. But the annual birth rate fell to eighty in 1930 and stayed there during the early Depression years; in 1936 it began to climb, reaching almost the peak rate of 1922. The total population exclusive of students rose from 5,500 in 1920 to a 1940 count of 6,400. Some of this modest increase may include people whose towns were flooded out of existence by Quabbin Reservoir, as some of their dead were reburied in South Amherst Cemetery and some of their houses were transported over the hills to be placed upon new Amherst foundations.

The cows in town numbered 1,350 head in 1921, declining to 970 in 1927. The Depression brought an actual increase in cattle to 1,450 in 1944. Amherst apparently went to the dogs during the Depression, from 500 in 1927 to 690 in 1933, leveling off to a high of 730 in 1943. In the good years of the 1920s only thirty elderly people were listed as poor and in need of public assistance, but a sharp increase in the number of poor persons began in 1926; by 1930 the town was spending $10,000 for aid to about 100 destitute families. When federal funds became available, as many as 235 families received large amounts of aid (in 1939). The social chaos of the Depression is shown in the arrest total of 114 tramps during 1936, each of whom spent a night in jail prior to his expulsion from town in the morning. Other federal aid came to Amherst in December 1933 to finance a large scale public works program under the direction of the late Stephen Puffer, Sr., who put the available labor to good use in road and sewer work. By 1936 this aid brought a monthly payroll of $5,600 to town in addition to food and clothing for the laborers. This activity under the federal Works Projects Administration was by 1940 a seemingly permanent aspect of town life.

Other significant public works which followed both the gradual growth and available monies included a central town dump site on old Belchertown Road in 1932, the transfer to the town of the former trolley car barn on South Pleasant Street for a municipal highway department, a primary sewage treatment plant (one of the first in western Massachusetts) in 1938, the purchase of the Triangle Street Playground in 1939, and the purchase by the town of the privately owned Amherst Water Company in 1941 for $600,000. This last item was bitterly opposed by Professor Clarence Eastman, the town moderator from 1926 to 1949, who saw public ownership of a private utility as another New Deal scheme, but Fred Hawley, president of the Amherst Savings Bank, was in favor of the purchase. Fiscally the town did well in the Depression, for the municipal indebtedness was decreased by half as new projects came out of the federal till. However, the debt did double in 1938 due to the sewer plant, sewer lines, and an addition to the High School.

Total valuation of real estate in Amherst (at about a third of actual value) rose from $5.5 million in 1920 to $12.5 million in 1928. During this time new housing starts were only six per year, with a constant tax rate until 1926, when a modest climb began. Yet housing starts at six per year extended through the Depression. The increase in total valuation did slow down in the thirties, with a $16.0 million amount recorded during World War II; half of this value was tax exempt as educational property.

During the 1936 flood, Amherst sent men and supplies to Hadley and Sunderland, two communities badly hurt by the Connecticut River claiming its flood plain. While Amherst escaped damage in the 1936 and 1938 flooding (there would be disaster were these floods to return today), the hurricane of 1938 did over one million dollars worth of damage to Amherst's street trees and utility poles.

The planning board returned once again in 1940 with a proposal to revive land use zoning which had been firmly rejected thirteen years earlier. It was a simple plan that set out a limited residence zone, a general residence zone, and a business zone. Houses could be built anywhere, apartments only in the two latter zones, and businesses only in the last. Building lots must have at least sixty or eighty feet of frontage, and standard setbacks from the street were specified. A zoning board of appeals was created to administer these provisions. The plan was explained as "a way of looking forward and protecting the town from conditions that might make Amherst less pleasant to live in or that might hurt property values." With this appeal for the preservation of property values and with more recent experience of communal action, the voters accepted essentially the same plan which they had decisively defeated in 1927.

This initial zoning by-law could have infringed only slightly on anyone's hopes for development of his property. By 1945 with the end of wartime prosperity, the problem which concerned Amherst's citizens was the possible return to the economic stagnation of the prewar years. The town created a postwar work planning board to grapple with the foreseeable return of unemployment.

GROWTH AND PLANNING BOARD FRUSTRATION

At first stagnation did seem to be the future for postwar Amherst. In 1945–47 only three new housing starts per year were recorded. The Central Vermont Railroad shut down passenger and express service to Amherst in 1946, opening the way for a new franchise to the Trailways Bus Lines. But by 1948 a time of growth had begun. The returning veterans of World War II provided the initial impetus. Amherst College in 1946 admitted the largest class in its history and gradually expanded the size of its student body and faculty by 15 percent. The newly retitled University of Massachusetts found its enrollment greatly increased when the emergency education program which had been at Fort Devens was closed down and all its students were returned to the Amherst campus. In 1947, under the leadership of Walter C. Jones, the town established a veterans housing project which promptly constructed twenty new houses on Memorial Drive for rent and later sale to veterans at low rates. A relative explosion of new housing starts occurred in 1948 and then continued at a steady rate of forty-three per year until 1963 when the second stage of the housing rocket ignited. By 1949 downtown traffic problems brought the first installation of parking meters. The population increase caused by the expansion of the university filled the available housing.

Due in part to town borrowing, the previously stable tax rate began to climb in 1945. It maintained a steady annual increase of about $3.60 per thousand dollar valuation through 1963. Meanwhile the property valuations themselves were increasing. Taxes were clearly upward bound. The finance committee was greatly concerned, and in 1954 the selectmen mourned, "The village is gone and the modern town is born." Yet, as Amherst entered a period of unprecedented growth, it was still business as usual as far as town planning was concerned. There was no vision of the future except the boosterism of the Chamber of Commerce and no effective regulatory machinery apart from the goodwill of the builders. Out of this confusion, interest began to develop in a town manager system of administration.

Modest expansion occurred in the late forties; the residential area of Struthersville just north of the university blossomed, and the town center expanded westerly, with new lots on Blue Hills Road, Dana Place, and several other streets that were planned but never made it to construction. To the east, Newell Court and Sunrise Avenue were built up.

The planning board felt powerless to deal with the typical small scale development that established new lots and a street based solely on the accident of past property lines rather than on the rationale of traffic patterns or human dynamics. These were the years of no effective control, when builders did what was right in their own eyes. Within several years the occupants of these new houses clamored for water mains, sewers, drainage, and paved streets; public funds had to go into these services which ought to have been provided initially by the private developers. Builders were therefore receiving a hidden subsidy, even as they argued against any government curbs on free enterprise such as the planning board might have imposed. These wide open years solidified an unfortunate tradition, as it were, in concrete. State laws restricting the planning board's activity weighed in heavily on the side of the developers. Few plans presented to the board were substantially revised or turned down. Growth was still outside the control of town planners.

And yet, in the midst of all this, a bureaucratic channel was established as early as 1951, which would become extremely important later on, when the planning board eventually grew some teeth. All zoning cases were turned over to the newly created zoning board of appeals. At first the ZBA heard few cases of any importance, so the shift in power was slow to develop. But develop it would.

A chronology of events in the 1950s reveals both a random approach to problems of growth and the gradual emergence of a constituency within the town which tried to increase the role of town planners. It is important to remember that it was not until 1953 that

Amherst town meeting, after sometimes acrimonious debate, voted in favor of hiring a town manager. Slowly other institutions and individuals emerged to control more actively the direction of town growth.

During the 1950s strip development occurred along the existing roads in Amherst, such as West Street, Strong Street, East Pleasant Street, and Leverett Road, as well as in Hadley on Route 9. The planning board was able to jawbone away one out-of-town developer in 1952; it also went on record in favor of new schools, for without them the town "would not be a desirable place to live." It also declared a desire to "slow the process of growth." New sewers at town expense followed development into Struthersville, Pelham Road, and Cushman. A move to squeeze out the residential area between the town center and the university by zoning it for business failed to get the support of the planning board and town meeting in 1953. The planning board was also greatly concerned about the student slum developing on Phillips Street. The need for new zoning was stressed again.

The area around the three town schools began to develop. The wet meadow on the south side of Chestnut Street was turned into houses in 1953. The Skillings land opened up into thirty deluxe lots on Hills Road and along the extension of North Whitney Street, called by its developers Red Gate Lane. (The planning board wanted it to retain North Whitney Street.) The Wildwood Cemetery Association took the opportunity to develop Wildwood Lane. From 1954 through 1956, East Pleasant Street was built with state aid. Sewers were extended into this area in 1951, establishing a keystone for future growth.

August 1955 was a wet time in Amherst. Hurricane Diane did a lot of damage, much of it unrecorded. Water covered Main Street, blocking Pelham Road, and the Belchertown Road embankment next to the Fort River bridge broke away, draining away some of the water upstream in one big road washout. In a sense, this hurricane helped build Echo Hill. William E. Aubin was driving in from Pelham with a house trailer in tow to enroll at the university. He was stopped on Pelham Road by the flood at the Fort River and had to pull his trailer into Center Street. He began talking with the owners there, one thing led to another, and by 1957 the Echo Hill project was begun.

The early effort in Echo Hill was a conventional plan of lots that fit well into the terrain, making good use of the existing forest cover. In these early years, Aubin worked for Wesley Wentworth, a local builder. The aggressive creativity of Aubin was early demonstrated when Wentworth told him to go out and fix up a particular house so that it would be fit for human habitation. Aubin did as he was told, and in so doing tore the house down to its basic frame to rebuild it. Wentworth was astonished, and the owner of the house was angry. The house was rebuilt at Wentworth's expense. Aubin's most significant effort would be later on in Echo Hill South.

In the early 1950s Walter C. Jones, serving as chairman of the town's water commissioners, administered the town's water supply. He was instrumental in extending the mains into outlying areas as well as in establishing a maintenance program on the watershed lands. William McConnell of the university forestry department began his service in those years—clearing the watershed of hardwoods and conducting timber sales. Jones retained Tighe & Bond Engineers to do a study on how to enlarge the water supply to keep pace with the growth generated by the university, and a new water main loop was extended into South Amherst center.

When Allen L. Torrey became town manager in 1954, one of his first tasks was to bring together the many divergent efforts to cope with the growth. Within a few years, he was able to reorganize the many separate activities, including the separate fiefdom of the water department, into a comprehensive public works department. After many years of service to the town directing the highway and sewer programs, Stephen P. Puffer, Sr. retired at the end of 1955. About this time Walter C. Jones left the water department. Soon a young veteran, Stanley P. Ziomek, whose wisdom and zeal helped mold this newly established department, was chosen as superintendent of public works. The problem of inadequate building regulations was partly solved late in the decade when an inspection service was established to control the quality and safety of structures, yet meaningful control was still not attained, since no building code was official. The first comprehensive town property atlas was finally published in 1957, to aid the assessors in the equalization of the tax burden.

One series of events during this period well illustrates the attitude of the time to settle for the short-term solution rather than the long view. A proposal to develop a water supply well field in Leverett was defeated at the Amherst town meeting. Yet during the summer of 1957, a severe water shortage developed. During July and August an emergency was declared, and water was pumped from Orient Springs in Pelham. Negotiations with Hadley came to nothing, when that town voted not to sell water to Amherst. By December 1958 the new South Amherst well field in Lawrence Swamp was in operation, furnishing a much needed source of water that solved the immediate problem. But Amherst's long-term water needs had not been addressed squarely, and the problems would recur.

In 1948 Ted Bacon embarked upon a long and important service to the town as a leading member of the planning board. He became chairman in 1949, succeeding Walter C. Jones, and that same year he began urging the town to review its goals and revise the zoning by-law of 1940. Yet his advice was ignored for fifteen years until the consequences of accelerating growth became apparent to everyone.

In 1958 the planning board under Ted Bacon's leadership again turned its effort to revising the zoning by-law now eighteen years old. Roland Greeley, a planning consultant, was retained to help in this task. Part of the work involved a definition of goals: What was growth to move toward? The board selected these priorities: to prevent the build-up in the outlying areas of town, thus preserving the rural character and eliminating the need to extend sewers and water mains; to encourage the growth close to town; to limit fraternity houses to a particular area; and to attract light industry to Amherst. To achieve these goals, density in housing would be a minimum of two-acre lots in the outlying areas and one-acre lots closer toward town. Land then zoned at a minimum of 15,000 square feet per lot would be changed to a minimum of 40,000 or 80,000 square feet. This meant that land held in speculation for development might be reduced considerably in its immediate market value.

Owners of large tracts of land telephoned town meeting members and encouraged them to vote no. At the annual town meeting of 1958 the vote fell short by 13 of the necessary two-thirds majority needed to pass. Bill Aubin introduced a motion to reconsider which carried. After more heated argument, Ted Bacon moved to eliminate the two-acre proviso so that the largest minimum lot size in all of town would be one acre. Two to one seemed to be adequate compromise, and the new by-law passed.

Soon after town meeting, Herbert Randolph, a onetime member

of the planning board in 1940, presented a petition to the town clerk to call a townwide referendum on the new zoning by-law. The League of Women Voters and the town boards supported the by-law. Bacon stated that this by-law was the last chance to control growth. The opposition sprang up with anonymous letters to the papers and slogans claiming that the working man could not afford to live in Amherst and that Amherst would become an exclusive bedroom community. Bacon responded in part:

Communities are going to grow regardless of what we do as citizens, and Amherst is going to grow faster than most of the surrounding communities. If we don't improve the zoning by-law very soon, we will shortly feel greatly increased taxes. We will wonder how Amherst could have become so crowded and so much like a typical city in such a short time.

The opposition argued the need to preserve the "freedom to use the property we own within the dictates of reason" and claimed that this vote would be another campaign on the "battleground between the home builders and the zoners," for "this by-law plays into Communist hands."

On the day of the balloting, 59 percent of the voters turned out to vote. The town meeting action was reversed by the voters, 1606 no to 1032 yes. Years of effort were wiped out as the by-law of 1940 continued in force. Suspicion of something radical combined with sufficient apathy about the issue to sustain the posture of no control on growth, a condition that allowed developers to do as they pleased.

While Amherst was dividing against itself, the state was proceeding with its overall highway network that would have a profound influence on the town. The construction of Interstate 91 would soon move Amherst very close to Springfield, and the new Route 116 bypass, built in 1958 as far south as Russell Street in Hadley, became a line of departure for future highway plans to the East and South.

EXPLOSIVE GROWTH AND LIMITED CONTROLS

Rejection by Amherst's citizens of the planning board's 1958 zoning by-law proposal returned the town to the minimal restrictions of 1940, regulations which had been designed in a depression period for a community of 6,400 residents whose rate of new housing units had averaged only six per year for two decades and at a time when the Massachusetts State College seemed to have stabilized at about 1,700 students. The planning board of 1960 knew that these provisions were already inadequate for a town of 13,718 residents (including some students) with a steady rate of growth over the past twelve years of forty-three new housing units per year. Much of this growth was a direct result of the developing new state university, which had over the same dozen years added 500 additional students annually for a total in 1960 of 6,500 and which had publicly announced its goal of reaching 10,000 by 1965.

Yet even the planning board did not fully envision in 1960 the scope of the development which Amherst would encounter during the coming decade. The newly appointed president of the university, John W. Lederle, could have foretold some of what lay ahead. Coming from the university system of Michigan, his mission was to raise the University of Massachusetts to the same level of excellence and service which had been attained in his home state. For him this meant not only fiscal autonomy for the university, which enabled it to compete for top faculty and administrators, but also the foreseeable growth of the university at Amherst to a level of twenty-five or thirty thousand students. He did not initially announce this goal, though he did make clear his judgment that the university should expand at a rate of 1,500 additional students annually in order to meet the needs of the young citizens of Massachusetts.

For the next ten years this inexorable statistic of growth, 1,500 new students per year along with the requisite new faculty, administrators, and staff, would transform the town and decisively shape the problems its planners, developers, officials, and citizens had to face. From an institution of 6,500 students with a faculty of fewer than 600 in 1960, the university grew by 1970 to 21,000 students with a faculty of 1,150. Meanwhile, Amherst College had officially expanded its student body by 200 students and its faculty by almost forty, while the new Hampshire College beginning in 1970 would add over 1,000 students and sixty faculty to the burgeoning community. By 1970 a report prepared by Nancy Eddy concluded that almost 3,000 new housing units had been constructed in Amherst during the preceding decade, a figure that more than doubled the housing units that had existed in Amherst in 1960. Further, a paper value had been created in that over 3,000 additional units had planning board and zoning board approval, but were not yet under construction. The story of the 1960s was that of hectic, hardworking efforts by the established leaders and boards in Amherst to maintain some semblance of control over a growth which in ten years had exceeded the total growth of the previous 220 years. It was a story of mingled success and failure. It produced popular acceptance of more far-reaching measures to regulate land use and private construction than the previous ideology would ever have entertained. It culminated by the late 1960s and the early 1970s in citizen movements which charged the established town leaders with not doing enough to control (or even to halt) the continuing development of Amherst, while land developers complained of ever increasing interference from government bureaucracies which hampered their rights as free citizens.

In the first few years of the 1960s several small steps were taken to accommodate the increasing pressures on the town. In 1960 the industrial and development commission was established to attract light industry to the town, in order to widen the tax base and diversify the community that was dependent for the most part on the education industry. But many long meetings brought nothing. The commission had little political encouragement or backing. In 1962 the town established the conservation commission to preserve selected areas of the town's open space. During the next decade, hundreds of acres were acquired (predominantly in Lawrence Swamp), and the commission became the manager of wetland control laws and a prime mover behind townwide wetland zoning.

Future growth in Mill Valley was enabled to a large degree through the activity of Norman Keddy, doing business as KV Realty, who developed Jeffrey Lane in 1958 with houses that were soon sold to moderate income families. As other dwellings on adjacent and nearby land were built, the old sewage filter beds off East Hadley Road next to the Fort River began to receive more sewage than could be treated. New sewers were built quickly, bypassing the old beds and flowing south to the West Street pumping station, the collection point for all sewage in Amherst south of the Boston & Maine tracks. From here the sewage was pumped to the treatment plant near the university. The West Street station was operational by 1964, just in time to avert significant pollution from failing septic tanks in the predominantly poor soil of South Amherst. Sanitary sewers were extended into South Amherst in 1968 to serve the Strategic Air Command alternate headquarters under Bear Mountain. Half a million dollars, a good part of it state aid, was spent on the new pumping station and major renovations at the sewer plant.

Of symbolic significance, in 1962 the town hall was remodeled.

The addition of new offices and meeting rooms signified a growing citizen interest in town affairs. But the interest continued to express itself ambivalently. That same year, the planning board and town government attempted once again to revise the zoning by-law—and failed. The point of contention was the proposed campus zone which, in spite of modifications made on the floor of town meeting by Ted Bacon, did not pass.

By 1963 the rate of housing starts had leaped to 130, a 200 percent increase over the previous rate of forty-three. This increased growth brought with it a demand for more municipal services which was reflected in the tax rate. Though the tax rate increases in each year subsequent to 1963 were almost half of the increase in previous years, a typical homeowner ended up paying more taxes in spite of the revaluations of 1963 and 1969, which caused a fairer distribution of the tax burden. One cheerful note is the rate at which the Amherst homeowner has paid for water, 34 cents from 1941 through 1976. The big water users, however, have had increased rates over the years. Meanwhile the tax pie grew each year, and the schools kept consuming bigger pieces, with less, on a percentage basis, going to general government. State and federal funds were used to keep the tax impact down.

The sudden and dramatic escalation of building in the early 1960s encouraged the planning board to persevere in its attempt to have new zoning by-laws passed. The year 1963 was known as the "year of the apartments": The zoning board of appeals handed out permits for four separate complexes that totaled 222 dwelling units, rejecting the construction of only forty units. The university had grown to ten thousand students about two years sooner than expected. All indications were that wide open growth would not only continue but increase in its pace. The proposed by-law was similar to that of 1958, but the minimum lot size for outlying areas was only 30,000 square feet instead of the 1958 compromise area of 43,560 square feet. Much open land could still be developed into apartments.

At the 1964 town meeting there were many new faces—young university faculty, many of whom came out of a liberal Democratic background. Perhaps some of the older town residents as well had begun to see the handwriting on the wall. The proposed by-law passed town meeting with a comfortable margin.

The opposition began a replay of its 1958 referendum vote,

cheered by the taste of victory remaining from a recent referendum defeating fluoridation of Amherst's water supply. But the zoning debate this time did not generate the bitterness of 1958. The town had made up its mind, and the referendum upheld the town meeting action. A vital land use reform had been accomplished. For the first time in the two centuries since the Hadley proprietors gave away Amherst in large farms and woodlots, the town asserted that public needs dictated certain limitations on the development of privately owned land. Development was no longer by right so much as it was by permission of the town acting upon the merits of each petition. The new by-law was as restrictive as state law and review by the attorney general would allow. Major land reform had been made possible by the 1964 vote, even if confusion about the actual goals of growth kept the full potential of the new by-law from being realized initially.

Immediately some development was deflected into adjacent towns, for distance from the university was offset by ease of development and still low tax rates. Yet applications for new buildings continued to pour in—Echo Hill South, Valley View, Eastwood, and Green Meadow. The stark University Park Apartments (a sixty-four-unit development) were constructed after approval from the zoning board of appeals.

The planning board followed up on its zoning victory by adopting in February 1965 a revised and greatly improved set of subdivision regulations. About this time, Amherst also adopted a building code which set minimum standards for dwellings. The adoption of this performance-type building code and the intense test it received during the next few boom years, under building inspector Chester Penza, became a major influence in the formulation of the present statewide code.

Many problems existed in the relationship between town inspectors and private construction crews. Several part-time inspectors spent many hours attempting to instill good utility standards into the developments—bona fide standards used by consultant engineers retained by the town. Each catch basin and every foot of sewer line was a battle, and without the support of a set of regulations and the ability to withhold occupancy, the few victories won were Pyrrhic indeed. On one occasion, an inspector was physically threatened with a crow bar; on another the tires of his car were deflated. However, in 1971 a solid set of regulations was adopted by the selectmen, and the incidence of physical combat diminished a great deal on all the job sites.

In 1966, recognizing the need for an overall statement of goals which would establish a rationale to pass judgment on individual requests from developers, the town retained Charles E. Downe of West Newton, Massachusetts to prepare a master plan for town development. The planning board found itself too occupied with day-to-day business to attempt such an overview on its own. Thirty thousand dollars later (some of which came from the federal government), Downe completed his plan. His 1969 report called for seven "village centers" to be distributed around the larger town center. Each village was to consist of dense housing and commercial facilities. The concentrated development would be in juxtaposition with open, undeveloped space between adjacent villages.

This plan was a tool, a set of guidelines. Attempts to turn it into a comprehensive by-law came in the 1970s. Meanwhile, the 1964 regulations remained in effect, and these gave the zoning board great influence, if not direct control, over the quality of development in the town. The board could turn down or modify poor development, but it could not of itself generate quality or creativity in the projects presented to it. Town planning in Amherst was still reactive, not initiatory. But because developers did have to obtain permits from the several boards, they were receptive to suggestions and sometimes drastic revisions proposed by members of the boards. Quality and creativity, from a town planner's point of view, sometimes did find their way into projects put before the town for approval.

In 1969 another significant step was taken in land use control when a proposal was made to town meeting to create a conservancy and watershed protection zone. This concept was the result of years of work by the planning board and conservation commission. It was to be a zone which included town conservation land (no problem there, for zoning is largely irrelevant on that land) and which also protected areas of land along the water courses of Amherst. That was a whole new idea—to ignore ownership lines and to consider the specific qualities of the land as to soil type, forest cover, water courses, and flood plains. The brooks, streams, swamps, and ponds of the town were to receive government protection for the first time since the European occupation. There was a bit of political expediency in the proposed regulations, the lesson of the 1958 zoning defeat not being forgotten. An exception was granted in the by-law for streams at road crossings which involved loss of frontage land that could be developed, a prime example being the land on the northwest corner of Belchertown and Gatehouse Roads. The significance of the exception for this area would emerge later on. In the meantime, the zone proposal was passed, and, though flawed, it was another landmark achievement.

Proponents of the new zoning regulations believed that deficiencies in the version passed by town meeting could be corrected in part by state legislation called the Hatch Act, which was designed to protect wetlands from improper development. But in these first years, the Hatch Act was clumsy and vague and accomplished more paper work than protection.

The actual track record in development control in Amherst subsequent to the 1964 by-law and the 1965 subdivision regulations is best seen in a review of selected projects:

● As Echo Hill (the northerly part) was being finished, Aubin began to gather together a design for Echo Hill South, a neighborhood with single-family dwellings, apartments, open space, and commercial areas. Per Nylen was his landscape architect in 1965 when the entire plan was presented to the town. Aubin was permitted to do pretty much as he liked, for no one liked to tangle with him, and his final products were attractive and earned him a great deal of national recognition. In order to build his "planned unit development," a change in the zoning by-law was required. The zoning change was approved in 1965 by town meeting, which allowed Aubin to develop a concept new to Amherst. By 1973 the development was finished except for a few houselots and a vacant piece of land on Belchertown Road.

As it turned out, this planned unit development had no commercial nucleus. Vacant land in the "center" of Belchertown Road was surrounded by dense condominium housing, with conventional lots on the periphery contiguous to commonly owned second-growth woods. On the other side of Belchertown Road, Ed Doleva, over the objections of the planning board, had convinced town meeting to rezone his farm to a commercial zone. The significance of this zone change became obvious when a much more ambitious developer, Otto Paparazzo, later moved into the picture. Whatever final development may happen in East Amherst, it will involve both Echo Hill and Amherst Fields with busy Route 9 going right down the middle of it. By 1976 neither Aubin's effort to create one of the first fully planned developments in New England nor Paparazzo's later effort across Belchertown Road to create one of the most imaginative developments in New England had fulfilled their original visions.

• One of the first subdivisions to be reviewed under the new zoning of 1964 was Eastwood, brought into being by one of the most colorful developers to operate in Amherst, Donald Grant. His story begins in Amherst with a new concept of mass production in dairy farming at his Fort Hill Farms on Stanley Street; this enterprise soon failed. Grant then cast his eye on the lucrative building trade. His first venture, in 1965, became the Eastwood development adjoining North Amherst cemetery. Having negotiated a land deal and made applications to the planning board for subdivision approval, the package crumbled in his hands at the public hearing, when one of the owners disavowed the inclusion of his land. Yet Grant reappeared with a similar scheme on a piecemeal basis which was approved, each piece at a time. While he used qualified people to plan and engineer his project, once the plans were approved they may as well have been thrown away. To keep his front-end cost down, he directed the construction himself, using outmoded equipment. Only on such chores as paving streets did Grant call in more qualified contractors.

In 1973 Grant took the planning board to court over an escrow account to correct some of the deficiencies of his older streets which had since become town ways. He lost, but so did the town. Eastwood at this writing is half built; the area to the northeast is in chaos as to future land use. The entire development is a testimony to Grant's onerous misfortune, as well as to the inability of new zoning by laws, regulations, and codes to insure sound construction.

• Kamins Circle was a good example of a bad development. Here the most lots possible were imposed on the terrain, and the soil conditions were ignored, as if the sand and stone of Echo Hill were here instead of the treacherous varved clay. In September 1972 the Fort River made a dramatic move and nearly dumped a house into the drink with a sudden landslide which dammed the river for several hours. Further upstream, another wet area was opened into lots on Dennis Drive in 1971. Three houses made it into completion before the sewer ban shut down activity.

• Pomeroy Court was first planned in 1967 and built in 1971. The developer was D. Ruben Pomeroy, an old resident of the town. With a panama hat, a hoe, and a cheerful smile, this octogenarian hobbled about giving personal directions to the contractor building the new road and bridge over Plum Brook. Early one morning, the foreman on the job was found near tears, sitting in the cab of his truck, while old Ruben outside, mad as hell, waved his hoe and shouted that the contractor was stealing his dirt! A representative of the town cooled the combatant down and read the handwritten contract; sure enough the contractor had overlooked a few unusual items therein. In accordance with the contract he began to truck in load after load of clean fill, and Ruben was all smiles again. One of the new houses on this street had to be temporarily abandoned by the builder when the sewer ban hit town, an example of the personal tragedy experienced by the small-time builder when the rules of the ballgame change in the fifth inning. The state finally gave permission for this house to tie into the sewers in July 1976.

As in 1960, efforts continued to build up paper value on land in Amherst before attracting a buyer. By 1966, for instance, a total of 567 apartment units had received permits from the zoning board but had not been built. These permits were then transferable and thus constituted a wealth given individual owners by the town. Before 1970 the zoning board with some timidity began to turn down requests for apartment units, having realized what was going on in the market place.

The North Slope of Mount Holyoke has been the scene of some hotly disputed development battles. In 1965, Pat Kamins made a deal with Earl Wales and brought in a preliminary plan of subdivision which was turned down for numerous reasons. Next in line came James Giard with his Southgate proposal next to Sanderson Lane. The town had purchased conservation land just to the south, thus the conservation commission entered the ranks. Giard, who is very mercurial, fought well and lost (he has since sold off some of the front lots). His subdivision was turned down in 1969.

Late in 1971, Long Mountain Realty Trust came in with a grand plan of lots going up the mountain all the way to the beginning of the "upright" slope, where even climbers have great difficulty. Turned down by the planning board, he took the town to court. In the meantime, the board of health adopted more stringent and detailed regulations which essentially made half of the proposed lots unbuildable even if approved. The status of the plan is moot, for the state purchased most of the land for conservation purposes in 1976 at a cost of $155,000.

ROAD CONSTRUCTION

The developed sections of Amherst were spared those highway construction activities which decimated so many town centers and country greens in the 1950s. Even while involved in zoning matters and by-laws, the planning board went on record in opposition to the southerly extension of the Route 116 Bypass that would have crossed back into South Amherst from Hadley and run up the mountain through the Notch to connect to the existing highway in South Hadley.

Amherst College continued its watchful attention on the condition of Route 9 through Amherst center, desiring no change that would add more traffic to the northern boundary of its campus. The university, assuming much about the identity of decision makers in town and their views, made an irrevocable decision on its campus layout when it constructed Massachusetts Avenue and located major new facilities close to North Pleasant Street.

In the fall of 1966 the Massachusetts Department of Public Works (MDPW), as part of its general improvement of Route 9 throughout the state, submitted to the town three alternate routes for a new highway, all of which went through South Amherst. The selectmen passed the proposal to the planning board for its recommendation. The planning board passed the question on to Charles Downe, the planning consultant. Of the three routes proposed, the most southerly was selected by Downe as the best (this line being the only one of the three that was outside the southerly view from Amherst College). The MDPW began work on highway plans and the approved route was apparently given sanction by being included in the master plan which became public in May 1969. The proposed highway followed a westerly extension of Potwine Lane, turned southeasterly and went cross country over Muddy Brook and Plum Brook, through South Orchard Drive, and then along the southerly limit of Lawrence Swamp north of Bay Road into Belchertown. The political response was severe. In July 1969 concerned residents of South Amherst signed a petition to halt the new road, and over 250 people showed up at a planning board meeting to protest the highway plan. The planning board was totally unprepared for this event; it suffered a loss of public credibility because of the deference it had shown to the MDPW as the experts. A shadow planning board was established by some of the protesting citizens, calling themselves the Amherst road proliferation committee. It soon presented its own planning response which opposed any relocation of Route 9. The MDPW conducted a general retreat in this matter, finding no political support for their plans.

In 1968 a town-university task force came into being to review various items of mutual concern, one of which was the proposal to close North Pleasant Street to auto traffic through the main campus. This group recommended that a short bypass be built along the easterly perimeter of the university which would connect to North Pleasant Street at both ends; the main campus would no longer be divided by a busy street. Town meeting approved this jug handle concept in 1969, and the MDPW began to design the road.

The town meeting of October 1970 felt the influence of the new environmental concerns committee, recently reorganized from the now defunct Amherst road proliferation committee. Other citizens reacted to lines drawn on the town map and protested new roads that came anywhere near their homes. The original bypass route around the university was voted down because of concerns about the destruction of Butterfield Terrace and the area northwest of Pokeberry Ridge. The moderator was instructed to form an ad hoc committee to study alternative proposals which might allow for North Pleasant Street to be closed. Thus the town created the traffic circulation committee (TCC) and tacitly acknowledged a failure on the part of the planning board to handle the difficult situation. By 1972 the town meeting had voted twice on the alternative put forward by the TCC. First it approved the Northeast Bypass route which made a clockwise sweep from Route 116 north of the university to the intersection of South East Street and Belchertown Road, though some residential owners objected to the adverse impact on the East Street Common. At a later meeting the town revised the easterly terminus to realign the bypass close to Salem Street and Shumway Street, to avoid crowding the area around the new Fort River School. The Northeast Bypass appeared to be as good as built. It made its way through various hearings and studies, and it had the full support of the TCC.

However, by 1976 residents of North Amherst were ready for a replay of the October 1970 town meeting. Led by Richard Minear, they raised the issue of safety for school children at Mark's Meadow and vented their antigrowth frustrations by calling into question the actual need for such a highway. Their lobbying was successful, and the May town meeting voted down the entire Northeast Bypass. Several years of planning were thereby nullified, and, in the bargain, the effectiveness of the new North Fire Station was put in question.

About the same time, the proposed reconstruction of Henry Street and the north end of North East Street was terminated by the combined actions of the planning board, with its jurisdiction over scenic roads, and the newly formed Cushman Historical Society. This latter group was still smarting from the 1972 rebuilding of the Bridge Street crossing of Cushman Brook by the MDPW. For the time being, road construction in Amherst was halted.

THE PAPARAZZO PROJECT

Apart from the master plan of 1969 (which had no legal authority in itself), no authoritative policy or by-law had been developed which could limit and direct the extent of growth in Amherst. Unless immediately affected as neighbors to some proposed development, townspeople seemed to accept without serious question the decisions made by the responsible officials in town hall. These officials were overwhelmed by the pressing needs for overseeing the technical quality of the new building projects and were restrained by state laws which favored development. They remained committed to concerns about the quality rather than the extent of growth.

Meanwhile, however, pressures were mounting toward an explosive debate in 1971 over the whole issue of the town's expansion. All of the latent uneasiness about the unprecedented growth rate of the 1960s, all of the mixed feelings Amherst's citizens harbored about the small town myth, all of the distrust emerging in the late 1960s toward established authorities came to focus upon the proposed development in east Amherst of Amherst Fields by Otto Paparazzo. This was clearly the most imaginative, most coherently planned, most strongly financed development ever to be attracted to Amherst. If the only issue was to be quality in planning and construction, the Paparazzo project was the culmination of those standards for which Amherst's officials had been pushing. But this proposal was also the most massive ever conceived for Amherst—2,200 building units in a mix of apartments, condominiums, and separate houses together with an extensive commercial village, some light industry, and a golf course. It posed dramatically and inescapably the questions of scale, of size, even of identity of the town. Could Amherst consciously accept an excellently designed development which would add almost 50 percent to the existing resident, off-campus population during the next decade?

The land in question had been largely ignored over the years, boxed in by the town dump, Belchertown Road, the Fort River, and the Central Vermont tracks. This land had never been good for crops. In the last hundred years its most noteworthy use was in supplying clay for brickmaking. During the last thirty years, the area was the site of frequent brush fires, spreading from the town dump. In 1968 the town installed the Brickyard wellfield on a site donated for this purpose by Louis Cohn and Sol Lavitt, developers from West Hartford. This rapidly completed new water supply helped to avert for a while a threatened water shortage, but it also helped to spur development in a long-neglected location. In 1969 Cohn and Lavitt received final permits for a conventional subdivision to be erected west of the dump. By 1970, although no construction at all had begun in the area, permits were outstanding not only for Cohn and Lavitt's subdivision but also for a commercial zone on land owned by Edward Doleva and for more apartments on land owned by Roy Conners.

Still, activity in this area might not have amounted to much except for the unusual impact made by a student report. Charles Downe's master plan, made public in the spring of 1969, had envisioned concentrating future development into seven village centers surrounding the town center itself. The village concept could minimize the cost of town services and at the same time help to maintain open space between villages. Paul Procopio, member of the planning board and the School of Landscape Architecture at the university, convinced the town manager that the next step was to design a specific plan for one or two of the future villages. Under a small grant from the town, therefore, David Webber, a graduate student at the School of Landscape Architecture, drew up an ambitious plan for a village in East Amherst, the most undeveloped and still malleable of all Downe's proposed village centers. The Webber Report called for a complete residential, recreational, commercial community of 10,000 people in some 3,000 housing units. He suggested that the existing parcels of land in the area should be combined either under single or group ownership to enable a rational, comprehensive plan for development of the whole East Amherst village. This report received wide publicity in local newspapers along with statements of commendation and support from various sources. Yet, like the Downe master plan itself, no official recognition ensued from any town meeting since neither proposal was ever officially presented for acceptance by that body.

Pushing ahead independently, Paul Procopio and Julius Fabos, colleagues both at the School of Landscape Architecture and in a private consulting firm, tried to unite the various landowners of the area into a common syndicate. Failing in this they began the search for a single developer capable of buying up all the necessary properties and imaginative enough to see the possibilities in the Webber Report. This search soon led them to Otto Paparazzo, most creative of the three brothers who had attracted national attention for the size, the originality, and the taste of Heritage Village, a complete retirement community they had constructed in Southbury, Connecticut. Reluctant at first, Paparazzo was encouraged to look seriously at Amherst by Joseph Derby, an enterprising Amherst graduate who had assisted in securing financing for Paparazzo's Connecticut ventures. Derby, who had also shared in the financing for the East Amherst parcel held by Cohn and Lavitt, was very excited by the Webber Report. Here was a town which had itself laid the groundwork for the kind of comprehensive planned development which fascinated Otto Paparazzo and his architect Warren Callister. Further encouragement came when Amherst College agreed to assist in putting together the full parcel of 650 acres for the project. When Walter Jones had first offered the college an option to buy his 250 acres in East Amherst, the trustees hesitated to get involved. After the Webber Report, Treasurer Kurt Hertzfeld was authorized to make the purchase and to exercise leadership in exploring a village development in this area which would protect the eastern approach to the college from haphazard exploitation and which seemed to be desired by the whole community.

By the fall of 1970 Paparazzo's designers were beginning to make preliminary sketches for the grand project to be unveiled in East

Amherst. Certainly he felt confident about his welcome there. Professional planners from the town itself had sought him out. The town manager had encouraged him. Joe Derby assured him that Amherst College's participation in the enterprise would carry great weight in town. Certainly, too, the prospect of enlisting Otto Paparazzo as developer to carry out the concepts already developed in Downe's master plan and in the Webber Report encouraged many of those who had been responsible for insuring quality in Amherst's growth. From the perspective of a town planner Paparazzo's large-scale project promised a significant advantage over smaller developments. The immediate demand for new housing in town would be met quickly and capably, and Amherst would have time afterwards to stand back, see where it was, determine where it should be going, and then adopt the necessary by-laws and other regulations to guide both the quality and the extent of future growth.

One afternoon in May 1971 a select group was invited to cocktails to view a presentation of the Paparazzo plan at the Alumni House at Amherst College. Members of the Paparazzo organization outlined their intentions for what would become Amherst Fields. Shortly afterwards the entire proposal was made, and at first there was little reaction. Paparazzo Associates moved forward, openly and with confidence. Applications were submitted to the zoning board of appeals. A preliminary plan with supporting documents went to the planning board as a first step to subdivision. A great land closing, extending into the evening hours, took place at the Registry of Deeds in Northampton. All the transactions to this point had been smiles and handshakes and overly casual. Later on, some acreage near the Belchertown line was found to be owned by other parties—but no matter, for it was on the periphery of the project. As the permit mill ground on, the public seemed to be accepting the proposal.

In July the first protests sounded. Richard Beamish and others began to attend the meetings of the zoning board of appeals which were focussing on the details of Amherst Fields. Much credit goes to Arnold Rhodes, who as chairman of the zoning board kept the open meetings from becoming outright shouting contests. His patience with the speech making, combined with exercises of authority from the chair kept the often heated proceedings free of police intervention! Opponents of Paparazzo sometimes viewed his flexibility and calm manner as part of the slick approach these "outsiders" had.

There was also a rising level of resentment about growth in general. Many in town did not have confidence in the ability of the local government to deal effectively with developers.

The first element of the complex to be cut out was the golf course, fought largely over the environmental pollution issue. And the original 2,200 dwelling unit complex around that golf course was cut down to 1,300 units around fields of goldenrod. The town agreed to give half a pie for a promise of not being taken to court for the whole pie; some hard political activity on and off the floor of town meeting accomplished this. Secondly, a subdivision plan of three main roads was approved, interconnecting Belchertown Road with Station Road and South East Street.

The town meeting also approved by a good majority three necessary zoning map revisions in the Amherst Fields area. Clearly the majority of town meeting favored this development, at least in its scaled-down version. A permit was finally issued under the Hatch Act to allow the main road to be built (this was one of the prolonged bloody engagements). The marching band of the antigrowth forces, now consolidated into the Amherst growth study committee, headed by Beamish, had paraded up the hill of public exposure, and marched back down again. But in retrospect, the committee had made its impact. Its legal proceedings against Paparazzo cost him over three thousand dollars per day in delay and untold damage in missing the opportunity both to get sewer permits and the tail end of the housing market just prior to the recession. Further, three specific sites on Old Farm Road were completely designed and approved for the federal 236 Program of subsidized housing for low and moderate income tenants. The developer spent many hours with town officials on the final design and makeup of this low income housing, which would have been built except for three reasons: the Amherst growth study committee's legal delays, followed by the sewer ban and President Nixon's impoundment of housing funds.

The national nosedive in housing sales was the reason that Amherst Fields (and other developments coming on line at the time) did not sell well, stopping after the construction of the Rusty Scupper Restaurant, the Living and Learning Centre day school, and the Ice Pond Condominiums. The creativity of the Paparazzo group was well displayed in this first work. The day school was the work of Paolo Soleri, who had done pioneer work in earth-cast concrete in

Arizona. On the Saturday the first concrete was poured, Soleri sat like a guru amid the reinforcing bars, while yards of concrete were hosed in all around him. Only the care of the frenzied foreman who was receiving instructions from all the directors of the Paparazzo group saved Soleri from getting a lapfull of cement. After all the pictures had been taken, Soleri was finally talked down, and the work proceeded in earnest.

One of the principals of the Paparazzo Associates, speaking in bitter hindsight, put his feelings this way: "We admit we made a mistake in telling Amherst citizens what we were going to do. The mistake was being too honest, the way we bungling, stumbling people are. Better we had said to hell with the townspeople, bought the land and the permits—and said we're going to build 165 units on so much acreage—and then when the people finally realized what had happened to them, we would have already completed our project and it would be too late." He further commented about members of the academic community who privately gave the Fields good marks in land use and who publicly never showed their faces at the meetings: "It's better to be loved publicly than privately, unless you're somebody's mistress."

It should be noted that these developers did what all developers do and attempted to cut some front-end costs in engineering support and underground construction. The quality of a sewer or water main does not sell a dwelling unit. But they were far less devious than other local developers had been before them. Furthermore, when they closed on the land they thought they already had sanitary sewerage and did not anticipate the costs of additional drainage construction.

It was the sewer ban in Amherst which finally halted Paparazzo's efforts until the recession appeared. The unprecedented growth of the late 1960s caused an overloading in the water supply and sewer system. The Brickyard well (rapidly developed as noted previously) was followed by the more deliberate construction of the second Lawrence Swamp well field in Belchertown which was fully operational by 1972. At the time of the Battle of Amherst Fields, water supply questions could not be brought in by the opposition as heavy artillery. Not so with the sewers. The Fields were particularly vulnerable to attack due to difficulties at the Stanley Street sewage pumping station. The overloaded town sewer system was continu-

ally dumping raw sewage in the Fort River at Stanley Street, in a
lagoon near Amherst Farmers Supply, and by the West Street pumping station. A lightly treated sewage effluent from the sewer plant
flowed into the Mill River in Hadley at several points and into Rus-
selville Brook, off River Drive. While government often moves
slowly, progress was being made by both the town and the state to
correct the pollution. Years of hard work and begging for federal
funds were about to pay off. The state had approved a preliminary
report including an eight million dollar new sewage treatment facility. The rebuilding of the Stanley Street pumping station and a new
sewage forcemain had reached the contract level. But though steps
were about to be taken to correct the pollution, the sewage was still
overflowing, and the condition was worsening.

The attention of many experts at the university and Hampshire
College became focused on the design aspects of the sewer problem
just at the time when the Amherst growth study committee was
raising the growth issue to broad public view in their attack on
Paparazzo. Political heat was applied to the sewer commissioners
(selectmen), questioning whether the plans for sewage treatment
were not too conventional and out-of-date, just at the time the
selectmen (sewer commissioners) were deluged with complaints
about not presiding more effectively over the town's growth.

Town officials then established the previously promised technical
advisory committee (TAC) that included many of the resident experts in the sanitary and environmental sciences. They also created a
select committee on goals (SCOG) that would gaze into the navel of
Amherst and try to solve the town's identity crisis. A new problem
was how to bring about a peace in the warfare over growth between
the developers, often seen as foreigners, living "out there," and the
local town residents. It is interesting to note, however, that through
this period there were many recent refugees from urban America
who joined the stop-growth chorus and sang songs about closing
down the gates of the town to keep latecomers out. They were
particularly evident in the growth study committee, to the an-
noyance of many older residents.

A third force now entered upon the field, not to do combat, but
to lobby for the rights of the communities downstream from
Amherst which were being flooded by the town's untreated sewage.
The water pollution control division (WPC) of the state Department

of Natural Resources worried that Amherst might join other communities along the river that ignored lawful schedules to correct pollution problems. Viewing the situation from Boston, the division became unnerved when Amherst's TAC began studying alternative methods of sewage treatment and seemed to be setting aside the plant design which had already been approved. Further, the committee's study was resulting in costly delay. The federal requirements were getting stiffer and more expensive to implement as each month went by with no construction beginning. For these and other reasons, the state WPC decided to make an example of Amherst, to force the town back into reality, and to warn other towns in the valley which might procrastinate about sewage treatment. The WPC ordered a halt to all new sewer connections in the town.

The move came as a complete surprise to most people in town. The state imposed the ban in two stages, first, at the Stanley Street pumping station (the direct target being Paparazzo), secondly, over the entire town some months later. The order first hit town in February 1973, and it stopped Paparazzo cold. Only after he got an approval from WPC to install a $300,000 temporary tertiary plant, a system similar to that for treating sewage going into a place like Lake Tahoe, Nevada, could he proceed; and by that time, according to Paparazzo, "We lost all our buyers." Meanwhile the ban had a direct effect on the fortunes of the remaining local builders and landowners. Some small builders left Amherst in bankruptcy. Some survived, many of these by skill of maneuver on the battlefield. Some builders thought about getting together to sue the town and the state, but joint action was never taken. Some went to Boston to try to "clarify" their case and get relief. Trade-offs emerged, with promises of "not to build here if I can build there." Jerald Gates was particularly successful in this way; he badgered approval out of Boston for the Winston Court condominiums.

At first there was a certain rationality to the limits of the ban; if a house was already under construction, it was free and clear. But this did not last for long. Within months the screws tightened, and some builders got caught by changes and clarifications to the order. The town manager had the onerous duty of administering the ban at town level. Some lawsuits finally did emerge that involved town and state officials, notably one by Don Grant. Another reason that a concerted reaction to the ban did not take place was the decline in actual housing sales, for the recession finally came to Amherst. At that point, availability of sewer lines became largely academic.

When the recession hit, Paparazzo's partner, the Connecticut General Life Insurance Co., bought all of his developed land for $1, leaving him a buy-back option if he could find a financial backer. Paparazzo recalled: "I lost over $1.4 million in cash, let alone three years of sweat and work." He further mused that, ironically, the sewer ban and bureaucratic delays may have saved him from worse disaster. "They did me a favor by clobbering me; if I had built 200 or 300 units before the recession, I would have been in serious trouble." In 1976 Paparazzo began to build houses for sale on land that would stay in his ownership. Asked what would happen if this novel approach failed, he responded, "I don't know where you can go from here—eat the land?"

AFTERMATH

Two significant developments in the 1970s can be traced to issues raised by the Paparazzo case. In 1971 the town began to investigate in detail the town's flood prone areas, in order to update water course protection. New aerial photos were flown in the spring of 1972. The planning board heard much argument the rest of the year as the new flood prone conservancy zone (FPC) was proposed. There were many profitable investments which were in danger of being "washed out" by this protective zoning. A major battle loomed between conservationists and developers. True to form, when the issue came before town meeting in October 1972, the zoning was voted down. But that December a fortuitous rainstorm washed away the light snow cover wherever the ten-year flood occurred. Photos taken the day after the storm compared so well with the proposed zone and provided such a dramatic evidence of its necessity that the bulk of meaningful objection was silenced. The FPC zone was established at the town meeting in March 1973, with only a few changes. Without the rainstorm, and the follow through by the staff of the town hall, the zone might never have passed.

The FPC zone was the first fruit of the select committee on goals, whose existence also had its origins in the Paparazzo controversy. Formed in 1972, SCOG grappled with the issues raised by the master plan of 1969. It received much public input from neighborhood meetings, widely distributed questionnaires, and research work by students. In makeup the SCOG was a cross section of the community, including academics and farmers, mechanics and housewives. SCOG finally issued a report which pictured a future Amherst having multiple village centers as satellites to the main town center, separated from each other by open spaces. A rural setting would be preserved on the multiple perimeters. Intensive development would occur only at each center. The heat of the Paparazzo combat tempered these concepts, and the proposals had more solidity to them than if they had emerged exclusively from enclaves of quiet academic thought. A comprehensive zoning by-law was prepared, based upon a consensus formed by a group of representative town citizens.

At the Olympian town meeting of May 1975, the new regulations came up for a vote. Evening after evening, the knock-down-drag-out debate continued. There was much boring repetition and some useful insight. Eventually a tired meeting called the question. The vote lost; a majority wanted the new zoning, but it could not muster the necessary two-thirds margin. The old guard that had been victorious in 1958—and many individuals were the same—"won" in May 1975. But the loss did not demoralize the planning board. Nor did the board cave in on any major issue in order to get half a loaf. It was all or nothing. It seemed to be only a matter of time before the new zoning would pass. In October 1975 the same proposal was before the town. The same speeches followed, the same interminable debate. And again the by-law lost, this time by one crucial single vote.

This review of town planning in Amherst has been somewhat critical at times of the will shown by Amherst to control its own destiny with respect to land use. The "man-sized town" has time and again adopted zoning by-laws which were too little and too late. The boards and commissions charged with controlling and directing growth have often been caught up in the present tactical situation and have not always concerned themselves with longer range strategic issues. Yet this is not the whole story. The individuals who have made the important decisions in town these last fifty years, even during the most recent decades of explosive growth, have not done badly. Look around us today in Amherst. The town is not "ruined." The fabric of land and buildings retains much that is beautiful. Some opportunities have been lost to preserve more of the "old" Amherst as the "new" Amherst grows apace. But we could have done worse. And there is still time for a responsible citizenry to become more positively and actively involved in the control and development of the land that remains to us. We can yet ensure that the Amherst of the future remains recognizable as the unique city on the hill it has always tried to be.

CHAPTER FIFTEEN

THE CHANGING CLIMATE OF AMHERST

PHILIP TRUMAN IVES

Born and reared in South Amherst, a graduate of Amherst College, Phil Ives has spent a lifetime in combining his affection for Amherst with his devotion to scientific research. His work within the biology department at the college has been supplemented by writing occasional historical essays and regular reports on the weather for the town newspaper. Here he brings to bear all his interests to write a valuable and unusually reliable essay on the changing climate in one place over an extended period of time.

Most of us who grew up before the middle of the twentieth century were raised on the dogma that nobody living a life of three-score-and-ten, or even four-score-and-ten years, in one locality, will experience any real change in the meteorological climate of that area. The prevailing view was that the variations in weather which occur over the period of a century or two are only random fluctuations around a stable mean. A stable climate was one of the few things that everyone seemed to be sure of.

As this century has progressed, however, a growing number of young climatologists has challenged that view. Some of them go so far as to proclaim that not only is our climate not stable, in this century it is actually "deteriorating." I find that too extreme: deteriorating is too loaded and too ambiguous a term to use in describing climate. But I have come into the opinion that good century-long weather records might show that, in some parts of the earth's temperate zones, this probably postpleistocene climate we are living in has not yet reached stability. If this is so, one should not be surprised or alarmed by the appearance of either regular or irregular climatic anomalies, lasting for several years, in the records of strategically located weather stations, of which Amherst, Massachusetts may just happen to be one.

The systematic recording of daily mean temperature and other weather data in Amherst has one of the longest continuous histories of any place in America. Ebenezer S. Snell, graduate of Amherst College in its first class and within a decade its Professor of Mathematics and Natural Philosophy (which was Science at that time), began recording precipitation, to the hundredth of an inch of water, in August 1835, and the daily mean temperature, to the tenth of a degree Fahrenheit, in March 1836. He continued to do this, with only brief interruptions, until his death in September 1876, and his daughters continued the records for the rest of the century. The site of these observations was the Snell residence on the corner of today's Snell and South Pleasant Streets, "100 rods" (500 meters) from the Amherst College campus.

In 1889 a standard weather station was established at the other end of town on the Aggie campus. (I never heard it called Mass. Aggie in the 1920s—it was always Aggie.) Run by the Massachusetts Agricultural Experiment Station (MAES), it soon became a contributor of meteorological information to the U.S. Weather Bureau, now the National Weather Service (NWS).

In the fall of 1948, to provide first-hand objective experience with weather phenomena for the sophomores in a new course, "The Evolution of the Earth and Man," weather and climate being prime factors in the evolution of both, a new weather station was established in front of the Biology Laboratory at Amherst College, and I was given the responsibility for its function. When the reduction of that year-long course to a single semester eliminated the "weather exercise" (it also included clouds and wind, the barometer, and humidity), I continued the temperature and precipitation records as part of my long-term study of the genetic structure of the South Amherst natural population of *Drosophila melanogaster,* the common fruit fly, which weather affects profoundly.

The MAES weather station ran into site difficulties as a result of the large and rapid building program at the University of Massachusetts in the 1950s. After it was moved off campus in December 1960, the new site proved to be unsatisfactory for temperature readings. As a result, the MAES stopped recording meteorological observations at the end of June 1966, but the NWS precipitation measurements continued close by at the town's waste treatment plant.

To provide comparative recent historical weather information for the students of the Evolution course, I used the data from the monthly meteorological bulletins published by the MAES, arranging the data as decade averages for the sixty years, 1889–1948, in the spring of 1949. Each spring thereafter the students compared the monthly averages they had helped to inscribe with the averages of the previous year whose weather they had experienced as freshmen and with the six decade averages from the MAES data. As it happened, the most spectacular warm period in the history of Amherst began in the fall of 1948. During the decade of the Evolution course five of the years were among the ten warmest on record, including the warmest three. Many of the students were quick to see and appreciate the exceptional and exciting nature of the weather they were experiencing and to grasp the idea that quite possibly climate is not as stable as the textbooks say.

When the original MAES site had to be abandoned in December 1960, I found, from a judicious use of our parallel data for November 1948–November 1960, that I could convert the monthly mean temperatures from the college station to a reasonable estimate of the monthly mean temperature which would have been recorded at the 1889–1960 site, within an accuracy of about ±0.5° F per month. There had been a shift in temperature level from "way above normal" to "below average" in the fall of 1955, giving me an array of cold as well as warm months to use in this conversion process. Accordingly, from December 1960 on I have routinely recorded this adjusted mean each month, together with the standard mean for the present college station site.

At the time that I set up the 1889–1948 decade averages, using the MAES data, I had learned that the earlier Snell data could not be used directly. Beginning before the NWS, Professor Snell had devised a different system for recording and calculating the daily mean temperature, and it would require much more time than was available to me then to convert his observations to useful form, if indeed that could be done at all. (I did not know then that recordings at the Snell site continued after 1888.) I marked that project as "the first thing to look into when I retire, if I can still add 2 and 3 and get 5 most of the time."

Retirement seemed then at least a century away, but time accelerates unbelievably in each succeeding decade of one's life, and so it was that only a few months later (it can't be twenty-six years!) I found myself in the Archives of the Frost Library at Amherst College, working over the Snell data.

During the 1890–1899 period at the Snell site not only were daily mean temperatures recorded, using the original Snell method, but standard minimum and maximum temperatures were also recorded, though they were not used in any way. Thus it became possible for me to calculate standard means for those 120 months of Snell records. From those means, I determined for each of the twelve calendar months the average difference (1) between the Snell mean and the standard mean and (2) between the Snell site and the MAES site. Finally, by combining those two differences I came up with the desired calibration factor for each calendar month, and I was able to convert all of the Snell means, March 1836 through December 1888, to numerical values comparable to those of the MAES site in the 1889–1960 period. As it turns out, the amount of calibration varies all the way from no change at all in the September Snell means, and a reduction of only 0.1° F in August, to a reduction of 1.6° F in both the January and February Snell means. For the year as a whole the average of the twelve monthly correction values came out to $-0.95°$ F, which I think can be safely evened off to $-1°$ F. Actually, after I had adjusted all of the individual monthly means, I used them for recalculating all of the annual means, and they constitute the data which became the most important result of this study, a graphic representation of Amherst's climate over a period of fourteen decades (see Figure 1).

In the figure each decade is represented by a pair of points, one the average annual mean temperature and the other the average inches of precipitation (including snow melt) in that decade. Lines connect these points simply to show the direction of change over the period of 137 years (through 1975).

The precipitation data are from the Snell site in decades 1–5, from the MAES site from January 1889 through June 1966, and from the NWS gauge at the town's waste treatment plant from July 1966 to date (through the cooperation and courtesy of Charles Gricius, the manager of the plant). The temperature data are from the published meteorological bulletins of the MAES from January 1889 through November 1960 (corrected for occasional errors of various kinds)

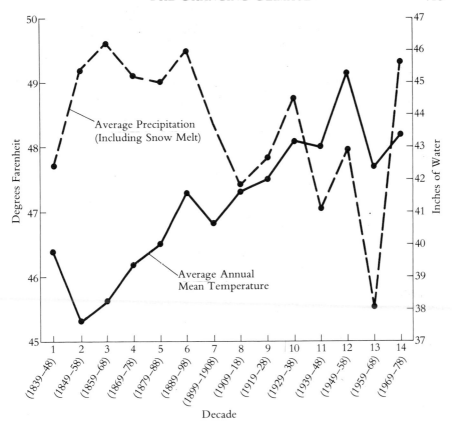

FIGURE 1.   THE CHANGING CLIMATE OF AMHERST, 1839–1975.

and from my calibrations of both the Snell data from 1839–1888 and
my own recordings at the Amherst College station from December
1960 to date.

The underlying assumption, which has to be made and accepted
on faith in interpreting these curves, is that there were no important
changes in methods, instruments, or the sites themselves, at any of
these locations, during their respective periods of use.

Accepting the above assumption, one sees in the temperature
curve a strong trend to a higher level of annual mean temperature
over the fourteen decade periods. The continuity of the trend was
interrupted by three declines, in decades 2, 7, and 13. Each of the last
two declines was preceded by a decade showing an apparently

steeper rise in temperature than average. Since the third decline the temperature seems to have risen again, with the decade 14 average currently second highest to that in decade 12. (I have attempted no statistical analysis of these data; this is purely a sight analysis of the curve.)

That decade 14 point suggests that, for Amherst at least, the threat of a return to the "Little Ice Age" temperature level of the middle centuries of this millenium has dissipated. I am not sure that the threat ever existed, outside of the news wire releases during some cold Januaries in 1968–1971.

Inevitably, in a strict division into decade periods, briefer and more extreme sets of years will either be hidden within a decade or overlap two decades. Thus, there was a five-year cold period over-lapping decades 2 and 3 which had an average annual mean temperature of 44.5° F with each year under 45° F. (That is nearly 2° F colder than any of the years in the very recent cold set that seems to have popularized the "deteriorating" school of climatologists.) Also, three of the four coldest winter quarters on record are buried in the decades 7 and 8 points. At the other extreme, the warm period of 1949–1955, which averaged 49.7° F on an annual basis, came in a decade with enough cold in 1956 and 1958 to hold that decade average down appreciably.

The precipitation curve is more irregular than the temperature one, but it has several interesting features. During the second half of the nineteenth century precipitation, in decade lumps, was remark-ably stable. During the twentieth century it displayed an erratic and possibly alarming decline into decade 13. There it seems to have bottomed out in what is probably the most spectacular anomaly of the 140-year period, the five years from July 1961 through June 1966 which had an average precipitation of only 31.28 inches per twelve-month period. None of those five "years" recorded over 34 inches. Since 1968 there seems to have been a complete recovery. Precipitation in the last seven years has been right up there at a level equal to the second half of the nineteenth century. (There are other interpretations possible for this apparent recovery, however, and only the data from several more decades will decide which one hap-pens to be right. The one I have suggested may well be wrong.)

The major point of this pair of curves is to show just how much the climate of Amherst did change from the mid-nineteenth to the mid-twentieth centuries in its two most important characteristics. These are hardly random variations. They may or may not be irregularly rhythmic shifts around a much longer term mean. It is impossible at this time to judge that possibility, in the absence of earlier systematic records of the kind pioneered by Professor Snell.

I have examined the decade changes also to see if perchance one or more seasons or months have contributed disproportionately to them. In general the data (not included in this report) show that this is not likely, at least not to any striking quantitative amount. But this does not mean that today's seasons have the same relative characteristics as formerly, following the 3° F rise in annual mean temperature in the last 120 years. That much rise in the means of the spring and fall months has clearly shortened the effective winter season by at least a month. There are senior citizens, life-long residents, who have the sense of this change in Amherst's climate during their lifetimes.

The change in the length of the winters was, of course, not a sudden one. And it was not accompanied by any reduction in snowfall that I can see. Professor Snell's own 1849–1875 seasonal totals for snow were enough like the extremely variable amounts that I have recorded in 1949–1975, within 100 rods of his house, that our series of seasonal totals could be interchanged and make no great difference. His average was 57.0 inches and mine 53.3 inches. There was, however, measurable snow seven times in October, the earliest storm amounting to 6 inches on 4 October 1841, at the Snell residence. No measurable October snow has fallen in the middle of town since 1875. On the other hand, the Snell site never recorded measurable snowfall in May. Many in Amherst today can recall a wet, sticky, damaging (to tobacco tenting) snow storm in the morning of 25 May 1967. In 1945 an inch fell on May 10–11. Snowfall in November and March was as irregular as now, but it usually lasted longer back then because of the generally lower temperatures.

There was no mild winter in the 1837–1888 period comparable to the ten mildest winters since that time. Curiously, both the change to warmer Marches and the appearance of the first notable mild winter seem to have been triggered by the Blizzard in mid–March 1888, the most intense snow storm in 140 years or more. (The Snell estimate was 32 inches of snow, most of it in about that number of hours, with the temperature dropping through the teens to a low of 8° F, and the wind at 40 mph.) The observer at the MAES noted that the

THE GREAT BLIZZARD OF '88 BURIED THE CENTER OF TOWN.

following winter, 1889, and the winter of 1890 were both mild in a way that not even the oldest inhabitants could remember for an earlier winter. Even today those winters are among the ten mildest in the 140 year span. After that cold blizzard month, the March average in decade 6 jumped 2° F above the prevailing averages of the preceding four decades and held that level until decade 9 when it jumped another degree to its current level, about 35° F. November's decade record is more erratic, but it jumped 2° F in decade 5, from 36° F to 38° F, then to 39° F in decade 8 and to its current 40° F level in decade 10.

The ability of winter to come on strong over a three-month period was not at all diminished, however, by this marked change in the quarter's adjacent months late in the nineteenth century. The winter quarter of 1918 (including December 1917) was 2° F colder than any winter quarter in the Snell periods; 1904 was second and 1905 fourth. And among the individual months, December 1917 and February 1934 were coldest in their categories. The latter was the coldest month in the 140 year period, 11.6° F, with the 11.9° F of January 1857 close behind. In our most recent series of colder years, the coldest month, January 1970 at 14.7° F, ranks only eighth coldest among the Januaries. The Decembers of 1958 and 1963 were also among the ten coldest Decembers.

Hot summers began earlier than mild winters. Professor Snell was both surprised and amazed in 1870 by the first hot, dry summer of his time. (He was born in 1801.) For the first time "crops withered." Actually, it was not unlike some of the drought periods of the most recent thirty-five year span in Amherst. Indeed, in our time a summer that doesn't brown lawns and wither (nonirrigated) gardens for at least a week or two is an exceptional summer. That itself suggests a significant change in our climate.

What made the hot summers of 1870 and 1876 stand out (they rate fourth and fifth behind 1949, 1973, and 1955 on the 140 year list) was the extreme cold that also came in that decade: 1875 was the coldest year on record, 1873 wasn't an awful lot warmer, and the summer of 1874 averaged 2° F colder than any summer in the last thirty-five years. The 1870s had a variable (deteriorating?) climate that the 1970s or any future decade will be hard put to equal.

The increasing warmth of June and August have served to make our hot summers longer. Except for 1870 and 1876 all the ten hottest summers have been recorded in the period 1937 to date.

The most destructive storm in Amherst's history, The Great New England Hurricane of 21 September 1938, had no apparent triggering effect here on a shift in the climate of a season, like the Blizzard of 12–13 March 1888, so far as I can see. It did usher in a quarter century in which southern New England, especially along its shores, was hit hard by many hurricanes and tropical storms. Only that first one was severely destructive here.

Professor Snell's marginal daily weather comments show no hurricanes. He did record several severe line squalls and thunderstorms with hurricane-force gusts that toppled trees and chimneys, similar to what we have had just about as often in my lifetime. Thunderstorms he almost invariably described as "powerful." His descriptions of the destructive effects of two violently windy hailstorms on 5 June 1845 and 31 July 1849 indicate that they were not far from being tornadoes. He lists two Connecticut River floods that carried away bridges, a devastating spring runoff on 1 May 1853, and a surprising "Great Freshet" on 28 January 1839 that must have been a January thaw of epic proportions.

I am unable to use the Snell data to calculate the span of the

EFFECTS OF THE HURRICANE OF SEPTEMBER 21, 1938. THE
SAMUEL FOWLER DICKINSON HOUSE (DAMAGED) AND ST.
BRIGID'S CHURCH

growing season in that half century. But so far as I can see for later
years, no real change has occurred in that respect. "First" and "last"
frost dates (measured in terms of freezing temperature at the weather
station) vary so broadly from year to year that the averages, first
week in May and first week in October, mean very little. So far as I
can determine there has been no change in the average week, using
periods of twenty-five years or so, from 1889 to date.

In addition to the decade curves I have prepared a table showing
the extremes reached by the months, quarters, and years during the
whole period—coldest, warmest, driest, wettest—and the cumula-
tive averages from Snell's earliest months through 1975. The extremes I don't mind, but I am reluctant to list the averages. I hope
that readers will recognize their limited usefulness, after looking
carefully at the decade distribution curves. It should be clear then,
even without going to archives for the individual monthly records,
that these long-term averages do not really apply to the months,
quarters, and years of the first five and last five decades.

TABLE 1. 1835–1975 AVERAGES AND EXTREMES FOR MEAN TEMPERATURE
AND PRECIPITATION

	Average °F	Coldest	Warmest	Average Precip- itation	Driest	Wettest
Year	47.1	43.3 1875	51.3 1949	43.48	29.87 1964	64.44 1888
Winter (Dec., Jan., Feb.)	24.8	16.9 1918	31.5 1953	9.89	4.16 1944	18.18 1898
Spring (Mar., Apr., May)	45.2	40.7 1875	51.2 1921	10.63	5.05 1941	20.40 1943
Summer (Jun., Jul., Aug.)	68.3	64.0 1903	73.2 1949	12.11	4.33 1882	25.45 1897
Fall (Sep., Oct., Nov.)	50.0	45.5 1871	54.2 1931	10.85	4.25 1965	21.92 1888
January	23.2	11.9 1857	34.2 1913	3.28	0.66 1970	7.15 1898
February	24.2	11.6 1934	33.5 1954	3.07	0.36 1877	8.12 1900
March	33.4	23.8 1843	44.5 1946	3.56	0.12 1915	8.28 1953
April	45.3	37.0 1874	52.1 1941	3.35	0.55 1941	9.02 1854
May	56.8	49.5 1917	63.4 1944	3.72	0.48 1903	8.72 1850
June	65.8	60.3 1903	71.5 1949	3.80	0.72 1949	11.69 1862
July	70.6	65.4 1860	76.0 1955	4.20	0.70 1929	14.51 1897
August	68.6	62.4 1904	73.7 1973	4.11	0.25 1882	16.10 1955
September	61.2	50.9 1857	68.3 1961	3.73	0.37 1865	14.55 1938
October	50.2	43.1 1841	57.4 1947	3.41	0.01 1924	11.36 1869
November	38.7	28.9 1873	46.2 1975	3.71	0.63 1917	8.64 1927
December	27.0	17.1 1917	36.9 1891	3.54	0.58 1943	8.81 1973

The averages give only the most general picture of the 140-year period, and that rather badly. Yet, who among us would not look first for the Average in any such presentation of 140-year data? We demand an Average. We linger on it. An Average suggests stability, a stability we need in a world where too often the only "average," the only certainty, seems to be that all things will continue to change—including the Climate of Amherst.

AN AMHERST BIBLIOGRAPHY

SHEILA RAINFORD

GENERAL

Allen, Mary Adele. *Around a Village Green: Sketches of Life in Amherst.* Northampton: The Kraushar Press, 1939.

Allen, Mary Adele. *The Boltwood House.* Amherst, 1937.

Amherst College. Archives, 1820–.

Amherst College. Special Collections.
About one half of Emily Dickinson's extant manuscripts; one of the largest Robert Frost collections in the world; and western Massachusetts imprints and authors.

Amherst Historical Society. Special Collections.
Miscellaneous documents, artifacts, and other memorabilia.

Amherst Historical Society. Oral History Project.
Interviews with individuals and small groups, begins 1976; available at The Jones Library.

Amherst, Town of. Town Records.
Available at the town hall.

Atkins, W. H. *Leave the Light Burning: South Amherst, Massachusetts.* Edited by Marjorie Atkins Elliott. McFarland, Wis.: Community Publications, 1973.

Bain, George W., and Meyerhoff, Howard A. *The Flow of Time in the Connecticut Valley.* Springfield, Mass.: Connecticut Valley Historical Museum, 1963. Rev. 1968.
A geological history.

Barnett, Edwin B. "Anatomy of Power in Amherst Politics." Honors thesis. Amherst College, 1949.

Beers, H. P. *Bibliographies in American History.* Rev. Ed. New York: The H. W. Wilson Company, 1942.

Bierstadt, Edwar. *Sunlight Pictures, Amherst.* New York, 1891.

Brawley, Peter E. "Catholics and Amherst: A Study of Problems and Ways of Surviving." Honors thesis. Amherst College, 1974.

[Brown, W. R.] *Amherst, Massachusetts, . . . A Home of Culture and Agriculture.* Amherst: Charles E. Ewell, n.d.

Bryant, Frederick C. "Birds of Amherst." Honors thesis. Amherst College, 1954.

Carpenter, Edward W., and Morehouse, Charles F. *The History of the Town of Amherst, Massachusetts.* Amherst: Press of Carpenter and Morehouse, 1896.
Our most lengthy and detailed history; first imprint has maps and photos; later copies do not have photos.

Chaplin, Davis. "Amherst's Negroes." Honors thesis. Amherst College, 1953.

Clark, Roger B. "The Effect of the Proposed Expansion of the University of Massachusetts Upon the Town of Amherst." Honors thesis. Amherst College, 1955.

Cochrane, James C. "The Anti-Slavery Movement in Hampshire County." Honors thesis. Amherst College, 1946.

Committee for a New England Bibliography, Inc. *Massachusetts: a Bibliography.* Boston: G. K. Hall and Company, 1976.

Daughters of the American Revolution, comps. *Amherst, Massachusetts: The Chronology of Events.* Amherst: Mary Mattoon Chapter, DAR, 1941. Rev. 1975.

Dickinson, Marquis F. *Historical Address Delivered at the Centennial Celebration, July 4, 1876.* Amherst, 1878.

Doubleday, William. "Amherst: A Community Study." Honors thesis. Amherst College, 1972.

Everts, Louis. *1869 History of the Connecticut Valley in Massachusetts.* Philadelphia, 1879.

Garden Club of Amherst. *Trees in Amherst.* Amherst: Hamilton I. Newell, Inc., 1975.

Guide to the Public Vital Records in Massachusetts. Boston: Historical Records Survey, 1942.

Hitchcock, Frederick H. *Handbook of Amherst, Massachusetts.* Amherst, 1894.

Hoffman, Edwina. "A Language Study of the Negro Community in Amherst, Massachusetts." Senior honors thesis. University of Massachusetts, 1968.

Holland, Josiah G. *History of Western Massachusetts*. 2 vols. Springfield, Mass.: Bowles Press, 1855.

Jameson, J. F., ed. *Records of the Town of Amherst from 1735 to 1788*. Amherst, 1884.

The Jones Library. Special Collections.
Extensive holdings of account books, journals, business directories, Amherst imprints and authors, genealogical materials, documents, photographs, and memorabilia relating to Amherst and its people.

Judd, Sylvester. *History of Hadley*. Springfield, Mass.: H. R. Huntting & Company, 1905. Facsimile. Somersworth, N.H.: New Hampshire Publishing Company, 1976.

Lower Pioneer Valley Regional Planning Commission. *Comprehensive Development Plan*. Washington, D.C.: Clearinghouse for Federal Scientific and Technical Information, 1971.
Development plans for Amherst and twelve other towns.

Lower Pioneer Valley Regional Planning Commission. *A Future for the Past: Historic Preservation in the Lower Pioneer Valley*. Springfield, Mass.: Lower Pioneer Valley Regional Planning Commission, 1974.

Martin, Margaret E. "Merchants and Trade of the Connecticut River Valley, 1750–1820." *Smith College Studies in History*, Vol. XXIII, No. 2 (January 1939).

Massachusetts, State of. Office of the Secretary of the Commonwealth. Census.
Begin 1837.

McKeon, Newton Felch, and Cowles, Katharine Conover. *Amherst, Massachusetts: Imprints 1825–1876*. Amherst: Amherst College Library, 1946.

Miller, J. A. "A Regional High School for Amherst." Honors thesis. Amherst College, 1954.

Niven, Jean Olive. "Place Names of Amherst and Belchertown, Massachusetts." Senior Honors Thesis, University of Massachusetts, 1974. Available at the town hall. Use with caution.

Norton, Paul F. *Amherst: a Guide to Its Architecture*. Amherst: Amherst Historical Society, 1975.

Pabst, Margaret Richards. "Agricultural Trends in the Connecticut Valley Region of Massachusetts, 1800–1900," *Smith College Studies in History*, Vol. XXVI, No. 1.

Parsons, W. G. "The Amherst Water Bureau." Honors thesis. Amherst College, 1950.

Picturesque Hampshire: a Supplement to the Quarter Centennial Journal. Northampton: Wade, Warner, and Company, 1890.

Rand, Frank Prentice. *Heart O' Town.* Amherst: E. L. Hildreth & Company, 1945.

Rand, Frank Prentice. *The Village of Amherst: a Landmark of Light.* Amherst: Amherst Historical Society, 1958.
Provides a general history in a conversational manner.

Roberts, Stephen X. "Amherst: If You Can't Do It Here. . . ?" Honors thesis. Amherst College, 1976.

See, Anna Phillips. *Amherst Past and Present.* Amherst: Tercentenary Committee, 1930.

Stearns, Alfred Ernest. *An Amherst Boyhood.* Amherst: Amherst College, 1946. Foreword by Chief Justice Harlan Stone.
Celebrates the 125th anniversary of Amherst College.

Thayer, Charles H. *History of the Stockbridge House at Massachusetts State College.* Amherst, 1936.

United States Census Bureau. 1st–10th Census, 1790–1880. Population schedules of the first through the tenth census of the United States. Washington: National Archives and Records Service, 1959–. Microfilm.
For Massachusetts, the University of Massachusetts library holds the microfilm edition of the original manuscript population schedules.

United States Census Bureau. 11th and 12th Censuses.
The original manuscript schedules for the eleventh census were destroyed by a fire in 1921. The schedules for the twelfth are in the National Archives and have been filmed under restrictions which confine their use to the National Archives and to Federal Records Centers.

United States Census Bureau. 13th and later Censuses.
Not yet available on microfilm. Published statistical summaries exist for all censuses and are widely available, but they do not contain nominal records (i.e., records relating to named individuals).

Walker, Alice M. *Ye Amherst Girl of Ye Olden Tyme.* Amherst, 1900.

Walker, Alice M. *Historic Homes of Amherst.* Amherst: Amherst Historical Society, 1905.

Walker, Alice M. *Sketches of Amherst History.* Amherst: Press of Carpenter and Morehouse, 1901.

Walker, Alice M. *Through Turkey Pass to Amherst and Beyond.* Amherst: Press of Carpenter and Morehouse, 1903.

Wikander, Lawrence E., et al. *The Hampshire History: Celebrating 300 Years of Hampshire County, Massachusetts*. Northampton: Hampshire County Commissioners, 1964.
Includes "Amherst" by Eleanor R. Dunn and Frank Prentice Rand, p. 11–23.

Your Amherst Government. Amherst: League of Women Voters, 1975.

REPORTS PUBLISHED BY AND FOR THE TOWN OF AMHERST

Amherst Schools. Minutes. July 4, 1889–January 25, 1902; April 12, 1902–November 2, 1914.
Manuscript in school department files.

Amherst Pelham Superintendency Union, Union #28. Minutes, 1901–1961.
Manuscript in school department files.

Amherst Redevelopment Authority Final Project Reports. Cambridge, Mass.: Center School Complex Consultants, 1973.

Annual Budget. Submitted by the town manager and boards. Gives breakdown of budgets for each department.

Annual Reports, 1852 to date. Each includes reports by the selectmen, school committee, and other town boards and committees.

Archives. Vault in town hall houses most town records.

Board of Selectmen Policy Manual, 1974.

Board of Selectmen Procedures Manual, 1974.

Comparative Valuation Lists, Real Estate, 1963–1964.

Government of the Town of Amherst, Massachusetts. Vol. 1.
Certain by-laws, with special acts, regulations, and statutes accepted or availed of by the town, 1972.

Herder, John H. *A Plan for Police Service in Amherst: A Management Study of the Police Department Amherst, Massachusetts*. Hampden, Conn., 1972.

Law Enforcement Study Committee, Summary of Recommendations. Hampden, Conn., 1972.

Official 1970 Amherst Real Estate Tax Valuations. Amherst: Amherst Bulletin, 1970.

Planning Board. *Comprehensive Plan, Amherst, Massachusetts*.
Charles E. Downe's report as planning consultant to the Amherst Planning Board of Massachusetts Department of Community Affairs, 1969.

Planning Board. *CBD Study, June 1969.*
Charles E. Downe's report as planning consultant concerning Amherst's Central Business District.

Planning Board. *East Amherst Village, 1970.*
Prepared by the Planning Collaborative for East Amherst Village, Hampshire Village, and South Amherst Village.

Select Committee on Goals. *Final Report of the Select Committee on Goals for Amherst: Amherst, Massachusetts.*
Prepared for the selectmen, January 29, 1973. Known as the SCOG Report.

South East School District of Amherst, District #8. Minutes. February 22, 1828–March 28, 1862.
Manuscript in files of school department.

Street List of Persons Twenty-one Years of Age and Over Residing in the Town of Amherst. 1921 to date.

Street List and Site Construction Standards, 1972.

Subdivision Planning Board Adopted February 2, 1972.

Town of Amherst Real Estate Valuations-1978. Amherst: Amherst Record 1978.
A special section of the Amherst Record, February 25, 1978.

Town Officers. *Town Report.* 1877 to date.

Zoning Board. *Zoning By-Laws.* Amended frequently.

BIOGRAPHY—GENERAL

Amherst Art Center. *Amherst Poets.* Amherst: Amherst Journal Record, 1959.

Amherst College. *Catalog of the Corporation, Faculty and Students.* Begins 1825.

Amherst College in Battle Dress. Amherst: Amherst College Press, 1944.

Bingham, Millicent Todd. "Contributions of Mabel Loomis Todd to the Town of Amherst." Address delivered at the fortieth anniversary of the founding of the Mary Mattoon Chapter of the Daughters of the American Revolution, November 1, 1934.

Boltwood, Lucius M. *Genealogies of Hadley Families, Embracing Early Settlers of the Towns of Hatfield, South Hadley, Amherst, and Granby.* Northampton: Metcalf & Company, Printers, 1862.

Cronenwett, Philip. "The Papers of Sidney Biehler Waugh, American Sculptor, 1904–1963." Finding aid prepared for The Jones Library in Amherst, 1977.
Includes a brief biography of Sidney Biehler Waugh.

Dwight, Clara. "Recollections of South Amherst."
A scrapbook compiled in Amherst, 1966. Available at The Jones and Munson Libraries.

Francis, Robert. *The Trouble with Francis*. Amherst: University of Massachusetts Press, 1971.

Feuss, Claude M., ed. *The Amherst Memorial Volume*. Amherst: Amherst College, 1926.
A record of contributions made by Amherst College and Amherst men in the World War, 1914–1918.

Feuss, Claude M. *Stanley King of Amherst*. New York: Columbia University Press, 1955.

Garis, Roger. *My Father Was Uncle Wiggily*. New York: McGraw-Hill, 1966.

Goodell, Henry Hill. "Amherst Writers: an Address Delivered Before the Amherst's Woman's Club, October 15, 1900." Additions by Dr. Frederick Tuckerman.
Typed manuscript at The Jones Library.

James, Edward T., et al, eds. "Mabel Loomis Todd." *Notable American Women, 1607–1950*, III, 468–69. Cambridge, Mass.: Belknap Press of Harvard University Press, 1971.

The Jones Library. Special Collections.
Extensive collection of manuscripts and memorabilia relating to Ray Stannard Baker (David Grayson), Emily Dickinson, Eugene Field, Robert Frost, Chief Justice Harlan Stone, Helen Hunt Jackson, Noah Webster, and others.

Lyman, Rev. George. *Addresses Commemorative of the Late Lieut. Enos Dickinson in the Church of South Amherst January 18, 1870*. Boston, 1870.

Lyman, Payson W. *Military Service of the Towns of Amherst, Belchertown, and Granby in the Revolutionary War*. Amherst, 1889.

Odell, Ruth. *Helen Hunt Jackson*. New York: D. Appleton-Century, 1939.

Todd, Millicent. *Mary E. Stearns*. Cambridge, Mass.: Riverside Press, 1909.

Tuckerman, Frederick. *Charles Anthony Goessman*. Cambridge, Mass.: Riverside Press, 1917.

Wade, Harold J. *Black Men of Amherst*. Amherst: Amherst College Press, 1976.

Walker, Alice M. *Mary Mattoon and Her Hero of the Revolution*. Amherst: Press of Carpenter and Morehouse, 1902.

Walker, Charles S. *Samuel Minot Jones: The Story of an Amherst Boy*. Amherst: The Jones Library, 1922.

Warfel, Harry Redcay. *Noah Webster: Schoolmaster to America*. New York: MacMillan, 1936.

Younger, Paul H. J. "Terras Irradient: A Study of Amherst College Missionaries in the Far East in the Nineteenth Century." Honors thesis. Amherst College, 1959.

BIOGRAPHY—RAY STANNARD BAKER (DAVID GRAYSON)

Bannister, Robert C., Jr. *Ray Stannard Baker: The Mind and Thought of a Progressive.* New Haven: Yale University Press, 1966.

Dyer, Walter A. *David Grayson: Adventurer.* New York: Doubleday, Doran, 1928. "The story of the author of *Adventures in Contentment, Friendship,* etc., as told by Walter A. Dyer."

Dyer, Walter A. "The Real David Grayson," *Mentor* (October, 1925): 1–18.

Memorial Service for Ray Stannard Baker. (At the Jones Library 8 September 1946.) Portland, Maine: The Southworth-Anthoensen Press, 1947. "Personal appreciation" speeches by George F. Whicher, Victor L. Butterfield, and Frank Prentice Rand.

Napier, Rachel Baker. *Ray Stannard Baker "David Grayson" a Bibliography.* Amherst: privately printed. 1943.
A listing of writings by Ray Stannard Baker as himself or as David Grayson prepared by his daughter. Has no biographical or critical section.

Rand, Frank Prentice. "The Myth and Magic of David Grayson." Amherst: The Jones Library, 1961.
An address for (Jones Library) Founder's Day, 26 October 1961.

Rand, Frank Prentice. *The Story of David Grayson.* Amherst: The Jones Library, 1963.

Rugg, Winnifred K. "Ray Stannard Baker and David Grayson." *Boston Evening Transcript,* December 31, 1932.

Semonche, John E. "Ray Stannard Baker," *A Quest for Democracy in Modern America, 1870–1918.* Chapel Hill: University of North Carolina Press, 1969.

BIOGRAPHY—EMILY DICKINSON

Bianchi, Martha Dickinson. *Emily Dickinson, Face to Face.* Boston: Houghton Mifflin Company, 1932.
Reminiscences by Emily Dickinson's niece, Mattie; experts state that this book is unreliable.

Bingham, Millicent Todd. *Ancestor's Brocades.* New York: Harper & Row, Publishers, 1945.
History of the publication of Emily Dickinson's poetry and letters.

Bingham, Millicent Todd. *Emily Dickinson, a Revelation.* New York: Harper & Row, Publishers, 1954.

Bingham, Millicent Todd. *Emily Dickinson's Home.* New York: Harper & Row, Publishers, 1955.
Life in Amherst and the Dickinson family, including letters of Edward Dickinson and his family.

Brose, N. H., Dupre, J. M., Kohler, W. T., and Mudge, J. M. *Emily Dickinson, Profile of the Poet as Cook.* Amherst: Guides at the Dickinson Homestead, 1976.
Selected recipes and biographical comment on the domestic life of the poet.

Emily Dickinson, a Bibliography. Amherst: The Jones Library, 1930. Foreword by George F. Whicher.

Hampson, Alfred Leete. *Emily Dickinson, a Bibliography.* Northampton: Hampshire Bookshop, 1930.

Jenkins, MacGregor. *Emily Dickinson, Friend and Neighbor.* Boston: Little, Brown, & Company, 1930.
Recollections of Jenkins' boyhood near the Dickinson family.

Johnson, Thomas H. and Ward, Theodora, eds. *The Letters of Emily Dickinson.* 3 vols. Cambridge, Mass.: The Belknap Press of Harvard University Press, 1958.
A complete, annotated collection.

Leyda, Jay. *The Years and Hours of Emily Dickinson.* 2 vols. New Haven: Yale University Press, 1960.
Chronology of events in the life of Emily Dickinson with her family.

Longsworth, Polly. *Emily Dickinson: Her Letter to the World.* New York: Thomas Y. Crowell Company, 1965.
Young people's biography.

MacLeish, Archibald, et al. *Emily Dickinson: Three Views.* Amherst: Amherst College Press, 1960.

Mudge, Jean McClure. *Emily Dickinson and the Image of Home.* Amherst: University of Massachusetts Press, 1975.

Sewall, Richard Benson, ed. *Emily Dickinson: a Collection of Critical Essays.* Englewood Cliffs, N.J.: Prentice-Hall, Inc., 1963.

Sewall, Richard Benson. *The Life of Emily Dickinson.* 2 vols. New York: Farrar, Straus and Giroux, 1974.
A definitive biography of the poet, her family, and the people in her world.

Waugh, Dorothy. *Emily Dickinson's Beloved: A Surmise.* New York: Vantage Press, 1976.
Scholarly presentation of Miss Waugh's theory.

Whicher, George F. *This Was a Poet*. New York: Charles Scribner's Sons, 1938.

BIOGRAPHY—EUGENE FIELD

Conrow, Robert. *Field Days: The Life, Times and Reputation of Eugene Field*. New York: Charles Scribner's Sons, 1974.

Dennis, Charles H. *Eugene Field's Creative Years*. New York: Doubleday, Page, 1924.

Fisher, Henry W. *Abroad With Mark Twain and Eugene Field*. New York: Nicholas L. Brown, 1922.

Phinney, W. R. *Eugene Field in Amherst*. 24 pp. typescript. Special collections. Amherst: Jones Library, n.d.

Thompson, Slason. *Eugene Field*. 2 vols. New York: Charles Scribner's Sons, 1901.

Wilson, Francis. *The Eugene Field I Knew*. New York: Charles Scribner's Sons, 1898.

BIOGRAPHY—ROBERT FROST

Amherst College. Special Collections. World's fourth largest Frost collection.

Clymer, W. B., Shubrick, and Green, Charles R. *Robert Frost: A Bibliography*. Amherst: Jones Library, 1937.

Coffin, Robert P. Tristram. *New Poets of New England: Frost and Robinson*. Baltimore: Johns Hopkins Press, 1938.

Cox, James M., ed. *Robert Frost: A Collection of Critical Essays*. Englewood Cliffs, N.J.: Prentice-Hall, 1966.

Francis, Robert. *Frost: A Time to Talk*. Amherst: University of Massachusetts Press, 1972. Conversations recorded by Robert Francis.

Frost, Robert. *The Letters of Robert Frost to Louis Untermeyer*. New York: Holt, Rinehart, and Winston, 1963. Foreword by Louis Untermeyer, editor.

Grade, Arnold, ed. *Family Letters of Robert Frost and Elinor Frost*. Albany, N.Y.: State University of New York Press, 1972.

Isaacs, Emily Elizabeth. *An Introduction to Robert Frost*. Denver: Alan Swallow, 1962.

Jennings, Elizabeth. *Frost*. Edinburgh: Oliver and Boyd, 1964.

Jones Library. Special Collections. World's third largest Frost collection.

Lathem, Edward Connery. *A Concordance to the Poetry of Robert Frost.* New York: Holt Information Systems, 1971.

Lathem, Edward Connery, ed. *Interviews with Robert Frost.* New York: Holt, Rinehart, and Winston, 1966.

Lathem, Edward Connery, ed. *The Poetry of Robert Frost.* New York: Holt, Rinehart, and Winston, 1969.

Lathem, Edward Connery. *Robert Frost 100.* Boston: David R. Godine, 1974. Description of a traveling exhibit to honor the poet during the centennial of his birth.

Lathem, Edward Connery, and Thompson, Lawrance, eds. *Robert Frost: Farm-Poultryman.* Hanover, N.H.: Dartmouth Publications, 1963.

Mertins, Marshall Louis. *Robert Frost: Life and Talks—Walking.* Norman, Okla.: University of Oklahoma Press, 1965.

Mertins, Louis, and Mertins, Esther. *The Intervals of Robert Frost: A Critical Bibliography.* Berkeley: University of California Press, 1947.

Munson, Gorham B. *Robert Frost: A Study in Sensibility and Good Sense.* New York: George H. Doran, 1927.

Reeve, Franklin D. *Robert Frost in Russia.* Boston: Little, Brown, 1964.

Sergeant, Elizabeth Shepley. *Robert Frost: The Trial by Existence.* New York: Holt, Rinehart, and Winston, 1960.

Smythe, Daniel. *Robert Frost Speaks.* New York: Twayne Publishers, 1964. Conversational interviews.

Squires, James Radcliffe. *The Major Themes of Robert Frost.* Ann Arbor: University of Michigan Press, 1963.

Sutton, William A., ed. *Newdick's Season of Frost: An Interrupted Biography of Robert Frost.* Albany, N.Y.: State University of New York Press, 1976. Biography based upon correspondence between Prof. Robert Newdick of Ohio State University and Robert Frost, with biographical notes made by Newdick.

Thompson, Lawrance. *Fire and Ice: The Art and Thought of Robert Frost.* New York: Holt, Rinehart, and Winston, 1942.

Thompson, Lawrance Roger. *Robert Frost: The Early Years, 1874–1915.* New York: Holt, Rinehart, and Winston, 1966.

Thompson, Lawrance. *Robert Frost: The Years of Triumph, 1915–1938.* New York: Holt, Rinehart, and Winston, 1970.

Thompson, Lawrance, and Winnick, R. H. *Robert Frost: The Later Years, 1938–1963.* New York: Holt, Rinehart, and Winston, 1976.

Thomson, Lawrance, ed. *Selected Letters of Robert Frost.* New York: Holt, Rinehart, and Winston, 1964.

CHURCHES

Cary, Harold W. *The Church in North Amherst, Massachusetts 1826–1976.* Amherst: North Congregational Church, 1976.

A Century of Service: A Brief History of the North Congregational Church Amherst, Massachusetts, 1826–1926. Amherst: Press of Carpenter and Morehouse, 1927.

The Compass. Periodical issued 1873 to 1877 by Grace Episcopal Church, Amherst, Massachusetts.

1826–1951: 125th Anniversary of the Founding of the North Congregational Church. Amherst: North Congregational Church, 1951.

Hawley, John A. *A Record of the Observation of the Two Hundredth Anniversary by the First Congregational Church.* Amherst, 1940.

Hawley, John A., and Rand, Frank Prentice. *The First Congregational Church in Amherst, 1739–1939.* Amherst, 1939.

An Historical Review: One Hundred and Fiftieth Anniversary of the First Church of Christ in Amherst, Massachusetts: November 7, 1889. Amherst: First Church of Christ in Amherst, 1890.

Huntington, F. D. *The Church, a Body and a Life: In a Commemorative Discourse on the Twenty-Fifth Anniversary of Grace Church, Amherst, Massachusetts, July 17, 1891.* Amherst, 1891.

Huntington, M. P. S. *Eighty-Five Years of Grace Church.* Amherst, 1951.

Ives, Philip T. *A Brief History of South Congregational Church in Amherst,* Rev. Ed. Amherst: South Congregational Church, 1969.

Johnson, George H. *Historical Manual of the North Congregational Church and Society, Amherst, Massachusetts.* Amherst, 1889.

Lindsey, Dr. Adrian. *The History of Wesley Methodist Church.* Amherst: Wesley Methodist Church, 1976.

North Congregational Church. *Diamond Jubilee of 1901 . . . North Congregational Church.* Fitchburg: Sentinel Printing Company, 1902.

Second Congregational Church. *Articles of Faith and Covenant.* Amherst: J. S. and C. Adams, Printers, 1827.

Second Congregational Church. *Manual of the Second Congregational Church.* Amherst: H. P. Montague, 1875.

Second Congregational Church. *Centennial Anniversary: Historical Discourse by the Pastor, Rev. George E. Fisher, at the Second Congregational Church, Amherst, Massachusetts, November 12, 1882. . . .* Amherst: Press of J. E. Williams, 1882.

Walker, Alice M. *The Story of a New England Country Church.* Amherst, 1901. Story of North Congregational Church.

Whicher, Mrs. Harriet. *Church Symbolism as Illustrated in Grace Episcopal Church, Amherst, Massachusetts, with Illustrations by Ralph C. Williams.* Amherst, 1945.

INSTITUTIONS

Amherst Academy. *Catalogue of the Officers and Students of Amherst Academy (1850–51).* Amherst: J. S. and C. Adams, Printers, 1850.

Amherst Academy. *Catalogue of the Officers and Students of Amherst Academy . . . 1858.* Northampton: Thomas Hale & Company, 1858.

Amherst Academy. *Laws of Amherst Academy for the Use of the Students.* Amherst: J. S. and C. Adams, Printers, 1827.

Amherst College. *Amherst Institution, from Official Documents, January 17, 1825; Petition of the Founders and Proprietors, Presented June 5, 1823.* Boston, n.d.

Amherst College. Archives. Begins 1820.
Contains unpublished materials relating to Amherst College and its development, honors theses, addresses, and a large photographic collection.

Amherst College. Special Collections.
Contains 50 percent of Emily Dickinson's extant manuscripts, one of the four largest collections in the world of books and manuscripts by and about Robert Frost, and a collection of western Massachusetts' imprints with emphasis on Amherst imprints and Amherst authors.

Amherst College. *Catalogue of the Corporation, Faculty, and Students.* Begins 1825.

Bigelow, William Pingry. *Amherst College Songs,* 2nd ed. Amherst: Alumni Council of Amherst, 1932.

Burgess, John William. *Reminiscences of an American Scholar: The Beginnings of Columbia University.* New York: Columbia University Press, 1934. Includes a brief history of Amherst College.

Canfield, F. Curtis. *The Seed and the Sowers: A Series of Chapel Talks on the History of Amherst College and a Play about Its Founding.* Amherst: Amherst College, 1955.

Cary, Harold W. *The University of Massachusetts: A History of One Hundred Years.* Amherst: University of Massachusetts Press, 1972.

Caswell, L. B. *Brief History of Massachusetts Agricultural College 1917.* Springfield, Mass.: F. A. Bassette Company, Printers, 1917.

Currier, Barbara. "Special Approaches of Women's Education: a Model Coeducational Program." Mimoegraph. Hampshire College., c.1966.

Cutting, George R. *Student Life at Amherst College.* Amherst, 1871.

Dakin, Winthrop S. *Historical Sketch of Amherst Savings Bank 1864–1964.* Amherst, 1964.

DeMott, Benjamin H. *Amherst and Other Institutions.* Amherst: Amherst College, 1955.

First National Bank of Amherst. *One Hundred Years of Commercial Banking in Amherst.* n.p., n.d. Available at the Frost Library.

Fletcher, William M, III. "Japanese Graduates of Amherst College and the Problem of Identity and Individuation." Honors thesis. Amherst College, 1968.

Fuess, Claude Moore. *Amherst, the Story of a New England College.* Boston: Little, Brown and Company, 1935.

Hammond, William Gardiner. *Remembrances of Amherst: An Undergraduate's Diary, 1846–1848.* Edited by George F. Whicher. New York: Columbia University Press, 1946.

Hampshire College, Documentary Slide Set. Amherst: Hampshire College, 1969, 1970, 1971–1973.
Contains slides of construction of first Hampshire College buildings in 1969 and scenes of campus and student life.

Hampshire College, Special Collections.
Miscellaneous memorabilia and unpublished manuscripts relating to Hampshire College.

Hewlett, Horace W., ed. *In Other Words: Amherst in Prose and Verse.* Amherst: Amherst College Press, 1964.

Hitchcock, Edward. *Reminiscences of Amherst College.* Amherst, 1871.

Hitchcock, Edward. *The Results of Anthropometry—As Determined From Measurements of the Students of Amherst College.* Amherst: Press of Carpenter and Morehouse, 1892.

Humphrey, Heman. *Sketches of the Early History of Amherst College.* Northampton, 1905.

Kennedy, Gail, ed. *Education at Amherst: The New Program.* Amherst: Amherst College Press, 1955.

King Stanley. *"The Consecrated Eminence": The Story of the Campus and Buildings of Amherst College.* Amherst: Amherst College, 1951.

King, Stanley. *History of the Endowment of Amherst College.* Amherst: Amherst College Press, 1950.

LeDuc, Thomas Harold Andre. *Piety and Intellect at Amherst College: 1865–1912.* New York: Columbia University Press, 1946.

Long, Kirk Edward. "Senior Year at Amherst: A Period of Transition." Honors thesis. Amherst College, 1965.

Messersmith, Andrew Kirk. "Amherst College Student Housing: A Systems Approach to Building." Honors thesis. Amherst College, 1973.

Mooty, David N., and Jenkins, Everett W., Jr. "Amherst College in Black and White: A Study of Student Racial Attitudes." Honors thesis. Amherst college, 1975.

Morgan, Charles Hill. *The Classical Collection at Amherst College*. Cambridge, Mass.: Archaeological Institute of America, 1967.

Morgan, Charles Hill. *The Development of the Art Collection of Amherst College, 1821–1971*. Amherst: Amherst College Press, 1964.

Newmann, Fred M. "The Influence of German Universities on Amherst College, 1854–1911." Honors thesis. Amherst, College, 1959.

Patterson, Franklin Kessel, and Longsworth, Charles R. *The Making of a College: Plans for a New Departure in Higher Education*. Cambridge, Mass.: M.I.T. Press, 1966. Rev. ed. 1975.
Hampshire College working paper. Revised edition includes "Report of the President, 1971–1974."

Peterson, George Edward. *The New England College in the Age of the University*. Amherst: Amherst College Press, 1964.

Rand, Frank Prentice. *The Jones Library in Amherst*. Amherst: The Jones Library, 1969.

Rand, Frank Prentice. *Yesterdays at Massachusetts State College*. Amherst: Associate Alumni of Massachusetts State College, 1933.

Riley, Herbert E. *An Amherst Book*. New York, 1906.

Taylor, Mark J. "The Role of Psychological Research in Higher Education: An Exploratory Empirical Study of the Reported Mode of Course Selection and Orientation to College of Amherst College Seniors." Honors thesis. Amherst College, 1958.

Taylor, Robert Saxton. *The Making of a Library: The Academic Library in Transition*. New York: Becker and Hayes, 1972.
Hampshire College working paper.

Tuckerman, Frederick. *Amherst Academy: A New England School of the Past 1814–1861*. Amherst: Trustees of Amherst Academy, 1929.

Tyler, J. M. *The First One Hundred Years of Amherst College*. n.p., n.d.

Tyler, William Seymour. *A History of Amherst College During the Administration of Its First Five Presidents from 1821 to 1891*. New York: F. H. Hitchcock, 1895.

University of Massachusetts. Archives.
Unpublished manuscripts and memorabilia relating to the development of the University of Massachusetts. All masters theses from 1896 and doctoral dissertations from 1911. Variety of mimeographed and printed items.

University of Massachusetts. Oral History Archives. Begins 1976.
Interviews of faculty, staff, and alumni individually and in groups.

Whicher, George F. *Mornings at 8:50: Brief Evocations of the Past for a College Audience.* Northampton: Hampshire Bookshop, 1950.

Whicher, George F., ed. *Remembrance of Amherst.* Amherst: Amherst College Press, 1946.

MAPS AND DIRECTORIES

Ainsworth, Gordon. *Amherst Town Atlas.* Deerfield, Mass., 1970.

Amherst, Town of. Surveys of the Town of Amherst. Made in 1784, 1812, 1830. The town hall has these and miscellaneous maps, the earliest of which is a handdrawn map c.1772.

Beers, Frederick W. *County Atlas of Hampshire, Massachusetts.* New York: Beers, 1873.
Actual surveys by and under the direction of F. W. Beers.

Board of Trade. *Amherst the Village Beautiful.* Amherst, 1892.

Burleigh, L. R., *Amherst, Mass. 1886.* Troy, N.Y.: The Burleigh Lith. Establishment.

French, Robin et al. *Amherst, Massachusetts Guide Map with Major Points of Importance.* Amherst, 1953.

Gay, W. B. *Gazetteer of Hampshire County, Massachusetts.* n.p., n.d.

Graham's Pocket Directory: Town of Amherst, Massachusetts. Willimantic, Conn.: Graham Press, 1898.

Gray, Alonzo, and Adams, Charles B. *A Map of Amherst.* Boston, 1833.

Jones, D. H. Various maps produced for distribution by D. H. Jones Real Estate agency. Begin c.1968.

Kestrel Trust. *Around and About Amherst: An Outdoor Guide to the Region Around Amherst, Massachusetts.* Amherst: Kestrel Trust, 1971.

McCloud & Williams Printers. *The Amherst Almanac: Containing Matters of Local Interest, Local Business Announcements; an Almanac Adapted for This Section, Also Some Pages of Miscellaneous Reading.* Amherst, 1878.

Manning, H. A. *Amherst, Hadley, and Hatfield Directory.* Northampton, Mass.: H. A. Manning Company, 1948, 1952, 1954, and 1957.

Price and Lee Company. *Amherst, Hadley, and Hatfield Directory.* New Haven, Conn., 1966.

Tighe and Bond. *Town of Amherst, Massachusetts.* Holyoke, 1972.

Walker, George H., and Company. *Atlas of Massachusetts.* Boston, 1891.

Walling, Henry F. *Maps of the County of Hampshire.* New York, 1860.

PERIODICALS

Amherst College Periodicals

Amherst College Biographical Record. 1822 to present.

Alumni Directory. 1954 to present.

Amherst Alumni Council News. 1927 to 1949.

Amherst, the College. 1962 to present.

Amherst: The College and Its Alumni. May 1949 to present.

Amherst Graduate's Quarterly. 1927 to 1949.

Amherst Student (Title varies.)
   Ichnolite. 1857–1862.
   Amherst College Magazine. 1862–1868.
   Amherst Student. February 1868–.

Gazette of Amherst College. June 25, 1943–June 23, 1944.

Horae Collegianae: A Literary Periodical Conducted by the Undergraduates of Amherst College. October 1837–August 1840.

University of Massachusetts Periodicals

The Alumnus. Title varies.
   Massachusetts Alumnus. September 1953–August 1970.
   The Alumnus. October 1970 to present.

Bulletin. Begins 1909. Includes reports issued as public documents.

Daily Collegian. Title varies. Student newspaper.
   Aggie Life October 1, 1890–October 16, 1901.
   College Signal November 16, 1901–June 16, 1914.
   Massachusetts Collegian September 15, 1914–May 19, 1961.
   Collegian September 15, 1961 to present.

The Index. Student yearbook. Begins 1869.

Massachusetts Review. Quarterly literary publication. Begins October 1959.

Miscellaneous Periodicals

Amherst Gazette and Family Miscellany. January 24–April 17, 1840.

Amherst Journal. Weekly newspaper. September 13, 1946–December 25, 1953, Merged with the *Amherst Record* to form the *Amherst Journal-Record* January 7, 1954.

Amherst Record. Title varies. Vol. I, No. 1 was September 13, 1844. Title change as follows:
Hampshire and Franklin Express. September 13, 1844–January 20, 1865.
Hampshire Express. January 27, 1865–April 30, 1868.
Amherst Record. May 7, 1868–December 24, 1953.
Amherst Journal-Record. January 1, 1954–December 31, 1964.
Amherst Record. January 7, 1965 to present.
Amherst College has the area's most complete collection.

Daily Express. April 19, 1862–July 16, 1862.
One-sheet flyer of Civil War news, from the railroad station telegraph line. At The Jones Library only.

Five College Cooperation. General information brochure published annually from 1967 to 1975 by the Five Colleges, Incorporated.

Five Colleges in Cooperation. General information brochure published by the Five Colleges, Incorporated 1976 and 1977.

Five College Newsletter. September 1968 to present.

Index